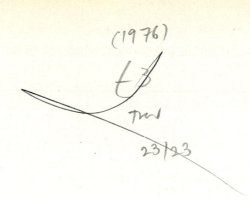

(1976)

23/23

THE GREAT
FIRE
OF LONDON

THE GREAT
FIRE
OF LONDON
AN ILLUSTRATED ACCOUNT

PETER BERRESFORD ELLIS

Designed by Michael Osborn

First published in Great Britain by
New English Library, Barnard's Inn,
Holborn, London EC1N 2JR in 1976

This book is set in Imprint 11/12pt
and 11pt Joanna italic

Printed in Great Britain by Thomson
Litho Ltd, East Kilbride, Scotland
Bound by Hunter & Foulis, Edinburgh

4500 32280

ACKNOWLEDGEMENTS

I would like to offer my warmest thanks to the
many people who helped me in my research for
this volume, especially those who aided me in my
search for illustrative material. In this respect
particular thanks must go to Frank Westwood who
toured the City of London with me looking for
remnants of seventeenth-century London. I would
also like to thank the following people: Ralph Hyde,
Keeper of Prints and Maps, Guildhall Library,
London; Miss Betty R. Masters, Deputy Keeper of
Records, Corporation of London Record Office;
Douglas Matthews, Deputy Librarian, The
London Library; Miss Diane Courtney,
Photographic Library, British Tourist Authority;
Miss Mary Allum, Photographic Department of the
British Museum; D. N. Cole, Librarian of the
Royal College of Physicians; R. Crayford, assistant
to the Clerk of the Works, St Paul's Cathedral;
Miss Caroline Pilkington, Librarian (Photographic
Survey) Courtauld Institute of Art; the Bishop of
London and Church Commissioners; Mrs S. M.
Hare of the Goldsmith's Hall; Miss Majorie E.
Crook, Publications Office of the Walker Art
Gallery, Liverpool; and the officers of the Fire
Protection Association. I would also add a special
thanks to the staff of the British Museum Reading
Room.

CONTENTS

'A WOMAN MIGHT PISS IT OUT!'

Sir Thomas Bludworth, Lord Mayor of London, on 2 September 1666.

Samuel Pepys (1633–1703)
Clerk of the *Acts of the Navy
Board* and diarist who left a
vivid day-by-day description
of the fire. He brought the first
news of its spread to Charles II.
NATIONAL PORTRAIT GALLERY

Charles II. He put his own life
in danger in trying to organise
the people of the City into fire-
fighting units. The
Corporation, in recognition of
his services, made him the
first reigning monarch to
receive the Freedom of the City.
Portrait by Sir Godfrey Kneller.
BY PERMISSION OF WALKER ART
GALLERY, LIVERPOOL

The Great Fire of London, 1666, from Wapping. Much is made of the flight of people and their goods. St Paul's stands in the background but the large building to its left is a figment of the painter's imagination. The spire of old St Mary le Bow stands on the horizon to the right of St Paul's.

A Contemporary View of the Fire from the West. Looking west from the riverside near the Temple, the Fire is seen at its height against the night sky. The moon rises over the Tower and London Bridge while to the left the ruins of the City are silhouetted against the flames. St Paul's Cathedral stands above the rest. In the foreground people are landing from boats with such of their possessions as they have been able to save. The painting is after Waggoner. GUILDHALL ART GALLERY

Sir Christopher Wren (1632–1723) was created 'Surveyor General and Principal Architect for rebuilding the whole City of London' after the fire. Wren devoted the last thirty years of his life to creating a new and beautiful City with St Paul's as his crowning achievement. NATIONAL PORTRAIT GALLERY

INTRODUCTION
The Victim

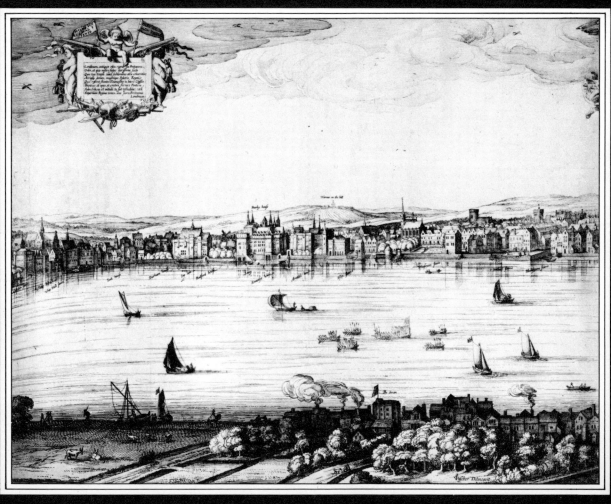

The four prints constitute
the complete panorama by Claesz Jans Visscher
made in 1616 of the City of London stretching from
the Tower to Whitehall.

Thomas Farynor, the King's baker, who kept his shop in Pudding Lane near London Bridge, afterwards swore that he had totally extinguished his oven fires before retiring to bed at ten o'clock that Saturday night. He was more than insistent on that point when he gave evidence to the Parliamentary Committee which had been set up to enquire into the causes of the great fire which had devastated the City of London during the first week of September 1666.

The fire, the biggest single calamity in the history of the City, had destroyed 13,200 houses, eighty-seven parish churches and six chapels, forty-four Company Halls, the Royal Exchange, the Custom House, St Paul's Cathedral, the Guildhall, the Bridewell and other City prisons, the Session House, four of London's bridges across the Thames and the Fleet, three City gates and made homeless 100,000 people (one sixth of the inhabitants). Londoners had given thanks that only four people had been killed by the fire, although the death toll from its indirect cause was much higher.

In the aftermath of the catastrophe Londoners were frightened and angry. They were frightened by the devastation of their capital, and angered by the loss of their houses and possessions, and they wanted a scapegoat to blame for the tragedy which had overtaken them.

Farynor was determined that it would not be him.

He need not have worried. The people had already decided upon the culprits: either the Dutch or French with whom England was at war, or Catholic agitators seeking to overthrow the

government. Many were sure that the fire was the result of a 'Popish Plot' similar to the conspiracy to blow up Parliament in 1605. It was even rumoured that Charles II's brother James, Duke of York, known to be ardent for the Catholic faith, had organised the burning and stood gloating over the flames.

The angry citizens of London recalled that the previous ten years had abounded with religious seers who foretold the destruction of London by fire, which was the vengeance of God on a heretical city. Eight years before, Walter Gostelo, in a booklet entitled *The Coming of God in Mercy, in Vengeance, Beginning with Fire, to Convert or Consume all this so Sinful City London*, likened the City to Sodom and Gomorrah and said, 'If fire make not ashes of the City, and thy bones also, conclude me a liar for ever.' In 1659 Daniel Baker had issued his *Certaine Warning for a Naked Heart* in which he said London would be destroyed by 'a fire, a consuming fire'. Catholics, Quakers, Presbyterians and other nonconformists seemed to unite in foretelling the destruction of England's capital. 'Most of our last year's almanacs,' recalled one writer in 1666, 'talked of fire in London.' Londoners were certain that a group of Catholics had decided to make the religious prophecy a reality in an attempt to overthrow the Protestant Government of the country.

A smaller section of the community wondered whether this was the long-awaited uprising by the republicans, unhappy at the Restoration of the monarchy six years earlier. They recalled that in April of that year Colonel John Rathbone and a

group of former Parliamentarian officers had been arrested and tried for conspiring to overthrow Charles and restore the Commonwealth. By a strange coincidence, the *London Gazette*, reporting the trial on 30 April, said that the republican coup involved the firing of London, which was to be done on 3 September. Eight republican officers of the old Commonwealth Army were executed.

But the average Londoner had no doubts that it was the Catholics who were to blame, aided, perhaps, by the Dutch and the French. The fact that the fire started as the result of carelessness in Farynor's bakery would not quell their anger and Farynor himself sought exoneration by insisting that he had not been negligent in dousing his fires that night. Only one thing would appease the City's anger. Blood.

And blood they had!

Within a few weeks of the fire a scapegoat was found and, following a farce of a trial at the October Sessions in the Old Bailey, a twenty-six-year-old French silversmith and watchmaker was executed at Tyburn, having been found guilty of causing the fire.

The Frenchman was Robert Hubert, a native of Rouen, whom the authorities claimed was a Catholic. The evidence indicated that he was, in reality, a French Huguenot. The basis of his conviction was a confession. His workmates told the authorities that Hubert was unbalanced; one of those individuals who will confess to crimes they did not commit either out of a death wish or a desire to achieve notoriety, a desire to be noticed in their otherwise humdrum existence.

James, Duke of York, Charles II's younger brother took
personal command of the fire-fighters in the City and displayed
great courage and determination in trying to bring the flames
under control. Thirty-five years old at the time, the Duke had
already won a reputation for bravery and dash that was sadly
lacking when, as James II, he was driven from the kingdom at
the fiasco of the Battle of the Boyne. His nephew, the Duke of
Monmouth, accused James of plotting the deliberate firing of
London as part of a Catholic plot to take over the kingdom.
NATIONAL PORTRAIT GALLERY

Hubert voluntarily told the authorities that he was the incendiary. His story was that he had just returned from Sweden in a ship which moored by St Katherine's Tower, near London Bridge, on 1 September. That Saturday night, 2 September, he and a companion, whom he identified as Stephen Peidloe, walked up Pudding Lane to Farynor's bakery. Here Peidloe handed him a fire-ball which he lit and put into the house through a window, using a long pole to place it.

When a puzzled Farynor told the court that no such window existed, Hubert promptly changed his story. In fact, he changed his story so many times, always to cover flaws detected in his previous stories, that it was obvious the man was lying. Henry Hyde, the second Earl of Clarendon, commented: 'Neither the judges, nor any present at the trial did believe him guilty; but that he was a poor distracted wretch, weary of his life, and chose to part with it that way.'

The final version of Hubert's confession, after it had also been proved that no Swedish vessel had been berthed at St Katherine's Tower in September, was that he had returned from Paris where he had been coerced into being an incendiary. He boasted that he had twenty-three conspirators under his command, although this figure rapidly dwindled to three on cross-examination. In one version of his story he claimed that he had been ordered to set fire to Whitehall Palace or, if that failed, to any building near it.

It was true that Hubert had, indeed, recently returned from France where it seemed he had been on a visit to his father in Rouen. The captain of the vessel, one Lawrence Peterson, was called to give evidence and he swore that *Hubert had not set foot on English soil until two days after the fire began.* A French merchant named Grace, who ran his business near St Andrew Undershaft, came forward to tell the court that Hubert had always been a 'perverse' person, unreliable and given to fantasy.

The only damning evidence in support of his own confession was the fact that Robert Hubert was able to identify the charred remains of Farynor's house as the one to which he had set fire. John Lowman, the keeper of the White Lion Gaol in Southwark, in which Hubert was held, told the court that he had taken Hubert to Pudding Lane and asked him to point out the house he had fired. This the young Frenchman was able to do. But by that time the house of Farynor had become a centre for sightseers as the spot where the terrible fire had started and was not difficult to pick out.

Lord Chief Justice Sir John Kelyng, who sat in judgement on the case, did not bother to point out just how fragile this evidence was.

The jury, carried away by public demands for vengeance, found Hubert guilty as charged. The young Frenchman appeared now, for the first time, to realise the consequences of his attempt at notoriety and started to protest his innocence. The writer of a letter to Sir Edward Mansell, dated 20 October, records how Hubert denied the charge. But the newsletters and broadsheets for popular consumption told how Hubert, the Protestant, had made his confession in the Catholic faith on the gallows and died admitting his guilt. The 'mopish besotted fellow', as the diarist Samuel Pepys described him, was hanged at Tyburn, the site of London's Marble Arch, within six weeks of the fire.

On 27 January 1667, the Parliamentary Committee investigating the fire, dismissed the notion that the City had been deliberately fired. They had carefully examined all the evidence, 'yet nothing hath been found to argue it to have been other than the hand of God upon us, a great wind, and the season so very dry'.

London had exacted its vengeance on an innocent man.

CHAPTER ONE

Sunday, 2 September 1666

Long Lane, Smithfield. John T. Smith
says that this house was constructed nearly two decades
before the Great Fire. 'It would,' he writes, 'be difficult perhaps to
exhibit a better assemblage of combustible materials than in
the wretched pile of buildings now before us.'
GUILDHALL LIBRARY

The long hot summer of 1666 was coming to an end in London. Citizens eagerly looked forward to the winter and the coming of rain, for the City was not a pleasant place in which to live. It badly needed rain for the houses were dry, tinder boxes, and the danger of fire was ever-constant. The long drought of the summer had lowered the springs and wells, and only a small volume of water reached the conduits which supplied the City with its water. But the fire hazards seemed insignificant compared with the dangers of a further outbreak of the bubonic plague. That terrible, horrific plague of the previous year (which had claimed the lives of 56,558 of the City's inhabitants) had almost died out, but still the rattle of the death cart and the harsh jangle of its warning bell could be heard in the cobbled streets. London had always suffered from fires but the plague was more frightening. The dry, dusty air created conditions in which germs could breed and spread. Increasing Londoners' anxieties was the fact that for several days now a wind had been blowing across the City from the

These views of Chancery Lane and Hosier Lane, Smithfield, show the timber framing, projecting portions and multiple storeys of City buildings at the time of the fire. In addition to the hazards of the narrow streets and inflammable materials there existed the danger of collapse of these top-heavy structures. The fire, in fact, ended only a few yards away from Hosier Lane.
GUILDHALL LIBRARY

east. John Dryden, the poet-playwright, called it 'the Belgian wind', a wind that would help to spread germs and disease across the City into the more prosperous western suburbs where the wealthy and influential lived.

It was the wind that would eventually destroy London.

The City of London of 1666 had outgrown the crowded square mile enclosed by its ancient walls. The actual 'square mile' was more of an oblong, being twice as long as it was wide. The area

[15]

surrounded by the walls had already taken on the shape of the commercial and trading centre while the more prosperous citizens sought to build their homes outside the City walls. The old walls surrounded London from the east, north and west, but along the south side, fronting on the River Thames, the walls gave way to a line of wooden warehouses and quays, crowded from the Tower of London in the east to the fortress at Blackfriars called Baynard's Castle.

Inside the City small houses crowded themselves between over fifty merchants' halls, thousands of shops and an incredible 109 parish churches, while dominating the City from the top of Ludgate Hill stood the great cathedral of St Paul's, which at one time had been the largest cathedral in Europe. The residential houses were, in the most part, over-crowded and insanitary; veritable breeding grounds for any pestilence. The streets for the most part, with the notable exception of Cheapside and Corn-hill, the social centres of the City, were tiny, narrow affairs. A man might stand in the centre of most of them and touch the walls of the houses on either side. The majority of the buildings were half-timbered constructions and many warehouses were entirely made from wood with thatched roofs.

In retrospect, it is surprising that the disaster of 1666 had not taken place earlier in the over-crowded, wooden-built City. As early as AD 1189, City ordnances had ruled that houses must be built of stone to decrease the fire hazards. They never were. In spite of further decrees and enacted laws the citizens of London still continued to erect timber-built constructions, and fires continued to break out with such regularity that they became regarded as a natural occurrence. One did not need to be a seer to foretell that London could be destroyed by a serious fire if its citizens did not take more interest in the welfare of their City. Even King Charles had written to the Lord Mayor on 11 April 1665, warning him of the perils of fire in the narrow streets and alleys and on the over-hanging houses built of wood in contravention of the various building acts.

By 1666 London had already grown from its medieval boundaries. Suburbs had sprung up on the south bank of the Thames in Southwark and Bermondsey which were linked to the City by London Bridge. The latter, completed in 1209 and considered to be the greatest engineering feat in the British Isles, was a stone bridge with nineteen arches spanning the Thames some 910 feet in length and over twenty feet in width. The roadway that crossed the bridge was twelve feet wide and on either side of it rose houses, overhanging the river,

supported by massive beams. Sometimes these precariously perched houses would fall into the river. They usually rose to a height of three or four storeys and were basically shops which sold all manner of goods. During one survey some 138 such shops were listed as being on the bridge and half-way along it was a chapel dedicated to St Thomas à Beckett.

The City had also extended along the north bank. The main growth had been towards the west, where houses spread into the suburbs along Fleet Street towards Westminster and northward on the west side of the River Fleet towards Holborn. To the immediate north of the City such expansion was checked by Moorfields, a badly drained boggy area which had been half-heartedly converted into a parkland for citizens in the time of James I. It was, however, described as 'a most noisome and offensive moorish ground, burrowed and crossed with deep stinking ditches and noisome common sewers'.

To the east, around Aldgate and Bishopsgate, more houses had sprung up and were following the roads which led to such isolated farming hamlets as Whitechapel, Stepney and Hoxton.

The Venetian ambassador had summarised London in these words:

The City of London renders itself truly worthy to be styled the metropolis of the kingdom, and the abode of royalty. It is three miles long and very densely populated. Two thirds of its extent consists in suburbs where the nobility and people also reside and where all the royal palaces, parks and gardens are situated. In the third part are the warehouses of the principal merchants from whom they select the chief magistrates of the City, called the Lord Mayor, and officials. There are also some good dwellings on the opposite shore, but less numerous.

They are connected by a very noble stone bridge of nineteen very lofty arches, on each side of which are convenient houses and shops, so that it has rather the air of a long suburb than a handsome structure such as a bridge.

Such was the City of London during that summer of 1666.

Saturday, 1 September, followed a succession of similar hot, dry days. It was the busiest day of the week from the viewpoint of most Londoners for it was the day when people received their wages and flocked into the City where willing hands soon helped them part with their money. At the end of the day most citizens had retired to bed exhausted and fallen into a deep sleep, oblivious to the easterly wind creaking the shop signs, tearing the shutters loose from their couplings, rustling the thatch and ripping dry leaves from the trees.

Thomas Farynor, the baker, his day's trading done, insisted that he drew his oven fires at ten o'clock and went to bed 'leaving his providence with his slippers'. He was positive that the bakery fires were totally extinguished. So positive, in fact, that he said he had wanted to light a candle about midnight and had gone down to his oven to see if there were any embers from which he could do so. He swore there were none. The fire was dead. When he was later asked whether a draught from an open door or window might have fanned an ember into flame, he declared that it was totally impossible. Until the day of his death, Farynor insisted that his house had been deliberately fired.

Shortly after two o'clock on the morning of Sunday, 2 September, Farynor's assistant was awoken with a choking sensation. The house was full of smoke. The assistant immediately aroused the baker who, in turn, woke his wife, Hanna, his son, Tom, his daughter and their maid. They 'felt themselves almost choked with smoke, and rising, did find the fire coming up the stairs, so that they rose to save themselves'. In spite of their haste, Farynor claimed that he had time to observe that the fire was nowhere near his oven nor the stack of firewood placed in his yard ready for the next day's baking. The flames cut off the Farynors' retreat

Pre-Fire London showing the area where the Fire started. An enlargement of a panorama of the City by Claesz Jans Vissner (see p 9) which shows the lack of space between buildings and the vast overcrowding of a small area. There was one church to every six acres of the City, with Company Halls or other public buildings almost as plentiful.
GUILDHALL LIBRARY

Wenclaus Hollar's map of London prior to the Great Fire. BRITISH MUSEUM

downstairs and so the baker led his family through a garret window across the roof to a neighbour's house.

Farynor's maid, however, was afraid of heights and was too scared to follow. She stayed behind.

The Great Fire of London soon claimed its first victim.

Farynor's bakery stood in Pudding Lane, a narrow little street which ran between Little Eastcheap and Thames Street, just to the east of London Bridge. John Stow, in his *Survey of London* (1598), described it in these words:

> Then have ye Rother Lane, or Red Rose Lane, of such sign there, now commonly called Pudding Lane, because the butchers of Eastcheap having their scalding houses for hogs there, and their puddings, with other filth of beasts, are voided down that way to their dung boats on the Thames. This lane stretched from Thames Street to Little Eastcheap, chiefly inhabited by basket-makers, turners and butchers.

Pudding Lane had not altered much since Stow's day. It was still a narrow cobbled lane, lined with tottering houses which ran unevenly down to

the Thames' banks. Farynor's house was situated ten doors up from Thames Street on the western side of the lane.

To the west of Pudding Lane, and running parallel to it, stood the main thoroughfare of Fish Street Hill, which led onto London Bridge. (Today's London Bridge now stands many yards to the west of the old bridge so that Fish Street Hill now leads only into Thames Street. In 1666 it was the principal thoroughfare into the city from south of the river). Directly behind Farynor's bakery, its yard and stables backing onto his house, stood the Star Inn, a well-known coaching stop. It was in the Star Inn's yard that a number of citizens gathered to watch Farynor's bakery aflame. It burnt for over an hour and allowed his next-door neighbours time to remove their household belongings before the fire caught hold of their houses.

Then the roof of Farynor's house suddenly collapsed in a shower of sparks and flying lighted timbers. The wind caught at them and sent them showering over the tavern yard, causing the spectators to scream and fly into Fish Street Hill. The yard and stables of the Star Inn were stocked with hay for the post horses as well as other combustible material and the inn itself was a magnificent structure of half-timber and intricate wooden galleries. Within seconds the inn was on fire and roaring in

Leadenhall Street showing the wood framing and cracked and crumbling plaster which were features of the houses during the Fire period. GUILDHALL LIBRARY

the high wind. Samuel Wiseman recorded the scene in verse.

> And now the doleful, dreadful, hideous note
> Of Fire! is screamed out with a deep
>   strained throat;
> Horror, and fear, and sad distracted cries
> Chide sloth away, and bid the sluggard rise;
> Most direful acclamations are let fly
> From every tongue, tears stand in every eye.

The inhabitants of Pudding Lane and Fish Street Hill came pouring into the streets to help douse the flames, urged by the alarm bell of nearby St Clements whose sexton had been dragged from his sleep by anxious citizens.

The Reverend Thomas Vincent recalled the scene:

> The fire begins, is quickly taken notice of, though in the midst of the night. Fire! Fire! Fire! doth resound the streets; many citizens start out of their sleep, look out of their windows; some dress themselves and run to the place. The Lord Mayor of the City comes with his officers, a confusion there is; counsel is taken; and London, so famous for wisdom and dexterity, can now find neither brain nor hands to prevent its ruin.

The Lord Mayor, Sir Thomas Bludworth, had been aroused at three o'clock. He was disgruntled at being fetched from his house in Maiden Lane, near Aldersgate, on the other side of the City. It would seem he was indecisive in moments of crisis. The diarist, Samuel Pepys, had already come into conflict with him and his estimation was 'a silly man, I think'. Bludworth was a vintner, son of an opulent turkey merchant who had risen to his position because he was 'a zealous person in the King's concernments'. He had been knighted at the Restoration for his Royalist sympathies and was elected Sheriff of London in 1662. From 1660–79 he was Member of Parliament for Southwark as well as being an Alderman of the City for the Aldersgate Ward. He had been the colonel of the Orange Regiment of Trained Bands and was colonel of the Yellow Regiment, which office he held until his death. The previous year he had been elected Master of the Vintner's Company. He was, by all accounts, a vain man. Now he stood observing the burning houses in Pudding Lane and Fish Street Hill and even as he watched, the church of St Margaret's, opposite the Star Inn in Fish Street Hill, caught ablaze.

'Pish!' observed the irritated Lord Mayor. 'A woman might piss it out.'

With that the Lord Mayor returned to his bed. There had been hundreds of fires before in the City, each burning itself out without much damage. Sir Thomas Bludworth was not particularly worried about another fire.

Towards dawn the fire was burning along the rows of timber-built houses, dry as chip after the summer drought, down Pudding Lane and Fish

[20]

A view of Wren's St Magnus Martyr, standing on the original site at the bottom of Fish Street Hill. St Magnus was the second church to perish in the flames.
JOHN BENTON-HARRIS

Street Hill towards the Thames. Fish Street Hill was a steeper hill in those days, where fishmongers, grocers and haberdashers carried on their trade. It was in a tavern in Fish Street Hill, in 1651, that Samuel Pepys and fifteen-year-old Elizabeth St Michel, the daughter of a penniless French artisan, celebrated their wedding breakfast. But now most of Fish Street Hill was ablaze, stretching down to where Thames Street (along which the Old Roman Wall of the City had run) cut across, running parallel to the river.

At the bottom of Fish Street Hill, just before it led onto London Bridge, stood the Church of St Magnus the Martyr where Henry Yevele, England's leading architect of the Middle Ages, lay buried. The lines of the fire raced over Thames Street and into the church. The parish clerk managed to save the old registers but in his haste he had to leave behind the vestry orders and also some money he had received for burials since the previous Lady Day. The flames caught fiercely at the church and leapt up into the high belfry. The rectory next door was also consumed.

At this time the fire might well have been checked by the use of the waterpumps housed in a waterhouse close by London Bridge. The waterhouse had been designed and built by Peter Marisi or Maurice, a Dutchman, in 1582. It utilised the rush of the river through the arches of the bridge for raising a supply of water to the houses around the Thames Street area. The engine and wheels could force the water along leaden pipes over the roof of St Magnus' church. But the fire had put the equipment out of action before the citizens thought of using it.

It was the flames shooting up the belfry of St Magnus the Martyr which was the first signal to the rest of London that a fire of unusual magnitude was taking place.

Some citizens had already seen the fire before dawn. A quarter of a mile away, in his house in Seething Lane, Samuel Pepys, the fastidious Clerk of the Acts of the Navy Board, was awakened by his maid, Jane, to see the fire. He recorded in his diary:

2nd (Lord's Day). Some of our maids sitting up late last night to get things ready against our feast today; Jane called us up about three in the morning, to tell us of a great fire they saw in the City. So I rose, and slipped on my night gown, and went to her window; and thought it to be on the back side of Mark Lane at the farthest; but, being unused to such fires as followed, I thought it far enough off; and so went to bed again, and to sleep.

Daylight found the fire being driven west and south by the wind. The roof of St Magnus the Martyr soon fell in and the flames were creeping onto London Bridge itself. There had been a fire on the bridge as recently as 1632 when the servant of a needlemaker had carelessly left a tub of hot ashes under the stairs of the house and was responsible for a fire which destroyed forty-two houses and burnt for eight hours. A devout parishioner of St Magnus, Sussana Chambers, had left the sum of twenty shillings a year for the parson to preach an annual sermon of thanksgiving that the fire had not destroyed the church.

A panoramic view of London before and after the Great Fire by Wenclaus Holler. BRITISH MUSEUM

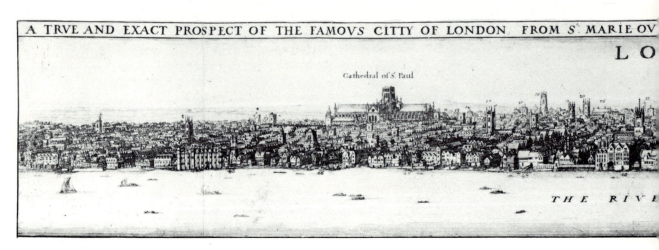

A TRVE AND EXACT PROSPECT OF THE FAMOVS CITTY OF LONDON FROM S.ᵗ MARIE OV

The flames that Sunday morning were following a similar course to the 1632 fire, burning across the gate house and destroying the houses that had been recently rebuilt on the charred remains. The flames from the roaring multi-storeyed houses on the bridge effectively blocked the road south, not only making it impossible for refugees to flee across the bridge into Southwark but also making it impossible for anyone who wanted to combat the flames to travel northwards. But the open space on the bridge which had served as a fire-break in 1632 also succeeded in halting the flames now. However, some sparks were borne on the wind into Southwark and set fire to a stable in Shoe Alley. The flames caught at two houses but the fire was soon stamped out when local men, more decisive than their compatriots in the City, pulled down a third house and created a successful fire-break.

According to Hugh Walpole (in his *Anecdotes of Painting*, 1786) a Holbein masterpiece perished in the flames of London Bridge that day. The German Hans Holbein (1497–1543) court painter to Henry VIII had lived in one of the houses on the bridge. Walpole recounts that:

The father of Lord Treasurer Oxford, passing over London Bridge, was caught in a shower and stepping into a goldsmith's for shelter found there a picture by Hans Holbein (who lived in that house) and family. He offered the goldsmith £100 for it, who consented to let him have it, but desired first to show it to some person. Immediately after happened the Fire of London and the picture was destroyed.

The fire was to destroy a third of the bridge but, luckily, did not spread across it. High above the south gate were the spikes on which the heads of traitors were impaled and John Dryden, inspired by the vision of these heads through the flames, wrote in his *Annus Mirabilis* (the only poem of worth inspired by the Great Fire):

The ghost of traitors from the Bridge descend,
With bold fanatic spectres to rejoice,
About the fire into a dance they bend
And sing this Sabbath's notes with feeble voice.

Samuel Pepys rose at seven o'clock, dressed himself and looked out of the window 'and saw the fire not so much as it was, and further off. By and by Jane comes and tells me that she hears that above 300 houses have been burned down tonight by the fire we saw, and that it is now burning down all Fish Street, by London Bridge'.

Pepys decided to walk to the Tower of London:

. . . and there got upon one of the high places. Sir J(ohn) Robinson's little boy going up with me; and there I did see the houses at that end of the bridge all on fire, and an infinite great fire on this and the other side of the bridge, which, among other people, did trouble me for poor little Michell and our Sarah on the Bridge. So down, with my heart full of trouble, to the Lieutenant of the Tower, who tells me that it began this morning in the King's baker's house in Pudding Lane, and that it has burned down St Magnus church and part of Fish Street already. So I went down to the waterside, and there got a boat, and

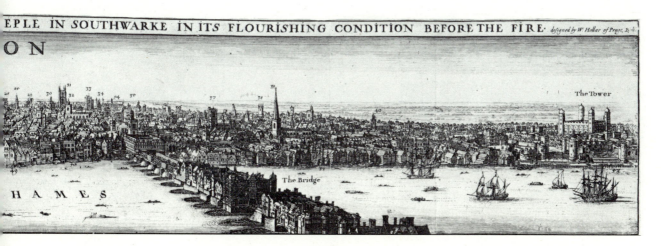

EPLE IN SOUTHWARKE IN ITS FLOURISHING CONDITION BEFORE THE FIRE. *designed by W. Hollar of Prage, 1647*

[23]

through the bridge, and there saw a lamentable fire. Poor Michell's house, as far as the Old Swann, already burnt away, and the fire running further.

From his strategic viewpoint in the boat, Samuel Pepys saw that the fire was now spreading west with appalling swiftness, whipped along by the wind. Everyone was endeavouring to remove their belongings, even flinging them into the river or trying to bring them off in small boats.

. . . poor people (wrote Pepys) staying in their houses as long as till the very fire touched them, and then running into boats, or clambering from one pair of stairs, by the waterside, to another. And among other things, the poor pigeons, I perceived, were loathed to leave their houses, but hovering about the windows and balconies till they burned their wings and fell down.

The Lord Mayor, Sir Thomas Bludworth, came back to the scene of the fire shortly after dawn as reports of its rapid spread continued to disturb his slumber. Bludworth remained an indecisive and pitiful figure who could do nothing more than wring his hands in agitation. If he had decided, at any time up until noon that Sunday, to pull down the houses and start creating fire-breaks, the impending disaster might well have been averted. Instead, when advisers put the solution before him, all he did was ask: 'Who shall pay for the charge of rebuilding the houses?' Also, he added when pressed further, he would have to get the owners' consent. It was true that an ancient London law decreed that any man who destroyed another's

house would have to pay for it to be rebuilt. But only an extreme bureaucratic mind would have held this up as a reason for inaction. Few people defended Bludworth's actions afterwards but among his defenders was John Evelyn of Greenwich who tried to absolve the Lord Mayor by saying it was the wealthy London merchants who obstructed him in his efforts to pull down buildings. According to Evelyn the merchants were 'tenacious and avaricious men, Aldermen, etc., who would not permit, because their houses must have been the first' to be destroyed. Chamberlayne, in the *Present State of England*, published in 1682, went so far as to blame the people for the spread of the fire. He claimed that Farynor was drunk and his neighbours were slothful and 'filled with drink and all in a dead sleep'.

The Fishmongers' Hall, on the west side of Fish Street Hill, by the bridge, was now well alight. The great building had once been Lord Fauchope's Thameside mansion but, at the end of the fifteenth century, it had been purchased by the Fishmongers' Company. Surrounding it lay a veritable tinder box of dilapidated timber houses, a slum which crowded upon the slope of ground from the Thameside to Thames Street, along the area then called Stock-fishmongers' Row, along the ancient fish-market quays to the water's edge. The slums were intersected by narrow foot-passages, Watergate, Churchyard Alley, Red Cross Alley etc. Here was the great danger area, the wharves with their store houses, cellars, sheds and warehouses, stocked with all manner of combustible goods – tallow, oil, spirits and hemp, goods brought up river by coasting vessels and traders. On the open wharves

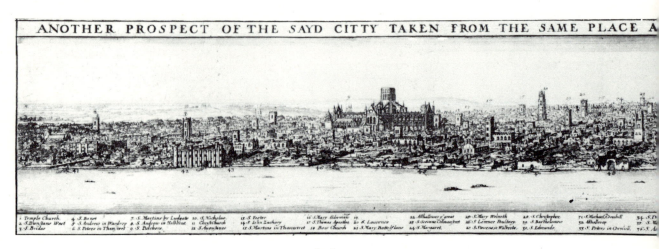

ANOTHER PROSPECT OF THE SAYD CITTY TAKEN FROM THE SAME PLACE A

John Evelyn (1620–1706), a diarist who took an active part in the fire-fighting at Holborn. A former student of Middle Temple, he proposed the idea for a Royal Society, of which he became secretary in 1672. An authority on numismatics, architecture and landscape gardening, he drew up a grandiose scheme for rebuilding the City of London while the City was still smouldering. NATIONAL PORTRAIT GALLERY

south of Thames Street lay hay, timber and coal. Within minutes the entire area was a mass of exploding flame, until it blazed from the bridge as far as the Steelyard.

The general trend of the fire was mostly westwards, although a sudden lull in the wind caused the flames to make a leap towards the east and brought destruction to St Botolph's church in Billingsgate.

A resident of Middle Temple knew nothing of the fire until nine o'clock that morning when, walking in the Temple gardens, he saw smoke from the direction of London Bridge. Curious, he turned into Fleet Street which was full of people running about in panic 'for it was already imagined the design of the French and Dutch in revenge of what our forces had lately done at Brandis upon the isle of Scheeling'.

Londoners had certainly been nervous that summer due to the war being waged against the Dutch. The war had broken out in 1664 and earlier that year the French had declared war on England in support of the United Provinces. It was purely a commercial war about imperial acquisitions. The English fleet was split into two commands, one under George Monck, now Duke of Albemarle, and the other under Prince Rupert. On 1 June Monck had met the Dutch fleet under the Admiral Michel de Ruyter under the shadow of the Downs. For four days anxious Londoners could distinctly hear the sound of gunfire as the two fleets battled it out. Amid the scream of shot and cries of the wounded, the two fleets fought each other to a standstill, both running out of ammunition and strength. As the fleets drew apart, both sides claimed a victory.

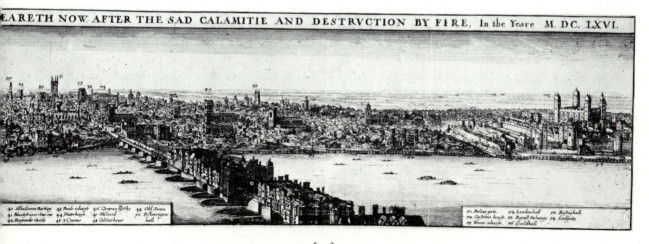

The Great Fire of London in 1666 by an Eye-Witness: The Scene from the South Bank by Thomas Wyck (1616-77) with old St Paul's (centre) amid the flames.

'Monck followed up, however, with an engagement off North Foreland and then destroyed the Dutch merchant fleet in Terschelling Roads. On the night of 8-9 August, English troops had landed on the islands of Vlie and Schelling and burnt the town of Brandaris, destroying it and setting fire to 160 Dutch merchantmen. To Londoners the fire appeared to be the enemy's revenge. Everyone who looked 'foreign' became a target for a fearful and hysterical mob.

The resident of Middle Temple recalled:

The riding of a hot headed fellow through the street (with more speed and fear than wit) crying Arm! Arm! had frightened most of the people out of the churches.

William Taswell, a pupil at Westminster School, was attending the morning service in Westminster Abbey that Sunday. The Abbey was crowded and he could only secure a place standing on the steps which led up to the pulpit. During the service, sometime between ten o'clock and eleven o'clock,

some people burst in with the news of the fire. '. . . without any ceremony,' recalled Taswell, 'I took my leave of the preacher, and having ascended Parliament Steps near the Thames, I soon perceived four boats crowded with objects of distress. These had escaped from the fire scarce under any other covering except that of a blanket.'

He continued, with slight exaggeration:

The wind was blowing strong eastward, the flames at last reached Westminster; I myself saw great flames carried up into the air at least three furlongs; these at last pitching upon and uniting themselves to various dry substances, set on fire houses very remote from each other in point of situation.

At no time either on that Sunday, nor later in the week, did the fire actually reach Westminster. Taswell was also a witness to the fear of the mob.

The ignorant and deluded mob who upon the occasion were hurried away with a kind of frenzy, vented forth their rage against the Roman Catholics and Frenchmen, imagining these incendiaries (as they thought) had thrown red hot balls into the houses.

[26]

A blacksmith in my presence, meeting an innocent Frenchman walking along the street, felled him instantly to the ground with an iron bar, I could not help seeing the innocent blood of this exotic flowing in a plentiful stream down to his ankles.

In another place I saw the incensed population divesting a French printer of all the goods in his shop, and, after having helped him off with many other things, levelling his house to the ground under this pretext, namely, that many thought himself was desirous of setting his own house on fire, that the conflagration might become more general. My brother told me he saw a Frenchman almost dismembered in Moorfields, because he carried balls of fire in a chest with him, when in truth they were only tennis balls.

In this interval of time, when the fury of the people burst forth with an irresistible torrent upon those unhappy objects of distress, a report on a sudden prevailed that four thousand French and Papists were in arms, intending to carry with them death and destruction, and increase the conflagration. Upon which every person, both in the city and suburbs, having procured some sort of weapon or other, instantly almost collected themselves to oppose this chimerical army.

It was a pity that the exertions of the Londoners were not put to a better use for, if the citizens collected themselves to oppose the mythical French army, they certainly did not collect themselves to fight the more immediate threat – the grim reality of the fire. The Thameside along by London Bridge, over a quarter-of-a-mile stretch, with its rookeries of stores and cellars, its low, dark, timber-built dwellings, rotting with age and neglect, was now one vast forest of flame. The fire burnt through house after house while the narrow passages prevented what few fire appliances that could be found by the more determined citizens from being brought into play. As one observer wrote: 'The engines had no liberty to play for the narrowness of the place and the crowd of people, but some of them were tumbled down in the river, and among the rest that of Clerkenwell, esteemed one of the best.'

By 10 am St Martin Orgar and St Michael Crooked Lane were alight. St Michael Crooked Lane contained the tomb of Sir William Walworth, a former Lord Mayor of London and member of the Fishmongers' Company, who achieved notoriety as the killer of Wat Tyler. The fire had consumed the Old Swann tavern in Old Swann Lane,

the Dyers' Hall, and had already raged across Coldharbour, destroying the Waterman's Hall. Also alight, to the north of the Steelyard, was All Hallows-the-More, the first church to set up the Royal Standard while General Monck was still undecided whether to bring about a restoration of the Stuart monarchy or govern England as a republic. Now this church was shattered by the intense heat, and part of its roofless shell was blown

A German fire-engine, thought to have been in use in London, dated from 1662. It was manually worked. SCIENCE MUSEUM

down by the wind. Later that day volunteers pulled down the end wall to avoid further danger. The steeple stood firm, however, and from the molten bell metal a new bell was cast in 1670.

On the river, Samuel Pepys stayed in his boat long enough to see:

. . . the fire rage every way, and nobody, to my sight, endeavouring to quench it, but to remove their goods, and leave all to the fire, and having seen it get as far as the Steelyard, and the wind mighty high and driving into the city, and everything after so long a drought, proving combustible, even the very stones of the churchs; and among other things, the poor steeple by which pretty Mrs — lived, and whereof my old schoolfellow Elborough is parson, taken in fire in the very top and there burned till it fell down.

This was a reference to the church of St Laurence Pountney. It stood on a hill overlooking the main fire area, just north of Thames Street. Its slender spire was one of the tallest in London and overlooked the centre of the City. As Pepys

Fishmongers Hall today: this stands slightly to the west of the original Hall converted from the Thamesside mansion of Lord Fanhope and purchased at the end of the fifteenth century by the Fishmongers' Company. It was the first of forty-four great Company Halls to be destroyed in the flames.

watched, live brands lodged by the wind melted through the lead roof and fired the timbers of the church. Another more poetic observer said the fire took hold of the steeple 'as if taking a view from that lofty place of what it intended suddenly to devour'. But Thomas Middleton, a surgeon, was to tell the Parliamentary Committee of investigation that 'I saw the fire break out from the inside of St Laurence Pountney steeple, when there was no fire near it. These and such observations begat in me a persuasion that the fire was maintained by design'.

The high spire of St Laurence Pountney became a blazing beacon for miles.

It was at this time, about eleven o'clock, that Samuel Pepys ordered his boatman to row him to Whitehall 'and there to the King's closet in the chapel, where people came about me, and I did give them an account which dismayed them all, and afterwards was carried to the King'.

Charles II was with his brother, the Duke of York, and the Secretary of State, Lord Arlington, plus several other ministers. Samuel Pepys quickly poured out his tale of the fire, what he had witnessed about the lack of organisation to fight it, and even suggested that unless His Majesty commanded houses to be pulled down to create firebreaks, nothing would stop the fire from getting completely out of control. Charles became a ball of action, issuing a steady stream of orders to his courtiers, establishing a system of couriers from the City to the palace to keep him in constant touch with the progress of the fire, and arranging for all available fire-fighting equipment to be sent into the City. He then ordered a royal coach for Pepys and told him to go and find the Lord Mayor and tell him to spare no houses but to pull down all necessary buildings before the fire. The Duke of York and Lord Arlington both told Pepys to assure the Lord Mayor that he could have as many companies of the King's Guards as he wanted to keep order and aid in the fire-fighting.

In a daze Pepys was driven back into the City but at St Paul's the coach was forced to halt by panicking citizens. Pepys alighted and continued on foot along Watling Street. The area was crammed with fearful people each fighting their way through the thick acrid smoke which was being blown up from the riverside. Pepys pushed on 'as well as I could, every creature coming away laden with goods to save, and here and there people carried away in beds'. The streets were 'full of nothing but people and horses with goods, ready to run over one another, and removing goods from one burned house to another'. The din was tremendous, the

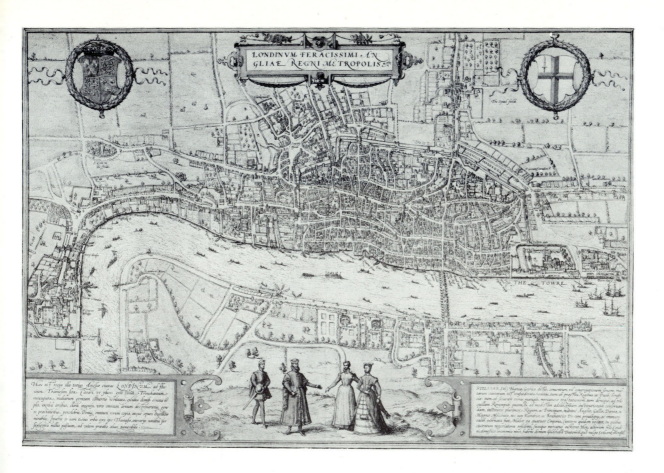

Pre-Fire London. A map of the City and suburbs made on a scale
of 17 ins to the mile by George Baum and Franciscus Hogenburg
and published in Civitates Orbis Terrarum in 1572.
GUILDHALL LIBRARY

rattle of handcarts, frightened whinnies of horses,
screams of women and general confusion, topped
by the great bells of St Paul's cathedral pealing out
the disaster warning. Pepys pushed against this tide
of humanity along Watling Street and from there
into Cannon Street.

It was in Cannon Street that Pepys met the Lord
Mayor. He was, says Pepys, 'like a man spent, with
a handkerchief about his neck. To the King's message he cried, like a fainting woman, 'Lord! What
can I do? I am spent: People will not obey me. I
have been pulling down houses, but the fire over-
takes us faster than we can do it!' Bludworth also
told Pepys that he must have more soldiers to help
and that he needed to go and refresh himself as he
had been up all night.

'So he left me,' wrote Pepys, 'and I him, and
walked home, seeing people almost distracted and
no manner of means used to quench the fire.'

Pepys decided there was nothing further he could
do on an empty stomach and went home to lunch.

It was not until after noon on Sunday that bands
of isolated but determined citizens seriously tried
to create fire-breaks by pulling down houses. But
they commenced their work without co-ordination
and also too close to the fire. And so, wind driven,
the fire crept back from the river to the numerous
courts and alleys which wound up the hill from
Thames Street, along quaint little places of medieval origin, like Duke's Foot Lane and Suffolk
House, which stood under the shadow of St
Laurence Pountney. Suffolk House had, in the
fourteenth century, belonged to Sir John Pountney, four times Lord Mayor of London, and then
to the Dukes of Exeter, Suffolk and Buckingham.
It was called 'The Manor of the Rose' and Shakespeare wrote of it in *Henry VIII* (Act I, Scene II)
when a surveyor says to the King:

Not long before your Highness sped to France
The Duke being at the Rose, within the parish
Saint Laurence Pountney, did of me demand
What was the speech among the Londoners
Concerning the French journey. . . .

Now the centuries-old house vanished in a mass
of flame. It had been acquired from the Earl of

Suffolk in 1561 by the Merchant Taylor Company which had established it as their grammar school. John Goad, the schoolmaster, at great personal risk, managed to save a portion of the library. Some eighteen months later he was teaching his scholars in a parish room by St Andrew Undershaft while a new school building was being built. Hector Forde, the head usher of the school, also conducted classes in the vestry house of St Katherine Cree, which escaped from the flames.

By midday on Sunday nearly half of Upper Thames Street was ablaze. But now disciplined bands were being gathered, although unco-ordinated, and these were posted under officers, 'watching', says Vincent, 'at every quarter for out-landish men, because of the general fears and jealousies and rumours that fire-balls were thrown into the houses by several of them to help on and provoke the too furious flames.'

The King's Guard marched into the City soon after noon and with them came Henry Bennet, Lord Arlington, Charles' Secretary of State. One spectator who stood watching the soldiers march past caught a glimpse of the Lord Mayor, Sir Thomas Bludworth. He was still in Cannon Street but 'on horseback, with few attendants, looking like one frightened out of his wits'. He was only seen once more in the City, on Wednesday super-vising the demolition of some houses at Cripple-gate, but he appears to slip into obscurity. He had become London's most disliked man. Pepys observed on 7 September that 'people do all the world over cry out at the simplicity of my Lord Mayor in general; and more particularly in this business of the fire, laying it all upon him'. Blud-worth's term of office expired in October and he was to die in relative obscurity in Camden House, Maiden Lane, in 1689. His daughter was to marry the infamous Judge George Jeffreys, Chief Justice and Lord Chancellor of England. The last glimpse we have of the man comes on 1 December, that year, when Pepys was walking up Thames Street. He met the former Lord Mayor and observed: 'Lord! the silly talk this silly fellow had . . . and complaining now that now, as everybody did lately in the fire, everybody endeavours to save himself and let the whole perish; but a very weak man he seems to be.'

A Dramatic Reconstruction of the Fire Scene: a coloured aquatint by J. C. Stadler after Philip J. Loutherbourg, published in 1799. This purports to show the scene during the Fire under one of the arches of London Bridge with citizens escaping as best they can with such possessions as they have been able to salvage. GUILDHALL LIBRARY

South-east view of a house in Sweedon's Passage, Grub Street,
which was finally pulled down in March 1805. The house was
built in 1650 and the artist, John T. Smith (1766-1833)
recalls that it was built of oak, chestnut, lath and plaster.

GUILDHALL LIBRARY

[32]

The fire was still spreading rapidly and Samuel Pepys, returning through the City after his lunch, observed in Upper Thames Street that:

There the flames were fed by tallow, oil, pitch, tar and even brandy in the shops and warehouses. Here I saw Mr Isaac Houblon, the handsome man prettily dressed and dirty at his door at Dowgate, receiving some of his brother's things, whose houses were on fire; and he says having been removed twice already; and he doubts, as it soon proved, that they must be, in a little time, removed from his house also, which was a sad consideration.

The flames were approaching Cannon Street and the people were 'now removing out of Cannon Street which received goods in the morning, into Lombard Street and further'.

King Charles and his brother James came down river that afternoon, rowed in the royal barge, and met Samuel Pepys at Queenhithe about 3 pm. Charles watched the blaze at Waterman's Hall from the roof of a tall house in one of the alleys beside The Three Cranes in Vintry. The Three Cranes was a well-known tavern, the oldest waterside tavern in London, although Pepys did not think much of it. He had dined there in January, 1662, and recorded that his party were crammed into a room which was 'such a narrow dog-hole . . . and a sorry, poor dinner it was too'. Charles was eager to direct the fire-fighting personally and had to be rebuked for placing his own life in jeopardy. He wanted to stop the fire at Queenhithe but, as Pepys observed:

. . . there was little that could be done, the fire coming upon them so fast. Good hopes there was of stopping it at The Three Cranes above and at St Botolph's Wharf below the bridge, if care be used, but the wind carries it into the City, so as we know not by the waterside what it does there.

Charles charged what members of the Privy Council and City magistrates who were at hand to defend the City. Sir Richard Browne, a former Lord Mayor and alderman, spoke to Charles and pointed out the laws governing the destruction of houses in the City boundaries. Charles dismissed this subject by saying that if anyone complained then they should file their complaints against him. Having tried to force some more constructive action on the City officials, Charles returned to Whitehall to await events. Pepys accompanied him

in the royal barge. The river, he observed, was now 'full of lighters and boats taking in goods, and good goods swimming in the water; and only I observed that hardly one lighter or boat in three had the goods of a house in it, but there was a pair of virginals (spinnets) in it'.

When Charles and the royal party arrived back at Whitehall Palace, they found William Lindsay, the Earl of Craven, waiting in some agitation. Craven was ever a man of action. After a long exile on the Continent for his support of the Royalist cause during the days of the Commonwealth and Protectorate, he had returned to England and taken a house in Drury Lane. During the plague he had stayed in London, refusing to join the royal court at Oxford, and devoting his time and money to tending to the wants of needy Londoners. This had endeared him to most citizens who respected him and trusted him. Craven was now demanding a Royal Warrant to give him permission to assist the Lord Mayor and magistrates of the City in fighting the fire. Charles accepted his offer of help with alacrity.

John Evelyn of Greenwich came to look at the fire that afternoon.

With my wife and son took coach and went to bankside in Southwark, where we beheld the dismal spectacle, the whole City in dreadful flames near the waterside, and now had consumed all the houses from the bridge, all Thames Street and upwards towards Cheapside, down to The Three Cranes, and so returned exceedingly astonished, what would become of the rest?

By 4 pm the fire on Fish Street Hill was within four houses of Eastcheap to the north and further on had entered the eastern end of Cannon Street. The Steelyard area was completely alight. The Steelyard was an area of three acres where the North German merchants of Hansa had their headquarters ever since Henry III granted them land there in 1259. The German merchants traded in such diverse goods as wheat, rye, grain, cables, ropes, masts, pitch, tea, linen, wax, steel, hemp, flax, etc. In fact, Steelyard was often referred to as a city within the City and it led an independent life. Sir Francis Drake once owned a house there. Now it was gone in a deluge of flames. And the great warehouses of the Hansa merchants were also ablaze. Stow described their great hall as 'built of stone; with three arched gates towards the street, the middlemost whereof is far bigger than the other, and is seldom opened, the other two be mured up'. The housemaster had just managed to escape with his clothes ablaze leaving two great masterpieces by Holbein to be devoured by the flames – *The Triumph of Riches* and *The Triumph of Poverty*. Afterwards it was rumoured that the pictures had been saved and removed to the Continent where they subsequently vanished.

Dusk was approaching the City now. A Spanish observer, whose account was published in Valencia a few weeks later, wrote:

Night approached: and the sun disappeared sooner than usual behind the thick clouds and fogs formed by the smoke; but it seemed to the onlookers that the day was returning with all its light, so widely was the fire spreading. The horror, fear, pity and confusion of that night – to relate them would be the work of days. Think of them: people wandering about the streets because their houses had been burnt, dazed by the thought of disaster; the fear of those in the districts towards which the flames were slowly making their way, the wind all the time fanning the flames and bringing the horror closer and keeping the remedy further away.

The anonymous resident of Middle Temple recalled:

That evening I was a second time on the water, and it was then the fire appeared with all the horror and dreadfulness imaginable; the flames afforded light enough to discover themselves, the black smoke, the building they so imminently threatened. The moon offered her light, too, but was so overcome by this greater; which not being able (by day) to contend with that of the sun had (as it were, in spite) by smoke lessened it. I came back at eight o'clock, leaving it then at The Three Cranes, which is distant from the bridge almost a fourth part of the space between the Temple and the bridge. At night more of the Life Guard and soldiers watched the City.

The resident of Middle Temple was not the only observer on the river that evening. Samuel Pepys left Whitehall Palace to walk to St James's Park where he joined his wife and his friends, John Creed and Mr Wood and his wife. Together they:

. . . walked to my boat; and there upon the water again, and to the fire up and down, it still increasing, and the wind great. So near the fire as we could for smoke; and all over the Thames, with one's face in the wind, you were almost burned with a shower of fire drops. This is very true; so as houses were burned by these drops and flakes of fire, three or four, nay, five or six houses, one from another. When we could endure no more upon the water, we to a little alehouse on Bankside, over against The Three Cranes, and there stayed till it grew dark almost, and saw the fire grow; and, as it grew darker, appeared more and more, and in corners and upon steeples, and between churches and houses, as far as we could see up the hill of the City, in a most horrid, malicious, bloody flame, not like the fine flame of an ordinary fire. We stayed till, it being darkish, we saw the fires as one entire arch of fire from this to the other side of the bridge, and in a bow up the hill for an arch of above a mile long; it made me weep to see it. The churches, the houses, and all on fire, and flaming at once, and a horrid noise the flames made, and the cracking of houses at their ruin. So home with a sad heart, and there to find everybody discoursing and lamenting it.

It was on the way back to Pepy's house in Seething Lane that it was noticed that the fire was now so strong that it was burning back *against the wind* towards the Tower of London along Lower Thames Street. If it continued thus it meant that Pepys was in the path of the fire. The Pepys' family spent most of the night packing their belongings and making ready their furniture to evacuate their house. At midnight Thomas Hayter, who was Pepys' clerk at the Navy Office, arrived to announce that his lodgings had been destroyed. 'We did put Mr. Hayter, poor man!, to bed a little, but he got very little rest, so much noise being in my house, taking down of goods.'

And while the Pepys family made ready for their evacuation, the fire raged on. The Boar's Head in Eastcheap was burned down, the famous tavern frequented by such literary talents as William Shakespeare, Ben Jonson and Richard Burbage. Shakespeare had immortalised the tavern as the scene of the drunken debaucheries of Sir John Falstaff, the tavern in which Mistress Quickly presided as hostess and Doll Tearsheet kept the customers happy. Now that, too, was gone.

The western edge of the fire had burnt up Downgate, then an open street leading steeply to

A view down Fish Street Hill today looking towards St Magnus Martyr and the Thames. At the time of the Great Fire this was the main thoroughfare south, out of the City, over London Bridge, which then stood at the bottom of the hill hard by the church, where the modern buildings are now sited.
JOHN BENTON-HARRIS

the water dock. Tallow Chandlers' Hall, Skinners' Hall and Innholders' Hall were destroyed. The Skinners' Hall had belonged to the Skinners' Company since 1441 and contained many treasures which, providentially, had been removed to Shoreditch before the flames caught.

The Post Office in Cloak Lane, Dowgate, was also destroyed.

Sir Philip Froude, the governor for the lessee, Katherine, Countess of Chesterfield, had left the Post Office at midnight, with his wife, and left it in the safe keeping of acting-postmaster James Hickes. Hickes was a phlegmatic man who did not frighten easily. He had remained in London during the plague, keeping the letter office open and attending to its business. It took much to force him to leave his post. But at one o'clock he realised the danger of the encroaching flames. With his wife and children, he packed what he could carry, and made his way through the burning streets to the Golden Lion in Red Cross Street, outside Cripplegate. At the Golden Lion he temporarily re-established the Post Office. He had saved several packets of post and letters of State received from the Chester and Irish mail coaches. These he sent to Sir James Williamson, Lord Arlington's secretary and editor of the *London Gazette*, with a note saying 'how we shall dispose our business only the wise God knows'.

Hickes sent his family to Barnet for safety as the fire spread. The Post Office in Cloak Lane was totally destroyed along with a secret apparatus for opening, copying and forging letters 'in the interests of the State'. This apparatus had been invented by Sir Samuel Morland, who was employed by Oliver Cromwell in his espionage system and placed in charge of the mails. Morland was, however, a double agent working for Charles Stuart.

On 4 September, acting postmaster Hickes wrote to his regional postmasters:

I am commanded to tell you letters from Ministers of State are to be sent hither to me, that I may convey them to the court. When the violence of the fire is over, some place will be fixed upon for a general correspondence.

And so, as Sunday, 2 September, the first day of the fire, drew to a close, London was burning from St Botolph's in Billingsgate, east of London Bridge, to Black Swan Alley, a few yards from Queenhithe, and northwards some three hundred yards to Eastcheap. It was a major fire but, so far, not a catastrophic one.

CHAPTER TWO

Monday, 3 September 1666

Admiral Sir William Penn,
a member of the Navy Board and Samuel Pepys neighbour.
He directed sailors in blowing up houses with
gunpowder to create fire-breaks.
NATIONAL PORTRAIT GALLERY

Monday was another hot, dry September day but with the wind still blowing, unabated, from the east and the fire extending rapidly north and west across the City, up Gracechurch Street and along Eastcheap and Cannon Street.

The majority of Londoners had been up all night, either watching the progress of the fire or fearfully packing their belongings like Samuel Pepys. He was still up at four o'clock that morning when 'my Lady Batten sent me a cart to carry away all my money and plate, and best things to Sir William Rider's at Bethnal Green, which I did, riding myself in my night gown in the cart; and Lord! to see how the streets and the highways are crowded with people running and riding, and getting of carts at any rate to fetch things away!'

Pepys, with his cart of belongings, drove out of the City by Aldgate along Whitechapel Road to Bethnal Green where Sir William Rider, a wealthy London merchant, lived in a house called Kirkby's Castle, a fantastic structure which was reputedly the setting for a famous ballad, ''The Beggar's Daughter of Bethnal Green'. Pepys found Sir William exhausted, having been up all night arranging to store the goods of his friends the Admirals Sir William Penn and Sir William Batten, who were two of Pepys' colleagues on the Navy Board. Pepys placed his belongings with the others. 'I am eased at my heart to have my treasures so well secured.'

Before six o'clock he had returned to Seething Lane and was aiding his wife, Elizabeth, in packing the more cumbersome pieces of furniture. He managed to hire a Mr. Tooker to take them away in a boat 'and we did carry them, myself some, over Tower Hill, which was by this time full of people's goods, bringing their goods hither; and down to the lighter, which lay at the next quay, above Tower Dock. And here was my neighbour's wife Mrs —, with her pretty child, and some few of her things which I did willingly give way to be saved with mine but there was no passing anything through the postern, the crowd was so great'.

Eventually, with the help of Elizabeth, Tom Hayter and his maids (with the exception of one maid, Mary Mercer, who had gone to help her mother whose house was in Fenchurch Street and in more immediate danger from the fire) Pepys loaded up the lighter. The goods were then transferred to the safety of the house of Sir George Carteret at Deptford. Sir George was another of Pepys' colleagues and Treasurer at the Navy Board.

With the dawning of Monday a new spirit seemed to take hold of the people of the City. The inhabitants seemed to recover from the apathy and indecision that had marked their attitudes on Sunday. John Evelyn had observed:

The conflagration was so universal, and the people so astonished, that from the beginning they hardly stirr'd to quench it, so as there was nothing heard but crying out and lamentation, and running about like distracted creatures, without at all attempting to save even their goods; such a strange consternation there was upon them, so as it burned both in breadth and length, the churches, public halls, exchange, hospitals, monuments and ornaments, leaping after a prodigious manner from house to house

Edward Montagu, Earl of Manchester. One of Charles II's Privy Councillors who was active in fighting the fire. At one stage he rode through the burning streets trying to connect water pipes.
NATIONAL PORTRAIT GALLERY

William Lindsay, Earl Craven, was a popular figure with Londoners. Rather than follow the Royal Court to Oxford during the dreadful plague year, he remained in London bringing help to the needy. A member of the Privy Council, as early as the first day of the fire he was urging Charles II to let him take charge of the fire-fighting.

NATIONAL PORTRAIT GALLERY

and street to street, at great distances one from the other, for the heat had even ignited the air, and prepared the materials to conceive the fire, which devoured after an incredible manner, houses and furniture and everything. Here we saw the Thames covered with goods floating, all the barges and boats laden with what some had time and courage to save, as on the other, the carts and etc.; carrying out to the fields, which for many miles were strewed with movables of all sorts, and tents erecting to shelter both people and what goods they could get away.

This Monday, however, the people did stir to quench the blaze. James, Duke of York, took direct command of the fire-fighting operations that morning. He appointed the Lords Craven, Manchester, Ashley, Belasyse and Harrison, all members of the Privy Council, as his lieutenants. A headquarters was established at Ely Place, Holborn, and fire posts were set up around the City's perimeter at Temple Bar, Clifford's Inn Gardens, Fetter Lane, Shoe Lane and Cow Lane in Smithfield. The posts were to be manned by the parish constables with one hundred civilian volunteers, aided by a military officer with a troop of thirty foot-soldiers. Command of each post was put in the hands of three justices of the peace and each post was to be provisioned with bread, cheese and beer to the value of £5. James also authorised a reward of one shilling for any man who was 'diligent at night' in giving warning of the fire's progress. Later that Monday further fire posts were established at Cripplegate, Aldersgate and in Coleman Street.

A manual fire-engine in use at the time known as the 'worm drive fire squirt' which first appeared about 1582.
SCIENCE MUSEUM

Orders were sent to the Lords Lieutenant of Middlesex, Surrey, Kent and Hertford to send in the county militias in order to help with crowd control, to prevent looting and to help in fighting the inferno. The first of these troops were marching into the City by early afternoon.

On Monday (wrote Vincent) Gracechurch Street is all in flames, with Lombard Street on the left hand, and part of Fenchurch Street on the right, the fire workers (though not so fast) against the wind that way: before it were pleasant and stately homes, behind it ruinous and desolate heaps. The burning was then in fashion of a bow, a dreadful bow it was, such as mine eyes never before had seen.

Near to The Three Cranes in Vintry, the fifteenth century Vintner's Hall with the company wharf and thirteen almshouses had vanished. Three other company halls were destroyed early that morning: – the Parish Clerks', the Plumbers' in Thames Street, and the Joyners' Hall. In the Plumbers' Hall a printing press and a library of valuable books were destroyed. Across Thames Street the flames had spread to the church of St

Martin Vintry and to St James Garlickhithe. The registers of St James dated back to 1535 and these were saved by an enterprising curate. The flames also crept up the nearby hill to the house which had once belonged to Richard Whittington, perhaps the most famous of London's Lord Mayors. Whittington was a wealthy merchant, a dealer in textiles, who became Lord Mayor four times, in 1396, 1397, 1406 and 1409. Nearby St Michael Paternoster Royal, which contained Whittington's tomb, was gutted and the Cutlers' Hall, close to it, in Cloak Lane, was also burnt down but a caretaker managed to save its extensive library and plate. And along the Thames, adding to the noxious smells, the fire spread to the buildings where trades such as soap-boiling and dyeing were carried out, causing steam and vile-smelling gases to rise from the vaults and pits.

By 10 am the fire was within four houses of Queenhithe, which once constituted half the port of London. The harbours of Billingsgate and Queenhithe used to serve all the wants of the medieval capital. Queenhithe used to make a deep indentation in the river bank behind which was a market. Early that morning Charles and James spent some time there and it seemed that Charles had great hopes of stopping the fire at this point. He personally encouraged a squad of men who were strenuously employed in pulling down houses, stripping the market of all combustible goods, in order to leave nothing to assist the spread of the fire. The King was there half-an-hour before returning to Whitehall. The efforts to create a fire-break were all in vain. An eye-witness wrote: 'After two hours' expectations we saw all these endeavours slighted by a leap which the fire made over twenty houses upon the turret of a house in Thames Street.' Soon after James called by the Navy Office in Seething Lane to ask advice. According to Pepys: 'The Duke of York came this day by the office, and spoke to us, and did ride with his Guard up and down the City to keep all quiet, he being now General, and having a care of all.'

The fire was increasing in noise and violence. The few hours' expansion since dawn had brought it to the City's wealthiest quarter, the intersection of Gracechurch Street and Lombard Street, where it continued to burn all day amid the rich houses of the merchants and bankers. Evelyn let his feelings run away with him when he wrote in his diary:

Oh, the miserable and calamitous spectacle! such as haply the world had not seen since the foundation of it, nor be outdone till the universal conflagration thereof. God grant mine eyes may

Sir Robert Vyner, one of London's wealthiest merchants, was sheriff of London during the Fire week. He had to flee from his house in Lombard Street. He later became Lord Mayor of the City and attributed the Fire to a deliberate plot on the part of Catholics to seize power. In 1674, during his mayoralty, he conferred the freedom of the City on Charles and his brother James in recognition of their action during the Fire week. In this engraving by Grignion from a drawing by Hayman, he is seen outside his house in Lombard Street in a far from sober state persuading Charles II to stay for more drinks.
GUILDHALL LIBRARY

never behold the like, who now saw about 10,000 houses all in one flame! The noise and cracking and thunder of the impetuous flames, the shrieking of women and children, the hurry of people, the fall of towers, houses and churches, was like a hideous storm; and the air all about so hot and inflamed, that at the last one was not able to approach it, so that they were forced to stand still, and let the flames burn on, which they did, for near two miles in length and one in breadth.

Evelyn's description was more emotional than accurate for at no time that Monday did the fire reach the proportions he claimed and at no time were 10,000 houses alight at the same time. However, it was true that the fire-fighters were not effective against the flames, although now and again they won a minor victory. In the east of the City, for example, young William Taswell had joined a group of fire-fighters raised by the Dean of Westminster.

On the next day (Monday) John Dolben, Bishop of Rochester and Dean of Westminster (who in the Civil War had frequently stood sentinel) collected his scholars together in a company, marching with them on foot to put a stop if possible to the conflagration. I was a kind of page to him, not being one of the number of King's scholars. We were employed many hours in fetching water from the back side of Saint Dunstan's church in the east where we happily extinguished the fire.

But because of the drought, because the wooden water pipes in the streets were burnt or broken, because the pumping houses at the north side of London Bridge lay in charred ruins, no water could be pumped into the City to aid the fire fighters in their task. Roads were hastily torn up to find sewers or to sink wells, elm trees were hollowed to form new pipes but the City cisterns were dry. It was obvious that the fire was totally out of control.

By 3 pm Lombard Street, the financial centre of London, was destroyed.

Lombard Street was a narrow, little street, with only a few feet of space separating each house. It was one of the most picturesque streets in London, its houses in timber frames with large casement windows, decorated by a wealth of gilt and coloured signs:– the Unicorn, the Grasshopper, the White Horse, the Golden Fleece, each proclaiming its merchant financiers. The street had been named after the many bankers and money-lenders from Lombardy, in Italy, who had settled in the area but

who had left the country again in the reign of Elizabeth. They left a permanent mark on English finance and the symbols £ s d derived from £ = lire; s = soldi; and d = denari. The Lombardy arms, three golden balls, became a symbol of money-lending. The merchants who lived in Lombard Street in 1666 governed the financial resources of the country; it was they who made it possible for the Government to conduct the war against the Dutch and French.

Sir Robert Vyner, elected Sheriff of London for that year, had his house in Lombard Street. It was one of the largest in the street, covering half an acre and situated next to St Mary Woolmoth church. Sir Robert was a prosperous goldsmith who would one day become Lord Mayor. He was responsible for providing the new regalia used at Charles II's coronation, including the St Edward Crown which is still part of the coronation ceremonial today. Sir Robert had been astute enough to have removed his household goods the day before, but nothing could save the destruction of his house.

The picturesque street was consumed with the church of St Edmund the Martyr and the fine old George Inn next door. The wealth of Lombard Street, its bounds and securities, had been hastily removed as the fire neared it and although the merchants were hard-hit and widely scattered, the fire brought no financial panic in its wake. Indeed, Evelyn in a letter to Sir Samuel Tuke on 29 September, noted that this was a happy sign for the country. However, one Dutch merchant wrote to his colleagues in Amsterdam: 'My house amongst others was burnt, by God's grace my books and letters of credit are at my house at Clapham but none know where I shall find the merchants who will pay me the moneys due'.

With Lombard Street a flaming mass, Cornhill and the Royal Exchange were threatened. Cornhill was a wide thoroughfare surrounded by narrow alleys which survived from medieval days. It was a favourite shopping centre of the fashionable and rich. Just off its spacious precincts, in St Michael's Alley, Pasqual Rosee had set up the first Coffee House in 1652 establishing a social fashion which spread all over London. As the flames drew near the Cornhill the citizens were organised in pulling down the south side of the street. It was believed that this would leave a large dry moat over which the fire could not pass. The stone church of St Peter's Cornhill and St Michael Archangel would, it was reasoned, also be bulwarks able to resist the flames.

Organising the fire-fighting at this point was the handsome eighteen-year-old Duke of Monmouth

James Scott, Duke of Monmouth,
Charles II's illegitimate son. The young Duke commanded
cavalry troops in the City to prevent looting and to keep order.
When he led his abortive uprising against his uncle, James,
he accused him of being the instigator of a plot to burn
down London for political gain.

NATIONAL PORTRAIT GALLERY

with a company of the King's Life Guard. James Scott had been recently publicly acknowledged by Charles as his natural son and elevated to the peerage. Monmouth was to lose his head for organising a rebellion against his uncle James II in 1685. Among the accusations he made against James was that he had deliberately started the fire.

The attempt to stop the fire at Cornhill was abortive. According to Vincent:

Now the flames break in upon Cornhill; that large and spacious street, and quickly cross the way by the train of wood that lay in the streets untaken away, which had been pulled down from houses to prevent its spreading, and so they lick up the whole street as they go; they mount up to the top of the highest houses; they descend down to the lowest vaults and cellars, and march along on both sides of the way, with such a roaring noise, as was never heard in the City of London; no stately building so great as to resist their fury...

And perhaps the greatest stately building in the City was Sir Thomas Gresham's Royal Exchange, standing conspicuous with its lofty square tower of stone, its great clock and its balconied galleries. Some £3,737 of Elizabeth's money had been spent on clearing the site to erect the building. It was Renaissance in detail but designed like a Dutch bourse round a courtyard and with a tall tower. It was a place where the merchants could conduct their business, pacing up and down among the elegant arcades, while above, on the upper levels, were nearly two hundred shops. Many foreign visitors remarked on the beauty of the Royal Exchange and King Christian IV of Denmark, a noted connoisseur of architecture, was much impressed with it when he visited it in 1606.

The Reverend Samuel Rolle wrote in his *Burning of London*, 1667:

[44]

LONDON.

London Verbrandt, or London on Fire. A contemporary
Dutch engraving. BRITISH MUSEUM

Here, if anywhere, might a man have seen the glory of the world in a monument, as the Devil showed it to Christ upon a high mountain. Was it not the great storehouse, whence the nobility and gentry of England were furnished with most of those costly things wherewith they did adorn either their closets or themselves? What artificial thing could entertain the senses and the fantasies of men that was not there to be had? Such was the delight that many gallants took in that magazine of all curious varieties that they could almost have dwelt there (going from shop to shop like bees from flower to flower). If they had but a fountain of money that could not have been drawn dry. I doubt not but a Mahomedan (who never expects other than sensible delight) would gladly have accepted of that place, and the treasures of it, for his heaven, and have thought there was none like it.

And now the Royal Exchange, 'the glory of the world', fell victim to the flames. Vincent recorded:

The Royal Exchange itself, the glory of the

merchants, is now invaded with much violence; and when once the fire was entered, how quickly did it run down the galleries, filling them with flames; then came down the stairs and compasseth the walls, giving forth flaming vollies, and filleth the court with sheets of fire; by and by, down fall all the kings upon their faces and the greater part of the stone building after them (the founder's statue only remaining) with such a noise as was dreadful and astonishing.

As Vincent noted, only Sir Thomas Gresham's statue remained untouched. Strangely enough, when the rebuilt Royal Exchange was destroyed once more by fire in 1838, the only thing to survive was Sir Thomas Gresham's statue once again.

Threadneedle Street was now aflame and St Benet Finke's church destroyed, some twenty-three churches were burning simultaneously across the City as whole streets of dwellings and shops added new fuel to the rapacious flames. Vincent wrote:

[45]

A statement by John Morgan, a clerk, that on 3 September 1666, while he was in the garret of a house in Fye Foot Lane, a fireball fell through the roof and set the house alight, yet the fire, at this time, was nowhere near Fye Foot Lane but still in Thames Street some distance away.

CORPORATION OF LONDON RECORDS OFFICE

Hon:ed Gentlmen

I whose name is undernamed: am desired by frinds of mine, to declare and attest unto you what I seen in ye late fatall destruction of ye once famous citty of London by the invincible fire, As I was in a frinds house in ffyfott Lane London on ye 3: of September in ye year 1666. where I was desired, to goe in to ye house to see how neare ye fire was. I went in with some folkes of ye house to their garrett ye was empty: standing their with the folkes a little while. Immediately their came a Wild fire-ball by my eares: who fell fiercely into ye Corner of ye Roome and pierced a hole in ye boards to ye bottome & then presently it woosd up in smoke & flames of fire. & I was faine to make hast downe and leap out of ye window two pair of stairs and others with me. yet ye maine fire was a good way off in Thames Street from ye house.

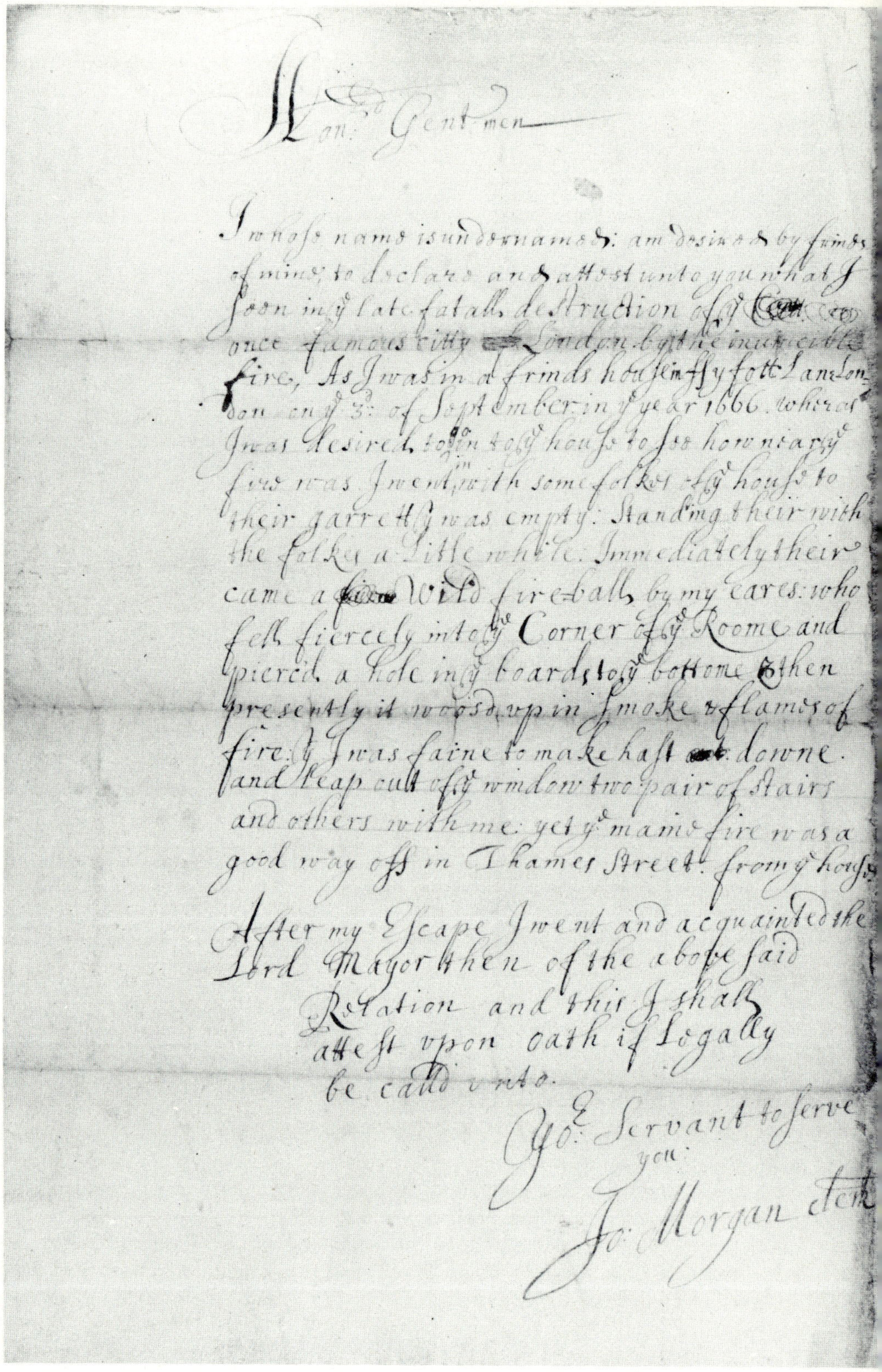

After my Escape I went and acquainted the Lord Mayor then of the above said Relation and this I shall attest upon oath if Legally be calld unto.

Yor Servant to serve you:

Jo: Morgan clerk

Rattle, rattle, rattle, was the noise which the fire struck upon the ear round about, as if there had been a thousand iron chariots beating upon the stones; and if you opened your eyes to the opening of the streets, where the fire was come, you might see in some places whole streets at once in flames, that issued forth, as if they had been so many great forges from the opposite windows, which folding together, were united together in one great flame throughout the whole street, and then you might see the houses tumble, tumble, tumble from one end of the street to the other with a great crash, leaving the foundations open to the view of the heavens . . . The yellow smoke of London ascendeth up to the heavens like the smoke of a great furnace; a smoke so great as darkened the sun at noon today! if at any time the sun peeped forth, it looked red like blood.

Evelyn estimated that the column of smoke must have risen and trailed fifty miles in length. That column of smoke was observed at Oxford by a Mr Locke who kept one of the first known meteorological registers. He made an entry on Monday: 'Dim reddish sunshine'. Several days later he added a note:– 'This unusual colour of the air, which without a cloud appearing made the sunbeams of a strange red rim light, was very remarkable. We had heard nothing of the fire of London. But it appeared afterwards to be the smoke of London, then burning, which driven this way by an easterly wind, caused this odd phenomenon.'

The wind blew all day. King Charles and his brother were repeatedly in the City trying to organise but it was difficult to control the general panic of the Londoners. This panic made many people hysterical against foreigners who, they imagined, were trying to destroy the City. That evening Michael Marsh, a company officer of the militia, arrested a Walloon at the Nag's Head in Leadenhall Street, merely because the man was carrying a lantern. Dawes Weymansel, a justice of the peace, swore he saw a foreigner arrested who had his pockets stuffed with incendiary devices. Such 'incendiary devices' usually turned out to be the most innocuous of belongings. Sir Edward Southcote's French servant was seized and Sir Edward only just managed to rescue him before he was lynched. Rumours of the arrival of a French or Dutch army, an uprising by Papists, or the like, caused fresh waves of hysteria to seize the crowds.

In Westminster Cornelius Riedveldt, a Dutch baker, was about to light his oven to prepare for the day's baking when people burst into his house crying that he was a foreigner about to destroy London. They dragged him out and were about to lynch him when the Duke of York rode by. Riedveldt was arrested and spent some weeks in the Westminster Gatehouse prison until he was cleared of suspicion. On his release he found that all his belongings and those of his family had been confiscated, including his house and shop. Penniless, he petitioned Lord Arlington in vain for compensation.

The worst incident of mob hysteria happened near Moorgate. A widow, trying to escape the fire into Moorfields, was attacked by a mob. She was carrying in her apron some baby chickens, perhaps the only things she had time to save before the flames enveloped her house. The crowd cried that the chickens were fire-balls. The woman was attacked and her breasts cut off, such was the hysterical frenzy of the mob.

Even the disciplined soldiers of the King's Guard were guilty of acts of violence. Denis de Repas wrote to Sir Edward Harley later that September that Charles and James 'had their corps de garde in several streets, and did knock down several strangers for not speaking good English. Some of them were armed with spits, some with bread staffs, and the captains with a broadsword'. De Repas blamed the London women for causing the hysteria. A Dutchman wrote at the time: 'Owing to the great fire which has taken place here, I have not dared to go out.'

By late afternoon the fire had greatly extended westward. It was in Cordwainer Street, Friday Street and Bread Street, leading to Cheapside. The Salters' Hall in Swithen Lane was burnt, an ancient building which had once belonged to the Priory of Tortington and was given to the Earl of Oxford by Henry VII. The fire had reached Derby House, granted in 1554 to the Heralds as their college of chivalry. The officers-at-arms had managed to save most of the ancient records of chivalry and these documents were given a temporary lodging in Whitehall by Charles. Woodmongers' Hall was alight, Cordwainers' Hall and Blacksmiths' Hall. Then Gerrard's Hall in Cheapside burst into flames. This was the site of the tomb of Gerrard the Giant, famous among London's fabled monsters. His vault survived to be destroyed by vandals in the nineteenth century.

Bucklesbury, the centre of the druggist trade, was also ablaze. This area was mainly occupied by apothecaries and took its name from the Buckle of Buckerel family who owned a mansion close by. Shakespeare mentions it through the mouth of Sir John Falstaff and refers to the smell of the drugs.

All Hallows, Star Lane. Left undamaged in the Fire, it was finally demolished, save for this tower, in 1870.

As the flames ignited the drugs the smell of Bucklesbury was worse than Shakespeare had conceived it.

It had been early that Monday when the majority of Londoners realised that this was no ordinary fire such as the many they had grown accustomed to. A panic started as they began to make for the open spaces round the City, Moorfields in the north and Tower Hill in the west. The majority made their way north to Moorfields and Finsbury Fields, large level spaces beyond the northern walls. Moorfields was the traditional drying place of the City's laundresses. Sir William Davenant had observed a few years earlier that Moorfields had consisted of 'acres of old linen, making a show like the fields of Carthagena when the fine months' shifts of the whole fleet are washt and spread'. Now the narrow streets which led towards the City gates were thronged with people and carts of various descriptions.

In some streets carts could not pass each other, in others crowds pushing this way and that and trying to save whatever they could, created panic. A further complication ensued. Against the tide of carts and people trying to get out of the narrow streets of London, there came a flood of entrepeneurs with empty carts, flooding into the City, in order to hire out their carts to these unfortunates at exorbitant rates.

> Now carts (wrote Vincent) and drays, and coaches, and horses, as many as could have entrance into the City were laden, and any money is given for help, five, ten, twenty and thirty pounds for a cart to bear forth into the fields some choice things which were ready to be consumed, and some of the countrymen did then offer in their extremity. I am mistaken if such money do not burn worse than the fire out of which it was rak'd.

Young William Taswell's parents were victims of the astute rogues who capitalised on the tragedy. He recalled:

> It could not be expected that my father's house should escape this almost general conflagration. They shared the same fate with others. But what rendered our loss still greater was this: certain persons, assuming the character of porters, but in reality nothing else but downright plunderers, came and offered their assistance in removing out goods. We accepted; but they so far availed themselves of our service as to steal goods to the value of forty pounds from us.

[48]

This engraving of *Winchester Street* by *London Wall* shows the type of narrow *streets* and *overhanging* upper storeys which contributes so much to the spread of the Fire. Drawn and etched by John T. Smith. GUILDHALL LIBRARY

E. Waterhous, in his *Short Narrative of the Fire*, recalled that:

Many had paid out their all on Saturday, their pay day, and those who had drained themselves were certainly put to great straits, being either forced to give one part (of their belongings) to carry away the rest or to leave all to the fire . . . Some I hope to have been very honest and reasonable, but into those honest and happy bands God knows many of my goods fell not, nor the goods of thousands more, but into the hands of those harpies that devoured all they took, and cried 'Give! Give! Give! never to return again.

The problem of the havoc and jams created by the carts moving belongings back and forth caused the magistrates to issue an order that Monday afternoon forbidding the admittance of carts into the City. It was also thought that this might compel Londoners to remain in the City to help assist the fire-fighters instead of fleeing into the surrounding countryside. The order was not enforceable so great was the panic of the crowd and the next day, Tuesday, the order was withdrawn.

The fire-fighters were working courageously in disciplined bands but their efforts were useless because of the high wind. As fast as they pulled down the houses before the fire, sparks were carried on the wind to anything up to half a mile so that the red-hot cinders would fall behind them and start new fires. And, indeed, quite apart from the wind, the fire created its own draughts in the tiny alleys, causing small fire storms. Waterhous observed that 'the fire carried the noise of a whirlwind in it, and was so informed with terror that it surprised the eyes and hearts of men with fear, as well as their houses and goods with flames'.

As night descended across the City the fire still raged unabated northward and westward. At 9 pm Baynard's Castle caught alight.

Samuel Wiseman, writing in his *Short Description of the Burning of London*, 1666, said: 'The flinty walls of Baynard's strong built castle, thought by the inhabitants that westward dwelt, a powerful garrison against the flames, yielded like a paper building to the fire.' Baynard's Castle had for centuries guarded the western side of the City, a sister fortress to the Tower on the eastern side.

It had been built by one of William the Conqueror's lieutenants and in 1111 it had passed into the hands of the de Clare family. In 1213 King John had attempted to destroy it because of the rebellion of its owner Robert Fitzwalter. Fire had almost destroyed it in 1428 but it had been rebuilt by Humphrey, Duke of Gloucester, and uncle of Henry VI. It was in Baynard's Castle that the notorious Richard Crookback, Richard of York, declared himself Richard III of England.

Henry VII had rebuilt it 'for the entertainment of any princes of great estate' and taken down many of its fortifications. One historical drama witnessed by the castle was the declaration by the Council of State for Mary Tudor. On 9 July 1553 the Duke of Northumberland had failed in his attempt to make his daughter-in-law, Lady Jane Grey, queen of England. The Council of State had slipped out of the Tower of London, barricaded themselves in Baynard's Castle, and declared Mary Tudor as queen.

Now the castle, its great walls rising directly out of the Thames, was permeated with a gloomy atmosphere and was hardly used, although Charles had dined there in 1661.

The flames leapt the old walls and caught at the dry wooden gables of the main building, which rose two floors. Soon all the turrets were pillars of flame. The old castle was still blazing at seven o'clock the next morning, some ten hours later. The *London Gazette*, which had its office in the grounds of the castle, had to be evacuated, its printing presses being left behind.

That night the fire was blazing from Baynard's Castle north to Leadenhall and Cornhill, and down to the river east of Billingsgate itself, where the flames had devoured the Custom House and was spreading among the drab warehouses and threatening the Clothworkers' and Bakers' Halls, and also the little colony of Genoese settlers who lived in Mincing Lane.

The eager flames consumed St Mildred Poultry, St Christopher-le-Stocks, St Bartholomew Exchange, the Grocers' Hall and the Mercers' Hall and chapel. However the stone walls of the Mercers' buildings did provide a temporary firebreak until dawn on Tuesday, but the company servants were not able to remove their plate and belongings. So strong was the heat of the fire that it melted the Mercers' plate so that 200lb of melted silver was afterwards recovered from the site. Nearby the Grocers' Hall had collapsed leaving one turret standing but, as providence would have it, that one turret contained all their records which had been stored there for safety.

Along Watling Street the flames were edging up the hill towards St Paul's Cathedral. People had lost count of the churches that had been consumed.

St Andrew Undershaft, Leadenhall, one of the few churches to survive the flames. JOHN BENTON-HARRIS

At Bread Street, where stood All Hallows church, someone had managed to save the parish register which recorded that at that church on 20 December 1608, 'was baptised John the sonne of John Milton the Scrivener'.

The only good news that night came from the north at Leadenhall. Against the high brick walls of Leadenhall the fire had been halted, unable to continue further, thus creating the first fully successful fire-break and saving the headquarters of the East India Company from extinction.

Leadenhall was one of the most important buildings in the City, a house with a leaden roof from which it received its name and which had been built in the late thirteenth or early fourteenth century. In 1411 Richard Whittington had given it to the City and in 1446 Simon Eyre built a granary on the site for the use of Londoners. Soon afterwards it became a market and has remained so, even today. In 1666 it was a large rectangular building, each corner having a turret with embattlements along the whole. The place served two purposes, as a market and as an arsenal for storing guns and ammunition.

The check the fire received at Leadenhall must have given faint cheer to the weary fire-fighters; at least the fire was not entirely invincible.

Throughout Monday night they worked hard at the futile task of creating fire-breaks, while thousands of Londoners still made a long procession through the City's gates into the open spaces where thousands more lay down beside their salvaged belongings and tried to sleep.

The fire was progressing rapidly westward and about midnight Lord Manchester and Lord Hollis made a hasty survey of the suburbs around Fleet Street, to the west of the Fleet River which bounded the western wall of the City. They ordered the pulling down of the houses in the Whitefriar area, seeing that it would not take long for the flames, now consuming Baynard's Castle, to leap the walls and spread through the suburbs towards Westminster itself.

Vincent recorded:

Monday night was a dreadful night, there was no darkness of night in London for the fire now shines about with a fearful blaze which yielded such lights in the streets, as it had been the sun at noon.

But if the people of London thought that Monday was a day of disaster then what was to come on Tuesday was a catastrophic day for the City.

CHAPTER THREE
Tuesday, 4 September 1666

Bas relief on the monument designed
by Caius Gabriel Cibber. It shows the idealised figure
of Charles II 'affording protection to the desolated City and freedom
to its rebuilders and inhabitants'. Charles, in Roman
dress, steps forward to help a fallen woman
representing London.
JOHN BENTON-HARRIS

Tuesday commenced dramatically with the destruction of Cheapside, one of the most beautiful and historical parts of the City, and continued with the burning of the Guildhall and St Paul's Cathedral, and the fire bursting through the City walls into the western suburbs around Fleet Street. It was to be the worst day of the fire.

Charles and his brother James were in the City at daybreak. The King, riding on horseback, did much to calm the panicking Londoners. At times he had no more than an attendant or two with him, and by word and example he encouraged those trying to pull down houses or throw water on the flames. He carried a pouch containing a hundred golden guineas which he gave to workmen as a reward and incentive to further efforts. Mud-splattered, stained with smoke and grime, never did Charles in his reign attain such a high standing among the people as he did during the days of the fire. Henry Griffith wrote to a relative:

> Some went to steal, others to look on, but all stood to the mercy of an enraged fire, which did in three days almost destroy the metropholist (sic) of our Isle, had not God of his infinite mercy stayed the fury thereof, which was done by his Majesty's and the Duke of York's singular care and pains, handling the water in buckets when they stood up to the ankles in water, and playing the engines for many hours together, as they did at the Temple and Cripplegate, which people seeing, fell to work with effect, having so good fellow labourers.

Lord Conway received a letter from a friend in the City to tell him:

> . . . all that is left, both of the City and suburbs, is acknowledged, under God, to be wholly due to the King and Duke of York, who, when citizens had abandoned all further care of the place, and were intent chiefly upon the preservation of their goods, undertook the work themselves and with incredible magnamity rode up and down, giving orders for the blowing up of houses with gunpowder, to make void spaces for the fire to die in, and standing still to see those orders executed, exposing their persons not only to the multitude, but to the very flames themselves, and the ruins of the buildings ready to fall upon them, and some times labouring with their own hands to give example to others; for which the people now pay them, as they ought to do, all possible reverence and admiration.

W. Sandys, attending the Duke of York, wrote to Viscount Scudmore at Lincoln that on Tuesday James was in the saddle from five o'clock in the morning until nearly midnight 'active and stirring in this business'. He went on:

> All orders signified nothing; had not the Duke been presented and forced all people to submit to his commands, by this time I am confident there had not been a house standing near White-

The Great Fire of London showing Ludgate in flames. The engraving is by John Stow. GUILDHALL LIBRARY

hall. The City (citizens) for the first rank they minded only for their own preservation; the middle sort so distracted and amazed that they did not know what they did; the poorer they minded nothing but pilfering; so the city was abandoned to the fire. The Duke on Tuesday, about twelve o'clock was environed with fire; the wind high, blowed such great flakes, and so far, that they fired Salisbury Court and several of the houses between that and Bridewell Dock,

so the Duke was forced to fly for it, and had almost been stifled with the heat.

Charles and James were not the only members of the Royal family to be up and abroad early on Tuesday. The Queen Mother, Henrietta Marie, was anxious for her safety at Somerset House. She managed to leave at six o'clock for Hampton Court. Henrietta Marie was able to worship in her faith at her own private Catholic chapel. A Spaniard attached to her household, who published an account of the fire at Valencia later that year, related with more piety than accuracy:

> . . . It was observed that, in view of the direction in which the flames were extending, the first building on which they would have had to fasten, and the one nearest to them, was the Roman Catholic Church which was allowed for use of the Queen Mother and her family and for the celebration of the Holy Sacrament. At this very point the onrush of the flames was arrested: and it is clear and certain that in this way the Almight (who is Lord of all the elements) wished to rebuke the blindness of those heretics, and to show in what respect he held the sovereign Sacrament of the Altar . . . Praised be God, who thus showed, and not for the first time, that He could make the flames respect those who loved Him.

The temporary fire-break at Mercers' Hall and chapel had held up the fire at the corner of Old Jewry and Poultry until five o'clock. Then, with a quick leap, the flames had by-passed Mercers' and were blazing along Cheapside itself. Cheapside was London's widest street, a market centre and head-quarters of the goldsmith trade. Its name derived from the old English word *céap*, meaning a bargain. The houses on either side rose to dizzy heights, many stood as high as four storeys. According to John Stow it had 'the most beautiful frame of fair houses and shops that be within the walls of London or elsewhere in England'. Paul Hentzer, a German traveller, had written:

> It (Cheapside) surpasses all the rest. There are to be seen in this street all sorts of gold and silver vessels, exposed to sale, as well as ancient and modern metals, as must surprise a man the first time he sees and considers them.

Cheapside was the wealthiest quarter of the City. On the south side of the thoroughfare stood London's most famous church, St Mary-le-Bow, named from the bows or arches of the Norman-built vault. To be born within the sound of Bow Bells gave the child the birthright to be a Londoner. From the ecclesiastical viewpoint it was second only to St Paul's. The church had a surprisingly violent history from its destruction in 1090 when a gale blew in its roof and killed many of its pari-

shioners, to being converted into a siege fortress by a supporter of John in 1196. Violence dogged its history from 1271 when a tower fell and killed many passers by, to its final destruction by high explosives in World War II.

Cheapside was more notable for its taverns, the Half Moon, the Mitre (Ben Johnson's favourite) and the Bull's Head which General Monck had made his headquarters in those momentous and uncertain days leading to the Restoration of the monarchy. But of all the Cheapside taverns it was the Mermaid that was the most famous. There such playwrights as William Shakespeare, Francis Beaumont, John Fletcher, John Ford, Christopher Marlowe, Thomas Middleton, Ben Jonson and John Webster gathered. 'What things have we seen done at the Mermaid!' wrote Francis Beaumont to Ben Jonson.

> What things have we seen
> Done at the Mermaid! heard words that have been
> So nimble, and so full of subtle flame,
> As if that every one from whence they came,
> Had meant to put his whole wit in a jest,
> And had resolv'd to live a fool the rest
> Of his dull life; then when there hath been thrown
> Wit able enough to justify the town
> For three days past; wit that might warrant be
> For the whole city to talk foolishly
> Till that were cancell'd; and when that was gone,
> We left an air behind us, which alone
> Was able to make the two next companies
> (Right witty, though but downright fools)
> more wise.

While others would declaim of the

> Souls of poets dead and gone,
> What Elysium have ye known,
> Happy field or mossy cavern,
> Choicer than the Mermaid Tavern?

Now the brutal flames were extinguishing some of London's greatest links with her literary history.

> Cheapside (wrote Vincent) is alight in a few hours' time; many fires meeting there, as in the centre; Sopar Lane, Bow Lane, Bread Street, Friday Street and Old Cheape, the fire comes up almost together and breaks furiously into Broad Street, and most of that side of the way was together in flames, a dreadful spectacle! And then partly by the fall of houses across the way,

the other side is so quickly kindled, and doth not stand long after.

The fire post in Coleman Street, where Sir John Harmer and a Colonel Fitzgerald were in command, was driven helplessly back before the flames. The fire, coming from Lothbury, advanced too fiercely and too rapidly for any halt to be made there. The fire spread very rapidly northward so that towards midday Guildhall itself, the massive medieval centre of London's administration, was threatened. Vincent recalled:

It was amazing to see, how it had spread itself several miles in compass, and amongst other things that night, the sight of the Guildhall was a fearful spectacle, which stood the whole body of it in view, for several hours together, after the fire had taken it without flames; (I suppose because the timber was such solid oak) in a bright shining coal, as if it had been a Palace of Gold or a great building of burnished brass.

Guildhall was the administrative heart of the City and it was there that all the civil courts were housed – the court of Common Council, court of the Lord Mayor and Aldermen, court of Hustings, court of Orphans, court of Sheriffs, court of Wardmote, court of Hallmote and the court of Requests or apprentices. The centre of this administrative headquarters was a great hall, 150 feet long, spanned by a hammerbeam roof. It had been built in 1411 at the order of the Lord Mayor, Thomas Knowles, and its paved floor was added by a bequest from the estate of Richard Whittington. Additions were made over a period of Mayor's chambers, a council chamber, and then a chapel, an almshouse for the use of seven poor citizens, which was added in 1430, and a large library which was also built by the executors of the estate of Dick Whittington.

The Guildhall contained a wealth of priceless city records and in the hurried evacuation thousands of records and documents were placed in the crypt beneath the Guildhall. Although the building burnt for up to twenty-four hours, mainly due to the heavy oak timbers out of which it was constructed, the amazing thing was that these records remained unharmed just a few feet below the blazing inferno.

Near to the Guildhall were many other company halls, such as the Basket Makers' and the Coopers', but people had begun to loose count of the number of halls which had been lost to the flames: Founders', Girdlers', Weavers', Masons', Haber-

Pepys Memorial in St Olave's Church, Seething Lane. Pepys was buried here on 5 June 1703, at 9 pm. It was the Church which he regarded as his parish one and where he attended worship the Sunday after the Fire.

dashers', Broderers', and Wax Chandlers'! By noon the fire had burnt right up to the northern walls of the City by Cripplegate. Cripplegate itself was saved only by the employment of gunpowder in blowing up the houses instead of the more lengthy process of pulling them down.

In the east of the City, in Seething Lane, Pepys had been up 'by break of day, to get away the remainder of my things: which I did by a lighter at the Irongate'. Samuel walked with Admiral Sir William Penn to Tower Street to see how the fire was progressing eastward. He saw 'the fire coming on in that narrow street with infinite fury'. Soon, he concluded, the fire would be at Seething Lane itself.

Pepys hurried back to find his neighbour Sir William Batten digging a pit in his garden in order to bury his wine there. Samuel 'took the opportunity of laying all the papers of my office that I could not otherwise dispose of. And in the evening Sir W(illiam) Penn and I did dig another, and put our wine into it; and I my parmazan cheese as well as my wine and some other things.' Pepys then had

The Earl of Shaftesbury who, as Lord Ashley, was a member of
the Privy Council and took an active part in the fire-fighting.
With Lord Hollis he intervened against a mob of hysterical
Londoners to save the life of the Portuguese ambassador who was
about to be lynched as a fire-raiser.

NATIONAL PORTRAIT GALLERY

an inspiration. Since Sunday some twenty-eight sailors had been helping in the demolishing of the houses and they had already advised on the use of gunpowder to blow them up rather than continue the lengthy process of pulling them down. According to Pepys:

I did propose for the sending up of all our workmen from the Woolwich and Deptford (Navy) Yards, none whereof yet appeared, and to write to Sir W(illiam) Coventry to have the Duke of York's permission to pull down houses, rather than lose this office, which would much hinder the King's business.

Pepys' prime objective was to save the Navy Office in Seething Lane and his own house, of course, with it. But the practise of blowing up houses first started that morning at Cripplegate. He wrote:

Now begins the practice of blowing up houses in Tower Street, those next the Tower, which at first did frighten people more than anything; but it stopped the fire where it was done, it bringing down the houses to the ground in the same places they stood, and then it was easy to quench what little fire was in it, though it kindled nothing almost.

More sailors to help in this project were brought in from the Fleet itself and more soldiers were also ordered into the City. The order forbidding carts to return to the City to bear away household goods was also rescinded and prices increased from ten shillings to £5 on the prices charged on Sunday and Monday. The average price for removing someone's belongings was as much as £40 or £50. Waterhous mentions one householder who paid £400 for the removal of his belongings.

An Italian, who published his account of the fire in Padua later that year, was moved by the misery of the people to write:

To one who watched, as from the top of a tower, the spectacle of the City burning, the miseries of this people were appalling. Like madmen, they exerted themselves to save such of their belongings as could most easily be removed, leaving the fire to consume all that remained, and making no effort to stay the flames. Men, women and children, of all ages and of all ranks, ran through the streets, their backs loaded with their most precious goods: and among them were carried many sick and disabled persons, who had been

A statement by B. Toller that on the Tuesday of the Fire he found three men, one of them 'a Frenchman in a Livery Suite', breaking into a Counting House at Holborn Bridge, and who, being questioned, said they had been sent by Lord Craven to advise people to get away quickly. On going into the yard of the Rose Inn, Toller ordered some men to cast down hay there into a ditch but they went away without answering and 'immediately . . . a small light burning like sulphur appeared and presently flashed over the hay like brimstone'. The fire spread rapidly and he believed the Rose Inn was deliberately fired. Dated 27 February 1668 and sworn 5 May 1668.
CORPORATION OF LONDON RECORDS OFFICE

driven from their houses by the fire. As they ran they made a heart rending murmer.

The fire was spreading nearer and nearer to the great cathedral of St Paul's. It had already swept to the north-west devouring the important Goldsmiths' Hall in Foster Lane. Although the Hall had stood upon this site for some years, the building standing in 1666 had only been erected some thirty years before and during the years of the Commonwealth and Protectorate it had housed the committee which dealt with sequestered Royalist estates. The building housed a number of monuments to the famous members of the goldsmith fraternity, men such as Drugo Barentine, a former Lord Mayor.

Now, just to the east of the towering cathedral building, St Paul's School caught alight and was soon destroyed with its valuable library, including the High Master's own collected of books. The fire continued to rage westward, preceeded by great showers of sparks and brands blown by the wind, all along Carter Lane on the south side of the Cathedral. Nearer to the river the Royal College of Physicians was consumed. Most of its charters, records, 140 books out of its library, a collection of surgical instruments, and the portraits of Drs Harvey and Fox, cut in haste from their frames by the Custos and Librarian, Dr Merrit, were saved.

By late afternoon St Paul's was an island completely surrounded by a veritable sea of flame.

The Sessions House in the Old Bailey was a smoking ruin. The debtors' prison, the Fleet, was evacuated and soon afterwards destroyed as was the Bridewell. The fire swept northward along the shanties that lined the Fleet River as far as Holborn. Ludgate was ablaze and also Newgate where the inmates of the notorious prison were taken to Southwark, although en route many of the prisoners managed to effect their escape.

As evening approached London lay buried under the pall of yellowish grey smoke. According to Vincent:

Now horrible is the flakes of fire that mount up in the sky, and the yellow smoke of London ascendeth up towards Heaven, like the smoke of a great furnace; a smoke so great, as darkened the sun at noonday. The cloud of smoke was so great that travellers did ride at noonday some miles together in the shadow thereof, though there were no other clouds besides to be seen in the sky.

Even at Enfield the fire was plainly visible. The wind that continued to blow carried debris across the countryside. As far away as Kensington the charred fragments fell over houses and gardens in a mantle of soot. A correspondent of Lord Conway wrote:

Had your lordship been at Kensington you would have thought – for five days together, for so long the Fire lasted – it had been Doomsday, and that the heavens themselves had been on fire; and the fearful cries and howlings of undone people did much increase the resemblance. The loss is inestimable. I believe there was never any such desolation by fire since the destruction of Jerusalem, nor will be till the last and general conflagration.

On Tuesday afternoon Lord Hollis and Lord Ashley stood at their fire post at Newgate Market when the saw a man being roughly manhandled by a mob. The two courtiers recognised the man as the Portuguese ambassador who could speak no English. On demanding what they were about, a citizen of some rank came forward and accused the ambassador of throwing a fire-ball into a house, which, he said, he had seen done with his own eyes. Lord Hollis interpreted the accusation to the amazed diplomat. It transpired that the ambassador, walking through the streets, had seen a piece of bread upon the ground and had picked it up and placed it on a window ledge. This arose from a current superstition among Portuguese people that it is lucky to pick up bread seen laying on the ground. The two courtiers managed to convince the mob that the ambassador was not a fire raiser.

Others were not so lucky.

In *Londens Puyn-Hoop*, a Dutchman living in London recorded that many foreigners were hanged on signposts by the frenzied mobs. Hair-raising rumours were still circulating about Papist uprisings and the march upon London by an army of Dutch and French which had miraculously risen to 50,000 soldiers. 'The inhabitants,' wrote an observer, 'of a whole street would run in a great tumult one way, so terrified men were with their apprehensions.' Many of London's foreign residents sought refuge in the house of Count de Molena, Spain's ambassador to Charles II's court, who lived at the Barbican. As one observer recorded, Count de Molena showed great humanity by opening his doors to Protestant Dutch and Catholic French alike. The Spanish writer recorded the scene:

Amid this welter of extreme misery, the greatest

Etiam periere Ruinæ

W. Hollar fecit A° 1666

St Paul's on fire; an engraving by Wenclaus Holler showing the Chapel on St Faith where London booksellers lost upward of £150,000 worth of books. BRITISH MUSEUM

crimes and most execrable atrocities were committed, particularly against the large number of foreigners who dwelt in London, many of whom were murdered. Others saved themselves as best they could from falling into the hands of the infuriated populace. (The Catholic ambassador on this occasion showed his great humanity by giving shelter to all who sought refuge.) Thefts took place openly during these turbulent days, arms were treacherously seized and as treacherously used and every kind of false testimony was borne in order that those who had been fortunate enough to save some part of their possessions might be the more easily robbed; and this was the fate, not of foreigners alone, but of Englishmen as well.

By sunset at 7 pm that Tuesday, the fire had completely broken through the western walls of the City and was burning along both sides of Fleet Street towards Chancery Lane. The church of St Bride's was gutted with the loss of part of its plate, and Axel Yard, where Pepys was born, was ablaze. Three-quarters of the City within the walls was in flames while the fire was burning over the walls from Cripplegate to the Thames.

And still towering untouched above the flames stood St Paul's Cathedral.

The cathedral was the crowning glory of the City, although Londoners treated it with little more than contempt. Laws had to be enacted forbidding the citizens to use the nave as a right of way for those too lazy to walk around the cathedral and to forbid the passage of mules or horses through the church. Shops had sprung up between the buttresses of the choir, and printing houses had been established in the vaults of the crypt.

The cathedral in its 1666 form had been started in 1087 on the ruins of a Saxon cathedral which had been destroyed in another fire. It looked much as Norwich Cathedral does today with a very long nave, a modest west front, transepts, and a short choir with a semi-circular apse. In 1221 the great central tower, 245 feet high, was added, and above this rose a lead-covered timber spire making an overall height of 449 feet. The Norman choir was demolished in 1256 and an English-style choir nearly as long as the nave was started giving the cathedral an overall length of 585 feet. It was, at that time, the largest cathedral in Europe. In 1561, for the third time in two centuries, the spire was struck by lightening and burnt down with most of the roof. The spire was not rebuilt and the tower was caped by a low pyramid shaped roof.

Because Londoners were not particularly concerned with the cathedral, it was allowed to fall into

[61]

A manual operated fire engine also dating from the Great Fire period. SCIENCE MUSEUM

a state of great dilapidation. The condition of the stonework became very decayed and a commission was set up by James I because the king was 'moved with such compassion to this decayed fabric, that for prevention of its near approaching ruin by the corroding quality of the coal smoke, especially in moist weather, whereunto it had long been subject'. The outcome of this inquiry into the condition of the cathedral was that Inigo Jones was employed to reface the exterior of the nave and transepts with new stonework.

The Civil War had witnessed great ill-treatment of the building and it had been made into a permanent barracks for 800 cavalry troopers. A sad fate for a cathedral which had witnessed so much history. It had been a place of great European pilgrimage in the Middle Ages, where pilgrims came to pray at the shrine of St Erkenwald, son of Offa, King of the East Angles, who was Bishop of London in 675 AD and canonised the year after his death. Erkenwald was London's own saint. Archbishop Laud had commented that St Paul's was now 'like a great skeleton, so pitifully handled that you might tell her ribs through her skin'.

In 1666 it had been decided that matters could not continue and that some restoration work should be carried out on the cathedral. Only the week before the fire, on 27 August, Dr Christopher Wren, John Evelyn, Humphrey Hinchman, the Bishop of London, and Dean Sancroft, had surveyed the building preparatory to its restoration. Already the central tower was surrounded by scaffolding and builders' material ready for the work to commence.

Now, as the cathedral stood, illuminated by the flickering tongues of the surrounding fire, blazing brands were borne on the wind to its roof. Martin, a bookseller in the Churchyard, saw the start of the fire which he afterwards recounted to Pepys. 'And he tells me that it took fire first upon the end of a board that, among others, was laid upon the roof instead of lead, the lead being broke off, and thence down lower and lower.' The dry timber forming the roof above the stone vault started to burn furiously and, at the same time, the builders' scaffolding around the cathedral caught alight.

The Spanish observer recalled:

At this point the king and his brother appeared on horseback, desirous of bringing some relief to the homeless people scattered about the streets, and wishing also to do something for the safety of the church whither they were called by considering for their blind religion. Not even the presence of royalty, however, could do more in the midst of that multitude than add to the confusion and difficulties. The fire was now universal, like Death himself, and respected neither sceptres or crowns. In the very sight of the King himself it proceeded to crown itself the conqueror of the highest part of the great building.

So great was the blaze that young William Taswell recorded:

. . . just after sunset at night, I went to the royal bridge in New Palace Yard at Westminster to take a fuller view of the fire. As I stood upon the bridge among others, I could not but observe the gradual approach of the fire towards that venerable fabric. About eight o'clock it broke out on the top of St Paul's Church, already scorched by the violent heat of the air, and lightning too, and before nine blazed so conspicuously as to enable me to read very clearly a sixteen mo. edition of Terence which I carried in my pocket.

Vincent is more dramatic in his account:

The church, though all of stone outward, though naked of houses about it, and though so high above all buildings in the City, yet within a while doth yield to the violent assaults of the conquering flames, and strangely takes fire at the top; now the lead melts and runs down, as if it had been snow before the sun; and the great beams and massy stones, with a great noise, fall on the pavement, and break though into Faith's Church underneath; now great flakes of stone scale, and peal off strangely from the side of the walls.

John Evelyn afterwards blames the builders' scaffolding for contributing to the disaster by aiding the flames to climb the great stone walls. He observed that the tremendous heat engendered by the inferno caused the stones to fly

. . . like grenadoes, the melting lead running down the streets in a stream, and the very pavements glowing with fiery redness, so as now horse nor man was able to tread on them, and the demolition had stopped all passages, so that no help could be applied. It was astonishing to see what immense stones the heat had in a manner calcined, so that all the ornaments, columns, friezes, capitals, and projectures of massy Portland stone flew off, even to the very roof, where a sheet of lead covering a great space (no less than six acres by measure) was totally melted.

It was this molten lead that made one of the most terrifying sights of the great fire, pouring, as it did, in a stream down Ludgate Hill. The blazing timbers of the roof smashed into the nave and choir, and the intense heat caused the Caen stone to be hurled through the air like cannon balls. The side walls of the aisle fell out, and the tombs of such notables as John of Gaunt, Sir Nicholas Bacon, Henry de Lacy and others were consumed.

Through most of this onset Charles and his brother James sat in silence on horseback, watching the flames devour the building.

The flames (wrote the Spanish eye-witness) seized upon the carved timber of which the church was in places composed, licked it up in a twinkling, and in a few hours left this marvellous building, the labour of many years, a smoking mass of lamentable ruins.

The west portico, designed by Inigo Jones, managed to withstand the flames but the cathedral was an inferno from end to end. The walls of the great nave and the choir and transepts seemed to be withstanding the shock of falling masonry but the furnace was systematically destroying some of London's finest monuments to its history. The tombs of the saints Erkenwald and Sebba, the tomb of King Ethelred the Unready and of the nobility of medieval London. Only Nicholas Stone's monument to John Donne, who died in 1631, managed to survive.

Pepys says the fire also entered the crypt. 'They first took fire from the Draper's side, by some timber houses that were burned, falling into the church.' Martin told him that 'one warehouse of books was saved under St Paul's; and there were several dogs found burned among the goods in the churchyard, and but for one man, which was an old man, that said he would go and save a blanket which he had in the church, and being weak, the fire overcame him'.

For the City of London that Tuesday night, the streets and surrounding districts were as bright as day, lit by the flaming spectacle of the great cathedral burning from end to end and completely dominating the vast, and still spreading, sea of flames about it. Vincent wrote:

Many thousands now have nowhere to lay their heads, and the fields are the only receptacle which they can find for themselves and their goods; most of the late inhabitants of London lie all night in the open air, with no other canopy over them, but that of Heaven.

The majority camped out again in Moorfields, Finsbury Fields, Tower Hill, and open spaces to the west such as St Giles' Fields.

Many without a rag, wrote Evelyn, or any necessary utensil, bed or board, who from delicateness, riches and easy accommodation in stately and well furnished houses were now reduced to the extremist misery and poverty.

The scene was dramatically painted by the poet John Dryden, whose *Annus Mirabilis*, was the only poetry of worth to be inspired by the flames. He recalled that night in these words:

Night came, but without darkness nor repose,
  A dismal picture of the general doom;
Where souls, distracted, when the trumpet blows,
  And half unready with their bodies come.

Those who have homes, when homes they do repair
  To a last lodging call their wandering friends:
Their short uneasy sleeps are broke with care,
  To look how near their own destruction tends:

Those who have none sit round where once it was,
  And with full eyes each wonted room require,
Haunting the yet warm ashes of the place,
  As murdered men walk where they did expire.

Some stir up coals and watch the vestal fire,
  Others in vain from sight of ruin run,
And, while through burning Labyrinths they retire,
  With loathing eye repeat what they would shun.

The most in fields like herded beasts lie down,
  To dews obnoxious on the grassy floor;
And while their babes in sleep their sorrows drown,
  Sad parents watch the remnants of their store.

All that Londoners could do was wait for what they felt was the inevitable total destruction of the city. The Pepys family were still in Seething Lane determined not to leave their house until the last possible moment. Pepys wrote in his diary:

This night Mrs Turner, who, poor woman, was removing her goods all this day, good goods, into the gardens, and knows not how to dispose of them, and her husband supped with my wife and me at night, in the office, upon a shoulder of mutton from the cook's without any napkin, or any thing in a sad manner, but were merry.

As the night drew on Samuel Pepys decided to snatch a cat-nap in the Navy Office, next to his house. 'I lay down in the office,' he wrote, 'again upon (William) Hewer's quilt, being mighty weary, and sore in my feet going till I was hardly able to stand.' And in a troubled state of mind he fell asleep.

Outside the wind was still unabated and the fire blazed as fiercely as ever.

CHAPTER FOUR

Wednesday, 5 September 1666

A statement made by John Powell
that on Wednesday of the Fire he learnt from people in
Fetter Lane that a man in woman's clothing had been caught
in the act of setting fire to a house there. The man confessed that he
was a Catholic. The people were about to lynch him when he
was rescued by some soldiers. The statement was
made on 5 May 1668.

Samuel Pepys had not been asleep long when his wife, Elizabeth, shook him awake. He wrote:

About two in the morning my wife calls me up, and tells me of new cries of Fire! It being come to Barking Church, which is at the bottom of our lane. I up, and finding it is so, resolved presently to take her away, and did, and took my gold, which was about £2,350. W. Hewer and Jane down to Proundy's boat to Woolwich; but, Lord, what a sad sight it was by moon-light to see the whole City almost on fire, that you might see it plain at Woolwich, as if you were by it.

And so, in the early hours of Wednesday, Pepys installed his wife at Woolwich, in the old lodgings she had lived in during the worst weeks of the plague the previous year. He left her with Will Hewer to help guard his £2,350 in gold and went back to London so that he could witness what he felt would surely be the death throes of the City. The wherryman rowed the boat along the Thames towards the great orange glow and Pepys noticed that the man was having a hard time in keeping the wherry in midstream. 'The wind's veered to the south,' explained the man in apology. Pepys sat a moment before he realised the significance of the remark. The easterly wind that had spread the fire had changed in direction and was now blowing the flames into extinction towards the river.

Was it possible that the worst was over?

In the western suburbs the fire-fighters were still struggling to prevent the spread of the flames westward. Having leapt across the Fleet River from Baynard's Castle the fire had spread through the Whitefriars area, then known as Alsatia. This was an area of narrow lanes bordered to the east by the Fleet, to the north by Fleet Street and Temple in the east. Here was a curious sanctuary for all the cut-throats in the kingdom – escaped felons, debtors, pick-pockets and murderers – all lived in a veritable rabbit warren of lanes, so narrow that a handcart could not be pushed along many of them.

Originally the area, from Whitefriars Street and the Temple, had been a monastery known as the White Friars' Priory. This had been pulled down at the time of the dissolution, although a few of its outbuildings still stood. On the site several large mansion houses were erected but, within a few years, their owners had moved out because they did

The only example left in London of late sixteenth century half-timbered houses at Holborn. These are typical of those destroyed in the Great Fire. JOHN BENTON-HARRIS

[66]

not find the area pleasant to live in surrounded as they were by the narrow slums, the haunt of all manner of criminals. Within a short space of time these mansions were converted into tenement houses containing as many as twenty to thirty families.

It seems that the criminals who lived in this squalid area of dram-shops, brothels, and dirty lodging houses, considered that the area kept its old monastic santcuary rights and even murderers who fled into the area were protected by the local population from capture. The civil powers were unable to keep any semblance of law and order in the area.

> . . . amidst a rabble so desperate no peace officer's life was in safety (wrote Macaulay). At the cry of Rescue! bullies with swords and cudgels, and termanant hags with spits and broomsticks, poured forth by hundreds; and the intruder was unfortunate if he escaped back into Fleet Street, hustled, stripped and pumped upon. Even the Warrant of the Chief Justice of England could not be executed without the help of a company of musketeers.

The playwright Shadwell depicted the area in *The Squire of Alsatia* which provided material for Sir Walter Scott's description in *The Fortunes of Nigel*. The entire area was destroyed and this was the one place which the authorities were not sorry to see consigned to the inferno.

In St Bride's parish only sixteen houses survived the flames, which spread northward to Shoe Lane which was quickly engulfed. It was in Shoe Lane that another casualty of the fire occurred when Paul Lowell, a deaf octogenarian watchmaker, refused to leave his house and business, saying he would rather perish among its burning timbers. His house, which stood behind the Globe Tavern, collapsed upon him not long afterwards.

A wall shut off the grounds of the Temple from the squalid streets of Alsatia and this, with the brick houses of King's Bench Walk, provided a temporary check to the fire. But not for long. The Inn of the Inner Temple, stretching from near Fleet Street to the Thames, was gutted, although amidst the debris the church of the Knights Templars was found standing with part of their hall, part of Fig Tree Court and the gateway into Fleet Street which had been rebuilt during the reign of James I. The flames rushed on to Middle Temple but were halted there after consuming only one building – Lamb Building.

The lawyers of the Temple had received plenty of warning to fight the fire but there appeared a lack of organisation. There was plenty of water available for them from the Thames but no appliances to prevent the fire spreading through the timber-framed houses which largely composed the Temple area. Most of the lawyers decided to evacuate the area rather than stay and try to save it. 'Neither boat, barge, cart nor coach is to be had, all the streets full of goods, and the fire flaming into the very 'Temple,' wrote J. Barker, one of the lawyers who managed to escape from his chambers with several of his law books.

Some of the greatests losses of documents occurred because that September week was part of the Long Vacation period when most of the lawyers were away and their chambers were locked. Lord Clarendon observed:

> . . . when the fire came where the lawyers had houses, as they had in many places, especially Serjeant Inn in Fleet Street, with that part of the Inner Temple that was next to it and White Friars, there was scarce a man to whom those lodgings appertained who was in town; so that whatsoever was there, their money, books and papers, besides the evidence of many men's estates deposited in their hands, were all burnt or lost, to a very great value.

Fleet Street had been almost completely reduced to ashes within the space of a few hours. The antiquarian, Mr Malcolm, in his *Londinium Redivivum*, observed that 'its greediness (the fire) was the cause of its own destruction' in this area. The flames had leapt over some houses and burnt a wooden one but was prevented by a brick house from proceeding further. Seizing the opportunity, the workers managed to pull down some buildings making a wide gap by the time the main body of the fire reached the spot.

Panic was spreading as far as Westminster. Buildings along the Strand were blown up with gunpowder and Somerset House was isolated. The 'people of quality' who dwelt in their fashionable houses along the Strand were now trying to clear their household belongings away up river beyond the reach of the fire. Many of them, not knowing what to do, just hung in doleful groups about the street. According to Lord Clarendon they were scarcely conscious of what they did and merely fled into the streets with their families so as not to be in their houses when the flames overtook them. Even Clarendon evacuated his house – Berkshire House – in Piccadilly. He wrote to Lord Winchilsea: 'We who live in the suburbs, preparing for the same

Gutielmus · Harvey · M·D·

Dr William Harvey. This portrait has an exciting history. It was
one of two portraits cut from its frame as the flames began to
engulf the Royal College of Physicians. The other portrait was
that of Dr Simon Fox which is now lost.
ROYAL COLLEGE OF PHYSICIANS

St Bartholomew the Great, Smithfield, was one of the few
churches to survive the Fire, described as 'a magnificent Norman
fragment'. BRITISH TOURIST AUTHORITY

fate, fled from our lodgings, and have hardly yet recovered our goods or our wits.'

The court was thrown into confusion and it seemed that Whitehall Palace itself would soon be threatened. Charles ordered that Sir John Denham's new house, on the site of what used to be Scotland Yard, should be unroofed preparatory to creating a fire-break. Courtiers began to pack their belongings.

In Chancery Lane the fire-fighters were still active and had pulled down the St John's Head tavern in Chancery Lane to act as a fire-break to stop its inferno spreading to Lincoln's Inn. All hope was abandoned, then the wind slackened, and veered to the south. Immediately messengers were sent to the exhausted Duke of York imploring more men to take advantage of the new situation. To the north the fire was being checked at Pie Corner, Smithfield, and at Holborn Bridge where it crossed the Fleet River.

Samuel Pepys arrived back at Seething Lane at 7 am, fully expecting to see his house and the adjoining Navy Office on fire. They were not. Nor was Barking Church alight. Instead the change of wind was pushing the fire back on itself and Sir William Penn, with squads of men from the navy Yards, had blown up several buildings before the flames. Pepys was delighted.

I up to the top of Barking Steeple, and there saw the saddest sight of desolation that I ever saw; everywhere great fires, oil cellars and brimstone and other things burning. I became afraid to stay there long, and therefore down again as fast as I could, the fire being spread as far as I could see; and to Sir William Penn's and there ate a piece of cold meat, having eaten nothing since Sunday but the remains of Sunday dinner.

At Sir William Penn's house Pepys met a Mr Young, a flag contractor to the Navy, and a Mr Whistler. They discussed the possibilities of the fire entering Seething Lane but decided that unless the wind changed drastically again there was little chance. The three of them then set out to explore what areas of the City they could, going along Fenchurch Street, Gracechurch Street and Lombard Street. 'The Exchange is a sad sight,' wrote Pepys, 'nothing standing there of all the statues and pillars but Sir Thomas Gresham's picture (statue) in a corner.'

Into Moorfields (our feet ready to burn walking through the town among the hot coals) and find that full of people, and poor wretches carrying their goods there, and everybody keeping his goods together by themselves and a great blessing it is to them that it is fair weather for them to keep abroad night and day; drank there, and paid twopence for a plain penny loaf. Thence homeward, having passed through Cheapside and Newgate Market, all burned, and see Anthony Joyce's house on fire. I also did see a poor cat taken out of a hole in a chimney joining to the wall of the Exchange, with the hair all burned off the body yet alive. So home at night and find there good hopes of saving our office; but great endeavours of watching all night, and having men ready; and so we lodge them in the office, and had drink and bread and cheese for them. And I lay down and slept a good night about midnight; though, when I rose, I heard that there had been a great alarm of French and Dutch being risen, which proved nothing.

That Wednesday Sir Thomas Bludworth, the Lord Mayor who thought a 'woman could piss it out', seemed more in control and was found directing the demolition of houses in Cripplegate.

Charles was concerned about the refugees crowding outside Cripplegate and issued orders that Wednesday for provisions to be sent to them. This was duly reported in the *London Gazette*:

Through this sad accident it is easy to be imagined how many persons were necessitated to remove themselves and goods into the open fields, where they were forced to continue some time, which could not work but compassion in the beholders, but His Majesty's care was most signal in this occasion, who, besides his personal pains, was frequent in consulting all ways for relieving those distressed persons, which produced so good effect, as well by His Majesty's proclamations, and the orders issued to neighbour justices of the peace to encourage the sending in provisions to the markets, which are publicly known, as by other directions, that when His Majesty, fearing lest other orders might not have been sufficient, had commanded the victualler of his Navy to send bread into Moorfields for the relief of the poor, which for the more speedy supply he sent in biscuit out of the sea stores; it was found that the markets had been already so well supplied that the people, being unaccustomed to that kind of bread, declined it, and so it was returned in great part to His Majesty's stores again, without any use made of it.

Late that Wednesday night some burning cinders from the charred remains of King's Bench Walk lodged in the roof of the Middle Temple Hall. It blazed up, and word was sent to the Duke of York, who was himself a Bencher of the Inner Temple, for aid. James rode immediately to the Temple and found that the gates had been locked by the lawyers who feared looters. It took some time before they grudging allowed him near the burning building. He finally managed to take charge and ordered the blowing up of the Paper House to stop the spread of the fire. James' gentleman attendant, W. Sandys, writing later to Lord Scudmore, recounted the following farcical incident:

The Duke of York found no way of saving the Temple Chapel and the Hall by the Chapel, but blowing up the Paper House in that court which experiment, if it had been used at first, might have saved a great many houses. One of the Templars, seeing gunpowder brought, came to the Duke and told him it was against the rules and charter of the Temple that any should blow that house with gunpowder, upon which Mr Germaine, the Duke's Master of Horse, took a good cudgel and beat the young lawyer to the purpose. There is no hope of knowing who this lawyer is, but the hope that he will bring an action of battery against Mr. Germaine.

Before the flames caught hold of the ancient hall of the Inner Temple, a seaman named Richard Rower climbed the roof with a soldier from Kingston and the two of them managed to beat the flames out. The exploit of the two men saved the building and Richard Rower was later rewarded with £10 by the grateful lawyers while the soldier received £2. J. Crouch celebrated in bad verse his exploit in his *Londinenses Lachrymae:*

... a brave seaman up the tiles did skip,
As nimbly as the cordage of a ship.
Bestrides the singed hall on its highest ridge
Moving as if he were on London Bridge,
Or on the narrow of a skullers' keel:
Feels neither head nor heart nor spirits reel.

The buildings were saved. This was the last fling of the fire before expiring and, as quickly as it had risen, the fire died away leaving a blackened smoking City to recover.

CHAPTER FIVE

Thursday, 6 September 1666

St Martin by Ludgate built by Sir Christopher Wren.
JOHN BENTON-HARRIS

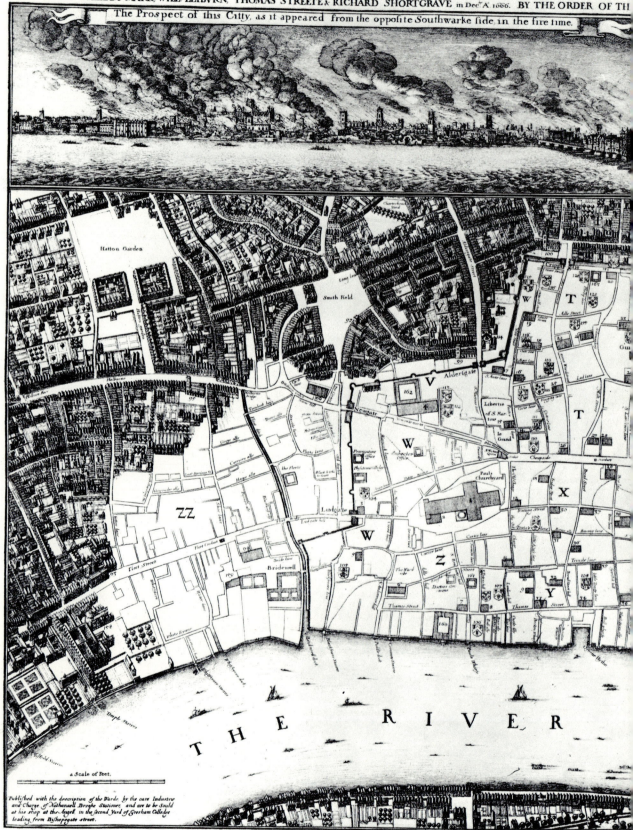

A survey showing the extent of the Great Fire, drawn by John Leake, based on the survey carried out by Leake, John Jennings, William Marr,

OF THE CITY OF LONDON FIRST DESCRIBED IN SIX PLATS BY IOHN LEAKE IOHN

ALDERMEN AND COMMON COVNCELL OF THE SAID CITY

Reduced here into one intire plat by Iohn Leake. the Citty Wall being added also. The places where the Halls stood are exprest by Coats of Armes, & all the Wards divided by pricks & Alphabet. &c

1 Cathedrall of S.t Paul	79 S. Iames Garlick hyth	76 S.t Hallowes
2 S. Gregory	44 S. Martin Vintry	77 S. Elens
3 Christ Church	45 S. Thomas Apostle	78 S. Catharin Cree Church
4 S. Martin by Ludgate	46 S. Antholine	79 S. Catharin Colman
5 S. Ann Blackfryers	47 S. Pancras	80 S. Denis Backchurch
6 S. Andrew in Wardrobe	48 S. Martin in Ironmonger	81 Grace Church
7 S. Bennet by Pauls wharfe	58 S. Clave	82 S. Leonard

THA MES

Part of Southwarke

Moore gate

Moore Fielde

THE TOWER

Tower hill

East Smith field

Tower wharfe

Beline gate

W: Hollar fecit. 1667.

Will Leyburn, Thomas Street and Richard Shortgrave, at the order of the Lord Mayor and Common Council of London in December 1666.

Young William Taswell was up early on Thursday.

Soon after sunrising I endeavoured to reach St Paul's. The ground was so hot as almost to scorch my shoes; and the air so intensely warm that unless I had stopped some time upon Fleet Bridge to rest myself, I must have fainted under the extreme langour of my spirits. After giving myself a little time to breathe I made the best of my way to St Paul's. And now let any person judge of the violent emotion I was in when I perceived the metal belonging to the bells melting; the ruinous condition of the walls; whole heaps of stone of a large circumference tumbling down with a noise just upon my feet, ready to crush me to death. I prepared myself for returning back again, having first loaded my pockets with several pieces of bell metal.

On my way home I saw several engines which were bringing up to its assistance all on fire, and those concerned with them escaping with great eagerness from the flames, which spread instantaneous almost like a wild-fire; and at last, accoutred with my sword and helmet, which I picked up among many others in the ruins, I traversed this torrid zone back again.

Before he did so, he came across a gruesome sight in St Paul's Churchyard.

. . . near the east walls of St Paul's a human body presented itself to me, parched up, as it were, with the flames; whole as to skin, meagre as to flesh, yellow as to colour. This was an old decrepit woman who fled here for safety, imagining the flames would not have reached her there. Her clothes were burnt, and every limb reduced to a coal.

According to a broadsheet the flames of St Paul's were still flaring brightly as late as Thursday night. The great library of books which the local booksellers had stored for safety in the chapel of St Faith, continued to smoulder for fully a week. The estimated value of the books destroyed was some £150,000. According to Taswell, the booksellers had strengthened and sealed the windows and doors of St Faith's, so certain were they that no spark would be able to get in. There were several conflicting accounts as to the destruction of the books. Pepys, who had the story from the booksellers Kirton and Martin, said that they caught fire when burning timbers and masonry fell through the arches of the chapel.

Pepys went to have a look at the cathedral that Thursday and noted 'a miserable sight of Paul's church, with all the roofs fallen, and the body of the choir fallen into St Faith's'.

The account published under the pseudonym Rege Sincera claims that the fire entered through the window of the chapel, setting fire to the pews and all the books stored there.

There is also a third conflicting tale, recorded in the State Papers and echoed by Lord Clarendon, that the books survived the general conflagration but the booksellers, anxious for their property, caused the chapel to be opened too early and that the books burst into flame as soon as air was emitted into the sealed chapel.

Never, claimed one observer, had there been such a destruction of literature since the burning of the great library at Alexandria.

F. Wright was moved to record the event in verse, published two years later:

See yet another Ruin; here were laid
    Choice authors, by the servants of the Muses;
And here to sacrilegious flames betray'd
    To spare or wit or temples fire refuses.

These half burnt papers lying here, needs must
    Be for the library of the dead mistook:
And for a scholar fain himself to dust
    Ashes of paper is a proper book.

Couldst thou not, Pauls, in thy vaults of stone,
    Preserve these papers from the tyrant flame?
When thou by paper, and by it alone,
    Art still preserv'd to triumph o're the same.

Were't not for books where had thy memory been?
    But that thou art, in Dugdale's learned story
And beautious illustrations to be seen,
    Thy name had been as lost as is thy glory.

The reference to Dugdale here is to Sir William Dugdale's *History of St Paul's Cathedral* of which 300 copies perished in the flames but, fortunately, several more copies survived. The bad verse inspired by the fire was legion.

The shattered cathedral became, that Thursday, an object for rich and poor alike to gather round and mourn. The Grand Duke Cosmo III of Tuscany, then a guest of Charles II, paused to look upon the smoking ruin later that day.

Of this stupendous fabric, he wrote later, there

St Benet Paul's Wharf. One of the churches rebuilt by Sir Christopher Wren. JOHN BENTON-HARRIS

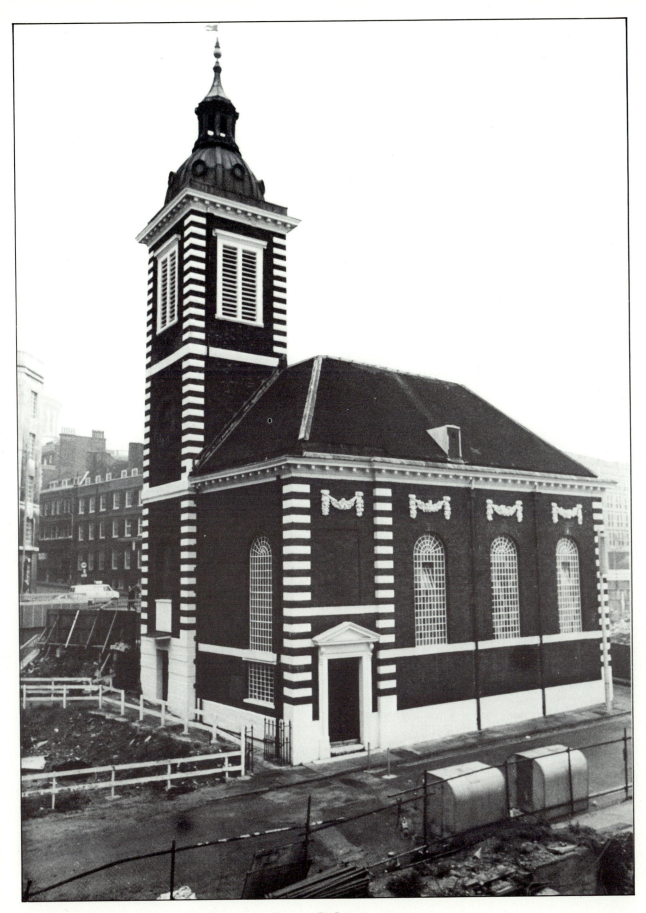

Orders of the Court of Common Council immediately following the Fire that the streets, lanes and passages be cleared of rubbish and obstructions by the inhabitants 'everyone before his own grounds'; that a Committee be appointed to consider means for the City's present subsistence and recovery with authority to apportion among the Freemen whose dwellings are destroyed such portion of Moorfields, the Artillery Ground and other open spaces as they think fit; that the Committee also look after the provision and repair of prisons; and that the Court meet weekly on *Wednesday* at Gresham House. Dated 10 September 1666.

is nothing now to contemplate except the vestiges of its ancient magnificence. One sees only a huge heap of stones cemented together by the lead with which the church was covered; this when melted fell among the ruins, which have entirely covered the relics of antiquity that were there formerly, and demolished many splendid monuments, both of Catholic bishops and other distinguished men, of which scarcely any trace is to be seen.

London lay a blackened, smouldering ruin with occasional little fires springing up here and there as air currents suddenly caught hold of smouldering wooden beams and fanned up a blaze. But the inferno had, at last, been quenched. And with the main danger over, Charles was able to give more attention to trying to calm the people's hysteria. About midday on Thursday he rode out to Moorfields to address the refugees there attended by a few gentlemen and members of his Life Guard. He addressed them sitting on horseback amid the litter of carts, tents and household goods, among which the Londoners stood or sat in bewildered silence.

According to W. Sandys, who accompanied him and faithfully reported his speech, Charles was direct. He told the people that the fire had been caused by the hand of God and not by any Popish plot nor by the French or the Dutch. It was an accident; no more. He had personally questioned several of the people arrested as suspected arsonists and found them innocent of the accusations. Anyway, he added, Londoners were strong enough to withstand any attack made by an enemy and he, Charles, had strength enough to defend London and he would live and die with them.

There was little to do now but to commence to clean up what remained of the capital. An extra 200 soldiers were drafted in from Hertford with pick-axes, spades and buckets to douse the smouldering ruins. More contingents arrived late from Kent, Middlesex and Surrey.

Charles wrote to Sir Thomas Bludworth ordering him to gather all the aldermen, magistrates and persons of quality 'to the end that there may be an appearance of magistracy and government'. Such persons would form a special committee with members of Charles' Privy Council to take care of the public welfare of the City. A meeting was scheduled for Monday, 10 September, at Gresham House, which was to serve as London's administrative centre for many months to come.

On Friday, 7 September, John Evelyn felt confident enough to leave his fire-fighting post at

Holborn and tour the City. He wrote in his diary later that day:

I went this morning on foot from Whitehall as far as London Bridge, through the late Fleet Street, Ludgate Hill by St. Paul's Cheapside, Exchange, Bishopsgate, Aldersgate and out to Moorfields, thence through Cornhill etc., with extraordinary difficulty, clambering over heaps of yet smoking rubbish, and frequently mistaking where I was: the ground under my feet so hot that it even burnt the soles of my shoes.

I was infinitely concerned to find that goodly church, St Paul's, now a sad ruin, and that beautiful portico (for structure comparable to any in Europe, as not long before repaired by the late King) now rent in pieces, flakes of vast stone split in sunder, and nothing remaining entire but the inscription in the architecture which showing by whom it was built, had not one letter defaced; which I could not but take notice of. It was astonishing to see what immense stones the heat had in a manner calcined, so as all the ornaments, columns, friezes, capitals and projectures of massy Portland stone flew off, even to the very roof. It was also observable that the lead over the altar at the east end was untouched, and among the divers monuments, the body of one bishop remained entire.

This bishop was Robert da Brabroke, a bishop of London and Lord Chancellor of England, who had been buried in St Paul's in 1404. The body was found intact 'teeth in the head, red hair on the head, beard and skin and nails on the toes and fingers, without cirecloth, enabling spices, or any other condite'. The body was stiff and could be stood on its feet without falling over, which the more ghoulish of the finders attempted. The remains were promptly removed to the Chapter House where they became the subject of an exhibition. As late as 1675 Londoners were able to see the remains of the bishop but soon after they were reinterred in Wren's cathedral.

Evelyn continued:

The ruins of the vaulted roof falling, broke into St Faith's. Thus lay in ashes that most venerable church, one of the most ancient pieces of early piety in the Christian world, besides near one hundred more. The lead, ironwork, bells, plate etc. melted; the exquisitely wrought Mercers Chapel, the sumptuous Exchange, the august fabric of Christ Church, all the rest of the Companies' Halls, splendid buildings, arches, entries,

all in dust; the fountains dried up and ruined, whilst the very waters remained boiling; the voragos of subterranean cellars, wells, and dungeons, formerly warehouses, still burning in stench and dark clouds of smoke; so that in five or six miles traversing about it I did not see one load of timber unconsumed, nor many stones but what were calcined white as snow.

The people, who now walked about the ruins, appeared like men in some dismal desert, or rather, in some great city laid waste by a cruel enemy; to which was added the stench that came from some poor creatures' bodies, beds and other combustible goods.

Vast iron chains of the City streets, hinges, bars and gates of prisons were many of them melted and reduced to cinders by the vehement heat. Nor was I yet able to pass through any of the narrow streets, but kept the widest; the ground and air, smoke and fiery vapour, continued so intense that my hair was almost singed, and my feet unsufferably surbated. The by-lanes and narrow streets were quite filled up with rubbish; nor could one have possibly known where he was, but by the ruins of some church, or hall that had some remarkable tower or pinnacle remaining.

I then went towards Islington and Highgate, where one might have seen 200,000 people of all ranks and degrees dispersed, and lying along by their heaps of what they could save from the fire, deploring their loss; and, though ready to perish for hunger and destitution, yet not asking one penny for relief, which to me appeared a stranger sight than any I had yet beheld. His Majesty and Council, indeed, took all imaginable care for their relief, by Proclamation for the country to come in and refresh them with provisions.

In the midst of all this calamity and confusion there was, I know not how, an alarm begun that the French and Dutch, with whom we were now in hostility, were not only landed but even entering the City. There was, in truth, some days before great suspicion of those two nations joining; and now that they had been the occasion of firing the town. This report did so terrify, that on a sudden there was such an uproar and tumult that they ran away from their goods, and taking what weapons they could come at, they could not be stopped from falling on some of those nations whom they casually met, without sense or reason. The clamour and peril grew so excessive that it made the whole Court amazed, and they did with infinite pains and great difficulty reduce and

appease the people, sending troops of soldiers and guards to cause them to retire into the fields again, where they were watched all this night. I left them pretty quiet, and came home sufficiently weary and broken. Their spirits thus a little calmed, and the affright abated, they now began to repair into the suburbs about the City, where such as had friends or opportunity got shelter for the present; to which his Majesty's Proclamation also invited them.

The first Sunday after the fire, 9 September, thousands of grimy, soot-stained citizens crowded into the surviving churches while many others attended services in the open air. Samuel Pepys went to St Olave in Hart Street, a fifteenth-century Perpendicular church dedicated to the king who helped Ethelred the Unready fight against the Danes at London Bridge in 1014. It was Pepys' parish church and he recorded that Sunday that 'our parson made a melancholy but good sermon; and many and most in the church cried, especially the women. The church was mighty full; but few of fashion and most strangers.'

The first rain for weeks fell on London that Sunday, almost symbolically. Now came a rainy season, with the rain pouring down for ten days without cessation during October. It was much needed. Charles was aware, however, of the dangers of complacency and he warned the City aldermen that there was still much combustible material in the City which was still smouldering in spite of the rain. He warned them to have a special watch kept in case of sudden flare-ups.

Indeed, Charles was proved right for the fires smouldering in cellars and vaults kept breaking out anew as late as six months after the fire! A newsletter of 29 September recorded that a warehouse near St Paul's, when opened, broke into flames. On 30 November John Aubrey saw a cellar opened at Holborn; 'and there were burning coals which burnt ever since the Great Fire; but being pent so close for air there was very little waste'. Pepys recorded several instances of such outbreaks, the last as late as 16 March 1667, when he wrote: 'The weather is now grown warm again, after much cold; and it is observable that within these eights day I did see smoke remaining, coming out of some cellars, from the late Great Fire, now above six months since.'

On Monday, 10 September, the Council of State,

The petition of Elizabeth Peacock, a widow, to the Lord Mayor of London because of hardship. The Horseshoe on Snow Hill, of which she is tenant, and on which her late husband spent £800, had been 'utterly consumed' leaving her and her three children with 'only 39s in money not so much as a stool to sit upon'. With some friends she has begun to build a small house upon a piece of ground allotted her in Smithfield but can make no progress because of lack of finance. Below a neighbour has witnessed the truth of her statement and the Lord Mayor, Sir William Bolton, has authorised a payment of £10.
CORPORATION OF LONDON RECORDS OFFICE

St Ethelburger. A pre-Norman church dedicated to a Saxon saint. It managed to escape the flames of 1666. JOHN BENTON-HARRIS

[Facsimile of handwritten Orders of the Court of Aldermen, dated 6 and 7 September 1666]

augmented by the aldermen, magistrates and other
London persons of quality, met at Gresham House
as ordered. The Royal Society, which had met there
since its foundation in 1662, was ejected but met at
Arundel House in the Strand, placed at its disposal
by the newly-elected president, Henry Howard,
later the sixth Duke of Norfolk.

The very first directive of the Council was an
order to the citizens of London to clear the streets
of the capital, the lanes and all public passages of
rubbish, and everyone was to be responsible for
clearing their own land. Until this order was completed, no work could be attempted on the ruins. In
each ward a booth was to be set up to which landowners were to bring details of the condition of
their property and a register was to be opened to
record all those who were willing to buy or sell land
in the City.

Most important was the rehousing of the
merchants in order that the financial and trading
life of the City could get underway again. A special
committee was established to appoint temporary
sites to merchants from which they could conduct
their business. This committee had to present a
draft of its proposals for a Bill in Parliament which
was done by 24 September. In the meantime
Gresham House itself became the centre where the
financiers and merchants could conduct their
business and where, says Pepys, 'infinity of people,
partly through novelty to see the new place, and
partly to find out and hear what is become of one
man or another', gathered. 'I met with many
people undone,' he continued, 'and more that have

At the Court at WHITEHALL the eighth of *May* 1667.

Prefent

The KING's moft Excellent *Majefty,*

His *Royal Highnefs* the Duke of YORK,
Lord Arch-Bifhop of *Canterbury,*
Lord Chancellor,
Lord Privy-Seal,

Duke of *Albemarle,*
Marquefs of *Dorchefter,*
Lord Chamberlain,
Earl of *Bridgwater,*
Earl of *Berkfhire,*
Earl of *Bathe,*

Earl of *Carlifle,*
Earl of *Craven,*
Earl of *Lauderdaill,*
Earl of *Middleton,*
Lord *Arlington,*
Lord *Afhley,*

Mr. Comptroller,
Mr. Secretary *Morice,*
Mr. Chancellor of the Dutchy,
Sir *William* Coventry.

An ORDER made by the Lord Mayor, Aldermen, and Common Council of the City of *London,* of the 29. of *April* laft paft, in the enfuing words, (viz.)

It is Ordered, That the Surveyors take fpecial care, that the Breaft-Summ... ...houfes do range of an equal height houfe with houfe, fo far as fhall be convenient, and there to make... ...tions.

And that they do encourage and give Directions to all Builders for orn... ...te and projections of the Front-Buildings be of rubbed Bricks; and that all the ... of rough Bricks neatly wrought, or all rubbed, at the difcretion of the Builder, or that ... inrich their Fronts as they pleafe.

That if any perfon or perfons fhall defire in any Street or Lane of Note to Build on each fide of the Street or Lane (oppofite one to the other) fix or more Houfes of the Third Rate, or that the upper Rooms or Garrets may be flat Roofs encompaffed with Battlements of Bricks covered with Stone, or Gable ends, or Rails, and Bannifters of Iron or Stone, or vary their Roofs for the greater ornament of Building; the Surveyors, or one of them, fhall certifie their opinions therein to the Committee for Re-building, who fhall have liberty to give leave for the fame, if they fee caufe.

That in all the Streets no Sign-pofts fhall hang crofs, but the Signs fhall be fixed againft the Balconies, or fome other convenient part of the Side of the houfe.

It is Ordered that a Poftern fhall be made on the North-fide of Newgate for Conveniency of Foot-paffengers, and that Holborn-Bridge fhall be enlarged to run ftraight on a bevil Line from the Timber-houfe on the North-fide thereof, known by the Sign of the Cock, to the Front of the Buildings at the Swan Inne on the faid North-fide of Holborn-hill.

Forafmuch as it is Provided in the late Act for Re-building, That the Surveyors fhall take care for the equal fetting out of all party-Walls and Piers, and no perfon be permitted to build till that be done; therefore, for prevention of any Erection in the taking of fuch Surveys, and of all Quarrells and Contentions that may arife between the Builders, it is Ordered, That no Builder fhall lay his Foundation, until the Surveyors, or one of them, (according to the Act) fhall view it, and fee the party-Walls and Piers equally fet out, and that all perfons obferve the Surveyors Directions concerning the Superftructure to be erected over the faid Foundation.

And that for the defraying that, and all other incident Charges of Meafuring, Staking out, taking the Levell, and Surveying the Streets and Ground, each Builder, before he lay his Foundation, or fuch Survey fhall be taken, do repair to the Chamber of London, and there enter his Name, with the place where his Building is to be fet out, and to pay to the Chamberlain the fumme of fix fhillings eight pence for every Foundation to be re-built. For which Mr. Chamberlain fhall give Acquittances: upon Receipt of which Acquittances the Surveyors fhall proceed to fet out fuch perfons Foundations.

And it is Ordered, That all perfons who have already laid any Foundations fhall forthwith pay into the Chamber of London fix fhillings eight pence for every Foundation.

And this Court is confenting and defirous that all ftreight and narrow Paffages, which fhall be found convenient for common Benefit and Accommodation, and fhall receive his MAJESTIE's Order and Approbation, fhall and may be Inlarged and made wider, and otherwife Altered, before the 20. day of May now next enfuing, as fhall be fitting for the Beauty, Ornament, and Conveniency thereof, and Staked and fet out accordingly.

Several late Inhabitants of Fleetftreet, intending to Re-build their houfes which did formerly ftand backward of other Foundations near adjoyning, and defiring liberty to advance their houfes, that the whole Front may run on a ftraight Line; the Committee did agree to the fame, if the Right Honourable the Lord High Chancellor of England and the other Lords fhall approve thereof, and procure his MAJESTIE's Approbation to the fame: and the Committee do defire liberty may be given for other perfons in other places, where it fhall be found convenient.

And it is Ordered, That the Committee for Re-building do prefent the Particulars aforefaid to the Right Honourable the Lord High Chancellor of England and the other Lords, and that the fame (if they receive his MAJESTIE's Approbation) fhall be forthwith Printed and Publifhed.

Which being this day reprefented to the Board by the Right Honourable the Lord High Chancellor of *England,* the fame was allowed and approved of; and it was Ordered that the fame be punctually obferved in every part thereof. And all perfons concerned are required and commanded to yield due obedience and conform themfelves thereunto. And that the faid Order be forthwith Printed and Publifhed.

Edw. Walker.

Printed by *James Flefher,* Printer to the Honourable City of LONDON.

An order made on 8 May 1667, by the Lord Mayor, Aldermen and Common Council of the City concerning the standards for the construction of new buildings.

extraordinary great losses.' Within a few days some 3,000 merchants were crowded round Gresham House trying to pick up the remnants of their shattered businesses. Dr Sprat, afterwards the Bishop of Rochester, wrote:

> They beheld the ashes of their houses, gates and temples without the least pusillanimity. If philosophers had done this, it had well become their profession of wisdom, if gentlemen, the nobleness of their breeding and blood would have required it; but that such greatness of heart should have been found among the obscure multitude is no doubt one of the most honourable events that ever happened. A new City is to be built, on the most advantageous seat of all Europe for trade and command.

Not every merchant viewed the destruction of their businesses with the equanimity that Dr Sprat thought universal. And not every merchant recovered from the fire. Many passed into the debtors' prisoners of Ludgate, Fleet and Marshalsea to end their days there. One such merchant, 'Philanthropus Philagathus', managed to raise sufficient funds to print a six-page appeal after nine years of suffering in a debtor's prison due to his losses in the fire. He claimed that he spoke for a great many former merchants who had lost everything in the fire and were now condemned to life in prison because they had no way of raising funds. He appealed to Charles and his Parliament for help.

> The aforesaid sufferers are, in another respect, worthy objects of your help and interposition for the stopping of the merciless fury of their creditors upon them, whereof the prisons about London are severe testimonies; as if they had been men marked out by Divine Vengeance merely to become a prey to their cruelty, and this countenanced by the Law, because of Debt, without any reflection upon the inevitable hand of God that disabled them.

'Philanthropus Philagathus' was appealing for his release four years after an Act of 1671 had been passed designed to relieve and release prisoners for debt impoverished by 'the sad and dreadful Fire'. Such an appeal proved that the Act had failed in its intent and still many were condemned to languish behind bars merely because they had lost their means of livelihood in the fire.

Markets were essential to the life of the citizens and as early as Thursday Leadenhall was appointed as the meat market, the place to buy fish, meal, hides and leather. On Thursdays, however, the market was to be given over to the clothiers. Stalls for the sale of vegetables were to be set up in Aldersgate Street and around the Pump in Bishopsgate Street. Outlying markets were temporarily formed by Royal Proclamation.

There was danger from the convicts who had managed to escape from the ruined prisons and one of the first priorities was to re-establish the security of the gaols. It was found possible to make swift repairs to Newgate and re-open a section of the prison. But Newgate was without a proper water supply until November. A wooden structure was set up in the ruins of the Sessions House in Old Bailey for gaol delivery and temporary prisons were established in any fairly secure room that could be found, rooms that were hastily fitted with bars and bolts, such as the lodgings of the Town Cryer over Aldersgate, from which he was turned out to make room for prisoners from the Poultry Compter.

Improvisation was the order of the day. Lord Bayning's house in Mark Lane was made into the temporary Custom House. The Excise Office was removed to Southampton Fields and the Post Office was established in Brydges Street, Covent Garden, although a few weeks later it was removed again into Bishopsgate Street.

The next most important thing was to provide relief for the impoverished citizens. Money to alleviate their suffering came pouring in from many sources. Several charitably disposed people had placed their homes at the disposal of the authorities to use as temporary lodgings for the homeless. Subscriptions were raised throughout the country. York sent £398; the merchants of Leghorn some £300; Marlborough, in Wiltshire, sent £50, while Lyme Regis, Dorset, collected £100. All over the country relief committees sent contributions both in money and kind. Lynn, in Norfolk, sent a

Christopher Wren's plan for rebuilding London. Wren conceived two plans, one west of the River Fleet centred on a piazza halfway along Fleet Street, and one for the City 'within the walls'. This commenced with a large triangular piazza in front of St Paul's Cathedral, from which two main roads fork on either side of the building. The northern one proceeds to Aldgate by the Royal Exchange. The southern one to the Tower past two more piazzas north of Dowgate and Billingsgate. A main road also runs from Newgate past Guildhall to the Royal Exchange, which would be in the centre of a large piazza surrounded by Bank, Post Office, Mint, Goldsmiths and Insurance Offices. The Commissioners for rebuilding rejected Wren's plan in the face of 'narrow spirited contests about identical property' but the real reason for not adopting it was the need to keep the City working and avoid the loss of leadership in world commerce. GUILDHALL LIBRARY

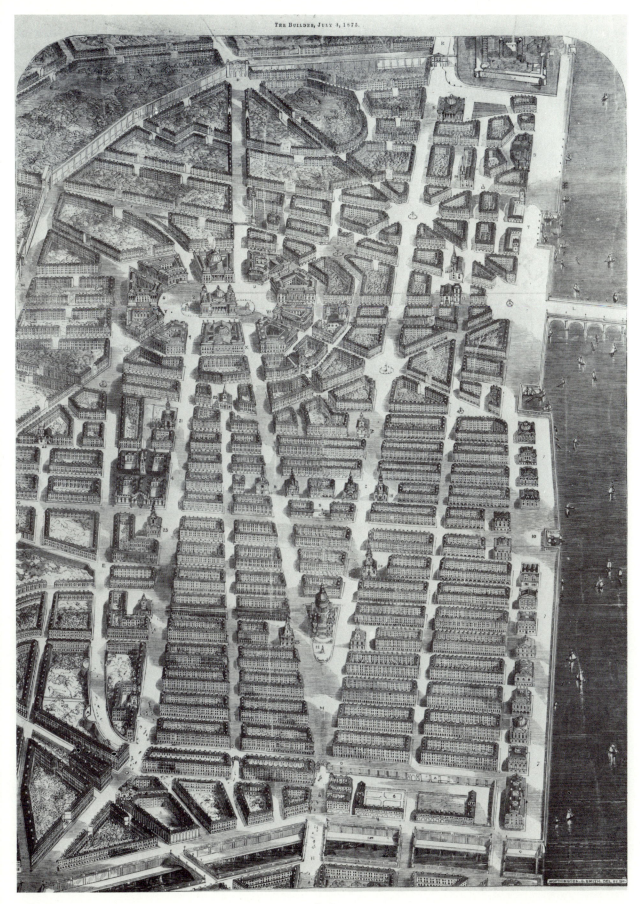

WORTHINGTON, G. SMITH, DEL. ET SM.

convoy of provisions to the ruined City. The saddest tale of bureaucratic stupidity came from Ireland. The Council of Ireland wrote to Lord Mayor Bludworth on 29 September wanting to assist the poor of London. Since money was scarce in Ireland, after ten years of the ruthless Cromwellian colonisation, the Council asked if the City would receive aid in the form of cattle. But under English law no cattle were allowed to be imported from Ireland, a way of keeping Irish trade subservient to England and no way was found around the law, not even to aid the homeless Londoners. The richer Ulster colonists managed to contribute £250. In addition to this there were many individual subscriptions such as £40 from the Countess of Devonshire and £42 15s from the Dean and Chapter of Lincoln Cathedral. Eventually the subscription reached the sum of £10,611.

Within a month of the fire Sir Thomas Bludworth's period as Lord Mayor came to an end. Londoners thought they were well rid of him. But although he was ineffectual during the fire he was at least an honest Lord Mayor. His successor, Sir William Bolton, sworn in on 29 October, was dishonest. Within a few months it was found that Bolton had been helping himself rather liberally to the relief fund and, pending an inquiry, was suspended from office and forbidden to attend the Court of Aldermen or any public function. It was not until 1668 that he was convicted of embezzling a large part of the relief fund.

On Thursday, 13 September, an enterprising Londoner started to rebuild his house at Blackfriars. He was promptly ordered to stop and a Royal Proclamation was issued the same day forbidding the rebuilding of houses. General regulations were going to be issued, Londoners were told, for the guidance of rebuilding in a uniform manner. The entire capital was to be rebuilt. As Dr. Sprat had said: 'A new City is to be built, on the most advantageous seat of all Europe for trade and command.' Henry Oldenburg wrote to his friend the Hon Robert Boyle: 'The citizens, instead of complaining, discourse almost of nothing but of a survey for rebuilding the City with bricks and large streets.'

There was one rumour that the capital might be moved elsewhere and the citizens of York wrote to the King requesting that York, as one of the oldest and most important city's in the kingdom, should be chosen as the capital. Londoners replied:– not until the Thames flowed under the Ouse Bridge. Charles himself dissuaded any further ideas along these lines by describing London as 'this our native City'. It was his aim, he said, that London should rise more magnificent than ever, 'making it rather appear to the world as purged with fire (in how lamentable a manner soever) to a wonderful beauty and comeliness, than consumed by it.' One thing was clear, that in the rebuilding of London,' no man whatsoever shall presume to erect any house or building, great or small, but of brick and stone.'

All eminent streets were to be of such a breadth, decreed Charles, that if one side were on fire there would be no danger of the other side catching alight. No streets were to be so narrow that it would be hard for people to pass in them, especially those streets that led towards the riverside. Most importantly, trades such as brewers, dyers, and soap makers, which emitted offensive odours and smoke, were to be removed to a special site.

Strangely enough Londoners were annoyed with the King's proclamation, wise as it was. They saw it as an interference with their liberty. Nevertheless, in spite of opposition created by the powerful merchant class, the provisions were accepted by the Council who, on 9 October, ruled that owners of houses had fourteen days left to clear the foundations of their property of rubbish and pile up bricks and stones preparatory to a survey for rebuilding.

But if the City of London was to be rebuilt then someone would have to be in charge of it. John Evelyn wanted to be that man. He wrote:

On the 13th (September) I presented His Majesty with a survey of the ruins, and a plot for a new City, with a discourse on it, whereupon, after dinner, His Majesty sent me into the Queen's Bedchamber, Her Majesty and the Duke only present, they examined each particular, and discoursed upon them for near a full hour, seeming to be extremely pleased with what I had so early thought on.

But Evelyn, as quick as he was in presenting his plan, had been beaten to the mark by Dr Christopher Wren, then deputy surveyor of His Majesty's Works. As London was still smouldering on Monday, 10 September, Wren had presented his plan for rebuilding to the King. Evelyn was to write ruefully to Sir Samuel Tuke: 'Dr Wren got a start of me, but both of us did coincide so frequently that His Majesty was not displeased.'

On 21 September, a third person entered the competition, Robert Hooke, then Reader of Mathematics at Gresham College, and perhaps the most brilliant experimental philosopher of the day. Hooke's proposal was to lay out the chief streets from east to west with other streets equally straight from north to south. It was utilitarian and, indeed,

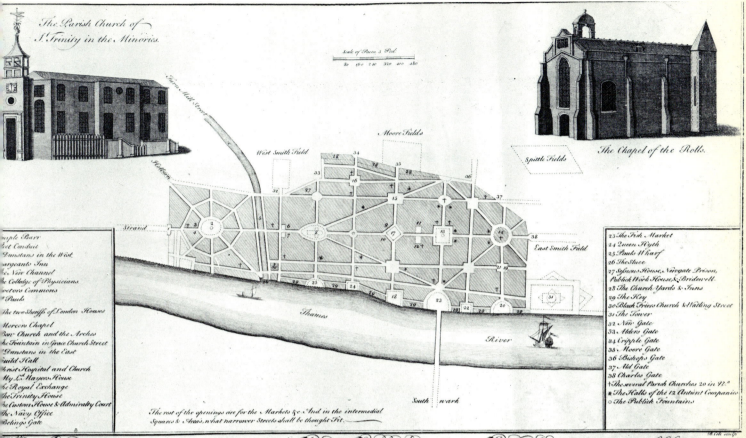

The Parish Church of St Trinity in the Minories.

The Chapel of the Rolls.

London Restored Or SIR IOHN EVELYN'S Plan for Rebuilding that Antient Metropolis after the Fire in 1666.

a prototype for the modern American city. However, it completely destroyed that little which remained of London's link with her past. Hooke certainly had a strong lobby behind him and his scheme was preferred by the Lord Mayor and his aldermen. It obtained for Hooke the job as City Surveyor.

John Evelyn's scheme was more continental in style. It involved the complete rebuilding of most of the City's streets with a straight highway running from Temple Bar in the west to St Dunstan's in the east with five large squares along its course. The first, coming from the west, was an oval, followed by an oval in which St Paul's Cathedral would stand. Thirdly would come a large square with Mansion House, fourthly a large piazza surrounded by colonnades and a fountain in the centre; and lastly a square enclosing St Dunstan's. At the east end of this highway was a triumphal arch called King Charles' Gate. From north to south six main streets would cut across the City. The Royal Exchange would be sited on the river front, just to the west of London Bridge. It was a very impressive plan but a very impractical one.

John Evelyn's plan for rebuilding London. The proposals by Evelyn differed from those of Wren although there are general similarities. They envisaged a main east and west street continuing from the Strand at Temple Bar, passing on either side of St Paul's and leaving the City to the east at a new gate dedicated to King Charles. Notable landmarks en route would be the Fleet Conduit, a palace for the Lord Mayor and a fountain in Gracechurch Street. At right angles to the mayoral palace would be a road from Moorgate to the Thames, with the Royal Exchange placed on the river bank. GUILDHALL LIBRARY

Wren's plan was similar to Evelyn's in many ways, except that Evelyn was, of course, an amateur architect, while Wren was a practising one. In his plan he made four principal objectives. Firstly, that the Royal Exchange should stand isolated on its existing site and would be 'the nave or centre of the town'. Secondly, greater significance would be given to St Paul's Cathedral. Thirdly, the bad communication across London Bridge would be improved. Fourthly, the river bank from Temple to the Tower would be cleared to construct a broad public quay.

A glance at Wren's plan (page 85) shows just how completely Wren would have destroyed the

[87]

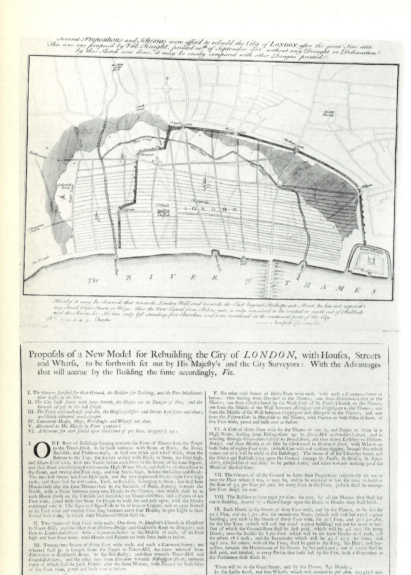

Valentine Knight's plan for rebuilding London, dated 20 September 1666. This plan led to the author's arrest because it included proposals for cutting a large canal for barge traffic through the City and securing large revenues for the King. The London Gazette commented 'as if his Majesty would draw a benefit to himself from so public a calamity of his people.'
GUILDHALL LIBRARY

old City. There was not one of the historic high-ways, such as Cheapside, Great Tower Street, or Thames Street, that he would have preserved. Fleet Street would have become unrecognisable and the Guildhall would have been totally destroyed and rebuilt.

At Ludgate Wren erected a triumphal arch to Charles II. A roadway ninety-feet-broad would have run up to St Paul's. The roadways crossing from south to south would have been about thirty feet in width but they would intersect with another ninety feet wide roadway running west to east, realigned from the old Cheapside. This road led straight to the Royal Exchange.

The frontage along the Thames was to be changed drastically. A public quay some forty-feet-wide would have extended all the way from the Temple Gardens to the Tower, along which would stand most of the rebuilt company halls. Outside the western wall of the City the old stinking Fleet River was to be remodelled into a beautiful and useful canal, passable by as many bridges as there were to be streets crossing it.

Wren's City would have been an architect's city, full of long vistas, and all the winding courts and narrow alleys banished.

Parliament was divided over the plans and finally Wren's scheme for the complete rebuilding was shelved as too Utopian. Not only that, but Parliament, mostly made up of merchants, was pressurised by a strong merchant's lobby who were anxious to rebuild as soon as possible lest trade be diverted to such places as Bristol, Hull or Southampton. Importantly, from their point of view – the question of the terrific cost of such a plan apart – Wren's idea made no provision for the growth of the city. His riverside quays would have shut out the enormous shipping and warehousing business and prevented ships and barges unloading at the water's edge direct into the warehouses that fronted the river from the Tower to Blackfriars.

Perhaps, from an architectural point of view, the greatest fault of Wren's plan lay in the fact that the streets crossed each other at every angle except the right-angle.

The one aspect of Wren's plan that was initially accepted was the need for the wider roads through the City. On 18 October a meeting of the Privy Council and the City Corporation's committees directed that a survey be taken for such highways from Aldersgate to the Thames, from Cripplegate

St James Galickhythe. Rebuilt by Wren, it was damaged during the Second World War but has now been restored.
JOHN BENTON-HARRIS

[88]

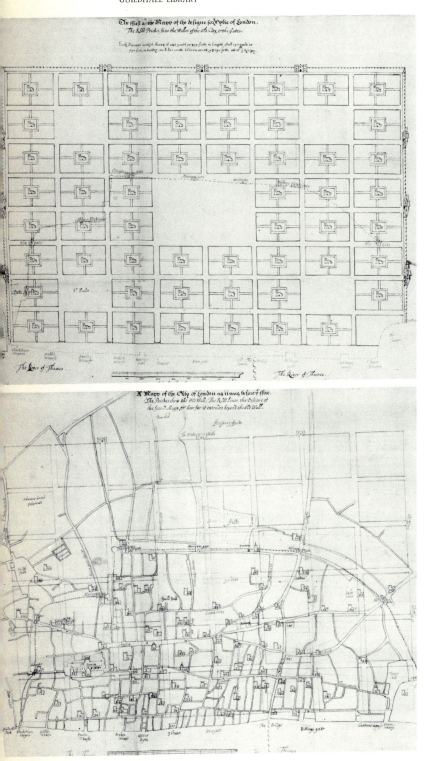

through Cheapside to the Thames, and from the Royal Exchange to the Thames and back to Moorgate. But it seemed that nothing came of this survey.

The debate continued until, on 5 February, 1667, a Rebuilding Act was passed in the Commons which stipulated that the City of London was to be rebuilt on the existing design of the town; all its historic streets were to be kept intact, as were the sites for most of its historic buildings. The impracticability of rebuilding the City except on the old foundation was agreed upon.

During the time Parliament were considering the three schemes of rebuilding, a Captain Valentine Knight of His Majesty's Service published a broadsheet containing proposals of his own. His scheme included the construction of a thirty-feet-wide canal through the City designed to carry barges from Billingsgate north to Fenchurch Street and west via Lothbury through to the Fleet River above Holborn Bridge. The value of this land would have been quite staggering and Captain Knight suggested that the prime advantage of the scheme would be that the King would receive £372,670 as a capital sum and £223,517 per annum.

Instead of gratitude that Captain Knight had his business interests at heart, Charles immediately ordered the man's arrest and lectured his subjects. 'As if,' said the *London Gazette*, 'His Majesty would draw a benefit to himself from so public a calamity of his people, of which his Majesty is known to have so deep sense, that he is pleased to seek rather by all means to give them ease under it.'

In prison, Captain Knight had time to reflect on the ingratitude of kings.

With the Rebuilding Act finally receiving the Royal Assent on 8 February 1667, it was announced that Dr Christopher Wren was to be appointed 'Surveyor General and Principal Architect for the rebuilding of the whole City, the Cathedral Church of St Paul's and all the principal churches, with other structures'. Working with him as his subordinates would be Robert Hooke, Peter Mills and Edward Jarman, with John Oliver and others as supervisors. Associated with Wren would be the King's Commissioners, Hugh May and a Mr Pratt.

All was now set to commence the great rebuilding scheme.

CHAPTER SIX

Who Was to Blame?

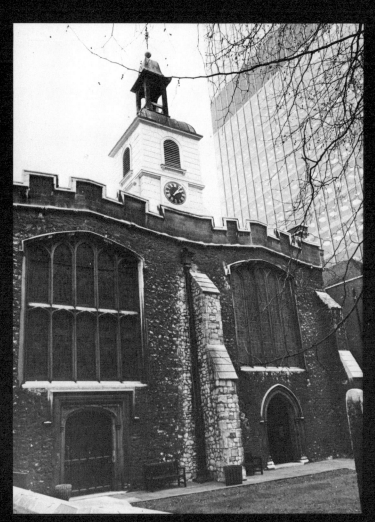

St Helen Bishopsgate, one of the few City churches to escape
entirely the flames of 1666.
JOHN BENTON-HARRIS

'And now we cry a plot, a plot, and 'twas treachery has done this unto us,' wrote Henry Griffith to his kinsman on 18 September. As early as the very first day of the fire Londoners were claiming that the City had been deliberately set ablaze and the blame was laid at the doors of the Catholics, Dutch and French. It is difficult to estimate how many unfortunate foreigners were done to death at the hands of hysterical London mobs such as the Frenchman who happened to be carrying some tennis balls which the angry people claimed were fireballs. The Italian eye-witness claimed that many of the foreigners resident in London were murdered, several were lynched on sign-posts. According to a Dutch reporter who recorded the incident of the murder of an old woman in Moorfields, 'All foreigners alike were held to be guilty, no discrimination being shown, and many who were well known to be of good character, and upon whom no suspicion could rest, were cast into prison.'

When, on Thursday, 6 September, Charles had tried to point out that the City's destruction had been the result of an accident, Londoners, inflamed with hatred, ignored him and demanded revenge on the people they suspected were the authors of their misfortune. Charles was greatly perturbed at this popular demand to throw the blame on the Catholics. It was already rumoured that he was too sympathetic towards Catholics and that his brother, the Duke of York, was too ardent for their faith. In face of the agitation he sent for the Lord Chief Justice, Sir John Kelyng, and commissioned him to conduct an investigation into the accusations.

Throughout the entire kingdom magistrates became busy arresting all foreigners who could give no good account of themselves. From West Cowes, John Lysle wrote a despatch to Sir James Williamson, the editor of the *London Gazette*, reporting that, 'since the Fire of London, both seamen and landsmen are rampant and outrageous for revenge upon the enemy'. And the public began to hear that the burning of London had been part of a great plan; 'that the plot was not only for London, but for the destruction of the principal cities and towns in England'.

The official narrative of the fire was published in the *London Gazette* Number 85, 3-10 September, 1666, the account being dated 8 September. The writer, on behalf of the Government, says that, notwithstanding all the suspicions, the way in which the fire burnt 'makes us conclude the whole was the effect of an unhappy chance, or to speak better, the heavy hand of God upon us for our sins, showing us the terror of his judgement...'

In spite of this official rebuttal of the rumours, the blame for the firing of London was laid at the doors of everyone who did not conform to the generally accepted principals of the time. Anabaptists, Quakers and other Nonconformists swiftly joined Catholics as suspects. The governor of Hull was soon busy arresting and banishing everyone from the city whose religion or politics he disagreed with. Similar measures were taken throughout the kingdom, arrest following arrest. Even the Royal Court became suspect, particularly James, and there were many ugly rumours of assassination plots.

The Lord Chief Justice gravely investigated the many suspects brought before him, and even took seriously the examination of one Edward Taylor, a ten-year-old apothecary's boy who swore that his father and uncle had destroyed the City between them. His uncle, he said, had given his father £7 to help him fire the City and they had put fire-balls into a house in Pudding Lane, in Thames Street, Fleet Street and the Royal Exchange . . . all on the same evening. 'The boy's age renders the whole suspected,' wrote an investigator on the statement, 'but it is to be put into my Lord Chief Justice's hands.'

Lord Clarendon recalled:

Many who were produced as if their testimony would remove all doubts made such senseless relations of what they had been told, without knowing the condition of the persons who told them, or where to find them, that it was a hard matter to forbear smiling at their evidence.

While the Lord Chief Justice was conducting his investigation, a young Frenchman, Robert Hubert, arrested at Romford in Essex, confessed that he was the incendiary who had fired the City. He was promptly sent to the White Lion Gaol in Southwark for interrogation. Here was a willing sacrifice to the fury of the Londoners. And so the twenty-six-year-old watchmaker from Rouen was hurried to his extinction. Afterwards, however, the Lord Chief Justice, who sat in judgement on the case, actually told King Charles that he did not believe a word of Hubert's confession. Charles discreetly did not interfere in case the people accused him of protecting Catholics, although it appears that Hubert was a Huguenot.

It was significant that the jury who found a 'True Bill' against Hubert consisted of Robert Penny, John Lowman (the gaoler at Southwark), Francis Gunn, Thomas Farriner, senior, Hanna Farriner,

The London Gazette.

Published by Authority.

From Monday, Septemb. 3. to Monday, Septemp. 10. 1666.

Whitehall, Sept. 8.

THe ordinary course of this Paper having been interrupted by a sad and lamentable accident of Fire lately hapned in the City of *London*: It hath been thought fit for satisfying the minds of so many of His Majesties good Subjects who must needs be concerned for the Issue of so great an accident to give this short, but true accompt of it.

On the second instant at one of the clock in the Morning there hapned to break out, a sad and deplorable Fire, in *Pudding-lane* neer *New Fishstreet*, which falling out at that hour of the night, and in a quarter of the Town so close built with wooden pitched houses, spread it self so far before day, and with such distraction to the inhabitants and neighbours, that care was not taken for the timely preventing the further diffusion of it, by pulling down houses, as ought to have been; so that this lamentable Fire in short time became too big to be mastred by any Engines or working neer it. It fell out most unhappily too, that a violent Easterly wind fomented it, and kept it burning all that day, and the night following, spreading it self up to *Grace-church street*, and downwards from *Cannon-street* to the Water-side as far as the *Three Cranes in the Vintrey.*

The people in all parts about it distracted by the vastness of it, and their particular care to carry away their goods, many attempts were made to prevent the spreading of it by pulling down Houses, and making great Intervals, but all in vain, the Fire seising upon the Timber and Rubbish and so continuing it self, even through those spaces, and raging in a bright flame all Monday and Tuesday, notwithstanding His Majesties own, and His Royal Highness's indesatigable and personal pains to apply all possible remedies to prevent it, calling upon and helping the people with their Guards; and a great number of Nobility and Gentry unweariedly assisting therein, for which they were required with a thousand blessings from the poor distressed people. By the favour of God the Wind slackned a little on Tuesday night & the Flames meeting with Brick-buildings at the Temple, by little and little it was observed to lose its force on that side, so that on Wednesday morning we began to hope well, and his Royal Highness never dispairing or slackning his personal care, wrought so well that day, assisted in some parts by the Lords of the Council before and behind it, that a stop was put to it at the *Temple-church*, neer *Holborn-bridge*, *Pye-corner*, *Aldersgate*, *Cripplegate*, neer the lower end of *Coleman-street*, at the end of *Basing-hall-street*, by the Postern, at the upper end of *Bishopsgate-street*, and *Leadenhall-street*, at the *Standard* in *Cornhill*, at the Church in *Fan-church-street*, neer *Clothworkers Hall* in *Mincing-lane*, at the middle of *Mark-lane*, and at the *Tower-dock.*

On Thursday by the blessing of God it was wholly beat down and extinguished. But so as that Evening it unhappily burst out again afresh at the *Temple*, by the falling of some sparks (as is supposed) upon a Pile of Wooden buildings; but his Royal Highness, who watched there that whole night in Person, by the great labours and diligence used, and especially by applying Powder to blow up the Houses about it, before day most happily mastered it.

Divers Strangers, Dutch and French were, during the fire, apprehended, upon suspicion that they contributed mischievously to it, who are all imprisoned, and Informations prepared to make a severe inquisition thereupon by my Lord Chief Justice *Keeling*, assisted by some of the Lords of the Privy Council, and some principal Members of the City, notwithstanding which suspicions, the manner of the burning all along in a train, and so blowen forwards in all its way by strong Winds, makes us conclude the whole was an effect of an unhappy chance, or to speak better, the heavy hand of God upon us for our sins, shewing us the terrour of his Judgment in thus raising the fire, and immediately after his miraculous and never enough to be acknowledged Mercy in putting a stop to it when we were in the last despair, and that all attempts for the quenching it however industriously pursued, seemed insufficient. His Majesty then sat hourly in Council, and ever since hath continued making rounds about the City in all parts of it where the danger and mischief was greatest, till this morning that he hath sent his Grace the Duke of *Albemarle*, whom he hath called for to assist him in this great occasion, to put his happy and successful hand to the finishing this memorable deliverance.

About the Tower the seasonable orders given for plucking down Houses to secure the Magazins of Powder, was more especially successful, that part being up the Wind, notwithstanding which it came almost to the very Gates of it, so as by this early provision, the several Stores of War lodged in the Tower were entirely saved: And we have further this infinite cause particularly to give God thanks, that the fire did not happen in any of those places where his Majesties Naval Stores are kept, so as tho it hath pleased God to visit us with his own hand, he hath not, by disfurnishing us with the means of carrying on the War, subjected us to our enemies.

It must be observed, that this fire happened in a part of the Town, where tho the Commodities were not very rich, yet they were so bulky that they could not well be removed, so that the Inhabitants of that part where it first began have sustained very great loss, but by the best enquiry we can make, the other parts of the Town, where the Commodities were of greater value, took the Alarum so early, that they saved most of their Goods of value, which possibly may have diminished the loss, tho some think, that if the whole industry of the Inhabitants had been applyed to the stopping of the fire, and not to the saving of their particular Goods, the success might have been much better, not only to the publick, but to many of them in their own particulars.

Through this sad Accident it is easie to be imagined how many persons were necessitated to remove themselves and Goods into the open fields, where they were forced to continue some time, which could not but work compassion in the beholders, but his Majesties care was most signal in this occasion, who, besides his personal pains, was frequent in consulting all wayes for relieving those distressed persons, which produced so good effect, aswell by his Majesties Proclamations, and the Orders issued to the Neighbour Justices of the Peace to encourage the sending in provisions to the Markets, which are publickly known, as by other directions, that when his Majesty, fearing lest other Orders might not yet have been sufficient, had commanded the Victualler of his Navy to send bread into *Moore-fields* out of the Sea Stores; it was found that the Markets had

Qqqq   been

[94]

Thomas Dagger, and Thomas Farriner, junior. In early documents the name of Thomas Farynor the baker is as 'Thomas Farriner the elder'. And so the man in whose house the fire started, by carelessness or accident, was instrumental in bringing to execution an innocent man.

The bill charged that Robert Hubert:

not having the fear of God before his eyes, but moved and led away by the instigation of the Devil, on the 2nd day of September, 18 Charles II, about the second hour of the night of that day, with force and arms etc., in London, to wit in the parish of St Margaret New Fish Street, in the ward of Billingsgate, London aforesaid, a fireball by the same Robert Hubert compounded and made with gunpowder, brimstone and other combustible materials, and by the same Robert then and there kindled and fired, then and there voluntarily, maliciously and feloniously did throw into the mansion house of one Thomas Farriner the elder, baker, set and being in Pudding Lane in the parish of the ward aforesaid; and with the fireball aforesaid by the same Robert Hubert thus, as aforesaid, kindled and fired, and thrown into the said mansion house, did then and there devilishly, feloniously, voluntarily, and of his malice aforethought set on fire, burn, and wholly destroy not only the said mansion of the aforesaid Thomas Farriner, but also a great number of churches and other mansion houses and buildings of thousands of lieges and subjects of our said Lord the King, set and being in the parish and ward aforesaid, and in the said city of London and the suburbs thereof, contrary to the peace of our said Lord the now King, his Crown and dignity.

As Lord Clarendon wrote:

And though no man could imagine any reason why a man should so desperately throw away his life, which he might have saved though he had been guilty, since he was only accused upon his own confession; yet neither the judges nor any present at the trial did believe him guilty, but that he was a poor distracted wretch, weary of his life, and chose to part with it in this way.

A petition to the Court of Common Council from citizens who believed the fire not only to reveal the 'imediate hand and justice of God' but also 'very much the malice and practice of men'. They asked the Court to entreat the House of Commons to renew its investigation into the causes of the Fire and re-appoint a Committee to receive such evidence 'as may discover the causes and fomenters thereof'. Presented on 15 November 1667.
GUILDHALL LIBRARY

Sir Hugh Wyndham (1603–84) was a judge in many cases arising out of disputed property in the special Court of the Fire Pleas. He was called to the Bar in 1629 and made Judge of the Common Pleas. In 1661 he became a member of Parliament for Minehead and became a Baron of the Exchequer in 1670.
GUILDHALL LIBRARY

Parliament had not been sitting at the time of the fire but it met for its new session on 18 September in Westminster. 'God be thanked,' said Charles, opening the session, 'for our meeting together in this place. Little time hath passed since we were almost in despair of having this place left to meet in. You see the dismal ruins the fire hath made; and nothing but a miracle of God's mercy could have preserved what is left from the same destruction.'

Seven days later the Parliament appointed its own committee to investigate the causes of the fire and Sir Robert Brook was made chairman. The first meeting of the committee was on 26 September with a brief 'to receive any considerable informations from divers and creditable persons about the matter wherewith they were instructed.' Two days later the House of Commons voted 'that the humble thanks of this House be given to his Majesty for his great care and endeavour to prevent the burning of London.' They then requested that Charles order the banishment of all Catholic priests, Jesuits in particular, and Charles had no option but to issue the necessary proclamation giving such priests until 10 December to quit the kingdom. Lord Arlington told the Earl of Sandwich: 'Your Excellency knows sufficiently the springs upon which the animosity to the Roman Catholics rises, and how hard it is for his Majesty to forebear declaring against them when the complaint ariseth from both Houses of Parliament.'

During one debate in the Commons Sir Richard Browne dramatically produced before members 'some desperate daggers, fit for massacres', two hundred of which, he declared, had been seized at the house of two French Catholics. A general search for arms was then made in the homes of all Catholics.

The Parliamentary Committee's report was presented to the Commons on 22 January and consisted solely of the evidence that they had heard, and merely a selection of that evidence at that. The report made no recommendation but was, if approved by the House, to be sent to the Council of State. Andrew Marvell, the poet, who was member for Hull, wrote to the city's mayor, R. Franke, to tell him that in his opinion the report was 'full of manifest testimony that the fire was of a wicked design'. The Commons forwarded the report to Charles and his Council with the customary plea that the report should be taken into account.

On 27 January 1667, the Council came to the conclusion that 'notwithstanding that many examinations have been taken with great care, by the Lords of the Council and his Majesty's Ministers,

yet nothing hath yet been found to argue it to have been other than the hand of God upon us, a great wind, and the season so very dry'.

Parliament accepted the decision and was prorogued on 8 February. The people, however, were not satisfied. As late as March they were demanding that the inquiry be re-opened. Selected editions of the report were published to inflame the populace against the Catholics. One such pamphlet, entitled *A True and Faithful Account of the Several Informations Exhibited to the Honourable Committee Appointed by Parliament to Inquire into the Late Dreadful Burning of the City of London*, went into five editions. 'The book appears to have been maliciously published by some Presbyterian hands, and

The Monument on Fish Street Hill, an oil painting attributed to J. Paul, copied from an engraving after Canaletto about 1750. The Corporation commissioned Wren to design a monument to stand on the site where the Fire began but it is, in fact, 130 feet from the site of Farynor's baker's shop in Pudding Lane. The monument actually stands on the site occupied by St Margaret's Church, Fish Street Hill.
GUILDHALL LIBRARY

may do harm, being approved of by some of that party,' wrote a magistrate who decided to confiscate all the copies found within his jurisdiction.

Many people now came forward with new tales of how they had seen foreigners throwing fire-balls into houses and shops in the City. A typical testimony was given by Dr John Packer who said:

. . . that he saw a person in the time of the Fire throw some combustible matter into a shop in the Old Bailey, which he thinks was the shop of an apothecary; and that immediately thereupon he saw a great smoke, and smelt a smell of brimstone. The person that did this immediately ran away; but upon the outcry of the people he was taken by the Guards.

Also, people began to recollect how they had been warned about the Fire from Catholics, French or Dutchmen, months beforehand. Mrs Elizabeth Styles told magistrates:

> . . . that in April last, in an eager discourse she had with a French servant of Sir Vere Fan, he hastily replied, 'You English maids will like the Frenchmen better when there is not a house left between Temple Bar and London Bridge.' To which she answered, 'I hope your eyes will never see that.' He replied, 'This will come to pass between June and October.'

All the stories were quite far-fetched although one story demonstrates how innocent remarks could be misinterpreted. It concerned Monsieur Belland, the King's Firework Master, who lived in Marylebone. M Belland was employed by the Office of Ordnance for making grenades as part of his duties as well as providing fireworks for the royal parties and fetes. Just before the fire he had brought a great quantity of incendiary material which he wanted in a great hurry. The citizen from whom he brought the material afterwards claimed that he had become suspicious.

> Mr Belland (said the citizen) what is the reason of your haste? Have you any show suddenly before the King? At which he blushed and would give no answer.
> Said the citizen: What kind of fire do you make? Only such as will crack and run?
> Belland answered: I make all sorts, some that will burn and make no crack at all, but will fly up in a pure body of flame higher than the top of Paul's and waver in the air.
> Said the citizen: Mr Belland, when you make your show shall I see it?
> Yes, said Belland, I promise you, and gave him his hand upon it.

This was regarded as a highly incriminating conversation. During the burning of London, this citizen and a colleague tracked down Belland to Whitehall Palace, where the Firework Master and his family had fled for safety against the mob hysteria. They managed to find Belland's son in the crowded corridors of the palace and told him: 'Both I and many thousand families more are the worse for you; for, you, under pretence of making fireworks for the King, have destroyed a famous City, and ruined a noble people.' At this M Belland appeared and threatened the two men with a law suit for that of which they had accused him. The citizens told Belland, 'You must give an account for what you have done,' and reported the matter to the authorities, adding, rather maliciously, that Belland was staying in the rooms of Lady Killegrew at Whitehall.

The authorities, quite rightfully, ignored the accusation, along with many more similar tales. It was only the diplomatic skill of Charles that prevented an outburst of religious persecution of Catholics. Parliament was still pressing for penal laws to be enacted such as those that were already in force in Ireland. Another Parliamentary Committee had already been set up to enquire 'touching the insolency of Popish priests and Jesuits and the increase of Popery'. The outburst of religious persecution was finally to break out in 1678 when Titus Oates claimed the revelation of a 'Popish Plot' in which eighty Jesuit friars were supposed to have fired the City. Londoners again demanded action against Catholics and on 10 January 1680, the House of Commons passed a resolution: 'That it is the opinion of this House that the City of London was burnt in the year 1666 by the Papists, designing thereby to introduce arbitrary power and Popery into this Kingdom.'

Not until 1830 was the truth finally admitted. London Corporation had decided to erect a monument to the fire on the site of St Margaret's in Fish Hill Street, which had been the first to perish in the flames. A Roman Doric column, designed by Christopher Wren, perhaps in collaboration with Robert Hooke, was sited some 130 feet from Farynor's bakery. The column was 202 feet in height and it was, at first, intended to be surmounted by a statue of Charles, but this was abandoned in favour of a brass urn from which flames emerged. A bas relief on the west side by Caius Gabriel Cibber showed Charles 'affording protection to the desolate City and freedom to its rebuilders and inhabitants'. An inscription on it erroneously boasted that London was rebuilt within three years.

The Lord Mayor of London at the time of the 'Popish Plot', Sir Patience Ward, decided to make an addition to the Monument, 'the better to preserve the memory of this dreadful visitation'. On the Monument itself was inscribed:

> The burning of this Protestant City was begun and carried on by the treachery and malice of the Popish faction, in order to the effecting their horrid plot for the extirpating the Protestant

The Monument to the
Great Fire, designed and
erected by Wren a few
years afterwards. It
consisted of a fluted Doric
column in Portland stone,
202 feet high,
surmounted by a vase of
flames, and has a staircase
inside it. The pediment
bears a bas-relief and the
plinth carried an
inscription blaming the
Catholics for starting the
fire, added in 1681
during the Titus Oates
alarms. This inscription
was removed in James II's
reign, recut in
William III's reign and
finally erased by an Act
of Common Council
in 1831.

JOHN BENTON-HARRIS

The stone tablet, now in the Guildhall Museum, accusing
Catholics of starting the Great Fire of 1666. It was originally
erected in 1681 at Number 25 Pudding Lane, the site of the
house in which the Fire broke out, near to the Monument. This
plaque was not removed until the mid-nineteenth century.
GUILDHALL LIBRARY

religion and English liberties, and to introduce
Popery and heresy.

A further inscription was placed on the site of
Farynor's bakery to emphasise the accusation.

Here by ye permission of heaven hell broke loose
upon this Protestant City from the malicious
Hearts of barbarous Papists, by ye hand of their
agent, Hubert, who confessed and on ye ruins
of this place declared the fact, for which he was
hanged (vizt.) that here began that dreadful fire,
which is described and perpetuated on and by
the neighbouring pillar.
Erected Anno 168(1) in the Majoralties of
  Sr Patience Ward Kt.

Patience Ward was commemorated for the deed
in verse by a namesake, Thomas Ward, in *England's
Reformation*, published in Hamburg in 1710. Titus
Oates, says Thomas Ward:

  . . . swore, with flaming faggot sticks,
  In sixteen hundred sixty-six
  That they through London took their marches,
  And burned the City down with torches;

Yet all invisible they were
Clad in their coats of Lapland air.
That sniffing Whig-Mayor Patience Ward,
To this damned lie had such regard,
That he his godly masons sent
T' engrave it round the Monument,
They did so; but let such things pass,
His men were fools, and he an ass.

Perhaps the more famous comment on the
inscription are the lines of Pope's couplet:

  Where London's column pointing at the skies,
    Like a tall bully, lifts the head, and lies . . .

When James came to the throne the words were
obliterated from the Monument but after the
'Glorious Revolution' and the accession of William
and Mary they were carved again, even deeper. The
lie was not finally removed from the Monument
until 1830. The nearby plaque was similarly
removed, concealed in a cellar, and finally presented
to the Guildhall Museum in 1876.

In examining the evidence it is impossible to
come to any other conclusion than that the fire
started because Thomas Farynor and his assistant,
after a hard day's trading, did not completely
extinguish their own fire and that a spark from the
fire, nurtured and blown by the wind, set light to
a pile of faggots by the side of the oven, put there

*St Katherine Cree, one of the few City churches to be left
undamaged by the Great Fire.* JOHN BENTON-HARRIS

The Old Wine Shades, the only City tavern to survive the Great Fire. Built in 1663, its timbers were impervious to the flames and it still stands in Martin Lane. JOHN BENTON-HARRIS

The George Inn, Southwark, a fifteenth century galleried coaching pub now owned by the National Trust. This inn is typical of the many that perished in the Great Fire, such as the Star Inn on Fish Hill Street which stood behind Tom Farynor's bakery.

JOHN BENTON-HARRIS

for relighting the fire in the morning. The Italian report came nearer to the truth when it recorded: 'The baker's boy, having placed some twigs in the oven to dry, about midnight on Saturday, they caught fire, setting the whole house ablaze.' Farynor's subsequent insistence that the bakery fire was out, that this pile of faggots (which he admitted was there) did not catch alight, was made out of fear in the light of Londoners' hysterical outbursts against plotters. His careful observations as to how the fire was burning, which he made after being dragged out of his bed in the middle of the night and finding his whole house ablaze so that his primary concern was to rush his family to safety over the rooftops, are a little too detailed to be believable. The fire of London was started by accident.

And what was the cost of this accident?

London had only one sixth of its area left habitable; the rest, including the suburbs to the west, were charred ruins as far as Temple Bar. Guildhall, the centre of the City's administration, was heaped in ruins although its main walls still stood. The justice courts, civil courts, and every prison had been destroyed while many of the prisoners had seized the opportunity to escape. In fact, as autumn turned to winter, a new menace arose among the ruins of the City. Crime became manifest and thieves and murderers, many of them escaped convicts, found that the cellars of the ruins and the deserted church vaults made excellent hideouts. The Postmaster James Hickes wrote:

There are many people found murdered and carried into the vaults among the ruins, as three last night as I hear, and it is supposed by hasty fellows that cry, 'Do you want a light ?' and carry links and that when they catch a man single, whip into a vault with him, knock him down, strip him from top to toe, blow out their links, and leave the person for dead . . . no person dare, after the close of evening, pass the streets among the ruins.

It is hard to know how many people perished in the fire. The first Bill of Mortality, published three weeks later, claimed a total of 704 deaths in the period including 104 from the plague. But the final published Bill of Mortality listed six people while most contemporary observers mention only four people: *One*, Thomas Farynor's maid; *two*, the old woman in St Paul's Churchyard seen by Taswell; *three*, the old man mentioned by Pepys and, *four*, Paul Lowell, the watchmaker of Shoe Lane. But John Evelyn, walking through the City, referred to 'the stench that came from some poor creatures' bodies'. On the other hand one must reject the estimate of the Spanish observer:

The dead numbered eight thousand: these were the sick and infirm, who were buried sooner than they expected amid dust and ashes, and the covetous ones – those who, in trying to save their effects, lost them and their own lives – and the daring people who, while trying to steal, were stolen away to Death.

It is true there were also cases of people who died of shock, such as the parishioner of St Botolph in Aldgate who dropped dead on Tower Hill during the fire 'being affrighted'. Five others were killed shortly after the fire by falling masonry and timbers while looking for salvage amongst the ruins. But the greatest number of deaths, although how great we do not know, were due to exposure. A large number of invalids, the frail and the sick, and pregnant women, had to undergo nights of exposure in open fields. It is thought that many hundreds died in this manner, although we can name only the poet James Shirley and his wife, driven from their home in Fleet Street, near Serjeant's Inn, who sought refuge in St Gile's-in-the-Fields and died of exposure, both on the same day, and were buried in St Gile's on 29 October. There were other deaths later, indirectly the cause of the fire, such as that of Richard Yrde, buried in St Mary Woolnoth's on 18 October 'being stifled in a house of office backside of Deputy Graham's house,' after the City was burnt'. Finally, adding to the death toll, were the numbers of unfortunate foreigners seized by the crowd and murdered in their hysterical rage; people such as the Frenchman whose tennis balls were claimed as fire-balls, and the old woman at Moorgate whose chickens were also claimed as fire-balls. On top of these came the judicial sacrifice, the execution of Robert Hubert.

One sixth of the population, 100,000 out of 600,000, including dwellers in the suburbs, were homeless. The Royal Exchange, the centre of London's international trade, and gathering place of merchants, was a smoking shell. Along the water's edge the boat stairs and wharves were unserviceable although, in spite of this, there was no shortage of the supply of foodstuffs for the citizens. An exact survey of the damage was needed.

Within days Jonas Moore and Ralph Gatrix, the City surveyors, set to work to assess the damage.

St Stephen Walbrook. This seventh-century church was destroyed in the Fire, rebuilt by Wren and then damaged by bombing in the Second World War. It has now been restored.
JOHN BENTON-HARRIS

Within the walls of the City they found that 373 acres had been burnt and outside the walls a further sixty-three acres and three rods were destroyed. Some 13,200 houses had been totally destroyed in over 400 streets and courts. The surveyors gave the number of churches burnt as eighty-nine while other authorities list eighty-seven. It is possible that the surveyors counted the full number of churches affected. The number totally destroyed seems to be eighty-four whereas three others were restored after substantial repairs. Some twenty-two churches were actually left unharmed by the fire, including eleven churches outside the City walls. There were also forty-four company halls listed as being destroyed. The entire area burnt was a mile-and-a-half long from Tower Wharf to the Temple by half-a-mile wide at its broadest point, reaching from the Thames to Cripplegate.

The first financial estimate of the damage seems to have been made by 'Rege Sincera' whose *Observations both Historical and Moral* was issued three weeks after the fire. He put the total cost of the damage at £7,370,000. His estimate is inaccurate in that it was made before the exact details of the surveyors' report were made known.

He records:

12,000 houses burnt, valued one with another at £25 a year's rent each, which at twelve year's purchase maketh £300, the whole amounting to:	£3,600,000
87 parochial churches, besides St Paul's, the six consecrated chapels, the Exchange, Guildhall, Custom House, the halls of the Companies, and other public buildings, amounting to half as much:	£1,800,000
The goods that every private man lost one with another, valued at half the value of the houses:	£1,800,000
About 20 wharves of coal and wood valued at £1,000 apiece:	£20,000
About 100,000 boats and barges, 1000 cart loads, with porters to remove the goods to and fro, as well for the houses that were burning as for those that stood in fear of it, at 20s. a load:	£150,000
In all	£7,370,000

Delaune, in *The Present State of London*, published in 1681, had access to all the surveyors' figures and he estimated the damage at £9,900,000 and adds that people should bear in mind the extra costs of private goods and moneys destroyed 'or pilfered away by those wicked wretches that made their gain by the common calamity'. He computed such losses at an extra £2,000,000. In an early eighteenth century history, edited by John Strype, there appears the first detailed estimate.

Houses burnt, 13,200 one with another at £25 rent at the low rate of twelve years' purchase:	£3,960,000
Eighty-seven parish churches at £8,000 each:	696,000
Six consecrated chapels at £2,000 each:	12,000
The Royal Exchange:	50,000
The Custom House:	10,000
Fifty-two halls of Companies, most of which were magnificent structures and palaces, at £1,500 each:	78,000
Three City gates at £3,000 each:	9,000
Gaol of Newgate:	15,000
Four stone bridges:	6,000
Sessions House:	7,000
Guildhall, with courts and offices belonging to it:	40,000
Blackwell Hall:	3,000
Bridewell:	5,000
Poultry Compter:	3,000
Wood Street Compter:	3,000
Towards rebuilding St Paul's Church, which at that time was new building, the stone-work being almost finished:	2,000,000
Wares, household-stuff, monies and movable goods lost and spoilt	2,000,000
Hire of porters, carts, waggons, barges, boats & etc for removing wares, household stuff & etc during the Fire, and some small time after:	20,000
Printed books and paper in shops and warehouses:	150,000
Wine, tobacco, sugar, plums & etc of which the City was at that time very full:	1,500,000
Cutting a navigable river to Holborn Bridge:	27,000
The Monument:	14,500
total sum	£10,788,500

St Sepulchre Without Newgate, partially destroyed in the Fire it was one of the three churches which was able to be repaired without entirely rebuilding it. On coming out of Newgate Gaol, the death cart would stop outside this church with the condemned while the bells tolled and the vicar would pray and give a nosegay of flowers to each of those about to be taken to be executed at Tyburn.
JOHN BENTON-HARRIS

This is the estimate that seems the most accurate and which was afterwards quoted by official sources but, in addition, the money paid to freeholders whose ground was acquired by the Corporation or State must be added and the cost of building wharves by the river, enlarging the old streets, making new ones and providing new market places, all of which must have greatly increased this figure.

Individual losses were also great but hard to estimate. Cases such as Alderman John Jefferies of Bread Street Ward, a former Member of Parliament for Brecknock, who had his warehouse of tobacco, valued at £20,000, burnt down. Then cases of wealthy merchants such as Thomas Catchmead, a fishmonger, who were reduced to beggary; although Catchmead, thanks to the intercession of luckier friends, was soon set up in business again. Not all the merchants were so lucky and many died in debtors' prisons.

The loss to English literature was inestimable. In terms of actually financial losses among the booksellers the figure has been put between £150,000 and £200,000. John Evelyn writing to Sir Samuel Tuke commented: 'Many noble impressions consumed by their trusting them to the churches, which will be an extraordinary detriment to the whole public of learning.' It has been suggested that many of the original drafts of Shakespeare's plays may have been destroyed in the fire. Certainly the rarity of the third folio of his works, printed in London in 1664, is due to the edition being almost totally destroyed in the fire.

The entire edition of the Polygot Bible, on which a committee of scholars had laboured for many years, was destroyed. A nine-volume edition of *Critici Sacre*, a compilation of works by eminent authors, was entirely destroyed leaving its publisher, Cornelius Bec, with a £13,000 loss to face. John Ogilby, a poet and printer of the period, was just about to publish an epic poem in twelve volumes entitled *Carolies* in honour of Charles I. The entire work was destroyed when Ogilby's printing house in King's Head Court, Shoe Lane, was destroyed. Ogilby had not the heart to try to rewrite his epic from memory.

Such were the losses created by the accident which occurred in Thomas Farynor's bakery.

CHAPTER SEVEN
The Rebuilding of London

The rebuilt Cathedral of St Paul's; an enlargement of the
panoramic view published in 1747 by Samuel and Nathaniel
Buck. The complete form of the rebuilt City appears in its fresh
state before it was encumbered by later building in the
nineteenth century.

A plan of the City rebuilt, made by John Overton in 1676. GUILDHALL LIBRARY

For the next thirty years Christopher Wren, 'Surveyor General and Principal Architect for rebuilding the whole City', devoted himself to his task. Wren was thirty-four years old when he was appointed and had been Professor of Astronomy and Geometry at Oxford University. He had spent his early life in the discipline of science but had also displayed great architectural skills with the designing of Pembroke College Chapel, Cambridge, and the Sheldonian Theatre. He had been appointed Deputy Surveyor General of the King's Works under Sir John Denham of whom it was written that 'though he may have, as most gentry, some knowledge of the theory of architecture, he can have none of the practice.' Indeed, Denham was a poet and royalist who had held Farnham Castle for Charles I in the Civil War. For his loyalty to the crown he was rewarded by his office and kept in office, so it would seem, because his young wife became mistress to James, Duke of York. Denham died in March, 1669, and was succeeded in office by Wren.

In order for Wren to commence his mammoth task, legislative measures had to be enacted first in order to clear the way. A special Court of Fire Judges had to be established to determine all differences between landlords and tenants, occupiers and others of the buildings burned or demolished in the fire. The Act became a negation of previous tenantry laws which existed and recognised that a special situation prevailed in London. The preamble was significant.

Whereas the greatest part of the houses in the City of London, and some in the suburbs thereof, have been burnt by the dreadful and dismal fire which happened in September last; many of the tenants, under tenants, or late occupiers whereof are liable unto suits and actions to compel them to repair and rebuild the same, and to pay their rents, as if the same had not been burnt, and are not relievable therein in any ordinary course of law, and great differences are like to arise concerning the said repairs, and new building of the said houses, and payment of rents; which if they should not be determined with all speed, and without charge, would much obstruct the rebuilding of the said City; And for that it is just, that everyone concerned should bear a proportional share of the loss, according to their several interests, wherein in respect of the multitude of cases, varying in their circumstances, no general rule can be prescribed; Be it therefore enacted etc . . .

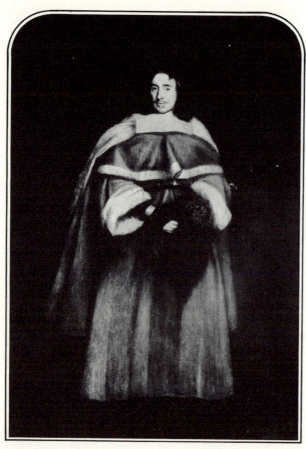

Sir Matthew Hale (1609–76) the Lord Chief Baron who drafted the legislation for the Rebuilding Acts. Called to the bar in 1636 he was created Judge of the Common Pleas by Cromwell in 1654 and became a member of Parliament for Alderney in that year and for Gloucester in 1660. Made Baron of the Exchequer in the same year he was a Commissioner for the trial of the Regicides. He was the first judge to offer his services to the City after the fire and became Chief Justice of the King's Bench in 1671., GUILDHALL LIBRARY

Landlords could not compel their tenants to take responsibility for the loss or damage of the property. But owners, impoverished by loss, were given incentive and compensation to rebuild. The basis of the legislation was: if a landlord could rebuild his property at his own expense, then he should do so. But if the landlord could not do so and the position of the tenant was such that he could provide the necessary funds, then the tenant should rebuild with the reward of an extension of his lease and reduction of his rent. If neither the tenant nor landlord could rebuild within three years, the sites would be sold to developers with the money from the transaction being paid to the landlord.

The Act was drafted by the Lord Chief Baron, Sir Matthew Hale, and was daringly conceived. It extinguished many sacred rights of property with which lawyers had invested land over the centuries. Dr Baxter wrote of Hale:

He was a man most precisely just, insomuch as I believe he would have lost all he had in the world rather than do an unjust act; patient in bearing the tedious speech which any man had to make for himself; the refuge of the subject who feared oppression. Every man who had a just cause was almost past fear if he could bring it before the court of assizes where he sat. He was the great pillar for the rebuilding of London. By his prudence and justice he removed a multitude of grave impediments.

The new legislation was certainly a great help to those who were at the mercy of extortionate landlords, some of whom were already threatening legal action if their rents were not paid, fire or no fire. Perhaps the worst example of this type of landlord was the Bishop of London, Humphrey Henchman or Hinchman, who made sure that he received every penny due him from booksellers and mercers in Paternoster Row. Henchman was warned that under the new legislation he could not pursue his rents but he dismissed the new Acts. He was brought before the courts for his contempt but claimed he was a Peer of Parliament and claimed Parliamentary privilege.

The Court of the Fire Judges sat for some years and gave its last judgement on 29 September 1672.

And so a new London began to rise out of the ashes.

'London rises again,' says the Monument, 'whether with greater speed or greater magnificence is doubtful, three short years complete that which was considered the work of an age.' The

Humphrey Henchman or Hinchman, Bishop of London in 1666.
Henchman displayed himself as one of the City's most extortionate
landlords by demanding rents from his tenants after his property,
which was extensive around St Paul's Cathedral, was totally
destroyed.

COURTAULD'S INSTITUTE OF ART with special permission of the Bishop of London
and Church Commissioners

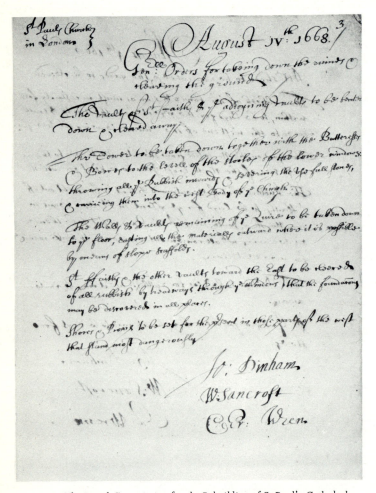

The Royal Commission for the Rebuilding of St Paul's Cathedral from the minute book of the general and committee meetings and showing the proposal for 'taking down the ruins and clearing the ground.' GUILDHALL LIBRARY

boast was grotesquely false for London's rebuilding took far more than 'three short years'.

Rebuilding had started early. Even before the Rebuilding Act and the establishment of the Court of the Fire Judges, Sir George Moore and other substantial landowners sought approval for a project to rebuild their property in Fleet Street. According to the *London Gazette* of 29 October 1666, this was granted and so Fleet Street became the first of the City's highways to be raised from the ruins and it was the first street in which new flagstone paving was completed. In addition to the new paving, as Fleet Street crossed into Ludgate Hill, the road was widened to forty-five feet.

Late in the eighteenth century, by the Inner Temple Gate, the Temple Exchange Coffee House still stood bearing upon its front a Latin inscription:

> You see before you
> The last house of the City in flames
> The first of the City to be restored:
> May this be favourable and fortunate
> For both City and house,
> Especially for those who are auspiciously
>   building.
>   Elizabeth Moore, owner of the site,
>   and
>   Thomas Tuckey, tenant.

It seems a fairly genuine claim although a chop house in Cannon Street also boasted to being the first house rebuilt after the fire and no doubt there were other claimants.

In March the City Surveyors were given the 'go-ahead' and the next month they staked out the first of the highways to be rebuilt near to St Paul's Cathedral. In May the staking out of plots for the rebuilding of the houses began. The chief streets had been cleared and the boundaries restored. People who had 'jumped the gun' were severely reprimanded and one man who had started to rebuild his house by Leadenhall, without official sanction, had to pull it down again because it did not comply with the Rebuilding Act.

On 23 October 1667, Charles went to the City in State, accompanied with his Life Guards, kettle drums and trumpets, and laid the first stone of the new Royal Exchange. The funds for the building were raised by the Mercers' Company and the Corporation of London. Charles himself had promised to rebuild the Custom House at his own expense and Wren was commissioned to design it. The work was completed in 1671 at a cost of

£10,000 only to be gutted by fire some forty-seven years later.

One of the most important works was that of the Guildhall. It was built at a cost of £37,422 and not completed until December, 1675. Wren again undertook the design and raised the height of its historic hall by twenty feet and constructed a new roof and gallery, as well as raising new buildings such as the Council Chamber, Parlour, Mayor's court, hall-keeper's house and others.

The rebuilding of the churches took a longer time and it was not until the Additional Rebuilding Act of 1670 that it was declared that only fifty-one of the eighty-eight churches destroyed were to be rebuilt. Until that date no church had been rebuilt although several damaged churches had been patched up, such as St Sepulchre in Holborn, whose parson paid £200 out of his own pocket to builders. In 1670 the rebuilding of the churches began in earnest, and one of the first churches to be restored was St Dunstan in the East at a cost of £1,075.

Wren recased most of his churches, the rebuilding of which had become his pet project, in Portland stone and utilised what materials remained from the ruins as foundation basis. The co-operation of parishioners was sought to raise money to aid in the cost of repairs and each church was asked to deposit £500 before rebuilding work could be started. The construction of St Mary le Bow, Cheapside, was accelerated by a gift of £2,000 from Lady Williamson which increased the rebuilding fund for the church to £2,385. Wren's building costs for the church, however, was £15,473.

By the year 1683 London had twenty-five of its new churches in use for public worship while

The rebuilt Cathedral of St Paul's; an enlargement of the panoramic view published in 1747 by Samuel and Nathaniel Buck. The complete form of the rebuilt City appears in its fresh state before it was encumbered by later building in the nineteenth century.
GUILDHALL LIBRARY

seventeen others were nearing completion. For designing and supervising the building of the fifty-one London churches, Christopher Wren received only £13,000. It has been said of Wren *Si monumentum requiris, circumspice* – if you would see his monument, look around. Look not just at the majesty of St Paul's Cathedral but the domed church of St Stephen Walbrook, the tower of St Mary le Bow, the steeple of St Bride's and the many other London buildings which carry the stamp of his genius.

By December, 1667, only 650 houses had been rebuilt. By the next year the figure had risen but only to 961 houses. By 1672 nearly all the housing sites had been rebuilt making an estimated 12,000 houses, most of them built within the space of four years.

The first public buildings to be rebuilt were the company halls. Forty-four of them had to be rebuilt which was as big an undertaking as the replacement of the churches. Only seven halls had escaped the flames and these opened their facilities to their less fortunate colleagues. The Carpenter's Hall gave rooms to the Goldsmiths, Drapers, Weavers and Feltmakers, while the Bricklayers' Hall housed the Coopers and the Leather Saddlers' Hall housed the Skinners, and so forth.

The bulk of the designs for the halls is attributed to Edward Jarman and the first of his halls were completed in 1668; the Butchers' Hall in Pudding Lane, the Cutlers' Hall in Cloak Lane and the Innholders' Hall in Dowgate. The following year the Plasterers' Hall, the Pewterers' Hall, the Goldsmiths' Hall and the Paint Stainers' Hall were ready. And each year new halls were erected until, finally, all the trades were housed once again.

The new Royal College of Physicians, started in 1670, designed by Wren, was opened in Warwick Lane. A poet called Garth wrote of the building:

A dome, majestic to the sight;
And sumptuous arches bear its oval height;
A golden globe placed high with artful skill,
Seems, to the distant eye, a gilded pill.

A new College of Arms was commenced in 1671 in what is now Queen Victoria Street and was completed in 1688. Inner Temple was rebuilt by a subscription raised from the barristers and Sir Robert Clayton financed the rebuilding of the south front

Warrant signed by the Archbishop of Canterbury and the Bishop of London for paying £494 7s 9¾d to Christopher Wren out of the money raised by impost on coals towards the rebuilding of the parish churches, dated 5 November 1688, and signed by Wren on 12 November. CORPORATION OF LONDON RECORDS OFFICE

St Paul's today. It was not until 1710, when Wren was in his seventy-eighth year, that the building work on the great Cathedral was finally completed at a cost of £747,600.
BRITISH TOURIST AUTHORITY

A panoramic view of the City around St Paul's today. The waste land in the foreground is the site of Baynard's Castle built in the time of William the Conqueror to guard the western approaches of the City, as a counterpart to the Tower in the east. Baynard's Castle was totally destroyed in the Fire. BRITISH TOURIST AUTHORITY

The City today, around Eastcheap, on which Fish Street Hill
and Pudding Lane emerge, where the Fire started.

of Christ's Hospital. Clayton donated £10,000 in
gratitude for his recovery from a dangerous illness.

The great clowning glory of the rebuilding was,
of course, St Paul's Cathedral.

The whole design of the churches and their
rebuilding rested on the shoulders of Wren himself. He designed and supervised work on no less
than fourteen churches in 1670 alone. In his match-
less group of designs he was more or less left without interference. However, with St Paul's, which
will always be associated with his name, he was
continually thwarted, his plans rejected and finally
he was removed from the supervision of his own
structure.

It had, at first, been thought that St Paul's could
be repaired with its existing structure for, although
gutted from end to end, the walls and even the
central tower still stood. Wren had advised against
this attitude and warned that the building was
extremely dangerous. He felt it would have to be
totally demolished and an entirely new cathedral

raised on the site. His advice was rejected and, after
the debris had been cleared, services were recom-
menced in the ruined nave, near the west door.

On 25 April 1668, came an alarming fall of
masonry which put an end to the services. Dean
Sancroft ruefully wrote to Wren: 'What you
whispered in my ear at your last coming hither, is
now come to pass. Our work at the west end of St
Paul's is fallen about our ears.' He continued:

Your quick eye discerned the walls and pillars
gone off their perpendiculars, and I believe other
defects, too, which are now exposed to every
common observer. The third pillar from the west,
at the south side, which they had now cased with
stone, fell with a sudden crash; the next, bigger
than the rest, stood alone, certain to fall, yet so
unsafe they dared not venture to take it down. In
short, the whole work of Inigo Jones was so
overloaded as to threaten a total wreck.

The only thing to do was to follow Wren's advice.
And so, on 25 July 1668, Charles issued a Royal
Warrant for the demolition of the eastern part of
the old cathedral. It was not until 1670 that the

authorities finally appreciated the need to demolish the entire structure and pulled down the wall of the nave. Wren was asked to submit designs 'handsome and noble' for the new cathedral.

Wren did so. The clergy of St Paul's did not like the designs. Wren produced a second design. The clergy were not enthusiastic and demanded a number of minor alterations. Finally, approval was given. In May 1674, Wren began to supervise the clearing of the site to build the foundations. The cathedral was to cost £747,600 and Wren's fee for the design and supervision was £200 a year.

The timber and stones of St Paul's were re-used in the rebuilding of the other London churches and some rubble went towards repairing the streets. The greater tower, 242 feet, leaning off the vertical, had to be demolished by gunpowder. It was not until 1686 that Inigo Jones' portico at the west end of the cathedral was finally demolished.

The Royal Warrant for permission to actually start the rebuilding was signed on 14 May 1675, nearly nine years after the fire. The new cathedral opened for its first public service on 2 December 1697, coinciding with the thanksgiving day for the peace of the Treaty of Ryswick, which ended the war between William of Orange's Grand Alliance and Louis of France and his allies.

It was not until 1710 that the cathedral was finally finished when Christopher Wren's son officially laid the highest stone of the cathedral on top of the lantern that surmounts the dome. His father, knighted in 1674, was still alive but he was not prepared at the age of seventy-eight to make the long and exhausting climb high above London, and watched the ceremony from below.

To the majority that watched that day, the Fire of London was either a dim memory or an historical event.

Out of London's greatest calamity, England's greatest architect was produced and duly rewarded with a knighthood. The knighthood had been made the same year that London had shown its appreciation of the work Charles II and his brother James had done during the fire week by making them freemen of the City. Charles became the first reigning monarch to be so honoured.

Strangely enough only one man was officially rewarded for his services in fighting the fire itself. This was Edmund Berry Godfrey, a justice of the peace for Westminster, who was knighted and received a gift of plate from Charles. According to the *London Gazette* of 18 September 1666, the reward was made in public acknowledgement of the eminent service done in suppressing the fire.

Godfrey was to win a greater distinction of being the magistrate to whom Titus Oates 'confessed' the Popish Plot. Soon after, Godfrey's body was found on Primrose Hill, having been run through with his own rapier.

The completion of St Paul's Cathedral in 1710 provides a greater reminder than the Monument itself of that week in September 1666, when the City was almost destroyed. The great cathedral, still dominating the City, must forever be a reminder of the circumstances from which it was raised as well as of the genius who raised it.

As the Spanish observer wrote:

An end was finally put to the devastation, but not to its memory, which must remain throughout the centuries, for it was one of the greatest fires of the kind which the world has ever known.

SELECTED BIBLIOGRAPHY

HISTORICAL DOCUMENTS: SEVENTEENTH AND EIGHTEENTH CENTURIES

BEDLOE, Captain W.: *Narrative of the Popish Plot & etc. of the Burning of London*. London 1679.

The Burning of London by the Papists: or a Memorial to Protestants of the Second of September. London ,1714.

DRYDEN, John: *Annus Mirabilis*. London, 1667.

EVELYN, John: *Diary and Correspondence*. Ed. William Bray, 4 vols. London, 1857.

FORD, Simon: *Poemata Londinensia Jam tandem Cosumata*. London, 1667-8.

Gazette de France Extraordinaire. Paris, 15 October 1666.

His Majesty's Declaration to His City of London upon the Occasion of the Late Calamity by the Lamentable Fire. London, 1666.

An Humble Remonstrance to the King and Parliament on Behalf of Many Decayed and Decaying Citizens and Families of London Occasioned Solely by the Late Dreadful Fire in the City. 'Philanthropus Philagathus' (pseudonymous author). London, 1675.

KNIGHT, Valentine: *Proposals for a New Model for Rebuilding London*. London, 1666.

Londens Puyn-hoop, oft Godts Handt over de selve in't verbranden der Stadt den 12-16 van Hefstnaent. Amsterdam, 1666.

London's Flames. London, 1679.

London Gazette. 3-10 September 1666.

London's Lamentations on its Destruction by a Consuming Fire. London, 1666.

London Verbrandt. Amsterdam, 1666.

Observations both Historical and Moral upon the Burning of London. 'Rege Sincera' (pseudonymous author). London, 1667.

Ondersoek van den Brand van London Door ordere des Parlaments van England. Amsterdam, 1667.

PEPYS, Samuel: *Diary*. Ed. Henry B. Wheatley. London, 1923.

Relacion Nueva y Verdadera del Formidable Incendio que ha Sucedido en la Grand Ciudad de Londres. Valencia, 1666.

Relatione esattissima del' Incendio Calamitoso della citta di Londa. Padua, 1666.

ROLLE, Samuel: *The Burning of London in the Year 1666*. London, 1668.

A Short and Serious Narrative of London's Fatal Fire . . . (& etc.). London, 1667.

SMITH, William: *De Urbis Londini Incendio Elegia*. London, 1667.

TASWELL, William: *Autobiography and Anecdotes, William Taswell DD, 1651-82*, Camden Society, circa 19th century.

A True and Exact Relation of the Most Dreadful and Remarkable Fire. London, 1666.

A True and Faithful Account of the Several Informations Exhibited to the Honourable Committee Appointed by Parliament. London, 1667.

VINCENT, Thomas: *God's Terrible Voice in the City*. London, 1670.

WATERHOUS, Edward: *A Short Narrative of the Late Dreadful Fire in London*. London, 1667.

WISEMAN, Samuel: *A Short Description of the Burning of London*. London, 1668.

NINETEENTH AND TWENTIETH CENTURY ACCOUNTS

BELL, Walter G.: *The Great Fire of London*. John Lane, The Bodley Head, 1920.

BURNET, Bishop Gilbert: *History of His Own Times*. 6 Vols. Clarendon Press, 1823.

CLARENDON, Edward Hyde, Earl of: *Life*. 3 vols. Oxford University Press, 1823.

HEARSEY, John E. N.: *London and the Great Fire*. John Murray, 1965.

STOW, John: *A Survey of London, 1603*. Everyman's Library, Dent, 1912.

INDEX

MY LIFE
AND
MY CARS

W. O. BENTLEY

HUTCHINSON OF LONDON

HUTCHINSON & CO (*Publishers*) LTD
178–202 Great Portland Street, London W1

London Melbourne Sydney
Auckland Bombay Toronto
Johannesburg New York

★

First published 1967

*This book has been set in Plantin, printed in Great Britain
on Antique Wove paper by Anchor Press, and
bound by Wm. Brendon, both of Tiptree, Essex*

CONTENTS

Also by W. O. Bentley

W.O. An autobiography
The Cars in my Life
An Illustrated History of the Bentley Car

ILLUSTRATIONS

Illustrations

W.O.'s NOTE

I first wrote my autobiography, with the close assistance of Richard Hough, during 1956 and 1957, and it was published under the title of *W.O. An Autobiography* early in 1958. People were very kind about it and it was reprinted a number of times. A few years later I wrote a book called *The Cars in my Life*, 'a hotch-potch of ideas on motor cars, motoring and the motor industry', as I called it at the time, which also included some memories of the cars I have driven during my motoring life. After that there was a book, mainly of photographs, called *An Illustrated History of the Bentley Car*.

What I have done now is to revise and bring up to date the first book, add some new material, and include quite a lot of the material about the cars and my own life from the second book, which is now out of print. This, then, if you will forgive the pretentious description, is a sort of 'definitive W.O.'

Some of the people who helped me, with their memories and notes, with the original *W.O.*, are now, alas, dead. All the same, I should like to record their names again, and repeat my earlier apology that for reasons of space it really isn't possible to include among them all those who gave such sterling service at the old Bentley Motors and Lagonda works in the 1920's, '30's and '40's: R. A. Clarke, George Duller, Jack Dunfee, Clive Gallop, H. Kensington Moir, Hubert Pike, R. S. Witchell, F. T. Burgess,

H. Varley, C. S. Sewell, S. S. Tresillian, W. G. Watson, D. Bastow, my brothers H. M. and A. H. Bentley, my sister 'Poppy'—and, of course, my wife Margaret.

W.O.B.

CHAPTER ONE

A Love of Locomotives

THE motor car seemed to me a disagreeable vehicle. Perhaps I should have realised the vast potentialities of internal combustion and recognised from my nursery days that it was to be the impelling force in my life. But the fact must be recorded that the motor car struck my young, literal mind as a slow, inefficient, draughty and anti-social means of transport. Motor cars splashed people with mud, frightened horses, irritated dogs and were a frightful nuisance to everybody.

Before I rode in a motor car I had reached the susceptible age of sixteen, when it might be thought that the horseless carriage would have stimulated my natural curiosity if not my sense of romance. In fact my first ride was taken in a sort of omnibus. I sat in this vehicle on one of the two facing wooden-slatted benches behind the driver. It was a Daimler, with tube ignition—I must have been a little interested to have noticed that—and I remember the journey to Inverness as being thoroughly uncomfortable, the absence of any sort of protection, solid tyres, elementary springing and rough roads all contributing towards this. It was a wretched journey.

In 1904 I had no time at all for the motor car. It was the locomotive that held my devoted love. If I responded to that Daimler with no more than a flicker of interest, the sight of one of Patrick Stirling's eight-foot singles could move me profoundly. Ever since I had been conscious that the world was full of these great roaring masterpieces of engineering I had been fascinated and excited by them, and they filled my dreams and my ambitions. A few weeks after that short, unimpressive journey I was on my way to Doncaster from King's Cross to fulfil these dreams and ambitions by becoming a premium apprentice at the Great Northern locomotive works.

The first fifteen years of my life were as calm, as lacking in crises and anxiety, as the following fifty years were to be eventful, anxious, often critical and nearly always exciting.

There were eleven of us—three girls, six boys, my mother and father—and an appropriate complement of servants in our Avenue Road house near Regent's Park in London, and I was the youngest by three years. The house survived until the 1940 bombing, when its numerous rambling rooms, solid walls, outhouses and stables were destroyed by a land-mine. The sight of its scarred ruins—all that remained of our noisy, happy home—made me rather sad when I saw them.

Our background was Yorkshire, direct paternally. But my maternal grandfather, Thomas Waterhouse, emigrated from Yorkshire to Australia in the early formative years of the colony, arriving in Adelaide a year or two after the city was founded, and promoted himself from the grocery trade to copper-mining and banking, and finally to philanthropy on a large scale. He returned to comfortable retirement in Hampstead and died there a few years later.

I was born at the usual disagreeably early hour on the morning of 16th September, 1888.

In early childhood my eight older brothers and sisters seemed to loom over me in almost overwhelming profusion, and yet there was indulgence; possibly more than was good for me. I didn't resent it. Except that I was always called Walter—an abominable name—I can recall no single childhood resentment. But I don't think I responded to this indulgent affection as warmly as my position as the Bentley baby demanded. In that fully populated, typically Victorian house I succeeded in being quiet and rather independent. I imagine myself at the age of five or six deeply involved in pulling something painstakingly to pieces, or equally painstakingly putting it together again, either in the big nursery we all shared or in my own bedroom.

My toys, of course, matched my interests, with a strong bias towards the mechanical. But there weren't many of them. No one had so many toys in the 1890s as they have today. But I did have a magnificent stationary steam-engine, given to me by an uncle, and heaven knows how many hours I spent with this treasured possession. Then there was a clockwork train set, probably crude by present-day standards, but I remember it as reliable and well made. I suppose shoddy toys must have been made sixty-five years ago, but I never saw any.

There were cricket and bicycles, later there were cameras, but in the final count it was the locomotive that reigned supreme. I can hardly remember our two nurses except their names, but my governess had a nephew who was an apprentice at Doncaster, reason enough for remembering her. This fact, plus my loyalty to Yorkshire and the Great Northern, settled Doncaster for me by the time I was eight, and I eventually landed up at the same digs as this envied, near-fabulous nephew. Walks with this governess nearly always tended to steer a course towards Loudoun Road, which at one point spanned the L.N.W.R., just outside the northern portals of the younger Stephenson's Primrose Hill tunnel. By careful timing we could catch the Scotsman getting into its stride as it bellowed out of the blackness and streamed past us towards Willesden. The station, now called West Hampstead, claimed hours and hours of my poor governess's time. Loudoun Road was in whistling distance one way from Avenue Road, Lord's a cricket-ball's throw the other way; but until the late 'nineties Loudoun Road had it every time.

Next door were the Thornhills, three boys and four girls as far as I remember, their ages parallel with ours. Geoffrey was the youngest and he was a train-fiend too. We spent hours together. Both our bedrooms were lined with copies of the *Railway Magazine* and the *Locomotive Magazine*, and railway books, and on the walls were photographs and paintings of locomotives. We were both utterly single-minded, and the fact that he was as sternly loyal to the L.N.W.R. (his father was chief engineer on the civil side, so I suppose this was only paternal loyalty) as I was to the Great Northern, added spice to our relationship.

Around my little cell of busy enthusiasm the bigger Bentley world rotated on its more important, more adult axis. I was aware of it, of course, though it didn't impinge very seriously on my privacy; and I suppose it was aware of me, a certain amount of affection mixed with its curiosity. I think I struck my brothers and sisters as rather aloof, which, considering they were between three and twelve years older, seems strange.

I remember no unpleasantness, no unhappiness at Avenue Road. I was very fond of my father and mother, and they were devoted to each other. I don't think my father was very good at business, and he retired early. I must have inherited my shyness from my father. He was terribly shy, which caused him to seem unsociable and retiring to outsiders; with us he was naturally good-humoured, just, and a good father, though I suppose you might call him a simple man. Anyway, his philosophy was a simple one which, with a strong religious base, suffered misfortune and accepted fortune with equal calm; everything in life being pre-ordained. He was short and held himself very upright, and always wore a little moustache. Once he had sported an imperial, but it didn't last long. I have no doubt that he was suddenly struck with self-consciousness about it.

My mother had a great warm-hearted personality, with a strong will and determination and a complete certainty about what she wanted from life, and, what was more important to her, what she wanted from life for us. She was one of those people who leave a strong impression on everyone they meet and wherever they go, and she certainly had a great influence on all of us.

We had long, glorious family holidays, the first I can remember at Bridlington, then at scattered improbable places like Stevenage and villages in Suffolk, usually in rented vicarages or country houses. Wroxham on the Norfolk Broads was a favourite place. We had a boat as well as a house there and took turns to sleep in the boat. We also took turns to sail it, mine being notable for their brevity.

I think I was about fourteen when H.M., who was nearest to me in years, and I push-biked 130 miles to Wroxham. We did it in a day. It was my first experience of independent travel over a long distance and it left me with a lasting impression of achievement and of having fulfilled—on a very small scale—one of man's fundamental longings; one which has, I think, been implanted unusually strongly in me. In my bicycle I had the means to express this longing, and the fact that I usually made a dead set for the nearest railway line, to watch the trains, is by the way; it took me there, when I liked and almost as fast as I liked. I loved my bicycle.

They were quite advanced machines by the 'nineties, and bicycling was not the hazardous business then that it is now. Even in St. John's Wood there was only scattered horse traffic; it was a wonderfully safe and efficient way of getting about. The first cycle I rode had solid tyres. Then at the age of nine, by dint of furious saving and with a contribution from my mother, I managed to buy a second-hand one of my own. This I would take to pieces with a frequency and thoroughness that terrified my mother. She would find me sitting on the ground surrounded by cogs and bearings and wheels which she never expected me to be able to get together again. But I was slower and more careful than she gave me credit for; I can remember a few crises but I always managed the reassembly in the end.

.   .   .   .   .

When the inevitable day arrived, I found the prospect of going to school intimidating. I have sometimes been called a stoic—and because I have not suffered a succession of nervous breakdowns there must be some truth in this—and the idea of leaving home for prep school at the age of ten probably affected a lot of boys who had never before left home, or been to day school for that matter, a good deal worse than it affected me. But I do remember being quite miserable when I was put on the school train with a great host of strange and extremely noisy boys, all of whom appeared to be on the most intimate terms with one another.

There were in fact sixty boys at Lambrook, trained to a severe standard of discipline by E. D. Mansfield, who had come from Clifton. In one form, and by one master especially, we were caned a great deal, and I had my proper share of it, mainly because I was so bad at lessons. I didn't like doing the things I didn't like and that was that. Besides this I was very slow at the lessons I did like, such as physics and chemistry, because I had to be satisfied that I understood the reason for every statement and argument. I was a great one for logical development, I had to see things through step by step, and if I missed one I had to go back to the beginning again. I had to know I was getting somewhere and I had to know why I was going, and this made for slow progress—and frequent canings.

For social success it was games that counted, of course, and for a while it looked as though my efforts were going to be equally disastrous on the rugger field. Games never came naturally to me and I really had to work hard and concentrate to achieve any sort of success. But cricket I enjoyed from the beginning. It had always been my first sport, Yorkshire has always been my first county and Wilfred Rhodes my first and greatest hero. I saw my first match at Lord's the summer before I went to school; Yorkshire were playing the M.C.C., and it was Rhodes's first match too.

To this day I take a lot of interest in the game and have over a hundred and fifty books on it. I'm only sorry it is taken so seriously now; the applause at the end of every maiden over, regardless of the quality of the bowling, strikes me as odd and undeserved. I like to do my own analyses of bowling on the number of balls bowled per wicket taken; every undistinguished maiden over deprives the fielding side's batsmen of valuable time for runs.

I've been lucky enough to see some of the epic matches of the past sixty years, and perhaps the greatest of all was the Oval Test Match against the Australians in 1902. I went there with my father on the last morning, when England, with 247 runs to get and three wickets down, early lost two more quick wickets. Then my hero, Jessop, came in, as always unperturbed by the situation. At once the match was transformed when 109 runs went up in the hour, and Jessop put England on the road to victory after slashing and stroking 104 in 75 minutes.

I think I have had more pure pleasure out of cricket than from almost anything else in life, and to get into the school eleven at Lambrook, go in first against a school at Reading and score 79 not out—as I did when I was twelve—gave me more satisfaction than anything that ever happened at Le Mans thirty years later. The other opener, incidentally, was S. S. Bonham-Carter, who later joined the Navy and (less shrimp-like than when I knew him) became a distinguished Admiral.

We had a wonderful gym at Lambrook. I enjoyed that, and I also won the school fives. Altogether I made out well enough in the fierce fight for games distinction, but it was a fight all the way; competition was red hot and a great deal depended on the result.

After a term or two I became accustomed to boarding-school and was able to accept it as a tiresome chore that took me away from my hobbies at home. But I never really got used to the sense of restriction, of being imprisoned, and above all I missed the freedom my bicycle gave me. At Lambrook we only went out for organised walks, and on Sunday to church, dressed in top-hats; and once a year to Ascot, a mile or two away, which sowed the seeds of my fundamental indifference to horse racing.

I don't remember any very close friends at Lambrook and I was probably as independent there as I had been at home. Nor do I remember any particular enemies, though I was horribly prone to getting into rows over bullying. That all started over two boys both of whom wore unorthodox clothes, and one of them had long curly hair, characteristics guaranteed to create trouble at a boys' school. Mass ragging soon developed in the playground against these two unfortunates in their early days, and this set my blood boiling. I went in with fists flailing, to the astonishment (but not I think discomfiture) of the attacking gang. I couldn't— nor can I to this day—tolerate any sort of bullying, physical or emotional. It is almost a passion with me, and one which has led me into many scraps, from prep school to middle age.

Apart from these episodes, and a few sporting highlights, Lambrook has not left me with many exciting memories. In spite of the discipline and the beatings it wasn't a formidable place. In fact we seemed to have spent a good deal of our brief spare time in such gentle pursuits as gardening our own little plots and, especially for me, photography. At the age of twelve I had been given a five-shilling box Brownie, which intrigued me vastly. I have always been devoted to gadgets, but photography soon left the 'gadgetry' class and became a real hobby. To take good photographs, to print and develop them myself in my own developing tank, was a constant challenge which I loved to accept. My first results were appalling, then I started to carry out my own research and experimentation and got better. I worked and worked away at that little Brownie and spent hours with it, becoming acutely depressed and angry when I took bad pictures and quietly excited when they turned out well. Oddly enough it was the master who was so severe and had been responsible for my canings who helped me most at school. A fellow enthusiast, he would show me some of the nicer points of the technique of printing. I still have some of those dim brown pictures—of cricket matches and buildings and boys—on which we worked together. In later years I think I must have wasted more money on photography than anything else, falling for that dangerous amateur's passion for ever more elaborate cameras and gadgets. I have now gone the full circle and my most recent purchase has provided me with the simplest possible equipment—with which I am taking the best photographs I have ever taken.

.   .   .   .

I suppose I was lucky to get to Clifton at all. My academic standard was still abysmal when my time at Lambrook was up, and I didn't deserve a place. But because my five brothers had all been there I suppose they felt they couldn't very well exclude the last Bentley. So in 1902 'the Bun' (my shape and my two black eyes got me that name) followed the others into Tait's house.

My brother H.M. was second in command at Tait's at Clifton when I went there in the autumn, and the three years between us assumed the proportions of a vast gulf. In fact I saw very little of him, though before I arrived he warned me about the dining-hall boxing, a traditional public school endurance test in which new boys were pitted against one another. 'A deuce of a lot depends on how you make out,' he told me, 'so give it all you've got.'

I practised like a fiend at the end of the holidays, so that when I came up against a formidable boy called Murray, for the bout in front of all the house, I was less depressed about my hopes than perhaps I should have been. I went at him like a demented monkey, energy and fanatical determination making up for any lack of finesse. It did the trick and I beat him—for the first and last time. I often boxed with him afterwards, but never got the better of him again.

Tait's was a converted private house in College Road, over-looking the playing fields. I think Clifton was a good school at that time, as it is today; but my life there followed a similar un-distinguished pattern to that at Lambrook. I hated nearly all the lessons, except chemistry and physics, at which I was quite good; but I seem to remember that the masters were either more tolerant or more resigned. Anyway I didn't get into so many rows, and on one epic occasion I actually got a 'Star' at chemistry. I again fought my way to a reasonable standard at most games, enjoying particularly the agility and concentration that fives demands. I threw myself into the rugger with sufficient enthusiasm to break my collar-bone, and I think both wrists. Cross-country running suited my temperament better than sprinting. It was a manage-able sort of challenge that I enjoyed, and the technique could be worked out to a slowly developing formula.

But above all, of course, it was the cricket I enjoyed most at Clifton. I worked like a Trojan at cricket and got into the house team in my second year—not for my bowling, though I did bowl three expensive overs, nor for my batting, described in the house records as 'showing some powers of defence', but for my fielding. I was no good in the outfield, where I think I must have lost my nerve or become self-conscious waiting for the ball to arrive. But I was very good in the slips. I scored only five runs in the sum-mer of 1904, batting on one great occasion for one hour for one run, but I caught out quite a few people and stopped enough balls to qualify for the report: 'a good field'. My second year in the team was a little less insignificant and I was opening bat—'a very consistent batsman, who watches the ball well'. I scored the second highest total of runs in the house, caught more catches than anyone else and actually took a few wickets.

I left Clifton early—at sixteen—to go to Doncaster, and never got out of the third form. I enjoyed my three years there well enough and made some good friends, like the little one-eyed Irishman Macnamara, and R. S. Witchell, now a director of E.N.V. gears, with whom I came into friendly contact again at Brooklands and at hill-climbs in the years before the war, and finally, of course, as works manager at Bentley Motors. Roy Fedden was also there, senior to me; he was later to become a distinguished designer, first with Straker-Squire and then with Bristol on aero engines.

It was during those last holidays in the summer of 1905 that I went up to stay at a farm in Scotland where one of my brothers was training for an agricultural career, and it was then that I made my first acquaintanceship with that tube-ignition Daimler bus. Its impact, as I have said, was negligible at the time, except in terms of mild discomfort. It was still locomotives for me— with all my heart and all my enthusiasm. At Doncaster I would have my fill of these entrancing great beasts!

CHAPTER TWO

On the Footplate

ONE alarum clock wasn't enough; it took two to get me out of bed at a quarter past five, and a cup of hot Bovril to bring me to consciousness. I then groped my way downstairs, lit the lamp of my bicycle, and wheeled it outside. It was pitch dark and bitterly cold when I mounted and pedalled off down Netherhall Road. There was a mile and a half to go across Doncaster to the plant and I was no longer half asleep when I left my bicycle and walked over the railway bridge and in through the gates, my ears numb, my eyes running with tears.

To be even thirty seconds late was an unforgivable crime. The Doncaster regime really was a tough one and you had to be a devoted disciple to survive it. The first session was from 6 to 8.15 a.m., when there was a break for breakfast; then a four-hour stretch to one o'clock, and the final one from 2 to 5.30 p.m. Including half Saturdays it was only just short of a sixty-hour week, and there was no slacking, no knocking off for cups of tea and gossips. It was hard going every day and the timekeeping and discipline were to military standards.

On our first morning the new premium apprentices started the day with a brief to-the-point lecture on what was going to happen to us, given by a little nondescript man with a drooping moustache. To utter even the curt words of welcome appeared to pain him, and he seemed relieved to pass us over, raw, bewildered and thoroughly intimidated, to the first foreman, Treece. From him we received an equally chilly reception and were impressed with the standards of discipline expected of us. 'At the plant six o'clock *means* six o'clock,' he told us.

The formidable Growcock, under whom we were to serve directly, seemed at first, through my seventeen-year-old eyes, to be more a sergeant-major than an under-foreman, and the two and three-year apprentices like battle-scarred old campaigners, worldly, knowledgeable and rather frightening. At first I hardly dared to open my mouth when they were around.

The purpose of this alarming reception became clear only after some time, when I could look back at it objectively. To the foremen premium apprentices were mostly 'softies', gently nurtured beings from well-to-do homes. That there would be some material worth developing from among them was a certainty; the difficulty was to discover it, and, to save everybody's time, this must be done as quickly as possible. It was rather like the ancient tribal custom of sorting out the potential warriors from the male youths. The first weeks at the plant were a testing time; those who were determined, keen and tough enough, survived the trial. Until they had, nothing was taken on trust.

It was no use pretending that there wasn't a barrier between the apprentices—sons of men who had lived all their working life on the Great Northern, bred and reared on locomotives—and the premium apprentices. The apprentices were paid five shillings a week from the day they started; premium apprentices paid their way in, a £75 premium for five years' slogging, though we did get this back in wages. I was ragged for my southern accent, even ribbed for being a snob, and there was plenty of horse-play. How you responded was watched carefully; if you came through—and just to be imitative wasn't good enough—the barrier dissolved and that was that.

Later, as a veteran, I had to help others through these tough early days. One of them was Gordon England, one of the earliest glider pilots, who became a big noise in the motor business. I had a lot to do with him in the Bentley Motors days, when the Doncaster period provided a strong link between us.

Once you were through and accepted you had only begun your lesson in human relations. Later I began to understand not only how to get on with the working man—that's not difficult—but also his mind: his pride, his conscientiousness, his loyalty, his attitude to life and his generosity. I've never met a group of men so generous as the apprentices and men at the plant. The time and trouble they took to help you over a problem that was holding you up were sometimes overwhelming; it seemed almost a point of honour that they should unravel it for you.

Doncaster had lived by trains for fifty years. There was very little else there but the construction and maintenance works; there were no coal mines huddled round the little town then, and almost everyone was connected with the Great Northern in one way or another. The main road crossed the line in the middle of the town, and that caused no one any trouble. Doncaster had been the birthplace of Edmund Denison, first Chairman of the Great Northern, and it was he who had been responsible for setting up the big plant there in 1853, incidentally bringing prosperity and a substantial increase in population to the town. He had tried to persuade his shareholders to pay for a church and school for his workmen, an uncharacteristic piece of misjudgement. Irate Victorians threw out his plan for the £8,000 church, and only allowed him his school with the utmost reluctance. It may not have been a very pretty place—railway towns rarely are—but I liked it, and there was pleasant country within easy bicycling distance.

The hierarchy at Doncaster in 1905 was tremendously impressive. There, in real life, as distant and awe-inspiring as stars to a dramatic student, but working in the same plant and from time to time even allowing themselves to be seen, were some of the great heroes of my boyhood. As locomotive superintendent, of course, there was Henry A. Ivatt, who had taken over this post from Patrick Stirling ten years before. Ivatt had been responsible for the first Atlantic-type locomotives to be built in this country; they marked a dramatic departure from Stirling's eight-foot and seven-foot-six singles, and were the linking design between the nineteenth-century express locomotive and the larger and more powerful superheated engines which were soon going to be needed on main lines.

Ivatt earned about £3,500 p.a. He was a tall, thin, very quiet man, much respected but not much liked because of his severity. I don't regard him now as a great designer; his main quality was his awareness of his own limitations, and because of this he knew he could not afford to make a mistake. Ivatt could never have survived a failure, and he never had one. This was in the strongest possible contrast to Nigel Gresley, then at twenty-nine already superintendent of the Carriage and Wagon works and due soon to succeed Ivatt. Gresley made many mistakes, but they were the mistakes of a genius and an original creator. Ivatt could never have produced the series of Gresley record-breaking Pacifics, which culminated in *Mallard*'s 126 m.p.h. run in 1938.

Also under Ivatt were F. Wintour, the works manager, and O. V. Bulleid, his personal assistant, who was to achieve a fame almost equal to Gresley's as head of the Southern Railway's locomotive department.

Among the premium apprentices I had some real friends. There was Pat Macguire, a distinctive six-foot-sixer, who made himself even more prominent by always being in the wrong place at the wrong time in the plant, and A. H. Peppercorn (of clerical stock, like so many railwaymen), who many years later became chief of the locomotive department.

I had no cause to complain about my contemporaries; I got on well with the foreman now; I admired, even hero-worshipped, the aristocrats. I had only one great sorrow and disappointment, made worse by its complete unexpectedness. Week after week, month after month went by, and I never even saw, let alone worked on, a locomotive. The only time I could catch a glimpse of one was when I sneaked out of the shop when the foreman wasn't looking—usually on the early morning shift—and poked around the erecting shops. For close-ups of my beloved engines, with all their grace, their sense of power, their speed and sound and movement that had made me their devoted slave for ten years or more, I should have done better to spend the day at Doncaster level-crossing. A year and a half passed before I got my hands on a locomotive. That was a bitter pill to swallow.

My first fitting work was on connecting rods in a shop at the far end of the top turnery, comparatively unskilled 'apprentice' labour. We had to put the radii and polish on the H sections, chipping away by hand at the sharp corners, trying to form an even cut of a quarter of an inch right along the eight corners of the H section without breaking the chip. It sounds tedious, but I found it fascinating. Afterwards the whole rod was filed up and the corners made into an even radius. All this exhausting and noisy work was done under the single (but eagle) eye of the charge hand, a fellow called Heap, who was all right if you did your best. His opposite number in the valve-motion part of the shop, Jack Bramley, was a wonderful and charming old man, well read, thoughtful, with a fine philosophy and a balanced view of life. I learnt a lot from him. I have another happy memory of his part of the works; my bench was against the window, and below was the main line, busy with 251 class Atlantics and sometimes one of the two surviving Stirling Singles.

It was a great advance to get into the foundry. There was something fundamental and creative about the foundry, with its huge cupolas, its heat and sand, and the sudden excitement when the delicate and highly skilled business of casting cylinders was taking place, a vivid, searing waterfall of molten metal. We worked on safe, simple stuff at first, things like maximum weight notices for goods wagons and carriage luggage-rack brackets. The birth from the furnaces of even these humdrum objects gave me enormous satisfaction, and I began to feel I was getting to the heart of things.

Gradually we moved around the plant, until we got into the engine-erecting shop. This was a red-letter day I'll never forget. Here were all the bits and pieces we had been working on, filing and polishing, chiselling and casting over the past months, like old friends seen suddenly in a new and more appropriate environment. To raise the morale of munition workers during the war, I believe they were sometimes taken to an airfield or Army depot, and there, to their delighted surprise, they would be shown little bolts or sprockets, tiny and apparently meaningless metal panels which they had been turning out by the hundreds of thousands, and which were now seen actually to have a purpose as an integral part of a tank or aeroplane. There was nothing wrong with my morale when I started work in the erecting shop; but it was a pleasantly cheering experience.

You had to be fit and muscular to stand up to the work there. To fit up, by hand, slide bars on which the crossheads ran, making them bear evenly along their whole length by filing the packing pieces at each end, called for brute strength as well as skill. But for sheer filth combined with hard work there was nothing to match taking a blast pipe out of a locomotive in the engine-repair shop. The blast pipe, a sort of exhaust pipe, directs the used steam up the chimney, and the flange at its base is secured by a series of nuts and studs which are always so corroded that they have to be split with a hammer and chisel. Everything is so awkwardly placed that every blind blow brings a fall of soot into your face, and every tenth blow lands on your hand.

The underside of a car after a few thousand miles is as hygienic as an operating theatre compared with a locomotive in for overhaul. The wonderful mixture of congealed grease, oil, mud and dust has to be seen to be believed. It sometimes took me ten minutes to scrape away the filth concealing the nuts I was looking for. It took even longer to scrape the accumulated filth of a day's work off my hands, arms and face.

Top: 'The Bun' at three

Middle right: As a premium apprentice at Doncaster

Middle left and bottom right: From two wheels to four. My first Sizaire-Naudin and my $3\frac{1}{2}$ h.p. Rex

The 1914 Tourist Trophy D.F.P., before the race

The 1914 Tourist Trophy D.F.P., during the race

Leroux does some last-minute checking on the 12/50 D.F.P. at Brooklands in 1914 while I look on

D.F.P. at Shelsley Walsh

This problem of dirt—a thing the layman is inclined to forget—and the fatigue from a ten-hour day in the plant just about settled the matter of evening entertainment. At Doncaster it hardly existed. At half past five I bicycled home, again in the dark in winter, to my digs with the Creaser sisters, the dear couple who looked after me so wonderfully well. After the prolonged business of cleaning and changing, I came down to a high tea—great spreads of chicken or pork pies or thick steaks, man's food for a ravenous young man. Then I might meet a friend or two, and as they were all quite as single-minded as I, we usually ended up on Doncaster platform talking shop.

I knew and liked as well as anyone there a fellow called G. C. Gowlland. He was an Army man from Woolwich on a course at the plant for a few months. He was a terrific rugger player, had played for Scotland and London Scottish as well as the Army, and at Doncaster he was equally keen on keeping fit as getting through his course. He soon had me at it too.

'Shovelling's about the quickest way of keeping the muscles in trim,' I suggested one day. 'Good training for the footplate too.'

He jumped at the idea, and the next morning we were in the foundry, offering to stoke the cupola. The men there were always delighted to see us; they would generously hand over their shovels and be equally generous with their advice on the correct mixture of pig-iron and coke to throw in. I still haven't heard of a better weight-reducer than stoking a cupola for an hour or two. Holding suitcases out at arms'-length in the train to London was another little self-imposed trial we endured.

There were more peaceful occasions with my Pathé gramophone. I fell for this in Clark's shop window in Doncaster and decided I had to have it. It was a very good machine, one of the early ones with a sapphire in the sound-box which eliminated the chore of changing needles. For the Pathé I accumulated quite a collection of records, ballet music and Faust mostly, and I reckon I got my money's worth from it. Music has always given me a lot of pleasure in spite of my technical ignorance. Rachmaninoff, Grieg, Tchaikovsky, Chopin; Layton and Johnstone, Tauber, Jean Sablon—my taste is catholic, but I do have my dislikes too!

On most Saturdays Gowlland and I made a dash for our digs at twelve o'clock, cleaned and changed and made the 1.03 London train with a few seconds to spare. Our special privilege tickets cost us only a few shillings and we were in Town for tea. Much as

I loved my work, it was a relief to get back to the clean comfort of Avenue Road and the family, and the gaiety and glitter of the Empire or the Palace with old friends had their charm after the severity and austerity of Doncaster. The 8.45 from King's Cross on Sunday evening brought me back, and it was some time after midnight when I walked out of the station and set off for Netherhall Road. I can still remember the sound of the church clocks chiming above the silent streets and the smell of the Don wafting all over the town.

By the beginning of 1909 I was ready for the footplate. Through all my childhood years, through prep school and Clifton, through three and a half years of sweat and dirt and grinding work at Doncaster, the burning ambition to get on to a locomotive's footplate had remained with me. You could call it, I suppose, my ultimate physical ambition, equal and parallel to the more intellectual ambition to design locomotives. By 1909 I was one of Ivatt's pupils, and among the privileges this brought was footplate experience as second fireman.

Until the summer of my first year at Doncaster, premium apprentices often went as first firemen on the footplate. In the middle of September that year I had seen off from the station the York train, with premium apprentice Talbot as fireman. With Driver Fleetwood, he had then fired the 6.50 York to Peterborough, where the pair had taken over the semi-fast King's Cross–Edinburgh mail train, No. 276 Atlantic. This train, which was due to stop at Grantham, came fast out of Stoke tunnel south of the town, ignored the distant Caution signal, and came pounding through the station and past the red light at the north signal-box. Fleetwood and Talbot, who both knew the line well and were thoroughly steady characters, were last seen, one on either side of the footplate, looking ahead; though other and less reliable eye-witnesses claimed to have seen them struggling together on the footplate as if Fleetwood had had a fit and Talbot was trying to minister to him.

At the junction north of the station, where the points were set against it, the engine left the rails, broke from the train and was almost destroyed. It was a miracle that only ten others were killed in the burning wreckage the Atlantic trailed behind it.

This disaster made a tremendous impact on us at Doncaster, of course. More experienced men than we argued hotly (and as fruitlessly) on the cause of it. Even the Board of Trade enquiry didn't settle the matter, and the Grantham crash remains one of the greatest railway mysteries. The one positive result it had was to prohibit premium apprentices from the footplate except as second firemen.

It was decided after all that my footplate experience should be taken at King's Cross, so I left Doncaster, with many regrets, and came south to London to work in the running sheds, and my two worlds were suddenly merged into one. For four years they had been quite separate: the harsh, rough, dirty, practical and classless world at the plant; and the comfort, gaiety and sociability of my Regent's Park life. Seen from Doncaster, Avenue Road often seemed as unreal as the overalled figures in the shops appeared when I was on leave in London. I had not realised how strong the contrast had been until it ceased to exist. At around six o'clock a filthy apparition would bicycle up the short gravel drive of the Bentley home and disappear inside to make himself fit for human company. When the weather was bad and I didn't use my bicycle, I crammed into the rush-hour Tube with my fellow commuters; it was particularly good fun to watch the varied reaction of the people who recognised me—or pretended they didn't.

Work at King's Cross was about the filthiest I ever got involved in during my apprenticeship. Routine maintenance was carried out in the running sheds, more serious overhauls and repainting being done at Doncaster. Examining fireboxes not only made you filthy, but roasted you as well. Fireboxes take a long time to cool down, too long to wait before the job has to be done.

My first footplate work was as second fireman on local goods trains, but I wouldn't have cared if it had been local shunting. This was the beginning of one of the fullest and happiest years of my life, and by the time I had worked up through local passenger trains to main-line expresses I was in my seventh heaven.

It is not often that childhood dreams mature into reality; it is rarer still for there to be no disappointment or disillusion when they do. I realise now how lucky I was that the sensation of being on the footplate of a Great Northern Atlantic, heading an express north out of London, was more thrilling and wonderful than I had ever thought it could have been. I was fascinated by the feeling of power as we pulled out of King's Cross, up the steep gradients and tunnels of north London, up the steady grind for another eleven miles to Potter's Bar, and by the sudden irresistible surge of acceleration when the track levelled off and fell away. There is nothing I know to compare with the sensation of rushing through the night without lights and with that soothing mechanical rhythm beating away continuously, even leading to a dangerous tendency to surrender to the power quivering beneath the steel floor. And then the signals flash into view, your absolute guide and master, and from time to time the lights of a town, the searing white flash of a station—and back into darkness.

My longest day was London to Leeds and back, on the return journey doing Wakefield to King's Cross non-stop for 175 miles. This was a total day's run of 400 miles, entailing a consumption of about seven tons of coal, every pound of it to be shovelled. Not a bad day's exercise.

All this was wonderful for keeping fit, and I don't think I've ever been so healthy in my life on all that fresh air and cold tea. Firing a locomotive isn't just a matter of throwing shovelfuls of coal into the box when the fire begins to look low. It would have taken me years to master the art, but I did learn something about keeping the pressure just right, anticipating requirements before coming, say, to a long up gradient, about dealing with poor coal, a dirty boiler, injector troubles and so on. I learnt a little about the art of driving too, but only a little, for it requires really uncommon skill. I have been on the footplate out of King's Cross in wet weather and with a heavy load when, in the smoke-laden blackness of the tunnels, the wheels have started to slip and, unless I actually leant out to feel the tunnel wall, there was no way of telling whether those 300 tons under the driver's care were moving backwards or forwards.

Oddly enough—and tragically too—this was how Cecil Kimber of M.G.s was killed. The train on which he was a passenger came slipping backwards out of the tunnel and his coach fouled the catch-points and upset. No one else was even hurt, I believe.

· · · · ·

Summer 1910. I had been working hard for five years. I was nearly twenty-two, my apprenticeship completed. It was a moment to take stock and reach a few conclusions about my future.

I wasn't at all sure that I liked what I saw ahead of me. Locomotives, as always, were nearest to my heart; familiarity had—if possible—improved relations between us. But, materially, what did they offer me? A job as a fitter, or at best the post of assistant to the assistant of the locomotive superintendent at King's Cross, with a maximum salary of £250 p.a. There were too few plum jobs, too long a waiting list for them when their present holders retired. And, like most young men of twenty-two, the material things of life interested me: gadgets, if you like, motor bicycles, some comforts and most of all the freedom from worry.

Suddenly, to my dismay, I realised that the railway was not going to be able to meet my wishes. Which way, then, was I going to turn? Over the past year or two, through my motor-cycle racing and other competition work (of which more later) I had at last become keenly aware of the internal combustion engine. A lot had happened since that trip in the Daimler up in Scotland. What had then seemed to me a tiresome and unreliable piece of machinery was now something to be reckoned with. The i.c. engine was carrying more and more people about the world, faster and more efficiently. It had even whisked a few people over the Channel. Internal combustion had to be taken seriously.

E. M. P. Boileau, who was on the staff of *The Autocar*, was an old friend of mine. Of all the people I knew he was obviously the best person to write to. He knew the motor business inside out. I suppose you can say that the letter I wrote him was quite a significant, even an important, one. Anyway, its results were important to me.

CHAPTER THREE

From two Wheels . . .

A LOT of people don't like motor bicycles, looking at them as I looked at the early cars as noisy, draughty and anti-social, and for the benefit of these and for people who are simply bored by them, all my motor bicycling—what you can call my 'two-wheel memoirs'—is concentrated in this chapter, which the reader can easily skip if he feels like it.

We have to go back a few years now, back to 1906 and to those somewhat rugged days at Doncaster. I have already mentioned my love for travelling and for covering great distances independently. One of the things I have always enjoyed most in life is to get out my maps (of which I have an enormous collection) and plot out a journey, imagining what the roads and the towns and villages are like, and then to carry out my itinerary. I don't think my delight in planned travel is unusual; certainly the excitement has not faded with the passing years, and remains with me as strongly as ever today.

At Doncaster the opportunities for travelling came rarely enough, but then one day I got hold of a copy of a magazine called *Motor Cycle*, and from its pages a wonderfully exciting new world opened up. A push-bike, it seemed, need not always be pushed; it could carry you along under the power of its engine, which helped you up the hills and allowed you to travel two or three times the distance in the same time. Neither the engine nor the additional speed it would give appealed in the least to me at first, the power striking me just as a very sensible means of exploiting an already admirable means of transport.

I thought about this motor bicycling for a time, and the more I thought the more I liked the idea. I bought and read more copies of *Motor Cycle*. Then, on one week-end leave in London, I went along to the nearest cycle shop, E. T. Morris's in the Finchley Road, where there were a lot of new and second-hand machines, both pedal and motorised. The one within my price range that I fancied the most was a 3-h.p. Quadrant, a belt-drive affair with a surface carburettor[1] and single-speed transmission. It must have been at least third- or fourth-hand for its registration number was an early one, A4667, and it had clearly seen a few years' service. Again after more thought and after discussing it with the family, I took the plunge, and came back to Avenue Road on it one evening, my self-consciousness changing to possessive pride when my brothers came out and looked over the machine admiringly and, I thought, even enviously. That little Quadrant was the first mechanically propelled vehicle any Bentley had ever owned, and I suppose it deserved this attention, just as in later years it had a lot to answer for.

Before long my brother A.W. had a Triumph and H.M. a Quadrant like mine, and we were going out at week-ends together, comparing notes and religiously reading page by page the weekly *Motor Cycle*. For a brief period motor cycles ruled out lives. I remember being envious of the Triumph's magneto and mechanically operated inlet valve, so obviously the engineering of that somewhat crude engine soon began to interest me. I have never been able to use any piece of machinery for long without having to pull it to pieces to see how it works.

The romantically inclined A.W., on the other hand, didn't care a scrap about what made the wheels go round, and it was just as characteristic of him that he should learn about—and become fascinated by—a record which has alas now become extinct: the End-to-End.

'You can't go much farther than that, can you?' I remember him saying of the Lands End to John O'Groats run, but as a practical proposition an attack on the record was quite absurd for someone who hadn't the least idea whether a cylinder worked inside a piston, or vice versa.

'You're not really thinking of tackling it?' asked H.M.; and was informed that of course he was.

It was also characteristic of A.W. that he should not only try but succeed, setting about the operation with the casual ease and transparent enjoyment that we loved in him. He set off from John O' Groats, driving a quite reliable machine but with the crudest

---

1. Many unkind things have been said about the surface carburettor, and it was a little tricky. But it was also very economical and worked well so long as you never let in more petrol by the needle valve than you could possibly use.

of lighting day and night over macadamed or dirt roads that were almost unsignposted, and arrived at Land's End tired but in comfortable time to take the record. A year or two later he took the End-to-End record for side-cars, with H.M. this time, equally soundly. Both were remarkable achievements which would not have been possible without an equally remarkable element of luck.

I took my Quadrant back to Doncaster by rail and used it there for getting about the town, continuing to take the Great Northern home at week-ends, until it occurred to me one day to do the journey by road. This may sound commonplace enough today, but it was a proposition to be considered carefully in 1906, with a machine with a top speed of less than 35 m.p.h., and the Great North Road a rough, narrow, second-rate highway. Anyway it was unusual enough to cause something of a sensation when I turned up at home, covered in dust and very tired, at nine o'clock one Saturday evening.

All this led naturally to the three of us joining the appropriate motor-cycling clubs, the Auto Cycle Union, the Motor Cycling Club and the North-West London Club, and taking part in their events. In fact we became rather ambitious, and A.W. even suggested that he and I should go in for the London–Edinburgh Trial. We must have been mad to consider it, for this was a major event in the calendar, supported by works' teams and professional drivers. However, A.W.'s infectious enthusiasm won the day as usual, and I found myself spending week-ends preparing our machines.

A.W., of course, went right through without any mechanical troubles and got a Gold Medal. As far as I was concerned, things went well enough until Newcastle, though I had arrived at each control only in the nick of time, which left me dependent for refreshment on the chocolate and apples and sandwiches I had in my pocket—and because of my meagre power I had had to pedal up every hill. I was just about all in when my rear tyre went flat somewhere around Morpeth, and I was ready to give up. But a good Samaritan in the shape of a fellow called Baddeley of the Newcastle club stopped and gave me a hand, so I was able to stagger on until I was actually in sight of Edinburgh—when my engine went dead. It was the wire to the contact-breaker this time. It had broken, and it was so tucked away that it was a major operation even to get at it. But I managed to mend it somehow, and tore off to arrive at the last control just in time. It was my first Gold Medal, and the hardest-earned of them all.

I got my moneys' worth out of that Quadrant all right. I don't remember what mileage I covered, but it included a tour of Scotland with A.W. and H.M. As soon as I could afford it I exchanged it for something better, and the next machine was a one-off made specially for me by the Quadrant hill-climb specialist, L. W. Bellinger, from a $3\frac{1}{2}$-h.p. engine, a lighter frame and other bits. It worked very well, but by 1908 I was converted to Rexs, which were no more reliable but much faster. The first was a 5-h.p. twin, an advanced machine with a particularly good frame design. Being hand-built Rexs varied a great deal, and you could be landed with a very bad one. I was lucky; mine was a good one. I had enormous fun with it, and it brought me Gold Medals in the London–Plymouth–London and Lands End-and-back Trials.

The following year it was a $3\frac{1}{2}$-h.p. Speed Model Rex, which was so fast that I got the wild idea that I might stand a chance in racing. Speed, you see, was beginning to get a grip on me. To the gentle charm of assisted propulsion on two wheels had been added the exhilaration and effortlessness of fast movement along the roads, which you can only appreciate to the full on a motor bicycle. Speed, as we all know, has a strong cumulative factor, and in no time at all I was experimenting with the rather unresponsive Quadrants and later the Rexs to try to obtain more m.p.h. When I was successful I derived enormous satisfaction from this mild tuning; and as a natural corollary when I thought seriously about speed events I tried to perfect in the same way my driving, and especially my cornering. Motor bicycles were regarded at that time with even graver suspicion than cars, and it was not always easy to find a clear, safe piece of road for this. The stretch between Barnet and Hatfield, we discovered, was the best around north London, and along here at night my great friend Jack Withers and I used to test our Rexs, and later our Indians, at speeds and under conditions that I prefer not to think about now.

Just as it is today, the Isle of Man Tourist Trophy was the premier event in the calendar, and—greatly daring—I entered my name for it, was accepted, and in due course took the boat to Douglas with my Rex. It was a wonderful course that extended across the width of the island and included every conceivable sort of corner and gradient. Wherever I went there were famous drivers I had read about and idolised, and every variety of fast machine. I was quite mad, I thought, to be pitting myself against this phalanx of works' entries and terribly experienced professionals.

Against the name W. O. Bentley in the 1909 records there is the bald and humbling entry: 'Crashed'. Actually I didn't survive a lap, overdoing it on one of the corners where over-hanging trees had left a film of dampness on the road. Half-way round I knew I wasn't going to make it, and there is little you can do about a dry-stone wall beyond waiting to hit it when you are skidding at 50 m.p.h. Luckily that wall was low enough, or I was tall enough, for me to take the brunt of the shock with my chest instead of my head, and I was only bruised and winded.

Brooklands had been open for two years by then and there were regular motor-cycling races there. One of the most important was the One-Hour in August, and in spite of the T.T. débâcle, I decided to have a go with the Rex. Motor cycling on Brooklands was not so uncomfortable as many people might imagine, firstly because the track was in quite good condition in those days, and also because we could not go very fast—sixty was about our maximum—and therefore never strayed up on to the rougher part near the top of the bankings. In fact that vast expanse of concrete was a little intimidating after the narrow I.O.M. roads.

I don't think I should have even finished, let alone managed to secure quite a good second, in that race if I had not incorporated a modification of my own in the Rex, which fed a film of oil into the carburettor by way of a little pipe from the crank-case. This made a tremendous difference to the performance; in fact after I told the Rex people about it, I rather think they incorporated it in all their models.

One of my last efforts on the $3\frac{1}{2}$ Speed Model Rex was the 6-Days Trial, a sustained and demanding event which took place mostly over the Welsh hills, the centre being Shrewsbury. Every day we went out on timed runs between controls and up some of those formidable hills. Like most trials it was regularity and not speed that counted, though the set speed up some of the mountains did take some keeping up. It was an interesting and enjoyable business, and from it I learnt a lot that was to come in useful when I transferred my loyalty to four wheels. Like the London–Edinburgh and most other trials there was no outright winner; it was a Gold Medal, a Silver one or nothing, and with 1,320 points out of a possible 1,335 I was lucky enough to qualify for the Gold.

One of my heroes at this time was Lee Evans, a superb rider in the Rex team who helped me a great deal in all my preparation and racing. Everything he said or did was right so far as I was concerned; so when he transferred to Indians, along I went too. The Indian was an American machine, and I suppose the Gilera of its day. It was a dream 'bike, with chain drive and terrific performance; but what I loved most about it was its silence. I have put up with a lot of noise in my time, but I don't like it, and I hate noise for the sake of noise. To me 70 m.p.h. in silence is far more creditable than a noisy 80 m.p.h. I am quite sure that the 1910 Indians were quieter than any air-cooled motor cycle on the market today, regardless of performance; and this feature was not only pleasant but useful at a time when the police were much hotter than they are today about noisy exhausts. In fact the rider of any modern air-cooled police motor bicycle would have been in court in no time before the First World War.

With this Indian, I thought, I really ought to be able to do something, for it was astonishingly fast as well as a beautiful machine to ride. Kop Hill Climb, the first thing I tried it on, proved this, and to my astonishment and terrific satisfaction I went up in 1 min. 27 sec., even beating several of the professionals there like Wells and Lee Evans on similar machines.

T.T. time came round again and I decided to sacrifice my holiday and have another crack. And I wasn't going to do anything silly this time. I had learnt a lot since the previous event both about riding and preparation, and it was going to be a case of 'No trouble's too much'. My ambition, like that of so many independent drivers since the earliest days of motor sport, was to beat the official works' team.

Well, I was unlucky, and I don't think for once it is unfair to say that. The Indian really was in fine fettle, as it ought to have been after all the time I had expended on it, and I think it was the fastest Indian on the island. The start was individual machine by machine, as it is today and was in the early T.T. car races, and I went off towards Ballacraine riding faster than I had ever ridden in my life. I passed Godfrey without too much trouble, and even got by Jack Marshall, the champion hill-climber, and completed the lap in 19 min. 27 sec., faster than all the Indians.

I was bursting with confidence and thoroughly enjoying myself on the second lap when suddenly my rear tyre burst, sending me in a terrific skid towards a wall. Here we go again, I thought, and maybe this time I shan't be so lucky! But I managed to pull up somehow on the verge, and when I had reorientated myself, took a look at the wheel. It was a terrible mess. The tube was in ribbons and the tyre had wrapped itself round and round the rim, damaging it hopelessly. There was nothing for it but to retire, horribly disappointed and cursing the makers of the tyres I had changed to (along with all the other Indians) the day before. The works' team had just the same trouble, and what should have been an Indian walk-over turned out a disaster, with only one finishing.

However, it wasn't a completely fruitless trip, for the next day there was the hill-climb up Snaefell. This time we used the old tyres and everything went swimmingly—especially for me, as I just managed to beat Lee Evans and Franklin and put up fastest time.

There was one more race and one more machine I should say a few words about. The race was the One-Hour T.T. at Brooklands, an all-Indian benefit with Bennet leading me home by half a mile. And the machine was the 5-h.p. Indian, which ran 1–2–3 in the next Isle of Man T.T. The attractions of the motor car were already getting a firm hold on me when I bought that big Indian, and I think I was probably prejudiced against it before I even sat in the saddle. Anyway, I didn't care for it, kept it for only a short time, and when I made the exchange it was for a 9-h.p. Riley car.

That was the end of motor cycling for me, at least for thirty-odd years. We are jumping a long way ahead if I mention the Francis Barnett here, but as I've said I would keep all my motor cycling in this chapter, perhaps I had better mention that it was a splendid little 98 c.c. machine bought originally in the interests of petrol economy in World War II when I had to travel daily between the Lagonda works and my home, and also add that it not only gave me a great deal of quiet excitement in my fifties, but also kept me entirely free from the common cold. In short, I can recommend motor cycling not only as an agreeable and exhilarating, but also an extremely healthy, means of transport.

. . . to Four Wheels

THE London taxi-cab has never been distinguished for advanced design or liveliness, and a 1910 two-cylinder Unic was perhaps an odd training ground for someone whose life was to be spent with high-performance machines. But my two years with those worthy sloggers[1] probably taught me as much as I could have learnt anywhere.

It all began with that letter to E. M. P. Boileau. He put me in touch with a man called Greathead who was the general manager of the National Motor Cab Company. So I went along to Hammersmith one day and landed myself the job of assistant to the second-in-command, a fellow called E. C. Esse, who really ran everything in the place except the finances, which Greathead kept under his wing. I liked Esse right away, liked his quiet, soothing manner and the feeling he gave of efficiency. He was very tall, with a bristling moustache and spectacles. Later we discovered our mutual passion for photography, and that helped to cement our friendship.

There were a lot of cab companies then, competition was fierce, and although the National had two hundred and fifty bright-red cabs, it was by no means the biggest. The little fish were always being eaten up by the bigger fish, and unless we were careful, I was warned, that could easily happen to us. Cab-running was a fine-marginal business. A healthy profit could be made, but any extravagance or wastefulness could convert this to a heavy loss in no time. Everything, in fact, depended on running efficiency; and this was where I came in. I was given the nominal rank of General Assistant, but actually I was a sort of odd-body cum efficiency specialist.

On my first morning I had a little lecture from Esse, who ex-

1. They were all landaulettes, with as generous luggage and passenger space as the modern cab, and as all-square and erect as the Americans imagine our cabs are today.

plained that the cabs were the company's property and responsibility, that we had to maintain them, overhaul them, service them every night, engage and pay the drivers.

'What we've got to do, Bentley,' he told me, 'is to try to cut down on the cost of these overhauls—in fact all our running costs.'

He led me out of his office, introduced me to some of the mechanics, to a few of the drivers waiting to go out, and to the great hefty tough nut, Colborn, who was in charge of them.

'And you must meet Hussein,' Esse said, leading me towards this formidable-looking Frenchman. 'He's our foreman. You'll find him quite unique.'

I was to have a lot to do with Hussein and wondered how I was going to get on with him. As things turned out we got on admirably. He was a good engineer, like so many Frenchmen, a good mechanic, and he became a good friend. He had only one weakness, and this was for absinthe. For weeks on end all would be quiet at Hammersmith; then suddenly, for no apparent reason, Hussein would get hold of a bottle, and all hell was let loose. He would drink prodigious quantities of it and go completely berserk, tearing round the shops brandishing an outsize spanner and threatening to 'Keel you all!' It was most alarming. But the next day he was as quiet and courteous as ever.

At Hammersmith the grounding I had had at Doncaster in the technique of human relations proved its value. Although I had no direct authority over the drivers, I had a lot to do with them, and I found them quite tricky at first. Cab drivers the world over are an independent race and the Hammersmith men were as independent as any. It was no good playing the heavy father, taking a 'holier-than-thou' attitude, or treating obstreperousness in a jocular 'one-of-the-boys' manner. Labour relations, for want of a better term, can be learnt only by experience, and I really can't define their formula, but it includes the ability to take a ribbing the right way. Sometimes—but only as a last resort—I would hail one of our cabs in the West End late at night, and then there would be no peace the next day. 'Bentley gallivanting round the bright lights again last night—coo, 'e's a masher, Bentley is!' There was never a dull moment with the drivers. They used to put up a ring at the works sometimes and have a few bouts. The antagonism was terrific and the standard of boxing very high. I used to bring friends along for a cheap show and it was always a roaring success. 'Much better than anything you see at the Wonderland,' they used to tell me.

The National cab drivers were a good and likeable bunch; but a few of them were a bit sharp, and one or two downright dishonest. These gave us an enormous amount of trouble because it was so difficult to pin down the culprits, let alone find any proof that we were being done. I got on to the first clue some time during my first few weeks when I was up in Birmingham on some mission or other and happened to see a red Unic carrying our registration numbers. I thought it was odd, a hundred-mile fare being almost beyond the capacity of the Unic anyway, and when I returned I checked on the records and found that this cab had recorded a total of forty-five miles for the day.

I reported my suspicions to Esse, who told me that he had known that this sort of thing had been going on for some time, but that he had had nothing concrete to go on. Even now it was not simply a matter of confronting the driver and accusing him. He would probably just deny it, put on an offended air and walk out. It was just as likely that a dozen of his cronies would follow him to General or one of our other competitors; and, there being no surplus of skilled cabbies, they would be welcomed with open arms.

Esse, Colborn and I set about our detective work with great discretion, and a silent battle of wits now ensued, with neither side acknowledging this state of cold war. Our own MI5 put us on to the next clue. The cab meters were operated through a cable from a scroll on the offside front wheel, and it took only a few minutes to change wheels in a quiet side street. They would then operate for the best part of a day with a 'faulty' meter. 'Sorry, sir, the meter's gone wrong, sir.' They probably added dramatic effect by banging the thing, muttering 'Must get it fixed,' and slipping into their pocket the agreed estimated fare for the trip, plus the tip. It was a highly profitable business, with all costs met by the firm.

We opened the attack by sealing the scroll and checking on all the seals every twenty-four hours. This was answered by pulling the tube carrying the cable down through the floor-boards and taking the pin out. We then sealed the tube. The opposition got round this one too. They were an ingenious bunch who were obviously enjoying this sport from sheer devilry as much as for the profit. We sealed the wheel nuts, sealed the cable, sealed half the nuts in desperation, until the cabs were going round with several pounds of dead-weight lead and wire on their chassis.

But they were still cheating us. It finally took months to find the answer, and I must have put in dozens of hours puzzling over it before quite by chance I discovered a minute hole in the glass over one of the meters. I saw at once that a needle could be delicately inserted through this and manipulated to hitch back the mileage figures. We knew that there were only a few specialists in London who could carry out such fine drilling work. For the next step we decided to call in professional aid.

I think our detective enjoyed the few days he spent with us. He was a cheerful fellow who quite entered into the spirit of the game. We dressed him as a driver and introduced him around the other men. The turnover of drivers being heavy, that went off all right. Then he went out on the trail. The operation, he eventually discovered, was a simple one, carried out at a little place near King's Cross for a modest sum. We thanked and paid our detective—and that was the end of the drain on our fare money. Our labour relations remained happy, and no word of accusation had been exchanged throughout the campaign.

That was the most exciting challenge I had at Hammersmith. Otherwise my two years with the National, whose motto might have been *ne quid nimis*, were mainly occupied with economy measures. Once a year the cabs had to be detached from their chassis and body and chassis overhauled for the police inspection and certification. This was a most expensive business, and I did battle with the coach-builder to bring down to the minimum the cost of his side of the operation. We streamlined the regular works maintenance and devised a new and rather revolutionary method of dealing with the worn dogs on the gears—by simply welding on new ones. Top gear on the Unic was a terror and sometimes nearly dislocated your wrist, which led to expensive dog wear. Fuel costs were a constant enemy, too, and the target for periodic harassing attacks. I spent hours with those carburettors, to the disapproval of the drivers who strongly resented losing any of their meagre performance. One major jet modification I installed in all the cabs aroused the strongest suspicion, and a hearty laugh and a word of reassurance were called for. 'Don't worry,' I told them, 'this'll give you just that extra power you want,' a deceit that matched even the meter-fiddling of some of the rogues among them.

40

At first I motor-biked to Hammersmith from Avenue Road, where I was still living with my family, but the lure of four wheels was becoming stronger and I was actually earning some money now instead of living off an allowance provided by my mother out of my future inheritance. Some of this new income went on the Riley, my first car, and, like most first cars, the one I remember best of all the many I have owned. It was a 9-h.p. water-cooled V-twin of 86 $\times$ 89 mm with the engine under the seat and placed centrally. Like the Grand Prix cars of today, it was neither a rear- nor a front-engined vehicle; but, unlike those successful machines, it did not hold the road very well, and with its wheelbase of 6 ft. 6 in. was a terrible skidder. The 'dreaded side-slip' which was the subject of such awesome conversation in those days occurred very frequently. It was quite a good little performer and accelerated forwards with an alacrity equalled only by its acceleration backwards, the latter being usually unpremeditated. It was, of course, chain-driven and, as was usual in those days, one was quite open to the elements. I wasn't really sorry to see it go.

I exchanged it at the Sizaire-Naudin concessionaires. Now I had some real performance and a more rewarding engine on which to work. The Sizaire-Naudin had a good record in Voiturette racing in France, and as soon as I had mine out on the road I began to see why. It had nice positive steering, held the road magnificently with its independent front suspension and was a joy at speed. It was a two-seater single-cylinder machine which was advanced in some respects, merely curious in others and thoroughly practical all through. It had a single-cylinder engine of 120 $\times$ 130 mm capacity which was astonishingly reliable and economical. Also, it always started—an unusual advantage at that time. Some forty years before a British manufacturer included such a refinement it had independent front suspension, on the sliding-column principle similar to that adopted by Lancia and Morgan in the 'twenties, with a transverse leaf spring. All this was very simple and effective and provided astonishingly good road-holding, although this could have been further improved if the manufacturer had not insisted on placing the gearbox in the back axle, which unnecessarily increased the unsprung weight. The Sizaire, incidentally, had quite a sporty reputation at this time and the car did very well in competition, especially the voiturette racing. I believe that a small Sizaire, driven by Naudin himself, won a sort of voiturette Targa Florio run on the Targa circuit in about 1906.

This single-cylinder Sizaire was followed by a four-cylinder car of the same make which I bought from the concessionaires, Jarrott and Letts, second-hand. This was a good car, too, but not nearly so satisfactory as the first one. Its four-stroke, four-cylinder, water-cooled engine was not quite so reliable, and it had a very noisy camshaft. But of course it was much faster than the earlier machine.

.   .   .   .   .

The year 1911 was happy and exciting. Life was opening up for me, and I liked what I saw. I was independent, the severity of apprenticeship behind me, with a comfortable home, a reasonable salary (augmented by racing tips of incredible accuracy from a driver at the works, who well deserved his 25% share of the winnings) and many good friends. There were Henry Wood Promenade Concerts at Queen's Hall, and of course music-halls at the Palace and Empire, with late suppers at the Piccadilly to the music of de Groot's orchestra to round off an evening. And there was Leonie Gore, Jack Withers' stepsister. Jack and I had many things in common, our strongest bond being first our Rex and Indian motor cycles and then our cars. We often ended up at his house at Maresfield Gardens, Hampstead, and there for the first time I met my future wife.

I can't say the response was very enthusiastic at first, and for some time there was a certain lack of balance between the affection we felt for one another. She was accustomed to the comforts of life, and I must have realised that at twenty-two I was in no position to give her what she expected. If I didn't, her parents made the fact clear to me. However, I was doggedly persistent, and prepared to wait.

Life may have been full and happy enough, and I enjoyed my job at Hammersmith, but I was not contented. For years the locomotive had monopolised my thoughts and ruled my ambitions. At the completion of my apprenticeship, and my departure from King's Cross, there had been no disillusionment. Like all first loves of childhood, warm with early memories and associations, the railway engine held a special place in my heart, and nothing would ever quite take its place. We remained friends after we

parted and have remained on the best of terms to this day. But
now the motor car, which I had once approached with caution,
perhaps still with a trace of suspicion and certainly with strictly
materialistic motives, had become firmly entrenched. Two hundred and fifty Unics—which grew to 500 during my term—a decidedly odd Riley and a Sizaire-Naudin had been mainly responsible for this. The attraction of the power and speed of the motor
car, the realisation of the independence and the means to take
you over a great distance that it offered, came to me at a period
of growing self-confidence and coincided with a keen wish to make
more money and to be my own master.

My chance came when I was ripe and eager for it, but quite
unexpectedly, in the early months of 1912. My brother, L.H.,
had decided that farming was an unprofitable business after all—
and from the way he managed it this was a natural conclusion—
and was looking round for something in which to invest his money.
H.M., glancing through the classified advertisements one day,
thought he might have found it. A firm called Lecoq and Fernie,
concessionaires for several French cars, was looking for a new
director, complete with money. H.M. went along to see if this
would do for his brother.

It was not a very satisfactory interview, with H.M. trying his
hardest to sell L.H. to Lecoq, the sharp and amusing director
who was also chairman and managing director of a firm of trunk
and suitcase manufacturers, Vuitton Trunks. Lecoq, H.M. reported later, appeared to have a single-minded interest in making
money, and he also got the impression that he was a good deal
more interested in making it out of luggage than motor
cars.

'You'd better come and see my fellow director, Fernie,' H.M.
was told. 'He knows much more about it than I do.'

Major Fernie was a different sort of proposition altogether, in
appearance resembling a caricature in *Punch* of the rough-riding
cavalry officer (which actually I think he had been), complete with
aggressive ginger moustache; a big, domineering man who
fancied himself as the straight-from-the-shoulder business man
who does not mince his words.

H.M. stood up to the verbal barrage well enough, but found
himself forced to agree that a half-hearted foray into farming
did not necessarily equip you for an active directorship in a
motor-car concession. The interview took an unexpected turn.

'Now what about you? Qualified chartered accountant—just the man we're looking for. Got any money?'

Embarrassed, H.M. stalled. 'Well, er—I'll think it over. It's rather difficult, you see . . .'

The outcome of all this led to a delicate family situation.

'But this is just the kind of opening Walter's been looking for.'

'And he's had the right kind of training for it.'

'What do they want an accountant for?'

H.M. agreed warmly with them all, and said he would not dream of depriving me of the chance. I said the same thing as emphatically in different words. Impasse.

Then H.M. grinned at me and said, 'Let's toss for it.'

At the time my whole future seemed to depend on that spinning coin, but as it turned out it was not very important that I won. Either way, I think, Lecoq and Fernie would have become Bentley and Bentley within a few months.

My share in the business cost me £2,000, which again came out of the money I would inherit when my mother died. I handed in my notice at the National Motor Cab Company, said good-bye to Greathead, Esse, Colborn, the gay quixotic Hussein, the motley army of drivers, the whole noisy, buzzing hive of hundreds of sturdy Unics. I was to miss certain things at the National, but I was content never again to peer under one of those identical red bonnets at one of those identical two-cylinder engines. After two years with them, to deal with another machine was a refreshingly exciting thought.

Lecoq and Fernie had the concession for three makes of French cars: Buchet, La Licorne and Doriet, Flandrin et Parent. But two were disposed of just before I arrived, and I was thankful it was the D.F.P. that had been retained. This French car interested me a great deal, and I thought it had real possibilities.

The first thing I did at the Hanover Street office was to sit down and wonder why any D.F.P.s at all had been sold; with the sort of promotion they had been receiving, with no road tests and no advertising, it was a miracle that they had kept up the rate to one a month. It said something for the word-of-mouth reputation of the car, I suppose, but I did see why they had inserted that invitation in the classified columns.

I began by trying to work up some sort of enthusiasm in Hanover Street, and it took only a week or two to discover that there wasn't any. Lecoq was too busy turning over profitable suitcases and trunks, and his partner appeared to have given up in despair long ago. The mask of the hard-driving business man fell away, revealing a noisy, bossy, ineffectual man—who tried to push me around. Now I hate being pushed as violently as I hate pushing others; it doesn't work with me, and I know it would never have brought results (or made for pleasant working conditions) if I had ever tried it on anyone working with me. I have never ordered anyone to do anything in all my life.

I made it amply clear to Lecoq that I was not going to be pushed around, and one way and another we exchanged quite a few words.

It would have been all too easy to slip into the general air of disillusionment in that office, and come to the conclusion that I had given up my job and thrown myself—and my money—into a dead concern. But I knew how profitable a good foreign-car concession could be; there were Charles Jarrott and Letts, Warwick Wright and many others to bear witness to this. And I knew business in the motor trade was good, and that the D.F.P. had virtually no competition on the British market. I was completely confident that this sporty little well-made French car could be sold in good numbers if it was only given a chance. D.F.P.s were excellent, reliable vehicles possessing the indefinable quality that makes certain cars a pleasure to drive, and always feel 'just right'. The steering and road-holding were first class and they were ruggedly built to stand up to the very harsh treatment all Frenchmen give their cars.

I talked things over with H.M. 'The company will never get anywhere with this man Fernie, and Lecoq's nothing but a sleeping partner,' I told him. 'A child of five knows more about selling motor cars than they do.'

Neither of us could understand why they had ever obtained the concession in the first place, and having obtained it, why they did not do something about it, or sell out.

'Do you think they would?' H.M. suddenly asked.

I said I thought it was worth investigating, and he already knew my opinion that there were tremendous possibilities in the D.F.P., and agreed with me.

'Let's go and ask them then,' H.M. said; and that is what we did.

I think Lecoq and Fernie were delighted when we opened negotiations for the purchase by H.M. of their share in the business.

Thinking about it now, I am sure that this is just what they had hoped would happen, and certainly their attempt to appear as reluctant vendors was not very convincing. Oh, but how those two could haggle! The negotiations were interminable, and before we had finished a couple of Lecoq's suitcases became involved in the bidding. In the end we took the suitcases and they took £2,000 from H.M. for their shares.

.   .   .   .   .

This was the most daring and momentous thing either H.M. or I had ever done. When all the document-signing and hand-shaking were over, we eyed one another nervously. We were twenty-four and twenty-seven, and had a £4,000 business (which was regarded—when it was regarded at all—as moribund) on our hands.

But we went home in a state of tremendous excitement and bursting with enthusiasm. Our chance had come, and we were going to build up this company, put the name of D.F.P. on the map and make a lot of money. There was nothing to hold us back now.

The new company of Bentley and Bentley moved in in March, 1912, with far too little working capital and far too much confidence. We kept the showrooms in Hanover Street; H.M., who was to look after the sales and business side, worked there with his secretary, while I moved into an old coach-house we rented from J. H. Easter, who did the body trimming for us, in New Street Mews off Upper Baker Street.[1] To work at Hanover Street as manager we had G. P. de Freville, an excellent man, whose inherent pessimism was no bad thing, for the bubbles of optimism in those early days needed puncturing from time to time. De Freville was a realist, and a worker. He had to be to survive the pressure, for we all worked at a tremendous pace for long hours week after week until we achieved our ambition and began to show a profit after the first six months. After the war, de Freville was to help launch the Alvis Car Company.

After a short time we got over from the French factory a little wizard called Leroux as head—and only—mechanic. Leroux was

1. Seven years later, in this same coach-house, the first 3-litre Bentley engine Ex 1 roared into life, to the alarm of the local inhabitants. Today there is a plaque on the wall commemorating the occasion (see page 79).

another tremendous worker whom we soon came to regard as the very backbone of Bentley and Bentley. He achieved prodigies of labour in the two and a half years he worked for us, acting as liaison with the factory, tuning and preparing the cars for competition work and riding as mechanic in races—an onerous and dangerous duty outside his routine work of checking over the chassis when they arrived from France, and servicing owners' cars.

Our first figures above the red line were not very imposing, but they did spur us on. There was no doubt that we were on the right track: selling the right product at the right price, and with some show of energy and initiative. We had three models in the catalogue, the 10–12 h.p., the 12–15 and the 16–20, at prices from £265 to £550, with a wide choice of bodywork. For this money the customer had absolutely top-quality West of England cloth upholstery, tailor-made especially for the car. The panel-beating was done by hand, of course, and the wooden frame-work and trim were made by real craftsmen carpenters who were dedicated to their calling. The painting took literally weeks, and each of the coats was hand-smoothed down after brushing and finished off with several coats of varnish. (In spite of all this attention, such has been the advance in the standards of materials for painting cars that I wouldn't change the cellulose finish on my cheap mass-produced car today for that which we used on the D.F.P.)

Incidentally, at New Street we had a wonderful old character who used to paint the fine decorative lines on the coach-work which were a *sine qua non* on any vehicle at that time. He was never, in my memory, anything but very drunk indeed, but with the aid of a supporting stick he painted the most beautiful fine lines with complete confidence and never the trace of a waver.

The 10–12 was a pleasant enough little motor car, a sporty two-seater with a well-raked windscreen and a fair turn of speed. We never pushed the 16–20, a heavy, sluggish car with little more character than dozens of British-made competitors. At one time I ran a fixed-head coupé. It had a very high centre of gravity and the engine, with its weak crankshaft, very long stroke and tendency to vibrate, was not nearly so satisfactory as the smaller cars in the range. But the 12–15 was a different proposition.

There was nothing available elsewhere quite like the 12–15 D.F.P., and it was on this model, that I had based my confidence in our future. In France it was considered a reliable, steady family four-seater; but then the French have always had different standards of performance from the English, and there were no cars of the same capacity on English roads then that could keep up with it. It was much livelier than the 12-h.p. Humber, but what made it even more interesting to me was the susceptibility of the 70 × 130 mm four-cylinder engine to tuning. There was a real potential here, and since H.M. and I had decided from the beginning that the quickest and most effective publicity came from racing and other competition work, it was on one of these engines that I set Leroux to work in May, easing things up generally and increasing the compression. I had my eye on the Aston hill-climb in June. I thought we had a chance of putting up a fair show.

.   .   .   .   .

It turned out a brilliantly fine Saturday morning, and the sun was already hot when Leonie and I set off for Tring in the open two-seater D.F.P. De Freville was there to see us away, full of encouragement of course, as usual. 'You'll get some nice dust up in the Chilterns today,' he told us with a shake of his head.

But he wished us luck, too, and this we were going to need. It was the first time I had ever tackled competition work on four wheels and I was feeling thoroughly nervous about the prospect of competing against experienced hill-climb drivers in one of the most important events of the season. I could face making a fool of myself in front of Leonie better than I could the prospect of failure with a machine we were working desperately to put on the map. There was an awful lot at stake, I realised, as we drove out through Hendon and Watford, and I thanked heaven that at least the weather was cheerful (to blazes with de Freville and his dust!) and the car was running beautifully.

A pleasant drive in a nice open car with your fiancée beside you cheers up most people, however, and I felt more hopeful about things when we got to Aston. But my optimism fell with a thump again after I had had a chance of looking round the other drivers and cars. In the gay party atmosphere everyone seemed to be on familiar terms with everyone else, they all seemed to 'belong' in the most natural way, and to be self-assured to a degree that at once depressed and exasperated me. I was glad H.M. was there (he had come up in another car on his own), and glad to have Leonie to ease the sense of isolation.

Most of the cars, I noticed, were foreign: Stoewers, De Dions, Oryxs, Chenard-Walckers, Le Guis and Pilots, together with several English Humbers and Scottish Arrol-Johnstons. In my class, the 2-litre Class 2, the virtually unassailable champion was W. G. Tuck, who always drove a Humber and was tester for that firm. Against him—and against a good deal of other potent machinery—I could see that my chances were not taken very seriously, and the defeatism I could feel rising up as I took my place in the queue leading to the start had to be firmly suppressed.

One after another we watched the 2-litre cars go away amid blasting exhaust roar and a scream of high revs that echoed against the high bank and rolled away through the beeches; and with each departure we moved closer to the starting line. It was an afternoon for record breaking, and Tuck and one of the Vinot drivers had already done very fast runs when I gently eased the D.F.P. on to the white line and drew on the hand-brake. Later I learnt every inch of the Aston climb, but at that moment I hadn't the least idea of the way the corners went beyond the general course described by the succession of dust trails that had preceeded me up the hill. I pulled down my goggles and hoped for the best.

Success or failure in hill-climbing is measured in tenths of seconds, which are usually gained or lost at certain points on the course. Because of the very steep initial gradient at Aston, it was the change from first to second a few yards from the line that counted. I had made a point of practising this frequently, and I snicked the lever back without touching the clutch and at revs for which the D.F.P. was never intended. Once away, my nerve-storm and self-consciousness seemed to disappear, and as the track levelled off and I changed to third, I could see the first left-hander ahead. It was third gear all the time then, with the right foot hard on the boards: up the rising gradient, through the sharp right-hander, and on and up to the finish at the top.

Leonie seemed to have enjoyed every wild second of the ride. When I pulled up she smiled through a mask of grey dust and congratulated me. In her innocence she even thought we must have broken the record.

Surely as a certain contradiction to her claim, the loudspeaker announcement came over a few moments later: 'Here is the time for Mr. W. O. Bentley's D.F.P. . . .' There was a horrible pause which I filled by trying to remember whether the time he had given was good or bad. Then: 'This is the fastest time of the day for Class 2 and is a record for a 2-litre car at Aston. It also makes the D.F.P. the day's winner on Formula.' So Leonie had been right after all!

We were wildly excited, and as we were congratulated from all sides, that acute sense of alienation, of being an interloper in a hostile world, subsided. I was going to enjoy giving the news to de Freville.

Aston marked among other things for me my first brush with Tuck in a ding-dong battle on a number of fields during the next two and a half years. As we drove away I sensed that he was already thirsting for revenge.

.   .   .   .   .

The success at Aston was a start, but it takes more than a class win at a hill-climb to establish a reputation. However, we took full advantage of this little effort by putting the car, with an accompanying notice, in the showrooms, booking some modest advertising space, and generally spreading the word about that, for those who liked it, there was real performance in the D.F.P. What was most important, it gave encouragement to our distributors and agents and supported my campaign which was opening new markets in the provinces.

D.F.P. had never had area distributors in the past, and one of the first things I had done was to go on a tour round the country trying to find them. It required a lot of persuasion and was the most exhausting work I had ever encountered. While the motor trade was nothing like the tightly knit, virtually impregnable organisation that it is today, by 1912 it had already formed a hard skin that was difficult to penetrate, and since March most of my life seemed to have been spent in dim, smoky hotel bars from Newcastle to Bristol, talking, talking, talking D.F.P. to dealers. I had not managed too badly with most of them, and already the results could be seen in the steadily growing stream of orders from those agents whom I had first persuaded to take appointments. Only in the Midlands did I strike real trouble. For some reason the fact that I had not 'come up through bicycles' seemed to stick in a few of the Midlanders' throats. I suppose fundamentally it was the old class barrier raising its ugly head, even if it was in inverted form. Heaven knows, I don't want to generalise about the Midlander, let alone condemn him, for I have a number of good friends in that part of the country. But this seems a good point at which to confess that I have never found business relations easy with some of the high-powered, straight-talking, as-good-as-the-next-man tycoons of the Midland car distributing trade. It is a thing I regret because, apart from anything else, both sides have suffered as a result.

It would be charitable to think that some interest in the D.F.P. by the motoring press was spontaneously aroused by our early competition successes, but it did happen that this coincided with our taking some advertising space. A decent interval passed after our first bookings, and then followed requests for test cars, and, shortly after, the reports were published.

We could not have asked for better—'an excellent turn of speed', 'splendid power and flexibility', a 'sweet clutch', 'smooth brakes'; and it had shown a 'meritorious performance' in competition. H.M. and I decided to take some more advertising, which we could not afford, but if these were the results, it was foolish to continue to rely solely on word-of-mouth good-will. We also had to have a stand at the Motor Show at Olympia, though this would stretch our resources to breaking point. For this, membership of the Society of Motor manufacturers and Traders was necessary, so we duly joined.

What we needed, I realised, was something to back up our first appearance at the Show, something beyond a success or two at hill-climbs. The idea of a special-bodied record-breaking D.F.P. had been forming in my mind for some time, and one day I put it to H.M.

'I've got my eyes on those Class B records,' I told him. 'We're getting nearly 70 m.p.h. out of the tuned 12–15. If we get Harrisons to work on a single-seat aluminium body, I think we might stand a chance.'

'It would be a good thing if we could pip Tuck again,' he agreed. 'But it'll take some doing.'

The Humber held all the records in this class, and I confess that spurred us on. Harrisons did a quick, neat job, and the humble 12–15 looked quite formidable in its new narrow polished aluminium suit, with streamlined tail astern and disc wheels. As before, we did no other modifications beyond increasing the compression and cleaning and loosening up with great care all round.

H.M., Leroux and I went down to Brooklands on November 9th, just after Tuck's records had been pipped by Reid's Arrol-Johnston, and with no spectators beyond Colonel Lindsay Lloyd, the timekeeper, I did a few warming-up laps and then cracked off.

You could call that first attempt a qualified success. Certainly we did not do all we had hoped for, but we gained a lot of useful experience, and we did manage to raise the ten-lap record from just over 60 m.p.h. to 66.78. We should have to be content with that for our Motor Show publicity.

.   .   .   .   .

An endurance trial that never got into any record book was a run of 635 miles that H.M. and I made on a sad mission. My brother Arthur—A.W.—a wonderful personality who seemed always to be overflowing with vivacity and enterprise and high spirits, died suddenly of a throat infection that modern drugs could have cured in a day or two. It was a great blow to the family, and especially to H.M., who was nearest to him in age and had the greatest affection for him. With his enormous sense of fun and humour, A.W. had a romantic streak, and he had expressed a wish that his ashes should be scattered in a valley near Achanalt in Ross and Cromarty where he had often spent happy fishing holidays.

I thought it would take H.M.'s mind off the funeral if we made this the occasion for an endurance run, and I knew the idea of a non-stop drive—and at that time 600 miles was a very long drive —would have appealed to Arthur. So we set off in a two-seater 12–15 D.F.P. at 2.45 one dark wet December afternoon, H.M. driving through the rain, without wipers of course, as far as Grantham, which we reached at 6.40. We refuelled, had a quick drink at the George, and I drove on to Doncaster. By this time our acetylene cylinder was getting low and the headlights were noticeably dimming, so we spent a fruitless half hour hunting up a new one.

Still in teeming rain and in pitch darkness, we reached Newcastle at two in the morning, driving on sidelights, gave up the hunt round the garages after an hour or so, and drove on again with an electric torch strapped to a front wing. We had a ten-minute stop at Berwick, then I drove straight through to Edinburgh, stopping there for breakfast—our only sit-down meal—and the acetylene.

There was snow on the Stirling hills when we left at noon, and soon we were deep in it up in the Grampians. But at least the weather cleared, and we had a moon to help us along the narrow, winding tracks that were marked as roads on the map. Inverness was reached at a quarter to eight in the evening, and there we stopped only for petrol and carried straight on past Beauly Firth, Loch Garve and Loch Luichart, arriving at Achanalt thirty-one hours after our start from London, dead tired and stiff and cramped, but feeling, I think, that we had done the right thing.

.   .   .   .   .

We struggled through the lean motoring months of 1912–13 and found we could face the new season with reasonable confidence. The little niche we had cut out for ourselves demanded a full competition programme, and we started off well by cleaning up at Aston as positively as the year before. At Shelsley Walsh, where the cars were not divided into classes, we clocked 1 min. 27 sec., which was better than some of the bigger cars and was not beaten by anything with a smaller engine.

At Brooklands I entered for the first time in a race, the Whitsun Handicap meeting, and came up against Tuck again. He just beat me into second place, and then followed this up by beating all the Class B records from the half mile to ten laps at speeds up to nearly 82 m.p.h. This made us think a bit; and led us to the conclusion that something more drastic than before would have to be done to the engine.

I decided I should have to go over to France to have words with M. Doriot, less to ask for advice than to discover whether he could incorporate any successful modifications we might make as standard on the 12–15s for English export. What we had in mind, besides raised compression, were improvements to the induction pipe and carburetion.

Our relations with the factory had been wonderful from the start; there was always the closest co-operation and they could never do enough for us. M. Doriot, a trifle bewildered at the performance we had squeezed from his homely little vehicles, had already visited us, and when I sat in his office at Courbevoie on the outskirts of Paris late in June, 1913, he jumped at my plan to produce for us a modified 12–15 for our sportier customers. I was certain, I told him, there would be a good demand for it.

While we were talking all this over, I noticed on Doriot's desk a little decorative piston, made of some alloy, which had obviously been given to D.F.P. as a souvenir paper-weight by the firm that did their foundry work. Doriot saw me pick it up before I left. 'Pretty, isn't it?' he said. 'Aluminium, you know.'

I agreed and said nothing. But on the way back to Paris my mind played on that paper-weight. In our record-breaking attempts we had got up to around 80 m.p.h., and there we had stuck, unable to squeeze any more power out of the engine. Piston failure had marked our stalling point; very light steel pistons broke their rings, cast-iron pistons cracked. That aluminium memento succeeded in keeping me awake all the way home, and I swept into Hanover Street like an over-excited schoolboy.

H.M. heard me out, eyeing me curiously, and proceeded to recommend caution. 'But I'm sure it's the answer,' I told him. 'And there's no harm in trying. I'm going back to investigate. I'd like to have a set cast to try out in the 12–15.'

At twenty-five it takes a lot to kill enthusiasm, and even Doriot's cold douche had no effect. 'They'll break and seize up before you're doing 2,000 r.p.m.,' he said. 'Aluminium's not suitable for the strains and stresses of that sort of work.'

'Well, I think you're wrong,' I told him. 'Anyway, just let me make a call at your foundry. All we can lose is the cost of a few pistons.'

The Corbin foundry showed more interest, worked out a formula of 12% copper to 88% aluminium, and agreed to cast some for experimental work.

The pistons were with us in a few weeks, and Leroux and I got to work. We ran them with plenty of clearance and found at once that we were getting more power, so we lightened them and ran them again—and got another improvement. Then we took a chance and lightened them again, increased the compression further; still we had no trouble. After more very thorough testing, we sent the good news to France and told them that we were ready to go ahead with the modified 12–15—to be called the Speed Model—and to back its introduction on the track.

The 12–40 Speed Model was to be outwardly distinguishable from the 12–15 by its wire wheels; mechanically the compression was to be higher, and of course the aluminium pistons were to be fitted as standard, though we were not going to advertise that. We thus became the first firm to use successfully and as standard equipment aluminium pistons, the performance from which puzzled many of our competitors and gave us a tremendous advantage.

In almost every respect they were a great advance, their only drawback being the noise they made when cold, the aluminium having a greater expansion coefficient and causing piston slap. We never had to alter the formula by even a half per cent, and it remained as the standard right through the war and well into the 'twenties in both aero and car engines. I never understood why our secret never leaked out. By the summer of 1914 there were quite a number of 12–40 D.F.P.s on the road. But the only hint was contained in an article in *The Autocar*, which suggested that some French foundry was thinking of making aluminium pistons and gave incorrect figures for the proposed formula.

Until that summer H.M. had rightly recommended extreme financial discretion, and we had been very careful, ploughing back nearly all our profits and keeping overheads to a minimum. But the 12–40 called for some modest expansion, and we got an assistant for Hanover Street and I got in a mechanic to work with Leroux, an old friend from the National Motor Cab Company called Jackson, who remained with us right through the Bentley Motors days. In addition, Doriot's young son came over to help us.

We tried out the 12–40 in the special body at Brooklands at the August B.A.R.C. meeting. Against some quite formidable opposition, we ran away with the Short Handicap race at 70.5 m.p.h., lapping once at 75.12, and a month later had another serious crack at Tuck's Class B records. This time we managed 82.38 for the half mile, 81.6 for the mile, and improved on the Humber's figures for the ten laps by over two miles an hour. This was very satisfactory, and I was just thinking that we would really have something to shout about at Olympia, where the 12–40 would be shown for the first time, and that we had settled with Mr. Tuck for a while, when the blighter reappeared on the scene with his tiny gold single-seater, and knocked all our records for six, taking the ten laps up to 79.63 and half mile to 83.53 m.p.h.

This was exasperating, and I was now determined to finish off the Humber once and for all. We put in some long hours at New

Street Mews, fitting two plugs to each cylinder, a Bosch dual magneto, and increasing the compression still further. Then we got busy with the drill and lightened the chassis all round. Finally we worked on the transmission, fitting the 10–12's lighter rear axle, which bent frighteningly, and using an open shaft instead of a torque tube. As a safety precaution I also did without a differential. Lambert had recently killed himself at Brooklands when his tyre burst, and sent him into a skid and turned him over. It was very likely that if the Talbot had not had a differential he would have probably been all right.

Successful record-breaking on very light machines in those days was often dependent on the wind. At Brooklands conditions were ideal when it was blowing strongly from the north-east; so that you got plenty of support from behind along the straight. It was often a tedious business waiting for a wind that might give you an extra two or three miles an hour, and I just did not have the time to spare to hang around the club-house.

On 14th February I took the single-seater out with Leroux, H.M. and young Doriot—and the wind, good and strong, was of course from the south-west.

'What's to stop us going round the wrong way?' I asked.

I had certainly never thought of this before; nor, it seemed, had the officials. The rules were consulted, but there did not appear to be anything to forbid lapping clockwise, and it was certainly the obvious thing to do on a timed run.

I did one or two trial laps and the ride was no more, though certainly no less, uncomfortable than on the more orthodox anticlockwise circuit. 'I think this is going to be all right,' I told H.M. when I drew in. 'I don't think there'll be any trouble except coming down the banking to the fork. That's very rough.'

I survived the bumps and that nasty turn, and the single-seater behaved faultlessly, to give us everything from the half mile at 89.7 m.p.h. to the ten laps; all of them better than the Class C records, too.

Tuck retired from the combat after that. This settled our record-breaking tussles, but the competition continued as keenly as ever on other fields. At the speed trials at Porthcawl, for instance, I beat him home in the class event, but in the open he got far enough ahead to spray me with wet sand—that sort of thing could happen at speed trials in those days—and just pipped me. Class 2 at Aston had become a D.F.P. benefit, and my fastest

The B.R.2, my best aero engine

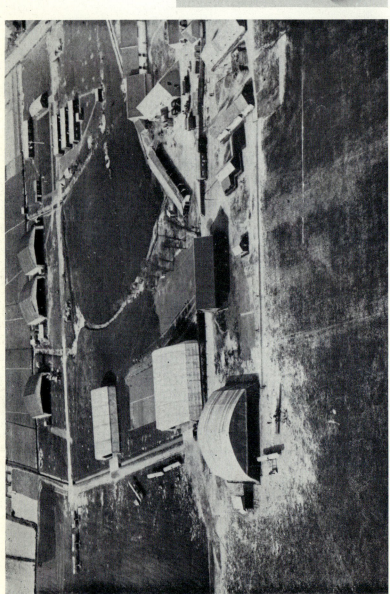

The R.N.A.S. station at Braydunes—and myself as a lieutenant

EX.1

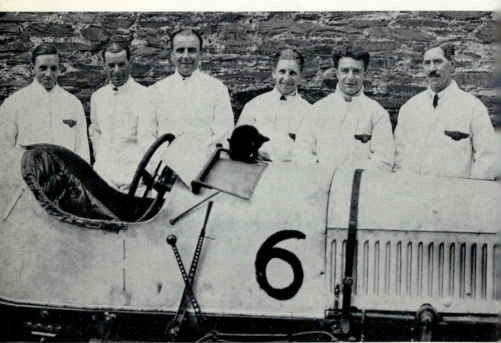

The 1922 Tourist Trophy team: the cars . . .
. . . and the drivers and mechanics. *Left to right :* Hawkes, Clement, myself, Pennell, Browning and
Saunders

time was backed up by Jack Withers' Formula win in another 12–40. Tuck would probably have beaten me at Caerphilly, but he misjudged one of the corners and as a consequence lost fastest time by 2 1/5th sec., with Jack Withers running third in his 12–40. Neither of us took the honours at the Leicestershire Hill Climb; they went to Fedden on the Straker-Squire after I lost my gear lever on that first violent change into second.

On one of our record attempts—I forget exactly which it was, but we were after the One-Hour—Dick Lisle was running simultaneously in his 3,817 c.c. Star for the Class E records. So that we should not get tangled up, I was sent away after Lisle had done half a lap, the timekeepers reckoning that at 81 m.p.h. he would gain fifty yards a lap and so would not have to pass the D.F.P. But instead, our little 2-litre machine began averaging around 83 m.p.h., and to Lisle's discomfiture I passed him quite soon.

We were all beginning to realise by then what a tremendous publicity-winning advantage there was in running a small car against bigger and more powerful machines. If you won, of course, as we did sometimes, then that was wonderful, and you shouted it from the roof-tops. 'David slays Goliath' was the headline theme then. But even if you did not, so long as you stayed the course, the innate British sympathy for the 'little man' who bravely battles against odds ensured the publicity. It was what I believe the Americans call 'psychology salesmanship'; Bentley and Bentley didn't have a name for it, but we knew we were on to a good thing.

It was this policy that decided us to enter for the fifth International Tourist Trophy race in the Isle of Man, which, after a lapse of five years, was due to take place on the 10th and 11th of June. It would be certain to get more publicity than any other race of the year, and in a car little over half as big as all the others I reckoned we should get the lion's share of it if we lasted out the 600 miles of rough roads and mountain climbing. It would be an expensive business, but worth it.

Half the motor trade and all the drivers and managers and designers one saw around the tracks congregated in the Isle of Man that June. I knew a lot of them by then, and many of them— Witchell, Frank Clement, Bianchi and Tony Vandervell—were my good friends. Tuck was there, too, of course, with the Humber team; and so were Louis Coatalen and Laurence Pomeroy with their Sunbeams and Vauxhalls. Coatalen was in his usual boisterous high spirits; Pomeroy was far less happy. He had had a lot of trouble with his Vauxhalls, and still had not settled satisfactorily the problem of his bolt-secured balance-weights. Testbed running had shown them satisfactory up to any speed, but the violent strains and stresses caused by rapid acceleration and deceleration in practice unfortunately told a different story.

Besides these two makes, there was a beautifully turned-out team of Belgian Minervas, led by their champion, Porporato, some fast Straker-Squires, and, among the less potent machinery, the Adlers and Stars and a single Hudson, suitably (or unsuitably, for it was a non-starter) modified by Rawlinson.

One or other of the Guinness brothers' Sunbeams was tipped as the likeliest winner. In spite of someone's charitable suggestion that D.F.P. stood for 'Deserves First Place' I had no illusions about our prospects. We were there for a very definite purpose, to stay the course, and unless nearly everybody else cracked up we did not stand a chance of a place.

The Isle of Man circuit was the one used by the motor bicycles today, with some severe gradients, hundreds of corners in its $37\frac{1}{2}$ miles, and one climb of 1,300-odd feet up the slopes of Snaefell; but its condition in 1914 was very different. Most of the roads were of loose stones, which turned to sticky mud in rain, and as it seemed to rain almost without cessation on that island, early morning practice was mostly uncomfortable. Leroux, Doriot junior—as mechanics—H.M. and I made up the team, and we had brought two cars with us on which we had lavished hours of preparation, one for practice and the other for me to drive in the race. Regulations demanded a wider track than was standard on the 12–40, so 16–22 axles were substituted, which added two hundredweight and made us substantially heavier than any of the other cars.

The rain stopped before the start, but it had been coming down heavily all night, and this, besides making the going sticky, caused the dust-laying sodium-chloride to penetrate behind our goggles and cause agonising pain to our eyes. But we lapped at around 47 m.p.h. without too much trouble, while the two Guinness Sunbeams, which had gone straight into the lead, went round about eight miles an hour faster. The first of the Vauxhalls was out within a few minutes, its balance-weights making a rapid penetration of the crank-case; and another followed it into retirement a lap or two later. Tuck was out by the third lap.

Later the sun came out, making things more cheerful, and we continued to circulate at a slightly higher speed and without a hint of trouble for the first 300 miles.

The second day was sunny and hot, so we changed tyres from steel-studded to non-skids before refuelling and set off, with the Guinness Sunbeams, the Minervas, Witchell's Straker-Squire and a couple of Minervas ahead of us, Clement's Straker-Squire, an Adler, Bianchi's Crossley and the surviving Vauxhall following behind. Apart from the weather, everything was much the same as on the previous day, with the sleeve-valve Minervas laying great smoke-screens from one side of the island to the other to add to the dust menace. At one point Leroux burnt his hand rather badly on the exhaust, but he did not say a word at the time and I did not find out till later. He really was the perfect mechanic to have on a long grind like this. Even when I overdid it on a corner—the heat and interminable noise must have made me momentarily careless—and went for a long broadside, he just raised a wry eyebrow and asked me solicitously if I was '*Un peu fatigué?*'

There were only six out of the twenty-three starters left at the end, with Bill Lee Guinness romping home with a ten-minute lead over the third Minerva. There was neither prize nor cup for the D.F.P., though at the presentation ceremony on the Thursday evening we did get a special medal. But things worked out just as we had hoped they would. For all the column-inches of free publicity and photographs we got in the popular newspapers as well as the motoring Press, we might almost have been first instead of last past the flag. Jack had taken on all the giants, and if he had not killed them all he had survived the holocaust. Variations on this theme made good stories, we realised, as we thumbed through the stack of Press clippings back in Hanover Street, and they all meant increased business for us. However, stories in the newspapers—even fairy stories—don't automatically sell motor cars; being stern realists, we set to work to squeeze every ounce of advantage out of our success.

.   .   .   .   .

One of the difficulties of writing an autobiography is to keep your own life in perspective with the great events. What are my affairs and ambitions compared with the earth-shaking achievements and catastrophes of the last half century? And of what importance is the fact that two World Wars and the international slump that separated them three times turned sour for me the sweet taste of success? Particularly because I was in no real physical danger in either war, nor in severe financial trouble in the crisis, I feel it is almost in bad taste to record that World War One killed the D.F.P., World War Two the V12 Lagonda, and that the repercussions of the Wall Street crash destroyed Bentley Motors.

The ironical thing about our effort in the T.T. was that the benefit from it lasted a bare eight weeks, and we never gathered our rich harvest. We issued a new catalogue, and even got our 'Tourist Trophy Model' on the market, in that short time; but that was as far as we could go before the curtain came down.

Leonie and I had married on New Year's Day and we had had a short honeymoon touring in the West Country, but we did not find time for a real holiday until the beginning of August, when the clouds were already rolling up and the storm seemed likely to break at any minute. On the 3rd we drove down to my 'in-laws' yacht at Southampton for the Cowes Regatta. There we saw work being rushed on some destroyers at Thornycrofts, and the atmosphere of drama and threatening disaster as Britain's ultimatum expired had already killed stone-cold the gaiety of the occasion. I decided to leave my wife on the yacht and set off back to London with my brother-in-law, Irwin Gore. We had lunch at the Bear in Farnham, and there, after the manager had politely refused to accept a five-pound note, we learnt we were at war.

The next day H.M. joined up as a Tommy. Half the Company was already gone, and there was an air of unreality in Hanover Street, and suddenly cars and motoring seemed as wildly inappropriate as yachts and regattas.

Ten days later our gallant Leroux was dead in Flanders.

CHAPTER FIVE

Aero Engines

To sit tight and wait seemed to me the wisest thing to do for the present. Two of my brothers had joined up and had been swept away on the first great wave of volunteers, but within days the Army was suffering from indigestion; thousands of trained men, whose skill was to be desperately missed later in specialist branches of the war machine, were being wasted in infantry regiments, and thousands more were being turned away at the recruiting offices. I did try to get into one of the armoured car brigades being formed, after contacting Rolls-Royce, who had switched at once to war work and had even requisitioned Silver Ghost chassis for conversion. They were in touch with the Army department responsible and told me where to go, but everyone was too busy coping with the rush and suggested I should come back in a few months when things had settled down.

Trading in new cars had more or less ceased, and there was only occasional servicing work at D.F.P. to keep us occupied. The one solid contribution I did have to offer, of course, was the aluminium piston, which I thought might be of value in aero engines and was still quite unknown to any other firm in England. To pass on the specification seemed a simple enough operation until I began to think about it. Security ruled out the spreading of it broadcast among the engine manufacturers, and I realised that I should have to tread carefully. Some weeks passed before I discovered the right person to call on. He was Commander Wilfrid Briggs, and he lived in one of the little temporary wooden huts put up on the top of Admiralty Arch.

Briggs' job was to build up an engine department for the rapidly expanding R.N.A.S., acting as liaison between the manufacturers and the Board of Admiralty. The advice I had been given was correct; he was the right man to talk to about aluminium pistons. The only officer in the Navy who could have been as clever as Briggs was the man who appointed him to this appallingly diffi-

61

cult post in which he had to deal with jealous, prickly engine-design departments that always knew best and often considered working for a service authority either as a favour or as beneath their dignity. He tackled bodies and individuals with an incredible tact that at once kept people happy and produced the results.

Briggs was to be my senior officer, adviser, nursemaid, champion and advocate, pacifier and moderator, for three and a half years. It wasn't until some time after my interview with him that I realised that he had me summed up and docketed within a few minutes, and from the moment I began working for him he handled me with a skill and subtlety which, allowing for the restrictions under which he worked, always got the best out of me. I owe him a great deal and am grateful to him for everything he did.

Briggs examined the piston I had brought with me and listened in silence while I did my sales talk. 'And what have you got to back up your claim?' he asked. 'It seems a remarkable thing that none of the big guns in the business have cottoned on to it after all this time.'

'It seems an odd thing to me too,' I agreed. 'I can't understand it. And I can't understand why it hasn't been developed in France. So far as I've discovered only D.F.P. know about it, and they only used it in the model they built specially for our market.'

He had heard of the D.F.P. and of some of the things we had done with it, but did not realise that we held all the Brooklands Class Records and had been virtually unbeaten in hill-climbs for a couple of years; least of all did he realise that the secret behind the power we had got out of the little engine was a new type of piston.

We talked technicalities together for a while, and then he said: 'We've got to spread the word around about this. It's obviously a development that's going to affect the work in all the big design departments. We'll have to tell them about it—but it must be done with discretion.'

Discretion meant that I had to do the job myself, he explained, and that I must have the authority of a King's Commission behind me.

'What on earth do you mean?' I asked.

'We must get you into uniform, Bentley,' Briggs said blandly; and a day or two later he telephoned: 'You're an officer now. Go to Gieves and get a uniform with two rings on it.'

Somewhat bewildered, I went along to South Molton Street

and did as I had been told, that excellent firm providing me with everything I needed off the peg. I stared at myself in the full-length glass, feeling a sense of unreality which became night-marish when I walked out, clutching a new pair of gloves, and received a smart salute from across the street. The reception from my wife on the doorstep was rather less impressive! 'What on earth's this?' she demanded.

The next day I was packed off to Derby where Rolls-Royce were making air-cooled Renault aero engines under licence, and working on a new design of their own. E. W. (later Lord) Hives was in charge of the experimental department, and, with a piston in my case, I called on him in his new office built on a sort of island surrounded by the factory's test track.

I hadn't met him before and liked him at once. In later years, and under sometimes trying circumstances, we were to see a lot of one another, but we always got on well. He examined my piston, listened to my story, and then called in his foundry specialist, Buchanan, to whom I gave the formula. Very sensibly, he made an analysis to check my figures, and then had some experimental castings made. Production went ahead with crisis urgency, and the result was that Rolls-Royce's first aero engine, the excellent water-cooled 200-h.p. Eagle, had aluminium instead of cast-iron or steel pistons.

The whole design of the Eagle aero engines' cylinder construction was also most fundamentally based on the results of a curious incident which occurred around the early part of 1915. A friend of a friend of mine tipped me off that one of the Mercedes racing cars, which had swept the board at the 1914 French Grand Prix, had got stuck in England at the beginning of the war, and that it still rested in the Mercedes showrooms in Long Acre in London. I could hardly credit the truth of this story, but thought that it ought to be investigated. So I told Briggs about it, and together we went along, representing the British Crown so to speak, with a 'search warrant'. The place was in a fine old mess, but down in the basement, half covered with sacking and old crates, lay the truth behind the story I had heard: a $4\frac{1}{2}$-litre Grand Prix Mercedes! We had it dug out, and soon it was being taken to pieces at the works of the people Briggs thought would make best use of it—Rolls-Royce at Derby.

It is common knowledge that all Rolls-Royce aero engines built during World War I owed quite a lot to this engine; in fact, Mercedes is reputed to have sent a facetious invoice to Derby while the war was at its height demanding a royalty payment. But that is doubtless an apocryphal story!

Stemming from their knowledge of the Mercedes Grand Prix engine (itself derived from Mercedes's early aero engines), and from their use of the aluminium piston, the Eagle was a brilliant success. Besides the pistons, its merit lay in the cooling and arrangement of their cylinders, in the design of the cylinders themselves, and, of course, as in all R-R products, in the detail design and workmanship which made them wonderfully reliable. The V12, 1,240-cu. in. engine had cylinders machined from steel forgings and spherical-shaped combustion chambers in which the valves were seated in the heads and surrounded by thin steel water jackets, also welded. This design gave excellent and really efficient cooling.

This may have been quite heavy and also expensive to manufacture but it represented a great advance, and accounted for the superiority of many of the Rolls-Royce aero engines during World War I, which in some of their final series were producing up to 400 b.h.p. Later on, Renault followed the same practice with their aero engines.

Word of the aluminium piston spread further. From Derby I went to Sunbeams at Wolverhampton where, because I knew the squat, jovial little Louis Coatalen well, the talk was on a more informal level. 'Bentley,' he said with a puckish grin, when I had finished, 'Bentley, you're one of the best salesmen I've ever met. I wouldn't have believed it could work, but I'll take your word for it.'

Louis did; and it was used in all the Sunbeam aero engines too.

. . . . .

Motoring did not entirely cease for me with the war, and I had some pleasant and amusing drives, especially during the early years. I had my 12–40 at first. In this I often went to Coventry from the Admiralty in London, and sometimes made the journey in under two hours, not a bad time even in the 1960s, with M1 to help—which shows that the little D.F.P. was no sluggard. But I made the trip so frequently and with rather less care for the engine than I should have done that I eventually put a con.

rod through the crank-case at Stony Stratford. That this did not happen earlier was a remarkable tribute to the durability of that fine old car.

Another car I ran during the 1914–18 war was an open, four-seater Cadillac V8 which I bought after I damaged my D.F.P. This was a very remarkable machine in many ways. It had a huge wooden steering wheel, and was very expensive on petrol at a time when this was rather scarce, although as I was working for a Government department this should not have unduly worried me. The Cadillac was one of the most flexible cars in top gear that I have ever driven and was astonishingly quiet. While some firms today boast that the passengers in their cars can hear only the clock at 100 m.p.h., the only mechanical sound from a Cadillac at a very creditable top speed was its fan. I used to love to take it to Derby and, starting in top gear, drive it at a slow walking pace round the Rolls-Royce works to show off its flexibility. This was really only a leg-pull, but it used to exasperate those present.

The engine dimensions were 79 × 130 mm, giving a capacity of 5,100 c.c., and it was, I believe, among the first V8s the Americans produced. The widely spaced three-speed gearbox was in unit with the engine, which was 'three-point suspended', forward by a ball-and-socket bearing. It had a three-bearing crankshaft, and a single central camshaft with eight cams, each operating two valves. Tungsten steel exhaust valves and tulip-shaped inlet valves were other interesting features, as was the two-cylinder tyre pump fitted at the front end of the dynamotor shaft, which included an oil-separating chamber to 'prevent oil being carried into the tyres with air'—a sensible enough precaution.

To drive in the Cadillac alone with the hood down was a strange sensation rather like navigating an empty barge along a canal. Its body was truly vast and with let-down seats that increased the passenger accommodation to seven. The detail work and standards of bodywork finish did not perhaps quite match up to its mechanical refinement, but the Cadillac did have its merits even if its petrol consumption was scarcely patriotic.

Then there was that other, and equally unusual American, the Franklin which I drove a lot at this time. Franklin was producing air-cooled six-cylinder cars half a century before General Motor's controversial Corvair; and this was how the contemporary advertising ran: 'How does "Franklin air-cooling" make a more powerful engine, and an abler car for less money?' and answered its own question, 'By creating a more efficient temperature in the combustion chambers than is possible in any other engine. By also getting rid of weight. By saving repair cost and weight cost, and by giving more day's work in a year.' Good sense, too!

The Franklin, which belonged to 'E' Section of the Admiralty, was a very pleasant motor, though its performance was negligible considering the size of its engine. It was also, I believed, very expensive for its time. It was cooled by a huge fan set in the flywheel, which drew air between the fine vertical cooling fins and the cylinders of sheet metal round the cylinders themselves. This cooling system was completely satisfactory and must have been a great advantage in the northern United States in winter weather. But the fan moaned rather, as it tends to do on all air-cooled cars, though why no one has got round this problem I cannot imagine. The Franklin had overhead valves operated by push rods and it had a wooden frame with huge full elliptic springs fore and aft.

·   ·   ·   ·   ·

The next sailing orders, for the rawest, most untrained commissioned officer in the service, took me up river to Chiswick, to the Gwynne factory, not far from my old National Motor Cab works.

Gwynnes were later known for that nice little car, the 'Eight', but at that time—as they do today—they specialised in marine and water pumps. They had, however, been astute and far-sighted enough to obtain the concession for the French Clerget aero engine just before the war and were then engaged in turning these out in large numbers for Sopwiths and Nieuports. Here I was to act as another link in the chain between the manufacturer and the Admiralty, for whom they were working under contract, and put in hand experimental work that would lead to the substitution of aluminium for iron pistons in the Clerget. 'They're to do what you tell 'em to do,' Briggs had told me, a simple enough brief which I received unsuspectingly.

Neville Gwynne, the good-looking chairman, appeared to welcome me. I gathered he was a man who had to be treated circumspectly, and I was a shade uncertain whether I should be able to command the tact and patience that would be called for. I was to deal more closely with Armitage, the works manager, and he was an easier proposition; I never had any trouble with him. Then

there was Aslin, Petty Officer Aslin, the senior of my staff of two.
Aslin, who was with me from the beginning to the end, was a gift
from the gods, a tremendous worker whom, even in those high-
pressure days, I found I had to hold back sometimes. He dedicated himself entirely to his job, never took any leave, and yet was
always tactful and cheerful. One meets these extraordinary men
from time to time, I find, and I count it as one of my blessings
that chance sent Aslin to me at a time when I desperately needed
his extraordinary qualities.

The Clerget was a rotary, a new form of aero engine to this
country, and one which at once caught my excited interest. The
rotary had a number of advantages over the more orthodox in-
line, radial or V-form engines. In a fighter the power/weight
ratio, coupled with reliability, is everything, and the rotary was—
and still is—the lightest form of piston aero engine for any given
capacity. Because of this it is not necessary to force up the power
output unduly with a high compression, and this of course gives it
great reliability. At that time one of the rotary's advantages also
created its own chief failing. The tip of a Clerget rotary was
doing about 150 m.p.h. at cruising revs, and in order to reduce
weight and centrifugal force loads the cylinders were finned and
made of very thin steel. This was splendid for cooling one side
of the cylinder, but the trailing edge, lacking the benefit of this
airstream, became so hot that it caused distortion. The French
got round this—or imagined they had—by fitting an obturator
piston ring, which was rather like a leather washer in a bicycle
pump, but made of a light alloy. It was very thin, very fragile and
very unreliable; and when it broke the piston seized at once. They
were giving a life of around fifteen hours in France, and this was
an expensive way to try to gain air supremacy over the Western
Front.

This wasn't the only trouble they were having at Gwynnes,
and the realisation that human lives were at stake began to worry
my conscience soon after I arrived. It is amazing how easy it is
to forget the responsibility you carry in a job far from the fighting line, involved in the day-to-day detail of your work and
cushioned by the normal comforts of home life in the evening. So
I was glad when the chance came to go out to France to see things
at first hand; and that first visit certainly had a profound effect on
my outlook, on my attitude to the war and to the men who were
fighting it, on my work on the weapons we were providing them

with, and I think, too, on the very fundamentals of my engineering philosophy.

The instructions I received were cryptic: we were losing far too many pilots through mechanical failures, and the cause was believed to be found in the wrist pins which were seizing up on the Clerget. I was to visit the squadrons near Dunkerque to investigate. I left Chiswick at once and arrived in France in a destroyer within a few hours.

This was the first of dozens of visits I made over the next three years. When the war began, there were two distinct and separately administered air arms, the R.N.A.S. and the R.F.C., under the Admiralty and War Office respectively. The factories, the story went, were split between the two by tossing a coin, and from the way things turned out this might even have been true. Anyway Gwynnes went to the R.N.A.S., nearly all of whose fighter and scout units were Clerget-powered in 1915; and it was to R.N.A.S. squadrons, stationed mainly between Ypres and Dunkerque, that most of my visits were made.

Feeling between the air arms was not too good and their relationship was soured by petty jealousies and rivalry that extended right up through the ranks and was nurtured by the false absurdity of the division. The R.N.A.S. squadrons seemed to me to be less smart, but they had better mechanics than the R.F.C., and on the whole I found them easier to work with.

Captain Charles Lamb was C.-in-C. of the R.N.A.S. overseas, a remarkably handsome, clean-cut man with iron-grey hair, whose H.Q. was at Marlo outside Dunkerque. In all my visits I found him consistently kind—almost fatherly—helpful and co-operative, and he never refused me anything for which I asked and always backed me 100% in any inter-departmental tiffs. I never understood why everyone called him cold, severe and difficult to approach (though all agreed that he was a magnificent commander), and no one could understand why he was so fatherly to me.

The formality of dinner in the mess with Lamb—an equally handsome Alsatian dog at his side—was frequently broken by shell-fire from a long-range German gun some twenty-seven miles away.

Under Lamb was Frank McClean, a young Commander and a less formidable and perhaps more cheerful figure than his senior, who had virtually started the R.N.A.S. with his own money some years earlier, when the Wright brothers were considered mythical figures and Louis Bleriot's effort a fluke or a fraud.

My trips always began at Marlo, and from there I travelled out to the various R.N.A.S. squadrons who were using our engines, talking to squadron commanders, pilots and mechanics freely, and getting at once from men who had just landed from reconnaissance flights or dog-fights detailed information on faults, and sorting out possible cures on the spot. This wasn't simply a time-saving convenience; the personal contact benefited both sides, the pilots feeling that they were dealing with at least well-intentioned and not entirely ignorant human beings instead of frustrating bureaucratic machines, while I was all the better for being (as I always was) frightened or moved—and impressed by the human element in our search for reliability and performance.

Sometimes it was quiet enough at the airfields, and I pulled engines to pieces, talked and drank, and was momentarily drawn into the squadrons' lives. At other times, when perhaps the Germans or the Allies were thrusting forward another few yards in some great offensive and the pilots were flying three or four missions a day, it was sheer hell. There was no romance about fighter work on the Western Front then, with five from one flight spiralling down in flames without parachutes, as happened on one visit; with grief, courage and fear thrown together in hectic drunken parties among the survivors in the evening; and with a fresh set of faces at every airfield on every visit, the previous ones already as dim and forlorn as in a fading group photograph. A visit to the squadrons was a drastic and positive cure for any lurking complacency.

I saw little of the fighting and was hardly ever in any real danger, though once or twice I thought I was. I should have gone on a bomber raid in a Handley-Page after dinner one night if my machine hadn't been unserviceable. Instead I went out in the moonlight to watch the others return, to meet a storm of screaming bombs. The cunning Hun had mixed in with our Handley-Pages and, guided by the landing-lights, pasted us to such good effect that the squadron were reduced to landing on the beach; a forerunner of the 'intruders' of the 1940s, proving again that there's nothing new in warfare!

There was often shelling, too. I was having a quiet cup of tea outside with the Canadian fighter ace, Mulock, one afternoon, when every gun in Flanders seemed to open up on us. Mulock, I noticed out of the corner of my eye, never stirred; Big Bertha herself could have gone off under his deck-chair and he wouldn't have spilt a drop. Then there was the occasional strafing, which always set the place buzzing like a stirred-up wasps' nest. The adjoining canal seemed to be the only retreat left to me when a Fokker came over one day, and after a terrific hundred-yard sprint with the bullets dancing behind me, in I went with a splash and huddled under the overhanging bank. The plane's next run across the airfield brought me company in the shape of Petty Officer Clarke, and side by side Bentley Motors' future head racing mechanic and I huddled among the rushes, teeth chattering. The pilot who sent us there, and helped to seal a warm friendship, was Baron von Richtofen himself. I almost felt a pang of regret when Brown in a Camel, powered by one of our B.R.1s, caught. him at last a year or two later.

I did fly sometimes, but, it appeared, never before they were assured there wasn't a Hun in the sky, and I was only really frightened once. This was on my first trip across the Channel, the one on which I was ordered because of the engine seizures, and which led up to this diversion from my account of the Gwynne factory.

Frank McClean took Aslin[1] and me to one of the squadrons having trouble with their Nieuports.

'Thank the Lord someone's doing something about this,' the C.O. greeted me. 'Flying the damn things is suicide.' He had already lost some of his best pilots so I could easily understand his abrupt manner.

We went off right away to work on one of the engines in the hangar, and after a few hours Aslin and I thought we had done the trick. I was wiping my hands on a bit of waste when the C.O. came up and asked us how we were getting on.

'I wouldn't mind going anywhere in this now,' I said wildly.

'Let's try and see then,' he said—without malice, even with a trace of merriment. 'You can go up on the dawn patrol tomorrow if you like.'

Some basic combat training would have helped in this situation, for I had never left the ground before, fired a shot in anger, nor even seen a Lewis gun, with which I was supposed to defend us from the roaming packs of Fokkers.

1. Poor Aslin was the most sea-sick petty officer in the Navy. He survived two trips and then I took pity on him and left him behind.

To the accompaniment of plenty of good-natured ribbing, I was instructed in the fundamentals of my weapon, dressed up like one of Scott's party, and put into the rear cockpit. We took off, turned into the rising sun, and made for the lines. I was convinced that the whole German Air Force was up there to meet us; the air was thick with planes, many of them under fire from anti-aircraft guns, and I prepared myself to swing the Lewis round from side to side in defence against the inevitable diving attack. I will swear to this day that I really did spot a black-crossed Fokker, but before I could do anything about it my pilot swung away and we went out to sea.

I had plenty of time to think about the icy water 5,000 feet below, waiting to receive me if we had been slipshod in our work the night before. There was a very strong head wind, and we seemed to take hours to get back, and the rough landing nearly finished me off. I struggled out of the cockpit a shivering wreck, trying to assume an air of calm, while the pilots clustered round, uttering wisecracks.

All that was quite good fun-and-games, but there was nothing humorous about what I found when we opened up the engine to assure ourselves that all was still well. Three of the con. rods were blue from the heat—their life could be measured in minutes.

To me the consequences of that discovery were profound, and from then on the appalling sense of responsibility hung over me and never left me for the rest of the war, the figure of a pilot killed by engine failure leaning over my shoulder, like some ghostly conscience, whenever I was at work.

.   .   .   .   .

The routine at Chiswick was ceaseless and gruelling, and for months on end I returned home useless for any sort of social life, and a poor companion to my wife in the brief moments when I saw her. It would have been something if I could have reserved all my energies for engineering, but any engineer who has tried will tell you how impossible this is. In spite of the position of authority I occupied, I was soon neck-deep in the politics, manœuvrings and jealousies that arise when an outsider is let into the design department. I managed to persuade Gwynnes to raise the compression, and, because they were ordered to, they accepted the aluminium piston, but I met a series of carefully contrived obstructions when I tried to improve the obturator ring and incorporate a cylinder with good conductivity formed of aluminium with a cast-iron liner shrunk into it which would equalise the temperature. This, I was convinced, would solve the major unbalanced heating problem in a rotary engine. But at this stage I think Gwynnes thought they were being led into an entirely new design to my specifications, which would mean dropping the French Clerget rotary. Besides, they were also occupied with a new rotary of their own, for which they had brought over a designer from France.

Gwynnes would, in fact, rather drop me than their Clerget, and they made this so amply clear that I was forced to put my case to Briggs.

Briggs knew what I was after; he knew, even before my call, that I was anxious to get ahead with my own rotary design; but, as tactful as ever, he suggested that I should return to Chiswick, work on one piston and cylinder to my specification and fit it to a Clerget to prove my case. Both as an engineering and diplomatic proposition, this required patience and ingenuity, but the results were as satisfactory to me as they were disturbing to Gwynnes.

I won't dwell on the tiresome consequences of the experiment, but I was soon back at the Admiralty to ask to be removed from Chiswick and to be allowed to develop my own aero engine design elsewhere. I thought for a while that Briggs was temporising, but he was only letting the clutch in slowly; soon the wheels were turning, and I was summoned back to his office and given my new orders.

'You're to take your bags to Coventry, Bentley,' he told me. 'Humbers have got all the facilities you'll want. They're only churning out Army bicycles—thousands and thousands of them —and terrible things like travelling kitchens. I think they're rather offended that they haven't been given something more challenging to test their mettle, so they'll welcome you with open arms.'

Briggs was right. Earl Russell, the Chairman (and Bertrand Russell's elder brother), Wright, in charge of the fitting shop, and Crundle, the chief tester, were bored stiff with the commonplace trivialities on their production lines and were delighted at the prospect of having an entirely new and exciting thing to get their teeth into. And so, of course, was Burgess, whom I had known in racing before the war. I was to have a lot to do with F. T. Burgess, head designer at Humbers—and draughtsman supreme. I soon recognised that we talked the same language, understood and appreciated the same things, and that he was a man in a thousand to have on design work. He had the most facile pencil of any man I have known, a pencil that flashed across the board in deft strokes, expressing in lines our ideas as quickly as the words were spoken. It was a wonderful sight to watch and the magic of it never failed to impress me, from those aero-engine days to the 'twenties when we worked together on the 3-, $4\frac{1}{2}$- and $6\frac{1}{2}$-litre Bentleys.

The other two with whom we were to be in close touch were the works manager, Niblett, a pleasant man who lacked only enthusiasm and what we considered a proper faith in rotaries; and Meason, the assistant works manager, a gay little live-wire of a man, bright, amusing and dead keen, about as strong a contrast to Niblett as you could imagine.

We settled down to work at once in the well-equipped drawing office, together with Aslin and his assistant, whom I had brought with me from Chiswick, and the first thing we did with our plans was to re-draw them. We were confident that the 120 $\times$ 162 mm nine-cylinder rotary was ahead of anything the Germans had; but in war you've got to be two steps ahead of the enemy, and at that time our air supremacy on the Western Front was very much in the balance. The new design, which we intended should leap-frog the 120 $\times$ 160 mm., was basically similar but larger and more powerful, with an anticipated output of over 200 h.p. With the design completed, I went to Briggs with the drawings.

He looked at me doubtfully. 'You're asking to run before you've shown you can walk,' he said.

I used all my persuasive powers, certain that we should go the whole way, and I think he agreed with me. But he was thinking of 'their Lordships', who had consented only reluctantly and under pressure to allow me to make a start at all.

'Let's see the first one running, then I'll do what I can,' he told me.

There were no greater difficulties in the design of the larger than the smaller engine; they were fundamentally similar. If the fighter squadrons had received the first batch of B.R.2s[1] in early 1917 instead of 1918 it is even possible that the war might have

---

1. Bentley Rotary. It was earlier given the less unromantic tags, 'The Bentley' and 'The Admiralty'. The final order for B.R.2s was 30,000.

been shortened. But that was not to be, and I went back to Coventry trying to console myself that I supposed we were lucky to have got the green light at all.

Harassed by Russell (as if we needed any spurring on!), we got the prototype on the test-bed by the early summer of 1916. Cracks were made later—which bothered me at the time—that the B.R.1 was an imitation Clerget. These originated from people who glanced only at the cam. mechanism, which of course was the first thing they saw and, for ease of production, was the only similar feature, and were probably incapable of differentiating even if they had bothered to look further. In fact the crank-case, crankshaft, method of securing the cylinders themselves as well as their heads, were all fundamentally different from the Clerget.

We had the usual early setbacks but they were mercifully few. After watching one of the prototype's runs until I was ready to drop, I went home to the King's Head Hotel where I lived in Coventry. I understood later why we had so many complaints of noise from the factory, for on that night the B.R.1's roar seemed to fill the streets, and it followed me up to my room and hummed in my ears as I tried to go to sleep. I must have dozed off momentarily because the next thing I remember was sitting up with a start, suddenly aware of a horrible silence.

I was back at the works in a few minutes, to find that a valve had broken. I saw that the repair work was carried out and retired, only to be woken up again. Again it was that valve, which was lasting just three hours; and again I went back to bed, wondering what we could do to remedy this fault.

Once more I dragged myself from my bed that night, and this time it was a case of third time unlucky. There was a serious crack round the flange where the induction pipes were bolted on to the cylinder—a fault to be overcome but hardly one to justify Russell's horrified exclamation the next morning.

'I hear your engine's burst!' he greeted me.

'What on earth do you mean?' I asked. 'It's nothing that can't be fixed in a few days.'

Well, we did cure the trouble, and the valve failures were solved by considerably lightening them. There were no more snags, and the B.R.1 was ready for the Admiralty Inspector (none other than the helpful S. C. H. 'Sammy' Davis) by the late summer and in production by the autumn. Later we raised the compression so that the Camels got more speed at heights above 10,000 feet;

and the only other modification we made originated from something of a mystery. One of the later experimental engines gave
more power than it should have done, and after taking it to pieces
and looking it over, we found a small leak in one of the induction
pipes. Secretly, and feeling rather like vandals, we drilled a 2-mm
hole in the top casting of the induction pipe in another engine—
and up went the power by 11 h.p. We sent the word round, and
fitters on every B.R. squadron were soon busy with little 2-mm.
drills.

With the success of the B.R.1 proved, Briggs got authority for
us to go ahead with the bigger unit without my having to ask him.
It was a comparatively simple operation to get the prototype
B.R.2 ready, the principle of the two designs being similar and
many of the parts interchangeable. All this became too big for
Humbers to cope with, so the Daimler factory was made the
B.R.2 headquarters to co-ordinate the huge construction programme, and Crossleys, Humbers and several other firms all became involved. The B.R.2 was in production for the new Sopwith
Snipes by the early spring of 1918, and output was running at
more than 120 a week by the summer.

All through the development and testing period I tried to keep
up my regular liaison visits to the squadrons. The pilots and
mechanics still depended on these for passing on any grouses or
suggestions, and though a few people tried to break up this
irregular state of affairs, I always had Captain Lamb behind me,
while Briggs turned the traditional naval blind eye. The only
time I got into serious trouble was when I short-circuited the
supply line.

I was over in France on 4 Squadron's airfield when I was
horrified to hear that four of their aircraft had failed to return.
Engine failure was suspected, and then news came in that two
of the machines had come down in fields—luckily on our side of
the line—and two on the beach. I dashed off at once to the nearest
one on the sands near Dunkerque and asked the discomfited pilot
what the trouble was.

Actually the diagnosis was straightforward: the spring in the
oil pump, which was made outside for us, was too hard and had
broken under pressure. With the old phantom spurring me on,
I raced back that afternoon, was at the factory in the evening, and
—with the magnificent co-operation of the foreman and his men
—had them at work on new springs by nightfall. They worked

right through the night on correctly tempered substitutes, copper-plated for recognition, and I was away with a suitcase of them in time to catch the train back to Town and the morning destroyer. The men on the squadron thought I had pulled some sort of trick on them.

The row began when the accounts department at the Admiralty received an invoice for the springs which lacked the usual authority reference of the Admiralty Inspector, and then everything had to come out. A letter was followed by an interview; I was really on the mat, reminded that I was subject to naval discipline, etc., etc. How had I got them over to France? In a *suitcase*? What authority did I have to use the destroyer, which was intended for . . .?

. . . . .

The great German last-fling offensive had expired and the weight of the Allied blows was at last making cracks in the enemy line. It was the summer of 1918; the B.R.2 was in full production. Briggs had been superseded in the big upheaval following the formation of the R.A.F., and his successor had pinned his faith to a new air-cooled radial engine which was intended to supplement the B.R.2 and had been put into hasty production, so hasty in fact that there was urgent need for new experimental work on it. I was asked to take over this post-production experimental work at the factory.

The new radial engine, I discovered, caught fire easily, was unreliable and ran far short on its power test at Farnborough. I didn't like it, and told my new C.O. what I thought of it.

'Bentley,' he said, 'I think you're just tired. And in any case it's natural for you to feel a certain prejudice.'

His first statement was all too true; the second made me so angry that it's a wonder that I ever got out of his office without committing violence.

That the war ended in November, before this radial reached the squadrons in any numbers, was merciful; and that my fears for it were realised gave me no satisfaction. It still succeeded in killing several good men, among them the brilliant test pilot, H. G. Hawker. His engine caught fire and he went straight in.

I was sent on leave before the armistice and, after a last tour of the squadrons, returned to Netherhall Gardens and my wife, suffering a good deal from the reaction. I was still nominally a two-ringer (possibly the longest-serving junior officer then, and certainly now, for I was never officially demobilised), my personnel of only two disqualifying me from promotion. That was all right, but the very low pay, on which I had to keep myself and a home going, had been a bit hard, and at one time I had had to appeal to Briggs for some assistance. The £1,000 tax-free gratuity he found for me helped things out, but no one could call me a war profiteer.

Money raised an uglier head two years later when I was invited to make a claim by the Royal Commission on Awards for the invention of the B.R.1 and B.R.2. My counsel was Douglas Hogg, K.C., later Lord Hailsham, and to back my case General Brooke-Popham and Sir William Brancker were there to give evidence to Mr. Justice Sargant and his Commission that the B.R.s were considerably superior to any other rotary used in the war and that it 'had improved both the strength and morale of the squadrons. Briggs was there to give support, too, and so were various other senior officers and much-decorated pilots. The opposition's claim was that, as a serving officer, I was merely carrying out my duties; and there was strong intervention from Gwynnes, too, who considered that they qualified for any award made as the original design had been conceived on their premises.

It was a beastly and tiresome business, the sort of situation at which I am not at my best, and after interminable delays I was granted £8,000—to the disgust of my counsel, who considered it such a niggardly pittance that he drastically reduced his fee, which would otherwise have about halved what I received. The last straw was the Inland Revenue's insistence that the claim was taxable, and this made me so angry that I determined to fight it. It was to be a test case, but a few days before it was due to be heard they capitulated. I was so disgusted by then that I don't think I even celebrated!

I had been married four and a half years but had seen very little of my wife during all this time. That her mother lived near her had helped, and when the Zeppelin bombing was at its worst (a high, steady barometer was an almost infallible indication of raids) I used to take the train down from Coventry in the evening, spend the night in Hampstead and return again in the morning. I now looked forward to some peace and quiet, and then with the war over—as it must be any day now—to preparing our plans for the formation of the company to produce the car we had been dreaming of for three years . . . even roughing out a few plans with Burgess as an occasional relaxation from the hurly-burly of rotaries at Coventry.

But if it held off its last blow for a few months, the war had not finished with me yet. Before my plans had materialised, before we had really got anywhere with our car, my wife died in the great Spanish 'flu epidemic that swept over shattered Europe.

CHAPTER SIX

Three-Litres

THE hospital matron was standing in the loft doorway, hands on hips, a formidable and displeased figure. 'Go and see what she wants,' I asked Gallop when I caught sight of her.

He came back in a few moments, a wry smile on his lips. Heaven knows how he had heard the indignant message he passed on to me through cupped hands: 'She says we're to stop this row at once. There's a man ill next door.'

'Tell her to go away,' I shouted back. What was the illness of one man? In here the birth of a new engine was taking place. 'A happy sound to die to—the exhaust roar of the first 3-litre Bentley engine!' someone remarked with awful irreverence later.

We gave it twenty minutes on the bench; then I told Nobby Clarke to switch off, and the gentle hum of traffic in Baker Street seemed a thousand miles away. Perhaps the poor man was really ill, though I fear my conscience wasn't struck till later. On that exciting morning in October, 1919, I had too many things on my mind.

.   .   .   .   .   .

On 20th January, 1919, Harry Varley, Burgess and I had sat down with nothing but a few bits of paper and some ideas in a small office on the top floor of a building in Conduit Street. There, to my instructions and to the accompaniment of endless technical talk, they had worked for nine months with hardly a break on the drawings of the design.

The seeds of it all had, of course, been sown during the war when I had decided that it just wasn't going to be enough for me to return to the agency business, profitable though it had been, and would be again. The creative instinct is strong in most engineers, and, just as I hadn't been satisfied for long to work on someone else's rotary engine, so I had to produce my own car.

79

Briefly, and without getting too technical, what I had in mind was a bigger engine than the D.F.P.'s, which was a good and sound little unit, but there was a limit to how much you could push it; it was not, in fact, a natural power-giver. An engine with overhead valves, and enough of them, a capacity of 3 litres, would be about right, so that we should not have to force it too much to start with; a reliable unit which would require the minimum of maintenance and would stand up to long distances at high speed.

It was possible in those days to drive long distances at high speed in this country, but it was with a particular eye on Continental roads that the 3-litre was designed. French roads in the 1920s were as straight, and as long, as they are today, but their surface was often appalling and at the same time there was a great temptation to drive fast. What we were aiming at was a car that could be pushed all day long at sixty or more miles an hour over almost any sort of road surface.

Many of the British designs at this time were perfectly all right for local trips and for pottering around. But pressed for any length of time, for perhaps a half-dozen laps round Brooklands at full throttle, and the low top gear and poor cooling would result in burnt-out valves or seized pistons. But the D.F.P. had shown me what could be done, in the French manner. I was determined that the 3-litre should stand up to long punishment, and for this each cylinder should have four valves, not too big, and with water all round for cooling. Equally important was to have water circulating closely round the plugs and cylinders, and, of course, a sensibly high top gear.

At the same time, this car, I decided, should sacrifice none of the merits of the good British touring car of the day. We made no attempt at originality or unorthodoxy in the 3-litre. This was impossible as well as undesirable because we had very little money for experimental work and no development department at all. We knew from the outset that we should have to take the best of what other people had done before us. But we also knew that we must not copy blindly, for that would have been fatal, however good the original product. 'We must take every little bit of every other product,' we told ourselves, 'examine it minutely and ask ourselves: "Why did they do it like this? Why didn't they do it like that?" "Ah yes, they were forced to do this because of so and so. It would have been fatal if they had done anything else." ' In this way we got a fascinating analytical view of the processes of thought that had resulted in a certain design feature in other engines. We simply did the logical thing and took it one stage further.

In the design of the 3-litre two distinguished motor cars influenced us more than any others. These were Henri's 1912 Peugeot and the 1914 Grand Prix Mercedes. I got to know a lot about the Mercedes engine when I used to visit Rolls-Royce at Derby. Our arrangement of the valve gear was rather similar to that used by Mercedes, driving through bevels to a single camshaft. The difference between the Mercedes layout and ours can be seen in these diagrams:

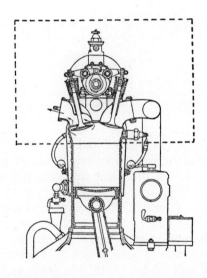

This had the advantage of direct action on the valves without the use of rockers, and the fact that you could put the plug in or near the centre of the crown or the hemispherical combustion space. We should have liked to follow Peugeot with twin overhead camshafts and a valve gear like this:

F

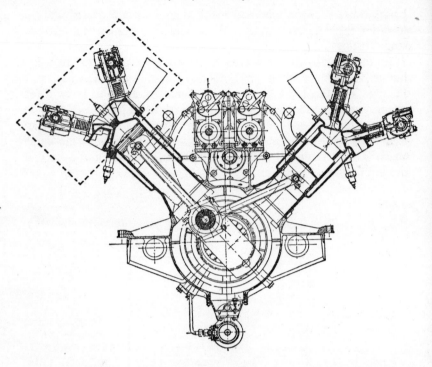

This was both more complicated and more efficient because there was less valve gear reciprocating weight and you could get your plug in the centre. On the debit side, though, two gear-driven camshafts at that time were rather noisy, and we were very conscious of the noise factor in what was to be essentially a touring car. As a result we had to use two plugs, one on each side, to get the same results. Later, more satisfactory camshaft drive methods than the train of gears which always chattered so noisily were discovered, and we felt justified in going back to twin chain-drive o.h.c. with the 2½-litre Lagonda.

Another thing we owed to the Mercedes was the bevel drive to the camshaft. The use of separate steel forgings in the welded-up ports and water jackets was not used, and the design of the cylinder block, which had several cover plates enabling you to be sure that the water passages were clear and free from sand, was our own idea. The lower half of the engine was our own original design, too, for which we owed nothing to anyone.

The gearbox was pretty straightforward, but later we had to

supply different ratios for different purposes when people started using the car for work for which it was never intended. Later still, Burgess and I had a go at synchromesh. We used the same principle of frictional synchronisation that later became so popular but we never got beyond the sketching stage. We still had no time for development and it would have taken years for just the two of us to get it right with the amount of time we could have devoted to it.

We also toyed at one stage with four-wheel hydraulic brakes. We didn't go as far as the brake shoe; our aim was to get equal pressure on all four wheels and we did work out a self-adjusting arrangement. But we were far too engrossed in other things to be able to spare the time. Instead we had to content ourselves with elaborating the Perrot principle which we eventually adopted.

For suspension, we were quite orthodox, with semi-elliptic front springing and a decent-length back spring for the open propeller shaft. Until the arrival of independent front suspension we suffered in common with everyone else from the limited travel we could allow the front springs.

Mercedes had used a torque tube, Peugeot an open carden shaft which took the torque on the back spring, a principle which we followed.

I have an all too clear memory of my first run in the prototype 3-litre in 1919. I was quite appalled by the noise; that was my first and most lasting impression. If you glance at the end of this book at the first road test of this car you will see that S. C. H. 'Sammy' Davis of *The Autocar*, who carried out this test, also referred in the kindest terms to this question of noise. The oil pump was the chief culprit, but, while I expected trouble here, I never thought it would make the din that half deafened me on that first trip. We had a form of dry sump lubrication in which the oil was pumped under pressure to the bearings by one pump and a second scavenge pump emptied the oil out of the sump and up into the tank on the dashboard. The gears of those pumps made a quite incredible noise.

Of course, everything made more noise in those days, a fact which is so easy to forget. The reasons for this were the permitted tolerances and the fact that the standard of machining, gear-cutting and general quality of design were all vastly inferior to what we expect today. Also, the actual mountings of the bevel gears, often through ignorance, were not sufficiently rigid, and the result of being off the correct pitch line was a terrible sort of hammering action. Believe it or not, I think that noise is one of the biggest enemies a designer has to fight; and I have spent a good many years in the field of battle, so I should know!

And what about the other things that struck me on that first run? I was pleased with the steering on the whole, and I think the 3-litre always had pleasantly light and precise steering considering the weight of the car and the year of its birth. The suspension, on the other hand, seemed far less satisfactory, and I knew we were going to have to work a lot on that. I was also pleased with the gearbox which never in fact gave serious trouble, and I found the car pleasant to handle through the corners and good on the road. Rather surprisingly, I also found that it was quite tractable in traffic. The brakes, on the other hand, were very noisy, chiefly because we used cast-iron shoes at first, but because of the unusually large drums they were very effective.

·   ·   ·   ·   ·

The market I had in mind for this car, which seemed likely to be as neglected as it had been before the war, was the fast sporting one. If the capital could be found, I thought we could meet it as successfully as we had between 1912 and 1914 with the D.F.P. The policy was a simple one. We were going to make a fast car, a good car, the best in its class; and when we had begun to show a profit and had obtained our own machine shop, then we would make a smaller, cheaper car—a bread-and-butter car in fact— as well.

Burgess, of course, I had known and worked with for years, and I have already told of his deftness and accuracy as a draughtsman. As hard a worker, as useful and with an even better theoretical knowledge, Harry Varley had been with Vauxhall and had done much good work there. These two worked on the drawing-board together, always efficiently, though later on perhaps rather less happily at times when their artistic temperaments got the better of them.

For several months Bentley Motors consisted of the three of us, while H.M. continued to look after D.F.P., making the money we were going to need. And he made a lot of it, about £20,000 in the first roaring boom twelve months after the armistice. Conditions were the same as they were in the late 1940s, with everybody wanting cars, everybody with money, and anybody who could turn out something with four wheels and an engine making it at a feverish rate. H.M. even had a relay of drivers working from the French factory, racing chassis as fast as they could go to the Channel ports.

This boom was all very nice, while it lasted, but it had an unsettling effect on us. It obviously couldn't last, and we wanted to be in on at least the tail end of it—which inevitably led to haste and frayed nerves. As we completed drawings for one part, so we had it made, a risky procedure we had to follow to save time. Anyone who has tried to make motor cars—or anything else for that matter—in boom times will know all about the frustrations and headaches involved in getting materials and in having anything made. With a four-year backlog to make up everyone had full order books, and there was hardly a factory in Britain seeking or even ready to welcome new customers. Here was our first difficulty. The second was not only much greater but almost inconceivable to anyone in the motor-car business today. We had to have *everything* made: gearbox, clutch, differential, bearings, stub axles—everything. There were no proprietary makes we could draw on, no ready-made back axles, no gearboxes, no universal joints complete with cardan shaft and so on. To design and build a new motor car in 1919 without substantial capital was like being cast on to a desert island with a penknife and orders to build a house.

The only people we could get to help us were at a works in Bristol. A man there called Peter Purves was wonderful at getting our stuff through, whipping the bits out by a compound of zeal, determination and bullying so efficiently that we decided we must have him for ourselves. 'Come and bustle for us,' I asked him one day. 'As a sort of liaison officer.' And he agreed. Purves had all the right qualifications—diplomacy, the ability to mix well, and intelligence. He became the company buyer later and stayed with us to the end.

As things progressed we had to get in more help, and next came Clive Gallop on the design side. Gallop had fought in France with the R.F.C. as a pilot. He had driven at Brooklands and—even more attractive to me—had worked for Peugeots. We had talked engines for hours in the past, in the same language and with identical enthusiasm, the first time on a train to the Midlands, and I think he had been half expecting the invitation I sent him in the summer of 1919. It was Gallop who helped to evolve the cam-shaft of the first 3-litre.

Jimmy Enstone was next, ex-Camel pilot, as Company Secretary, and then, with all the blueprints complete and most of the parts made, along came 'Nobby' Clarke. You'll remember our little flight from the Hun in the shape of the strafing Richtofen when we took refuge neck-deep in the water of a French canal; but that wasn't the only occasion on which I had met Nobby. Number 4 Squadron, the first to get B.R.s, was my favourite, and I had had frequent contact with Petty Officer Clarke, the chief mechanic. It was as future head mechanic of Bentley Motors that I had kept my eye on him, and by a piece of happy telepathy or something, he wrote to me from his home in Kent. 'Why don't you call to see us?' I answered his letter of enquiry. 'We need someone to put this engine together.' By September he was doing just that in the loft above the D.F.P. service station in New Street Mews which we had then taken over, and doing it with all the skill and dexterity I had expected from him.

Thanks to high-pressure work and co-operation all round, that engine took shape with remarkable rapidity. There it sat on its roughly knocked-together bench, with its single magneto and large pre-war Claudel racing carburettor, all glinting aluminium and copper, and around it we all assembled, like the members of some sect drawn together to witness an ancient rite.

'Let's try and start it now,' I said to Gallop—and the manner in which it didn't has been told by others so I won't linger over the awful anxiety while Clarke tested the valve timing and fiddled with the carburettor. Benzole did the trick—and at once the three-inch exhaust was bellowing and the straight-tooth gears screaming with enough noise to awaken the dead. . . .

.   .   .   .   .

Well, we were over the first hurdle, but it was a long, long course. The next thing was to get the engine in a chassis and have the married pair ready to be presented at the first post-war Olympia Show in November. We even managed that, after a fashion. The gearbox turned up from Moss Gears, the rear axle, of banjo tubing, from the National Projectile Company, and so on. We tried to get the crank-case out of the Coventry firm who were making it, but they couldn't finish it in time and so we made do with a dummy. The cam casing was of wood, too, and though we had the valves in there was no valve gear. But it still looked quite impressive and created a lot of interest in spite of the fact that we were tucked away in a corner, and some of the more knowledgeable poked about rather embarrassingly. Today you could get away with a ply-wood shell for a motor car, but in those days a lot of people either knew or liked to pretend that they knew something about engineering, and you had to be prepared for technical questions.

That Show was a wild affair, with the hall packed all day, an atmosphere of abandon in the air as the crowds searched for something they could blow their money on. There were people begging to be allowed to put down as much as £200 deposit on the strength of our semi-mock-up: a sellers' market gone berserk. But we weren't having any of their money, badly as we needed it, until we had something more substantial to offer them.

Somewhat breathless as well as encouraged after all this, we took our precious Ex. 1 back to New Street Mews, and then to the D.F.P. showrooms where, as our sole exhibit, it attracted more attention from passers-by in our window.

I thought until I started writing this book that I was the first person to take a Bentley on to the road, but it seems that I was wrong. Clarke tells of a precautionary move to ensure that all was well made by Gallop very early on the morning I was to take her out. There were no seats yet, and Clarke and Gallop packed themselves into a sort of cocoon of warehouse coats, and in some trepidation—and at some 3,000 r.p.m.—made their way out of the Mews into Baker Street in first gear, emitting an ear-splitting row into the still morning air. After a short interval and with the car slowing perceptibly, passenger turned to driver, to discover he had all but disappeared. Most of the coats had wrapped themselves round the exposed prop. shaft, and were about to be joined by Gallop himself. My drive, however, was so uneventful that I can remember nothing at all about it.

The noise was obviously one of the first things we should have to do something about. Some people like it, and there are apparently more of them about today than there were then, but we weren't going to make our fortunes out of people who liked noise; and in any case it offended me. The straight-tooth gears and the scavenger oil pump were the chief culprits, and for the production cars we decided to drop the dry-sump lubrication and

87

go over to orthodox wet sump, though this wasn't altogether satisfactory either, and the 3-litre ended up with a special tank separated entirely from the sump. We also, incidentally, went over to a three-cam cam-shaft with separate exhaust rockers, added a second magneto, and swapped the Claudel for a five-jet Smith.

Three hundred and sixty-seven days—and I record the figure now with some astonishment—after Varley, Burgess and I had our first session, *The Autocar* published its first road test, a highly satisfactory one written in the unmistakable style of 'Sammy' Davis. Besides the richly effective but not altogether relevant adjectives and classical analogies regarding 'speed' in general, the handling, the brakes, the comfort, and especially the sheer performance, were all highly praised, and the noise from the oil-pump drive was forgiven as a fault 'inseparable from the first chassis of a new design'. It stretched over two pages and there were three impressive photographs. How I wished we had had the cars we could have sold a dozen times over as a result of that piece of publicity!

What we probably ought to have done at this stage was to turn out three prototype chassis and use these to find someone to capitalise adequately a new company. Production might then have gone ahead from a properly equipped works where we could have been self-supporting instead of dependent—as we always were—on outside firms. Perhaps that boom can be blamed for our decision to go ahead on our own, struggling for a dozen years to show the profit necessary before we could go to the public and form a public company. We were greedy, I suppose, or perhaps too independently minded. An entire chapter of this book could be written about our financial crises; instead you will find them cropping up like festering boils all through this Bentley Motors period, just as they racked us persistently for twelve years with hardly a moment of peace.

H.M. was at that time trying to get the finances on to some sort of footing that would make it possible for us to build or buy a works, for all we had so far were the drawing-offices in Conduit Street and the little place in New Street Mews. I think almost everyone thought that these ought to be somewhere in the Midlands, where we should be in close touch with the supplying firms on whom we were to be dependent, but I wasn't having that. Put it down to prejudice if you like, and I think my decision was prob-

Previous page: Tourist Trophy, 1922. Frank Clement at Ballig Bridge in the rain

Pit stop during our first 'crack' at Le Mans . . .
. . . and the team cars in 1925. The pits this year were on the other side of the circuit

The end of the journey. This is how 'the slug' looked the next morning after the abortive record-breaking attempt at Montlhery

My first and last drive as riding mechanic. With 'Tim' Birkin at Ards, after the ordeal

1927 Le Mans—the White House Corner crash . . .

. . . and the sole survivor, entering the Savoy for the celebrations

ably a wrong one, but I was insistent that London should be our headquarters—if we could find the right place. This didn't prove easy, and in the end we were reduced to buying a plot of land in Oxgate Lane, Cricklewood, near the Welsh Harp. This was bordered at that time by fields and rolling countryside, and on it we erected a small brick building for the assembly of the next three experimental cars.

The year 1920 was one of some development and much frustration when a deuce of a lot of money went out and none at all came in, and the soft sales situation began very slowly to harden as we were forced to increase our overheads. To build those first cars we had to take on more labour, and more mechanics at Cricklewood meant that we had to have a works manager, while our new experimental department again required someone to manage it.

If we had more than our share of bad luck in those early days, and if we made more mistakes than we ought to have done, we were at least blessed by exceptionally good staff. R. S. Witchell, works manager for the entire life of Bentley Motors, was another R.F.C. man, and I have already told how I met him before the war, and was at school with him at Clifton and later dashed up many a hill after his Straker-Squire. Everybody respected Witchell, and there was never during all his time any labour trouble; he was an ideal man for the job, sound, steady and completely fair-minded. He and Frank Clement, with his light-hearted, devil-may-care attitude to life, made a strongly contrasting but a surprisingly well-matched pair. Clement, too, had been with Straker-Squire, and his racing experience was at least the equal of Witchell's. He looked after the experimental department, later helped on the testing and sales side, and was, of course, always our Number One professional driver.

Then there were the mechanics whom Clarke took on, nearly all as boys: Stan Ivermee, who was to follow me to Rolls-Royce, then to Lagondas; Jack Sopp, one of this country's greatest racing mechanics today; Wally Hassan, now a distinguished engineer; Saunders, father and son; Jackson, Puddephat, Howard, Martin, Pryke, and others all loyal and first-class men, and a credit to Clarke's talent for selection. The young Lord Settrington, today the Duke of Richmond and Gordon, a vigorous supporter of motor racing, came along later to the service station as an ordinary mechanic. It was the only way to learn the engineering business, he sensibly decided, and after we agreed that he should work under an assumed name, he turned up conscientiously with the other men at eight o'clock every morning. It was a long time before rumours began to circulate around the works, and the first suggestion that his secret was out came to him when he was prostrated on the oily floor under a 3-litre's differential. ' 'Ave you 'eard, Charlie?' he overheard. ' 'Ear there's a bloody Lord in 'ere.'

A drawing-office went up at Cricklewood in the autumn, and Varley and Burgess moved into it. The offices were alongside, and now we began to look around for some showrooms—just in case, one day, we should have something to show in them. Hanover Street had brought us fortune in the past and it seemed a good omen when we took a lease on excellent premises there. Showrooms demanded a sales organisation as well as something to sell, and here we had a small ready-made unit—again thanks to D.F.P. With our expansion, H.M. had sold the concession (and just in time, for the French firm went bust soon after), and we had his salesmen ready and willing to shift their loyalties to the new *marque*. A. F. C. Hillstead, an excellent salesman who could drive so beautifully that he could have sold a lorry as a limousine to a duchess, became sales manager under H.M.; and under him was a nice young man called Hugh Kevill-Davies, who had had a tough time as a P.O.W. for most of the war, and was to become one of the most successful car salesmen in the country.

That was the line-up in the summer of 1921, and on the whole it was a satisfactory one. Later on the inevitable little personal differences would inevitably show themselves, leading to the occasional resignation, and there were to be some difficulties in the sales-production-design relationship. For the present, however, we had no cars over which to disagree, and the single-minded aim—to get them on the market—united us.

．　　　．　　　．　　　．　　　．

One morning in September, 1921, a tough, smart, short-set young man turned up at the works. I went out to meet him, and took him over to the low 3-litre coupé that was standing waiting for him. 'Let us know if anything goes wrong, Noel,' I said to him. 'You've got a five-year guarantee, don't forget.' He looked the car carefully all over, raised the bonnet and cast an experienced eye over the engine, got into the driving seat and drove away. Our first customer had taken delivery of our first production car.

The choice of this first customer was a tricky and important one. He would naturally be sympathetic to the sort of car we were producing or he wouldn't be paying over £1,000 for his model. But he also had to be something of a social butterfly who would mix in the best social strata and spread the good word far and wide, and something of an engineer who could appreciate the qualities of his car, talk about them authoritatively, and come back to explain any snags to us.

Noel Van Raalte was very rich. He owned Brownsea Island, among his properties, and put up the money for K.L.G. plugs. He was very sociable. And besides his excellent mechanical knowledge, he had also had racing experience, which had begun while he was still an undergraduate, when he had taken part in those memorable races in reverse gear round the streets of Cambridge, in a Grand Prix Mercedes.

If there were any weak spots in our car, we were confident that they would show up in the hands of Van Raalte. I thought he would make an excellent testing and propaganda tool.

Everybody went back to work feeling encouraged and much more hopeful about the future. Inside, six more chassis were nearing completion.

CHAPTER SEVEN

Bentley Racing

IF THERE was one subject on which we never had any argument through all the crises and storms of Bentley Motors, through disagreeable board meeting after disagreeable board meeting, it was on our racing programme. Directors and chairmen came and went, sometimes at a bewildering rate, but, even when I was no longer managing director, I remained in control of the racing side of the business. No one ever attempted to dispute that competition success was the cheapest way of selling cars—and how could they? Time and again we got front-page lead headlines and as much as 200 column inches in the daily Press for one race, and even in our most active and successful year, when we couldn't put a foot wrong, the racing side cost us less than £2,500.[1]

The racing policy—as soon as we could afford one—was a part of the very foundations of Bentley Motors, for the two vital purposes of testing and publicising our cars, and as you will see later, there is nothing contradictory in the fact that we were successful in both roles and yet still failed to survive; though I will be the first to agree that there is an important lesson to be learned in this apparent contradiction. Pre-war racing with D.F.P. had been a useful training ground, and the war years, and especially the months between the armistice and the production of Ex. 1, had given me the chance to formulate my general ideas on racing. These altered from time to time but remained basically the same, and perhaps I should put them down here and now in their simplest terms for the record.

First, we never entered for a race (except for the '22 T.T.

1. The figures for 1924–5 to 1928–9 were £833, £2,412, £3,369, £2,616 and £2,487, after allowance had been made for prize and starting money, and manufacturers' and fuel and oil companies' bonuses. During the same period the money spent on Press advertising varied from between two and five times this amount.

trial effort) unless we thought we would win, and if we won we liked to do so at the lowest possible speed in order to preserve our cars and keep our true maximum performance from our competitors. We were in racing not for the glory and heroics but strictly for business, and sprints, 'garden-party' affairs round little circuits, handicap events on winding circuits without a decent straight on which we could take advantage of our superior speed, were all out. A small car can go round a corner as fast as or faster than a large car, which is all too often baulked by the babies—unintentionally of course—on winding or narrow roads. What sort of use could these races be to us? The Ards T.T.s, with their complicated handicapping, in which we never entered officially, proved our point exactly, for only once were they won by a big-engined car.

In later years, when we were getting all the publicity we could ask for, this policy became more inflexible, for we knew only too well that the news that Bentleys had lost—or had crashed or blown up—would take precedence even over the announcement of the winning car. 'Bentley *Doesn't* Win' became a sort of nightmare headline to me, underlining the hideous consequences of possible failure!

The Brooklands 500-mile and Double-Twelve races were just right. And so, of course, was Le Mans, with its long straight, and the advantage it gave a comparatively large engine which has not been unduly pushed. Again the results proved our point: time and again at Le Mans cars have finished in descending order of engine size, as in the most recent (at the time of writing). We got such a hold on the Sarthe race that by degrees we succeeded in driving out the opposition, the most successful and economical way I know of winning a race, and one which, because the engines were so little stressed, sometimes eliminated the need to take them down afterwards, though Clarke nearly always did so just to satisfy himself. I would have been perfectly content to see our cars circulating round Le Mans in inglorious solo solitude so long as the *Daily Mail* gave us their front page on Monday morning!

The second formula for success: sound, painstakingly meticulous preparation. 'Everything split-pinned, nothing too much trouble' might have been our motto. Clarke never let us have a car until he had been over it personally, end to end, inside and out, and when a man of his temperament had done his job, the drivers could feel that vital confidence in a machine on which their lives were to depend for a long time.

As to the drivers, we were fortunate in always having a mile-long waiting list which included the best amateurs of the day. The final choice for the team was always mine, and I was looking for drivers who were fast and steady and untemperamental, who would do as they were told, and who, if they didn't win and bring us the publicity, would survive to the finish to fulfil our second requirement and provide us with the evidence of any faults or weaknesses.

Next in importance I would put our pit-work, as applied to drivers and mechanics. Fast, efficient pit-work giving an advantage of three-quarters of a minute over a near rival (and we did better than that sometimes) could represent a saving of more than a mile and cause just that extra strain on your rival in attempting to make good the loss that could blow up his engine. I'll have more to say about our methods later.

We started off quietly and tentatively, using Ex. 2, a nine-foot chassis with a two-seater body, and with Frank Clement, the obvious choice, as driver. He had been using Brooklands for months for testing and had already put up speeds of over 90 m.p.h. with the fully equipped car when we took it down for the 1921 Essex Car Club and Whitsun meetings in May, and got a fairly comfortable first in one of the races. But we still had far too much to do, and far too little money, for there to be any sort of programme yet, and we did nothing further that year.

Oddly enough the famous American Indianapolis 500 miles was the first major event in which we entered; it was also our first major error. It was an expensive business sending the profesisonal driver, Hawkes, and a mechanic with the car across the Atlantic, but apart from the usual intention of winning, we were anxious to show the Americans what we were doing. So far as the race went, we just weren't fast enough, but we finished, which was more than a lot of the cars did, and we created quite a good impression. Indianapolis had been dominated by European cars, but it was becoming too specialised a race for anyone but experienced natives to stand a chance in it, a state of affairs that was to endure until the 1960s.

The same reasoning that had led us to enter the little D.F.P. for the 1914 Tourist Trophy race decided us now to put in a full team for the 1922 Isle of Man event, the first one since the war.

In 1914 we had stolen much of the winning Sunbeam's thunder by keeping ahead of a lot of bigger cars and finishing, one of the six survivors out of twenty-three starters, 'among the big boys'. This time we hoped to do the same thing by finishing, as a team, as the only genuine 'touring' cars in a field consisting entirely of specially built 3-litre racing cars. If we won—then that would be splendid. But our primary motive was to put the cars in the public eye and get them talked about.

Early in the year, Clement took over four of the production chassis from the works and began working on them in the experimental shop. Modifications weren't to be elaborate, but they were to be carried out with infinite care: high-compression pistons, a racing carburettor, an outside exhaust system, and a smaller, flat radiator. The two-seater body was as non-standard as it was unlovely, with the spare wheel concealed in the 'streamlined' tail. But they were our first-team cars and we were proud of them.

We had sent a similar car over for the Indianapolis 500 on 30th May; as the T.T. was on 22nd June it was touch-and-go whether Hawkes would get back in time, and he only just made the first practice.

The Manx circuit hadn't changed much in the eight years since I had last driven on it; it was still very rough, with constantly changing surfaces, each, it seemed, with lower skid-resisting properties than the last, a riotous variety of corners and narrow, hump-backed bridges, and a road width that often appeared to be endangering all four hub caps simultaneously against the island's dry-stone walls. But what fun it was, especially that sweep down from the mountains, sometimes breaking out of cloud like a diving aeroplane!

There weren't so many familiar faces among the bars and hotel lounges of Douglas as there had been in 1914. Four years of war was one cause; another was the curious nature of the race, which permitted out-and-out racing cars with a capacity limit of 3 litres when the International Grand Prix formula limit was 2 litres. Entries for this odd-race-out were consequently sparse, and I doubt if there would have been any at all if it hadn't been an international event carrying with it some prestige and tradition. De Hane Segrave, the French professional, Chassagne, and 'Bill' Guinness were there as the official Sunbeam drivers, along with *le patron* himself, Louis Coatalen. Then there were M. C. Park, Payne and Swaine, the Vauxhall drivers, non-competing drivers of varying eminence, and two whose future fortunes were later to be tied up closely with Bentley Motors.

One of these was the Marquis of Casa Maury, an international sportsman, a dark, dashing gentleman of pleasure and business, of Colombian origin I think, who was later to become the company's joint managing director and to follow our racing programme with keen personal interest. He was down to drive one of the leaping fleet little Bugattis in the 1,500 c.c. Trophy that was to be run off simultaneously with the T.T. in order to fill out the thin field, and he did very well in it, too, coming in third behind the Talbot-Darracqs of 'Algy' Guinness and Divo, and only 6 m.p.h. slower than the winning Sunbeam in the main event.

I don't remember meeting Maury in Douglas; but if I had never met Bertie Kensington Moir again I would always have remembered my first conversation with him. As it turned out, Bertie served Bentley Motors with distinction, at the wheel, in the pits, and in the service station. The T.T. was all over and we were on our way home in the *Castle Mona* when we were introduced and exchanged drinks. Bertie, with his vast good humour, his ebullience and warm, generous heart (aside from his storehouse of tales, false and true), was a person one never forgets. We talked about our experiences of the day before, when Bertie had had fun with the famous Aston Martin, 'Bunny', in the 1,500 race before a valve put him out, and we talked clear across the Irish Sea, through the night and through quite a few more drinks.

In the cold light of dawn on Liverpool docks I asked him if he would like to join us.

'I think that would be a very good idea,' he said, obviously delighted at the idea.

The I.O.M. T.T.s were usually pretty wet affairs, but I think 1922 was the wettest of them all, and we all knew we were in for an uncomfortable ride, in spite of the three-ply mudguards we had wired above the front off-side wheels. Park was the first away at half past nine in a Vauxhall, followed by Clement with Saunders as riding mechanic in Number One Bentley, and Segrave. I was fifth off, with Pennel crouching down beside me in the passenger seat. Almost at once the floor-boards of my car worked loose, making the unspeakable discomfort of the rain seem almost insignificant, and before the lap was out—a lap in which I somehow managed to go faster than all the Vauxhalls and the other Bentleys—the floor was no more. Try it one day, driving for a mile or two with your feet supported solely by the control pedals. You'll see what I mean by its being hard work; and I had five more hours ahead of me.

Just to cheer me on, Simon Orde, a friend of Clement's who was managing our pit, chose that moment to hang out the faster sign for me. I was so cross that I got the sulks and never glanced at the pit again until the end of the race, which caused me to lose third place by 6 sec. to a Vauxhall: the warning that he was closing was there for me to see and I had plenty of reserve in hand, but I never glanced at it. Later on in the race most of the giant outside exhaust broke loose, nearly gassing and roasting Pennel, and for some reason giving us additional silence. Altogether it was quite a race.

Clement put up a very good performance in Number 3 and was only four minutes behind Chassagne at the finish, while Hawkes, who lost his plug and all his water early on—and caused a sensation in the grandstand when he added cold water to a red-hot radiator—pulled well up again and came in fifth, which secured for us the team prize.

The T.T. was an introductory—an experimental race if you like—for us, and the results were very pleasing. We issued a rather splendid brochure afterwards, full of photographs and impressive statistics to show potential customers that in the 3-litre they had a car that could be as docile as a limousine and yet could also compete on equal terms with the fastest stripped racing cars of the day. We then offered the three team cars for sale, and they went in a flash, at very satisfactory figures.

.   .   .   .   .   .

The T.T. result and the excellent publicity we had received from it cheered up the board and made things almost pleasant for me at the next meeting. I can see now why I dreaded these monthly board meetings, why I always found them so uncomfortable and resented the loss of time from what I considered the real work; and why I was a good deal to blame for the unhappy atmosphere that hung over them.

Money in life, as they say, is a great comforter, and nowhere does this worn platitude apply more strongly than at company board meetings. I am not exaggerating when I say that we never

G   97

gathered together at Hanover Street with feelings of confidence in the financial position. Usually we were deep in a crisis, and often it was so critical that we had to face the total inability to pay the following week's wages. That is the first thing to remember about board meetings.

The quality of the board was the next factor. Because we were always under-capitalised in those early days, we were not in a position to pick and choose our directors, and some whom we persuaded to invest in our motor car were sharp men with improbable backgrounds, who were totally out of touch with the car business in general and our sort of car business in particular, with its emphasis on reputation and long-term customer goodwill. Cars are still booming, there's money in cars, let's build cars —any old cars will do—quickly: that was the attitude of some of them, and of course any sort of get-rich-quick policy was totally alien to our way of thinking.

After a few rows of varying degrees of unpleasantness, most of this riff-raff became impatient, demanded their money back and got out. We weren't sorry to see them go; our fault, I suppose, lay in not being able to pick and choose more selectively and in some way in being out of touch with the more solid sources of capital in the City and in the accepted Midland motor area.

A man called Boston was our first chairman, but he lasted only until the minor depression of 1923 (which of course hit us particularly hard just when we were getting the first chassis on to the market), when Stuart de la Rue took over. He owned the famous playing-card firm, which also printed bank notes and sundry other things on a large scale, and had a great deal of money. He came in, like so many of the really useful men, because of his interest in cars, especially our sort of car: a small, florid, fiery little man and a real enthusiast in everything he took up.

W. S. Keigwin was one of the more helpful of the early directors, a society man who was very useful at introducing the right sort of customer, but not always quite so sound at finding the right sort of people to put up money, a task to which he applied himself industriously. Guy Peck, who had been with de la Rues, and subsequently with the Aircraft Manufacturing Company, became an admirable general manager.

As a working director and head of the service department, when we got that side going, there was Hubert Pike, who came in early and stayed right to the end, proving an absolute boon, always getting on well with the customers and establishing himself as a vital link between us and them. I still have an enormous folder of customers' letters, many of whom have a special word of praise for their reception at the service station from Pike, and his second-in-command, Bertie Moir. Pike had been at prep school with me, had been at Humbers during the war, and afterwards had had a D.F.P., so our association was already particularly close. Pike was also adept at finding capital, but I remember him with especial warmth as the man who used to make my speeches for me at those tedious (and to me intimidating) business functions.

These, and several others whose names I have now forgotten, I remember with warmth and affection from those trying early years. Most of the others I prefer to forget, especially the gentleman whose departure we would gladly have hastened if we could have afforded to, who suggested as a condition of continued support that he should take a substantial commission on each car our sales department sold. Drastic retribution for this blackmail came to him on the Stamford–Grantham road one night when he drove flat out into the rear of a stationary lorry.

A natural corollary to our uncertain capital position was the question of overheads and expenditure. I was determined that when we bought machinery and equipment for the works, experimental and service departments, then it should be of the very best; bearing in mind the motor car and the reputation we were attempting to build, any other policy would have been folly. But there were always those who would niggle and nag, demanding economies, constantly pressing for the second-rate for a car we were to advertise and sell as the finest in its class, opposing the expenditure of money on vital equipment. There was one early and particularly sharp exchange over the purchase of a dynamometer when we were assembling the experimental chassis. Here we were, building a high-quality, high-performance sports car, and we were expected somehow to manage without any instrument with which to measure the horse-power! This was the sort of silliness that irritated me beyond endurance.

The trouble was that Bentley Motors was everything to me. All my ambitions were contained in that car, and the designing, building and perfecting of it were my whole life, occupying all my waking thoughts and every minute of my days. In those critical formative years of the company, when the loss of my wife still lay heavily on me and there was no gentle cushion of domesticity to support me and absorb the shock of the reaction after a hard day's work, I am sure I was not easy company. I was taciturn, unresponsive and over-sensitive to criticism, and in the intimacy of the board room these characteristics became more marked and I was at my worst.

Normally if I was cross, dissatisfied with something, or if I disagreed with someone, I might either mutter inaudibly or express myself in total silence, all of which was perfectly understood by the men at the works; I hated rows and violent words, which were nervously exhausting and took your mind off your work. Unfortunately I couldn't do this in board meetings; I was supposed to talk and explain and justify, feeling all the time I was being forced to make excuses for myself and others when I felt that none was required, begging for things which should have been offered, always on the defensive, a situation I detest.

And all the time was the feeling that I was letting down the works people, who were crying out for equipment and material and facilities to do their job better. Nor were matters helped by the fact that I was the only director with any engineering qualifications, and in the final issue the board was therefore obliged to accept my word: an unhealthy situation.

As time went on we got into the inevitable dilemma of any company dependent on outside firms for its supplies which becomes more and more seriously behind in its payment to them, and more and more at the mercy of the few who will continue to extend credit. We got seriously into the hands of the people who supplied us with our raw materials, who at one time were squeezing us so tightly that we lost all strength to argue, being forced to accept ever higher quotations as the price of continuing supplies. This was the sort of subject on the agenda that made me dread and detest board-meeting days.

I may be giving the impression that meetings of directors of Bentley Motors in the early days were unremitting shouting matches, which would not be true. There were always many routine matters of a day-to-day nature to be discussed, on which I was as silent as possible, my thoughts, I confess, often far away on current technical problems.

CHAPTER EIGHT

Bentley Clientele

W ITH the D.F.P. we had proved that there was an enthusiastic public willing to pay well for the privilege of speed, good handling, and also perhaps the distinction of ownership that that French car provided. I said earlier that the market we had in mind for the Bentley was the fast, sporting one. We were confident that if we could sell a good many slightly tuned French family cars on the strength of their performance and pleasant handling qualities, then the marketing of an open high-performance quality car should not present too many difficulties. All cars were selling easily when we began, and of course there were far more young and youngish men with money thirty-five years ago than there are now. The competition within our range was negligible. We were, in fact, though we didn't know it at the time, starting a cult which had a certain parallel in the United States in the early 1950s. It would be an absurd over-simplification to say that the Bentley initiated the sports-car tradition in this country; but I think it is true that, because we specialised exclusively in the manufacture of high-performance cars, because our racing successes received more publicity than those of any other make of car, the name of Bentley became so closely identified with the term 'sports car' that they became popularly synonymous.

The romantic association of the car with speed, the constant references to it in the Press and as the normal transport of fictional heroes from Bulldog Drummond to Ian Fleming's *James Bond* of today, all helped to create the false impression that the Bentley was the only sports car, so that any fast, open machine was popularly thought of as a Bentley, and anyone driving one as rather dashing.

The Bentley creed is a vast field for exploration for the social historian studying the 'roaring 'twenties'. I am not here concerned with sociology, nor am I concerned with the respective merits of the Bentley and its competitors, but only with the curious fact that the Bentley car, the Bentley Boys, the Bentley tradition, actually came to represent in the minds of many something of the very spirit of a decade.

However, in 1923 we were still little known, struggling furiously with the problem of making the cars as well as selling them, and with neither the time nor the money to consider a full competition programme. Our customers were mostly sporting industrialists and business men, with a sprinkling of rich society young men, such as the very young Prince George, who had had a D.F.P. and came along and exchanged it (with the balance in cash) for a 3-litre, the first of many transactions we had with him.

Later, when our clientele expanded, our register began to look like an anthology of *Debrett* and the *Directory of Directors*. Tallulah Bankhead, Gertrude Lawrence, Beatrice Lillie all had Bentleys, and it became almost a routine for visiting American film and stage stars—and many Eastern potentates and European royalty too—to go home with one. Jack Buchanan was one of our staunchest supporters and had the very first production 8-litre, the Prince of Wales a 4½ saloon.

We were then producing a chassis for an open two- or four-seater body, and at first our customers were of the rugged, open-air-loving type to whom you would naturally expect to sell this kind of car. But it wasn't long before disturbing things began to happen and we heard of people putting on impossibly heavy closed bodywork for which the chassis was never intended. We never thought of the 3-litre as a closed car, and certainly not as a town carriage, and this was the function for which some misguided people were using it, in spite of its four-cylinder engine and the vibration, particularly on the over-run, which soon set up rattles in the clumsy and elaborate saloon bodywork of the time.

To extend the chassis beyond its original 9 ft. 9½ in. to 10 ft. 10 in. in order to accommodate a roomier body and closed coachwork was an unnatural distortion of the design, which would certainly lower the performance. But this was what we were forced to do under pressure from the sales people, who were only reflecting the public's requirements. I regarded this purely as a stop-gap arrangement before we could get down to the design of a six-cylinder car with a greater engine capacity to fill the role adequately. Already, you see, we were having to adjust our policy to meet the taste of our customers, and to expand our clientele. By the autumn of 1923 we were listing, besides the two-seater and four-seater Speed Models on the original short wheel-base and for the first time with the red enamel background to the radiator badge, five forms of standard bodywork on the long chassis, ranging from the open four-seater at £1,225 to the four-door Double Saloon, with seats for seven, at £1,415 which was an imposing-looking vehicle if you like but very distinct from the original conception of the Bentley we had formed four years earlier.

We could afford little on advertising in those days; for our goodwill and reputation we were dependent on the recommendations of our customers and agents and distributors, and on the whole we were singularly fortunate in these. The personal enthusiasm of our customers, who felt that in buying a car they had established a personal stake in the firm, who would visit us at the works and service department for long technical discussions, was remarkable. We owed a tremendous debt for the good word they spread in conversation and by practical demonstration of the car in competition.

I suppose the person to whom we owed most was John Duff, a young enthusiast who had been born in China and had established himself as one of our London agents. Duff, a man with tremendous guts and determination, had bought a standard short-chassis 3-litre, had done some work on the engine himself, stripped off the wings and taken it to Brooklands to chase the D-class records. Driving single-handed on the 28th September, 1922, he had comfortably taken everything from the Three-Hour to the 1,000 miles at speeds of around 88 m.p.h., which did us a lot of good.

A few months later he called in at Hanover Street and told H.M. and Hillstead that he had heard that the French were planning a race at Le Mans to run for twenty-four hours and that he wanted to enter.

H.M. passed the information on to me. 'He wants us to back him, prepare the car, provide him with a mechanic and co-driver, and generally give him our blessing,' he told me. 'What do you think?'

'I think the whole thing's crazy,' was my comment. 'Nobody'll finish. Cars aren't designed to stand that sort of strain for twenty-four hours.' That was what I thought of Le Mans.

But Duff was a very persuasive man who was used to getting

his way. Finally we agreed that Clement's experimental department should help prepare his 3-litre tourer for the race, and that
Clement himself and Saunders and Bezzant should go over to Le
Mans with him. No other British manufacturer was supporting
the event, and I thought they were probably very wise; I viewed
the whole thing with the gravest suspicion.

The race was on a Saturday, the start four in the afternoon, as
it is today. By Friday morning I was already in a fever of anxiety
and suffering from a very bad conscience, and in the afternoon I
could stand it no longer. In spite of the promise I had made myself, I drove over from the works to Hanover Street, where I
found Hillstead.

'Come on,' I told him. 'We've got to go and see this stupid race.
We'll take the night boat.'

He was delighted at the prospect even though we had to travel
by train, turning up at Le Mans at midday, a few hours before
the start, and to the great surprise of Clement and Duff.

After a few hours in the pit I decided that this wasn't at all
stupid; that it was, in fact, very exciting. Before darkness fell and
the acetylene arc lamps at the corners were turned on, Le Mans
was beginning to get into my blood. By midnight, with the cars
pounding past the stand with their lights on—my first sight of
racing in the dark—I was quite certain that this was the best race
I had ever seen.

The rugged course with its long straights exactly suited the
Bentley, and though the rough, rain-sodden surface had caused
Clement to lose one of his headlamps, he was well up in the field
against the strong opposition of a lot of 5.3-litre Excelsiors, 3.5-
litre Lorraines and 3-litre Chenard et Walckers. There was no
sleep for me that night, and at daybreak Duff was running a good
second until he overdid things at Mulsanne. However, Clement
made up for that by breaking the lap record several times, finally
setting it at 66.69 m.p.h. Another flying stone intervened at this
point—it's difficult for the racing driver of today to imagine what
a menace they were—and punctured the Bentley's fuel tank. The
announcement of this mishap was treated by the French as
a great joke, it being the stock excuse for mechanical failure, and
Duff's panting arrival at the pits was roundly and ironically
cheered. However, they were quite prepared to accept the truth
and respond with genuine cheers when Clement dashed off on a
bicycle with a couple of cans, brought the car to the pits, and suc-

ceeded in mending the hole by the time-honoured chewing-gum method.

I was never more surprised and delighted than when we came in fourth in that first somewhat casual and slap-happy effort.

.   .   .   .   .

The only relaxation I ever had during the entire Bentley Motors period that remotely resembled a holiday was on Continental tests of the cars. In these extended runs all over France, up and down the passes to test the cooling and at high speed for hundreds of miles at a stretch, I could combine my love for travelling over great distances with something that was useful.

I put up huge mileages in those years, so that I think it is reasonable to claim that I drove every model of our cars farther than anyone else; at the wheel I could not only beat out from the car any possible troubles, but I also found it the most fruitful place to think out the answers to them. On the first 8-litre, years later, I once drove from Dieppe to Cannes in the day, without having to switch on the lights, cruising at around 85 m.p.h. for hour after hour by myself, chewing a few apples and sandwiches on the way. That was memorable motoring.

It was as a result of these trips that I became the Francophile I am today. I learnt from France that there was such a thing as a sun that rises and sets in a cloudless sky day after day, to refresh me, fill me with new vigour—and burn me to a nice shade of nut brown. I also learnt to love the free, friendly, classless people, their chateaux and cathedrals, their towns and hotels and food and wine. I have always been too busy (or lazy) to learn their language properly, but I love it all the same, and can even be temped into talking it, so long as there are no other English people around. My idea of heaven has always been to take a car across the Channel and drive along those incomparable roads to the south—and the Mediterranean sun.

The first test run took Hillstead and me conveniently to Tours, a few days after Le Mans, where the French Grand Prix was taking place; so we can both claim to be among the few English people to have witnessed the first major Grand Prix to be won by an Englishman in a British car. Bill Guinness chasing the Fiats until they cracked up one after the other and then blowing up, as he and everyone else expected, to let Segrave through on the Sunbeam, was something worth seeing.

We combined another test run with the French Grand Prix (which was also the European Grand Prix) in 1924, this time with the experimental prototype 4¼-litre six-cylinder car, which we had previously taken to Le Mans, the chassis of which we camouflaged with a monstrous Freestone and Webb Weymann body and an extraordinarily ugly hexagonal radiator, the whole, to the perplexity of the customers, being registered as 'The Sun'.

This time we had a full load: Witchell, Bertie Moir, a man from Hoopers the coach-builders called Michaelis, and myself. It was quite a hilarious outward journey, for we seemed to get lost frequently and only Michaelis could—and did vociferously —claim any knowledge of French. *'Quel est la route pour . . .?'* spoken in an uncommonly deep-voiced English accent, punctuated our journey at frequent intervals, to the accompaniment of irreverent laughter.

The race at Lyons justified the journey, with Ascari well in the lead coming in for a final pit stop just before the end, and then, with his valves burnt out, being unable to start, letting Campari through on another P2 Alfa-Romeo after the Sunbeams had failed.

We were running that 4¼ six-cylinder on the new Dunlop balloon tyres, which made the drive very comfortable on a pressure of a mere 16 lb., but also very unsafe under an all-up weight of 2 tons 11 cwt. They were bursting in the most alarming manner every hundred miles or so, and by Lyons we had got through all our spares and had to telegraph Dunlops to fly some more out to Tours by Imperial Airways.

It was on the way back from that race, and while we were running I think on the very last of those balloon covers, that we caught sight of another car, as unusual as ours, converging on our Route Nationale and trailing a cloud of dust. It was going very fast and which of us was going to get to the Y junction ahead first appeared questionable. The arrival was in fact simultaneous, with neither of us giving way to the other.

The car I now recognised as a Rolls-Royce, but like no Rolls I had seen before—until I remembered that the company had produced their prototype Phantom 1 o.h.v. car at almost the same time as we completed the experimental six-cylinder. By an extraordinary coincidence we had crossed one another's tracks on our proving trials at the same moment in the centre of the vast landmass of France; and in spite of our camouflage we had been identified after a quick suspicious glance by their crew as readily as we had recognised them.

This was not a chance to be missed. I put my foot flat on the floor, and the speedometer needle of the $4\frac{1}{4}$, which had been showing a cruising speed of around 65 m.p.h., leapt up towards the eighties. The Rolls driver took similar measures—and along we went, continuing side by side between the poplars on the deserted road, for mile after mile, neither car giving an inch to the other, up the hills and down the other side.

There was not a half mile an hour between us, and I suppose we should have continued like this all the way to the Channel coast if the cap of one of the Rolls' crew hadn't blown off and gone spinning away into the dust cloud in our wake, obliging them to pull up after a dozen or so miles. I was quite relieved to see them draw back, having had anxious thoughts about those Dunlops.

Back at the works there was an extended post-mortem on the behaviour of the car, and it was at a meeting between Burgess, Bertie Moir and myself that we decided, because the Rolls-Royce would almost certainly be increasing its power in order to claim superiority over us and we were in any case dissatisfied with the power, particularly at the lower end, that we had better keep two steps ahead and increase our capacity to $6\frac{1}{2}$ litres. And that was how the $6\frac{1}{2}$ was born, out of a chance meeting with our closest competitor.

On the eleven and twelve-foot wheel-base of the $6\frac{1}{2}$ it was possible to put anything from a two-seater to a hearse body with complete assurance of comfort and smoothness. The $6\frac{1}{2}$ and the later competition version on the short chassis, the Speed Six, were perhaps the most successful cars we made,[1] and to our great satisfaction both were faster than the Continental Phantom, the big sporting Rolls-Royce.

The cylinder block and the valve gear were the same as the 3-litre's, but to make it quieter we altered the cam-shaft drive. We also had to do something about the general roughness of the engine, which was very marked on the early production models. We cured this (we were too ashamed to confess at the time but I don't see that it matters now) by setting the engine on very carefully camouflaged rubber mountings. I think the $6\frac{1}{2}$ must have had the first rubber-mounted engine, and it was a very success-

1. *See* Appendix III.

ful makeshift, giving us silence in a car that already had astonishing flexibility and reliability. Only once did we have to touch a 6½ engine during a race.

It was again left to Duff to fly the Bentley flag at Le Mans in 1924, though this time he was given works assistance with greater readiness and we all felt more closely identified with his solo effort, while I went over with Moir and Hillstead to keep an eye on the pit.

That we won that year, taking the race fairly comfortably from an otherwise all-French field of new 4-litre Chenard et Walckers, Bignans and Lorraines, was an excellent thing for us, for the importance of Le Mans was already recognised. But it also had a bad effect on us, causing our previous healthy modesty to give way to over-confidence. This is too easy for words, was our conclusion. And, as we were to discover to our cost, there is nothing so calculated to send you off on the slippery slope of failure as cocksureness in motor racing. There were to be Bentleys at Le Mans next year, in greater strength, but it was to be a long time, and there were to be many changes in the Company and the cars, before we were to take the chequered flag on the Sarthe circuit again.

.   .   .   .   .

Amateur wireless was giving me a lot of fun in my few free evenings around this time. My old passion for gadgetry—and a friend called Spottiswoode—led me into the pleasures and perplexities of the wireless set. Spottiswoode had introduced me, back in 1921, to McMichael, from whose shop in Kilburn I bought the bits and pieces to make my first set. To my astonishment, this worked, and after joining the Wireless Society of London, I was granted the privilege of a licence—and they weren't easy to get in those days. Until the British Broadcasting Company began operations in 1924, there were only the occasional transmissions from Marconis at Chelmsford, and the Eiffel Tower and American time signals to listen to, but though I continued to build my own ever-more-elaborate sets, the magic naturally began to fade as broadcasting became more popular.

CHAPTER NINE

Bentley Boys

BENTLEY MOTORS lived for just twelve years, and I don't think many companies can have built up during such a short period a comparable fund of legend and myth, story and anecdote. The very nature of the firm and its products, which by chance perfectly matched popular taste in the 'twenties, was one reason for this. The Company's activities, particularly in its racing, attracted the public's fancy and added a touch of colour, of vicarious glamour and excitement to drab lives.

I think it all began with the coming of the Bentley Boys. Their arrival and the recognition and growth of their legend cannot be timed from any particular date; the corps grew slowly, shedding some members and gathering new recruits on the way as our racing activity increased. I suppose in all this nebulous band of drivers, whose club-houses were Mayfair and Brooklands and whose 24-hour Annual General Meeting took place at Le Mans, totalled perhaps twenty. But of these a number were very part-time, driving perhaps only once for us; the hard core was made up of only a dozen or so, and most of these were sporting men of independent means. The public liked to imagine them living in expensive Mayfair flats with several mistresses and, of course, several very fast Bentleys, drinking champagne in night clubs, playing the horses and the Stock Exchange, and beating furiously around racing tracks at the week-end. Of at least several of them this was not such an inaccurate picture.

There will be more about the Bentley Boys later, both on and off the track, but they were such a fascinating crowd that it might be interesting to look at some of them individually.

I think the first one I ought to mention is 'Benjy', the late J. Dudley Benjafield, M.D., bacteriologist and later Harley Street consultant, tough, thick-set, totally bald and wonderful fun at all times except perhaps during the hours immediately before a race. Benjy worried, a useful asset in a racing driver, and if his pit work sometimes bordered on the ludicrous (I don't think Benjy ever finally discovered which way the hub caps should be rotated on a Bentley!) he was a grand driver who forgot all his worries about his car and how he would perform once he got going.

I put Benjy first because, apart from Duff, who in any case drove privately and was in the trade, he was our first outside driver. It was our 1924 Le Mans victory that brought him to Hanover Street where he bought first a long-chassis 3 litre on which he placed a saloon body large enough to kill all performance, and then the red two-seater with the nine-foot chassis which Clement had raced in 1923. This provided him with the speed he wanted, and with it he raced with such energy at Brookland that we invited him to share the seat of a 3-litre at Le Mans the following year. After that he drove for us at Le Mans in 1926, 1927, 1928 and 1929, in the Six-Hour and Double-Twelve at Brooklands and in a number of other less important events.

Benjy was one of our steadiest and most reliable drivers and an equally strong supporter of off-duty fun-and-games.

Birkin, with the enthusiasm that he put into everything, created his own legend. To many schoolboys the slight figure of Tim Birkin—Sir H. R. S. Birkin, Bart.—at the wheel, with silk scarf flying in the wind, represented the ultimate in courage, excitement and glamour, the Bentley Boy *par excellence*.

I think Tim's money came from Nottingham lace; anyway he never had to do much work for it, and from the end of the war until he died in 1933 he devoted most of his working time to cars and racing.

We first came in touch with him when he bought a post-war D.F.P. with the idea of attacking my old B-class records at Brooklands, and he first drove for us at the Brooklands Six-Hour race in 1927. Tim's weaknesses were his love of playing to the gallery and his complete ruthlessness with his cars; I know of nobody before or since who could tear up a piece of machinery so swiftly and completely as Tim. During his brief, terrific duel with Caracciola in the early stages of the 1930 Le Mans, he threw a tread just after passing the Mercedes on the grass verge, and then to everyone's horror, instead of coming in to change the wheel, continued on the canvas without dropping speed. When he was finally forced to come in he was down to the rim with the mudguard smashed all over the place; and shortly afterwards he brought the steaming, long-suffering 4½ in again, ostensibly to hand over to his co-driver.

By 1930 two could work on the car, and Chassagne was leaping over the counter and making for the oil filler with the can when Tim's characteristic stuttering voice interrupted him. Standing on the tarmac beside his car, and pointing at the near red-hot sump, he called out with almost triumphant resignation: 'Ch-ch-chassagne, don't w-w-waste t-t-time. P-p-put it in th-th-through that bl-bl-bloody great h-h-hole there.' It was sound advice, too; the hole the con rod had made through the crank-case could have taken Bertie Moir's fist.

I'm afraid that was the sort of treatment Tim's cars had to put up with. But there's no question that he was a magnificent driver, absolutely without fear and with an iron determination, who—while there was anything left of his car—continued to drive it flat out and with only one end in view.

He lived equally furiously off the track, his fondness for the dramatic and unexpected having surprising and often excruciatingly funny results. Life was never dull with Tim around, if only because of the abundance and wide variety of his girl friends.

He wasn't with the regular team for long, one of his many enthusiasms being for the supercharger, which he quite mistakenly thought would make the 4½ a better and faster car. I'll have more to say later about the 'blower' which did us a certain amount of damage, confining myself at this stage to the fact that Tim, under the patronage of the Hon. Dorothy Paget, was by 1929 running a team of much-modified Bentleys in competition with us, which naturally resulted in our seeing less of him.

Tim won twice at Le Mans, once in the Speed Six for us with Barnato in 1929, and again in 1931 in a 2.3 blown Alfa-Romeo, a make of car he did very well with in his last years.

Incidentally, Tim was not killed while racing. Most people believe he died of his burns after a smash in the 1933 Tripoli Grand Prix, but in fact he only just touched his bare arm against the exhaust at the pits during practice—while reaching into the cockpit to retrieve his cigarette-lighter. His arm was still bandaged when he arrived in London six days later, but it was with general septicæmia following mosquito-bite poisoning that he picked up in Tripoli (he had contracted malaria in Palestine during the war) that he was admitted to the Countess Carnarvon Nursing Home, where he died on June 22nd. I saw him for the last time at a party he gave at Ciros, at which he turned up late after having his arm dressed, a few days before he died.

Glen Kidston was a born adventurer, rough, tough, sharp, and as fearless as Birkin. I think I was the only person never to receive the rough edge of his tongue, which could certainly be very sharp at times, and we always got on well together. Glen was a traditional naval officer type, quieter than most of the others and very amenable to discipline. Thick-set, with very powerful shoulders, and good looking, his life seemed to consist of one hair-raising incident after another.

Besides driving at Brooklands and elsewhere with great verve on Grand Prix straight-eight Bugattis and Salmsons, he did a lot of flying. He was in one of the early London–Paris airliners when it got lost in a fog. As it began grazing the tree-tops, Glen braced himself for the crash, and in the subsequent fire smashed his way through the fuselage with his fists and was the only survivor.

He had an equally miraculous escape from his submarine, which became caught in the mud of the sea bed, and only came to the surface long after all hope had been given up.

I shall never forget the sight of his Speed Six in the 1929 T.T. straddled across the hedge after one of the longest and most incident-filled skids in the history of motor racing. He got out of that without a scratch too. He drove for us at Le Mans in 1929, put up fastest time in the Irish Grand Prix that year, and won at Le Mans with Barnato in 1930. He had many other drives, including less fortunate ones with the 'blowers', and he was not only fast, but one of the steadiest drivers we had.

Glen's luck finally broke when he was in Africa. He had just taken the London–Cape Town record, and was touring the Union in his little Moth, which was heavily overloaded with unstrapped baggage. Bumpy weather set it loose in the fuselage, and the plane suddenly broke to pieces in mid-air without giving him a chance to get out.

Jack and Clive Dunfee were the tall, good-looking sons of Colonel Vickers Dunfee, c.b.e., a well-known figure in the City, where he was responsible for the creation of the City of London Police Reserve, and became its commandant. Jack and Clive both had to work for their livings, and I think they found the pace rather fast sometimes. After all, Barnato was spending money at a tremendous rate, and even Tim Birkin, Glen Kidston and Bernard Rubin's scale of spending at that time took some living up to.

The Dunfees had quite enough to buy themselves racing cars, however, and Jack had done some outstanding work at Brooklands and on the Continent in 3-litre straight-eight Ballots and 2-litre blown Grand Prix Sunbeams before he drove for us; and Clive, a shade quieter and also less experienced than the determined, irrepressible Jack, on an Austro-Daimler and an Alfa-Romeo.

When Clive got married to Jane Baxter he gave up racing, but came back again, very much out of practice, for the 1932 500-mile race at Brooklands, in which he shared a car with his brother. Both his wife and Jack were among the thousands who saw the 8-litre Bentley go over the top of the banking, and kill the driver. That was the last race for Jack, too; and it is on theatre programmes that his name is now so often seen.

S. C. H. 'Sammy' Davis, as Sports Editor of *The Autocar*, was not strictly an amateur, and of course he drove many other makes at this time, but he obviously qualified as one of the most active Bentley Boys, if only for his and Benjafield's effort with the 3-litre in 1927, when they brought the sole survivor from the White House Corner holocaust home to victory.

Sammy was a figure in the racing business for so long that a meeting at which one did not see him pacing about, sporting his inevitable black beret, asking questions, exchanging jokes, on familiar terms with everyone, was unimaginable. Sammy was celebrated as a somewhat severe pit manager in his own right, and even wrote a book on the subject, which perhaps made it harder for him to accept orders in the Bentley team. However, the records speak for themselves: he drove for us three times at Le Mans, and took second place for us in the 1929 and 1930 Double-Twelves.

George Duller split his loyalty between horses and motor cars; he was equally happy with either so long as they went fast, and if less consistent and more excitable than some, he was a very useful driver to have in the team as he had the happy knack of bringing things back on to a harmonious level at difficult moments with his bright and breezy casual manner and steady refusal to take offence. He shared a ride in the 'black' Le Mans of 1926 with Frank Clement, was second into the 1927 White House tangle, vaulting the hedge from the cockpit of his 3-litre in his best steeplechasing style, and notched up the first $4\frac{1}{2}$'s win with Clement again in the Grand Prix de Paris at Montlhery in 1927.

He once partnered Baron d'Erlanger, international banker, international playboy, whose wit and dry humour left an indelible mark in spite of his brief stay with us; the Baron and George together, one sardonically imperturbable and accepting the other's slapstick and practical jokes with a poker face, made an unforgettable pair.

It was Barnato who encouraged us to bring Bernard Rubin, a friend of his, into the team, and together they partnered the winning car at Le Mans in 1928 after the terrific tussle with the Stutz. Rubin was an immensely rich Australian who, like most of the others, was in it *pour le sport* and enjoyed himself with gusto.

Then there was Dick Watney, who drove once for us and had a difficult time sharing the car with Clement, who was about two feet shorter; L. G. Callingham, also a once-only driver; and, of course, dear old 'Chass'. Jean Chassagne had been in the game since goodness knows when; he had certainly been driving fast cars when Edward VII was on the throne. A lifetime as a pro had taught this quiet little grey-haired Frenchman all the tricks, and while there may have been more vivid, faster drivers than he, you would never find him at a loss in any situation and he was as canny as they come. Chass, who had driven for Coatalen against us in the 1922 T.T. and the 1925 Le Mans, would work for anyone, anywhere, any time, and could always be relied upon. Poor Chass; he finished up in the hands of the Nazis, who gave him such a wretched time during the last war that he died.

Frank Clement was, of course, our professional full-time driver; I've mentioned him several times already, and, although he lacked the amateur status of the others, he matched their spirit completely and also drove consistently well, particularly with the 3 and 4½ cars, and with much success and in more races than any of them. The short, squat, mischievous-faced Clement, with his unmatched technical knowledge, was a tremendous asset to the team from that first win at Brooklands in 1921 to the 1930 Le Mans, and he was in the winning car in four major races during this time. His pit work, incidentally, was the least spectacular, the calmest and the fastest. Frank was too methodical ever to get flustered.

Bertie Moir's fund of outrageous and improbable stories, punctuated by demoniac laughter of a unique timbre, were essential ingredients of the Bentley Boys' life blood. After competing in a couple of Georges Boillot Cup races and a Le Mans with us, Bertie was off racing for several years 'for domestic reasons', returning to the cockpit in the 1930 T.T. by bringing a blower 4½ into first place in class. During his 'rest period' Bertie did a lot to help us on the racing side, looking after the pit at Le Mans in 1926 and 1927. He did much towards developing a policy of procedure and technique which made ours the fastest team of its day, and achieving this efficiency by a form of enlightened discipline which surprised people who had seen the light-hearted Bertie only off duty.

And lastly Barnato, the best driver we ever had, and, I consider, the best British driver of his day. I shall have more to say about Woolf Barnato and the leading role he took in Bentley Motors and its downfall. But it is as a driver that we want to consider him now, and to understand him in this role it is necessary to know something about him as a man.

'Babe' Barnato's background was, to say the least, colourful. His grandfather, with the uncompromising name of Isaac Isaacs, was a shopkeeper in the East End of London in the mid-Victorian years. His son Barnett, a dashing, fiery fellow with a driving ambition, assumed the familiar Christian name of Barney, changing his surname to Barnato, and at the age of twenty-one, with nothing more than some slight stage experience and £25 in his pocket, went out to join his brother in Kimberley and make his fortune. In this he was prodigiously successful, buying a claim in the Kimberley Diamond Mine and floating companies with pioneering abandon. After reaching an amalgamation agreement with Cecil Rhodes, which gave them joint control of all the Kimberley diamond mines, he set about digging for gold on the Rand. By the 1890s he was fabulously rich, chairman of the Barnato Consolidated Mining Company, the Barnato Bank, and numerous other concerns. His son, Woolf, was just two years old when he brought him back from Cape Town, and on a calm June night off the African coast Barney disappeared overboard. Suicide was the verdict; but Barney Barnato had no worries to cause him to take his own life, and there were many who benefited from his death.

Babe inherited all his father's canniness and business acumen, and to this he added a love for the spectacular and the dramatic in both his business and private lives. As a sportsman he was a determined, almost dedicated perfectionist, and with his great physical strength, keen eye and razor-sharp reactions he was out-standing at anything he took up. His vitality and restlessness, his complete self-assurance and boyish, appealing appearance, gave him an irresistible charm. It is not surprising that most women threw themselves at him (a thing he always enjoyed) and that he was married three times: in 1915 to the American, Dorothy Mait-land, by whom he had two daughters, to Jackie Claridge, the daughter of a Californian coal magnate in 1932, by whom he had two sons, and again a few months before he died in 1948.

Babe was the epitome of the international sportsman-financier-playboy, and no one can have had more fun in living this role. Of Kidston he once wrote:

'He was the *beau ideal* of a sportsman. The word fear had been expunged from his dictionary . . . a resourceful and gal-lant driver with a flair for any kind of mechanism—a combina-ion of tender hands and a keen judgement plus that indefinable will to win that means so much . . . the most perfect host . . . and a good talker and a better listener. . . . A man about town when in the mood, a man of action in another.'

The words of this obituary of Kidston which appeared in the *Daily Telegraph* in 1931 over Babe's name could have been writ-ten for his own seventeen years later.

Having once determined, after careful thought, to take up a sport, he applied himself with religious concentration, starting from the most elementary principles, learning every step by his own experience and disregarding all second-hand advice. He once wagered £500 to £100 that he would reduce his golf handicap from seven to scratch in a year, and of course he was successful. When he took up cricket he was being tried as wicket-keeper for Surrey within months and played for that County several times. He took a fancy for horse breeding in the 1930s, and the Arden-run Stables were soon producing winners. At a party in Cannes —cruising in the Mediterranean was one of his pleasures—he once wagered that he could beat the Blue Train back to London. Although he liked his drink as well as most of his set and could consume a bottle or two of champagne without any trouble, it wasn't in his nature to make rash bets even when he was drunk, and he would never dream of driving under the influence.

Cold sober, he set off in his 6½ Bentley when the message came through from a friend at the station that the express was drawing out, drove straight through non-stop to Calais, where he took the next boat to Dover and was in his flat four hours before the boat train pulled into Victoria. This was the sort of challenge Babe enjoyed.

His consuming passion in life was to excel, and whether it was in athletics (his physique made him a natural heavy-weight boxer), speed boat or motor racing, he was always successful. 'I think the danger of motor racing is greatly over-rated,' he once wrote. 'It is not as dangerous as it seems.' And he considered life insurance as being 'not worth while'. But he was as shrewd and imaginative in his attitude towards racing as he was towards his business, and took precious few risks. Babe knew very well the sort of racing to avoid, and after weighing up the odds would turn down certain drives, just as he didn't care for track work and avoided the more dangerous events. What made him such an outstanding driver were his keen eye and judgement, his courage, discretion and self-discipline. He was never flustered and never looked as if he was in a hurry. At Mulsanne Corner on the Le Mans circuit it took a stop-watch to prove that he was the fastest driver round, and not the slowest as he appeared to be.

Babe was the only driver in my knowledge who *never* made a mistake, and he always drove to the book, keeping perfect position in the field, and religiously within the permitted revs, following all instructions to the letter. As Chairman of Bentley Motors at a time when I was still in charge of the racing but no longer even managing director, our relations might well have become delicate, and a man of less substantial character than Babe could have made conditions impossible by perhaps attempting to over-rule me. But as a driver he regarded himself as an ordinary member of the team, accepting if need be the second-string car without demur, and suggesting by his manner and his attitude that it was something of a privilege that he had even been included at all.

At the 1928 Le Mans, in which he drove the slowest team car, I had told him to keep station just behind Brisson's Stutz, judging that this would probably rattle the ultra-temperamental Frenchman. For lap after lap he did this, suffering periodic showers of stones when Brisson deliberately wagged his tail, until he was unable to stand these insults any longer and squeezed past the Stutz right in front of the packed stands, offside wheels in the gutter spraying up fountains of water, and with his fingers raised in the appropriate gesture. I joined in the laughter at this, then gave instructions for him to be slowed; but the next time he came round he had automatically resumed his position, satisfied that he had made his point.

This brings us to the matter of discipline in the Bentley team, and I'm going to break off to say a word or two about my relationship with the Bentley Boys.

It was a curious one, being part father-confessor, part schoolmaster, who was always happy to climb down from the rostrum to join in any classroom foolery. On duty these young men (who were not all that younger than me) accepted my leadership and the racing discipline completely because they accepted the fact that if they didn't it would be the end of their unpaid services, the vacancy being filled promptly by one of the numerous contenders for a place in the team.

Although I had to refuse a lot of invitations because I hadn't the money to return hospitality on their lavish scale—nor the time for that matter—I fitted in well enough at their parties and always enjoyed myself. When they were not yachting in the Mediterranean, ski-ing in Switzerland, shooting in Scotland, or just playing in Cannes or Le Touquet or Paris, the parties were often held in Grosvenor Square, the south-east side of which was known to every London bobby and taxi driver as 'Bentley's Corner'. Here, parked in the square which had no parking problem thirty years ago, were to be seen usually half a dozen or a dozen green 4½-, 6½- or 8-litre Bentleys (the limousines for town transport occupied by chauffeurs) outside the adjoining flats of Birkin, Barnato, Rubin and Kidston—*la crème de la crème* of the Bentley Boys. On other nights there were usually informal gatherings at the Grosvenor, the Ritz, Claridges or one of the more intimate new night clubs. When I could afford it I enjoyed these too.

An odd but a happy relationship, in fact; but on the other hand their girl friends could be something of a menace. At races I saw to it that the drivers kept them well under control and well out of sight—which meant out of the pits. Socially it was not so easy, their variety and abundance often being an embarrassment. On three occasions, I remember, I was begged by three different drivers to meet 'the most wonderful woman you've ever met, W.O.', and each time it was the same 'wonderful woman'. We knew each other pretty well by coffee at the end of the third meal.

Babe Barnato remains the only driver who has entered the classic three times—three successive times—and won it on each occasion. To have failed at Le Mans would have been an unbearable rebuff, Babe being inclined to take failure as a self-inflicted insult.

It is difficult to say which was his finest drive, for he won many times at Brooklands too; I think honours are probably evenly shared between the 1928 race, which he won after a terrific duel with the Stutz, with cracked frame and dry radiator, and 1930 when he and Kidston battled for $10\frac{1}{2}$ hours against Caracciola and Werner. For eighteen laps, in the early stage, too, when he was constantly passing and being held up on the corners by small cars, Babe's lap time varied by less than 15 secs.

'I don't do any training for a race,' he once said. 'I keep moderately fit, hunting in the winter, cricket and golf in the summer. But of course you oughtn't to have too bright a time just before, not too many parties. . . .' After it was all over, however, it was a different matter. Once he celebrated with one of his outsize parties at which all the waiters were dressed as drivers, complete with helmet and goggles. Another, and perhaps the most lavish and memorable he ever gave, was at Ardenrun, near Lingfield, his vast red-brick mansion in Sussex, which Babe called his country residence, but I thought was more like the Savoy, swarming as it always was with maids and footmen and valets in every corridor. Ardenrun was no place for a quiet week-end, and never knew one during his tenure; its end, like its closing years, was sensational and dramatic, a fire razing it to the ground one night.

I've still got the invitation to that Grand Prix de Danse in June, 1929, to celebrate Barnato's second and Bentley's fourth victory, lavishly decorated with drawings of inebriated Bentley Boys being pursued by Eton-cropped flappers in short-length evening dress. The bars are shown as specially built pits flanking the front drive which is—and was in the event—dangerously alive with fast cars.

Intending 'competitors' had to supply such personal details as cubic capacity and hobbies, and charabancs were provided 'for the convenience of those competitors or passengers whose cars are ditched or docked' from Grosvenor Square.

The hours were the usual 10 p.m. to 6 a.m., but the gaiety had still not faded long past dawn, when the prizes for the prettiest girls were awarded. A wild drive down the drive in No. 1 Bentley, 'Driver: Barnato or Birkin-au choix', was first prize. 'Safety belts and police whistles must be worn' was the condition of winning the consolation prize—the same ride, with Benjafield at the wheel.

By such happy means did Barnato manage to get through eight or nine hundred pounds a week, when the pound was worth four or five times its value today.

Babe, always a big-car man, began his Brooklands racing with a vast 8-litre Locomobile he had brought back from America. He had gone on to score a number of firsts in the following four years with Talbot, Wolseley, a garish Calthorpe and a Mercedes, becoming a Bentley customer in 1925, when he bought a short-chassis 3 litre on which Jarvis fitted a very pretty two-seater polished aluminium body. With this car, the prototype of the later 100-m.p.h. catalogue model, Babe won several major races at Brooklands, and, partnered by Duff, raised the world 3-litre 24-hour record in September, 1925, to 95.03 m.p.h.

It was at about this time that his seven-year lawsuit over the famous 'Barnato millions' was settled in his favour—and the Bentley finances were *in extremis*. Already a convert to our cars, could he, I wondered, be persuaded to extend his interest to our finances as other less affluent enthusiasts had done in the past? He was already sympathetic to our cause and there appeared to be a good chance that here might be the source of capital we so desperately needed.

One night I went round to his flat and, over a whiskey and soda, told him our troubles.

'You know things haven't been easy, Babe,' I began, and he nodded. He knew a great deal more than I had suspected about our business side and was soon asking a lot of searching questions about sales, publicity and our future plans.

It is probable, I think, that if I hadn't opened up first he would have come along to me instead.

Anyway, towards the close of 1925 it really began to look possible that the critical years of barrel-scraping, of loans and extended credit and incessant worry, were at an end; that a new and more hopeful era was opening for Bentley Motors under the comforting shelter of 'Barnato's millions'.

The Bentley Boys, 1927, at Le Mans. *Left to right:* 'Sammy' Davis, myself, Frank Clement, 'Benjy', Leslie Callingham and George Duller

Pipe-smoking engineers at work—on the V12 engine. *Left to right:* Charles Sewell, myself, Bastow, Kemmish and Ivermee

Preparing one of the V12s for the 1939 Le Mans

Margaret, my wife

Thirty-five years later: a line-up of 'Cricklewood' Bentleys in the lane outside my house 6

And (*below*) I pose for the owner beside his 'Crewe' Continental Bentley (*copyright W. Mayne*)

CHAPTER TEN

Bentley Disasters

I THINK it would probably be tedious to say any more about the series of financial crises which came about at the time of the introduction of the six-cylinder 6½-litre car. There wasn't a day without anxiety and when we did not have to confront the dilemma of having a new model which we knew we could sell, and at a substantially higher profit than the 3-litre, but which was so expensive to get out of the experimental and into the production stage that on several occasions I was certain we were going to go under and drown.

But before we go back to Barnato and the second phase of Bentley Motors, I think it is worth mentioning briefly what happened to our cars and those who drove them after that rather breathless moment when John Duff brought his 3-litre first over the line at Le Mans in June 1924. None of our racing was very distinguished—of several events I am thoroughly ashamed; but there was always a certain amount of fun, and we were learning—that was the important thing, we were learning.

Now that we've entered the Le Mans era this seems a good moment to say a few general words about the race as it was in the 'twenties. First of all it was a genuine and very severely regulated production sports-car race for full four-seaters with virtually no permitted modifications to the engine or chassis. Hoods had not only to be carried, but in the early years the cars had to be driven with them up for twenty laps, and ballast equivalent to three passengers had to be carried right through the race. Then not only did all spares and tools have to be carried in the car, but only the driver was allowed to refuel the car and carry out all maintenance and repairs.

Secondly, the road was everywhere so narrow that there was often scarcely room for cars to pass, and had a very rough surface which often used to break up entirely on the corners. No attempt was made to bank or smooth out the corners or clear the verges of obstructions, and of course until 1929 the road went right into the suburbs of Le Mans itself, with a 12-m.p.h. hairpin to negotiate, giving a total lap distance nearly $2\frac{1}{2}$ miles longer than today's.

All this, together with numerous other factors like the quality of fuel and tyres available, has to be borne in mind when comparing the fastest Bentley lap speed at Le Mans of 89.7 m.p.h. with that, some twenty years later after the Second World War, of 96.7 m.p.h. on a billiard-table-smooth road with wide, gently banked corners.

·   ·   ·   ·   ·

Prompted by our success in a race that had already achieved the stature of the premier sports-car event in the calendar, Louis Coatalen decided to enter a couple of his 3-litre six-cylinder Sunbeams in the 1925 Le Mans; and so for the first time we weren't going to be the only British contenders, and for the first and last time we were to be faced with serious British opposition. The situation, with Segrave, Duller, Davis and Chassagne making up the rival team (three of them later becoming Bentley 'regulars'), matched on our side with equal ebullience by Bertie Moir, Benjy, Frank Clement and John Duff, led to much leg-pulling, although the issue to both sides was an all-important one.

There was practice at dawn that year, and the pits were on the Hunaudieres Straight. There, at an early hour, we would find Segrave, looking even more dour and pessimistic than usual, a perfect target for our coarse humour; and there was always entertainment to be had at Mulsanne, watching him wrestling his way round, his mouth shaping the most dreadful oaths.

That year there was good cause for his depression. Something was seriously amiss with the Sunbeams, and they had had to be sent for attention by Dr. Coatalen in Paris, while the drivers were making do in practice with a standard touring Talbot-Darracq. This car was in the pits, awaiting the arrival of de Hane, and Duller and I were by ourselves in the Hippodrome Café, gazing idly at the car, when George suddenly said, 'Let's give the old boy something to cheer him up, W.O.'

When I asked him what he meant, he simply beckoned to me to follow, and in a very short time had made a neat adjustment to the choke cable so that it was operated by the accelerator pedal.

Segrave turned up a few minutes later, nodded towards us, made a few sour remarks about things in general, started up the makeshift vehicle on which he was supposed to accustom himself to the course, and drove away. When he left us he was trailing only a largish black cloud, but long after he had spluttered out of sight a great smoke screen was ascending above the distant pines towards Mulsanne.

I think it is generally known why we failed that year, giving the race to one of the $3\frac{1}{2}$-litre Lorraines. We had carried out careful fuel consumption tests, but with the hood folded, forgetting that the first twenty laps had to be covered with it raised, the additional air resistance playing havoc with our calculations. On top of this Bertie Moir opened the round with a tremendous tussle with Segrave, the two cars way out in front of the rest of the field, their hoods flapping and billowing in a 100-m.p.h. gale.

Bertie at his most determined was very determined indeed, and I should of course have slowed him down. Instead of which, after only nineteen laps he failed to appear, and was next seen making the long trek back to the pits on foot, leaving behind a perfectly good Bentley with a bone-dry tank.

When Duff was faced with the same predicament a few laps later, he responded in a less inhibited way towards the refuelling regulations. His approach to the pit was at a run, panting out as he arrived, 'I want some more petrol, W.O.'

'Of course you can't,' I told him brusquely. 'You know it's not allowed.'

'It's my car and I'll do what I damn well like with it,' he replied, grabbing a can and disappearing before I could stop him.

It wasn't for another thirty years that I discovered just what happened after that. The car was surrounded by officials when he got back to it, he told me, and it took a good deal of ingenuity and patience to distract their attention long enough for him to pour petrol into the autovac to take him to the pits, at once resuming work on a perfectly sound petrol pipe line.

Clement took over the car later, working his way up through the field and getting in front of the last surviving Sunbeam, until some forty laps later when he had to retire with carburettor trouble. And that was the end of the first 'black' Le Mans for us.

.   .   .   .   .

Before the next Le Mans came round there was a good deal of Bentley record-breaking activity. In those days, when sheer speed and endurance counted for much more with the public than it does now, even comparatively unspectacular records being rewarded with headlines in the papers, it was sound policy to have a go at records from time to time, quite apart from the valuable experience it gave us. We learnt an awful lot, for instance, from the attack we made on the 'D' class records at Montlhery in the spring of 1926.

The car we took out to France in March was a nine-foot chassis 3-litre, for which Gordon England had provided a very light, beautifully streamlined single-seater body, so simple that it could be taken off or put on again in ten minutes.

We had some merry, but strictly non-professional excitement in Paris on the way out. The party consisted of Barnato, Benjy, Frank Clement, George Duller, Bertie Moir and myself—and a friend of Barnato's whom we shall call Brown. Now Babe numbered some gay young men among his friends, but none could match the spirit of Brown, especially in Paris in the spring, in already quite light-hearted company.

After a good dinner at the Carlton Hotel in the Champs Elysées, everyone said they were going out to see the bright lights; Bertie and I were too tired and decided we would go to bed.

During the course of the night they all kept drifting back, singly and in pairs, in various stages of inebriation—all except Brown, who had last been seen making off in the opposite direction to the Champs Elysées with an intent expression on his face. At half past four in the morning I was knocked up by the night porter; the British Embassy was on the line, the voice at the other end informing me that a certain Mr. Brown, believed to be of our party, was in debt to the tune of £26 at a house of ill-fame, and would we please go along with the money and bail him out.

Bertie and I, far too cross to feel like Good Samaritans, took a taxi to the address, where we were at first warmly welcomed as new customers, and, after explanations and the payment of the debt, were handed Brown's clothes. Brown, however, was still in far too excitable a state to leave the premises voluntarily, and Bertie and I were finally reduced to frog-marching him down the front steps and into the waiting taxi.

Even that wasn't the end. The night was yet young for Mr.

Brown, who hopped out at the first red (traffic) lights. We never caught him, and saw no more of him until the next morning when we bailed him out again—from the Gendarmerie this time.

What we were after at Montlhery was the 24-hour record, which Barnato and Duff had taken the previous September in Duff's own 3-litre Bentley, and above all the 24-hour record at above 100 m.p.h. The prestige to be gained from travelling at 100 m.p.h. for a day and a night in a 3-litre car would be enormous, and at that time, with financial crises raging worse than ever and a horribly blank two-year interval since we had had any sort of competition success, we desperately needed something to shout about.

The luck wasn't with us that year, though, the worst year I think in Bentley Motors' history. The drivers complained that the sorbo-on-aluminium seat was too uncomfortable, and after I tried it out, incidentally having no trouble in putting over 100 miles into the hour, I agreed with them. It wasn't the track surface that caused this discomfort, it was more the shape of the seat. The trouble with the track, though of course it is very much rougher today, was that it was too smooth. At Montlhery we found ourselves during the testing period running at constant revs all the time, and this brought its own curious trouble with universal joints which failed to get lubricated because they never altered their position.

We had our first crack on 31st March, survived for rather over twelve hours, and took a dozen or so records at speeds of around 100 to 104 m.p.h. before the engine burst. A month later, and after a lot more work, we tried again, improved slightly on our previous times, until the engine went again.

This was infuriating. I really had set my heart on the 24 hours at over 100 m.p.h. and I was certain the car was easily capable of it. Nobby Clarke and his men installed another new engine, and we gave this an exhaustive test.

The valves were the cause of the trouble, repeatedly breaking up and falling into the cylinder. We just couldn't understand this, and in the end I got Clarke to put the oscilloscope on to it. This revealed that the valves were fluttering wildly at dead on 3,250 r.p.m. We had, in fact, hit a 'valve spring period', and we couldn't think what to do about it. The simple cure would have been to fit larger tyres, but this was no good either as there was a primary cam-shaft period between 3,150 and 3,250 r.p.m. In the end we fitted smaller tyres and went up to 3,450, which the engine seemed to stand quite happily and which would give us the speed we would need.

Still everything went wrong; even the weather was as nasty as it could be, and after waiting several days for a clearance, it was still looking threatening when Barnato went off just before midday. He did the first hour at just over 104 m.p.h., and then it began to rain, the rain turned to hail, a strong wind arose, turned to a gale, and it became dark ages before it should have done.

We huddled in the pit, a frozen, sodden group, while the little streamlined Bentley pounded round and round the steeply banked white concrete circuit for hour after hour. Without headlights, and guided only by market lanterns, the car with its trailing cloud of spume and spray gave the eerie impression of a piece of mechanism on a huge machine that is under control only by some engineering miracle. It seemed impossible that human hands were guiding it.

In spite of the diabolical conditions Barnato and Clement managed to do the first 1,000 miles at over 100 m.p.h., and there was no question that we had a lot in hand if only the weather would give us a chance.

Early in the morning Barnato came in from his second spell, after succeeding in putting the average up to 101 m.p.h., and I could see that even he was just about all in. So together we went back to the hotel in my car, had a good stiff drink and a wash, and got into some dry clothes. Duller was at the wheel then, and I could hear him easily while I shaved, the engine note fading only slightly as he came down from the banking on the far side of the track.

Suddenly the engine died and at once cut clean out, reminding me momentarily of that night crisis in Coventry when the B.R.1. was on its bench test. I rushed out of the bathroom, downstairs and out into the forecourt to the car. I could hear that the engine had restarted by the time I had jumped in, and I sat there with my finger on the button, holding my breath, waiting.

A few seconds later the engine note expired again, and there was complete silence until I could bear it no longer and drove off flat out for the track. There was still a horrible quietness when I pulled up at the pit, and, even more curious, there was Duller, who should have been driving, running down the track. Of the car there was no sign at all.

Saunders appeared from behind the pit, and together we found it in the end, completely wrecked, upside down in the ditch bordering the road circuit which branched off from the fast banked track at Montlhery. And underneath it, apparently dead, was one of our mechanics, Wally Hassan.

It wasn't till some time later that we could piece together what had happened. Duller, it appeared, had got into a nasty skid at the top of the banking, had gone through 360 degrees several times and had eventually come to rest, with the engine stalled, on the grass. Very shaken, and already tired and sopping wet, he had re-started and driven into the pit and got out, intending to get someone else to take over. But there was no one there; everyone else had, like Barnato and I, gone off for a clean-up and something to eat, leaving Hassan and Saunders to look after things.

Wally today is a very distinguished engineer, with magnificent work behind him at Jaguars and Coventry-Climax, but in those days he was very young, very keen and very ambitious. He had also had very little driving experience, but, seeing Duller arriving looking so groggy and obviously incapable of driving again for a while, he had decided that this was his opportunity to show what he could do and save the day for us at the same time. Before Duller could prevent him, Hassan was in the driving seat, had started up and was away.

You had to be a very good driver to handle that sensitive short-chassis light car on greasy concrete at around the 100 mark, and I think it is to young Hassan's credit that he managed a third of a lap before he got into a long slide, which took him through the barrier on to the road circuit, twice over and over—and into the ditch.

Of course he had done what he had thought was the right thing, but in merely getting into the cockpit he had broken the regulations, and any records after a non-registered driver had taken over would not have been recognised.

Somehow Saunders and I got his limp body into the car, still uncertain whether or not he was alive, and drove off to the nearest doctor's house. He wasn't very helpful, informing us by sign language and Gallic shoulder shrugs that he could do nothing, so, by this time feeling rather desperate, we rang up the American Hospital. 'Bring him along—we'll look after him,' they told us promptly; and we drove the now semi-conscious Hassan as gently as possible into Paris. They kept him for three weeks in a private room, and then refused to take a penny for their services.

I had been determined that the Bentley should be the first car to do a hundred miles for a day and a night, and after we had sorted out all our mechanical problems there had been nothing to stop us—except the awful weather combining with a piece of well-intentioned foolishness. We had failed, and it was a failure I felt more deeply than any other in the Bentley Company's history.

Incidentally, Hassan wasn't the only casualty of that unfortunate affair in France, for I developed congestion of the lungs while we were working on the car. Like most people, I particularly dislike getting ill abroad, where everything is unfamiliar and you don't feel you can trust anyone who doesn't even talk your own language. One morning a sinister-looking nun marched into my room with a black bag, turned me firmly over on to my front and, still in complete silence, stuck a dozen little glass flasks all over my back, filling them with something nasty-smelling and very inflammable, and then setting fire to them.

Bertie Moir, doubtless attracted by my cries for help, came in in the middle of the operation. The expression of horror on his chubby face made me forget the agony, and my laughter set all the little glass flasks a-tinkling like sleigh bells.

Curiously enough this mediaeval witchcraft did the trick all right. The vacuum created when the oxygen was exhausted by the flames in the cups must have drawn out the poison in some mysterious manner, leaving me with a mass of scars but with cleared lungs.

.   .   .   .   .

There are no excuses for failure in motor racing, though we all continue to try to justify ourselves; and it is especially tempting to attempt self-justification to your own board of directors after the expenditure of much time, effort and money. I felt very badly about our Le Mans failure in 1926, which, following the 24-hour record disaster, was a serious blow to the Company, and one which could have been avoided.

Probably our first mistake was to carry out our record attempt at Montlhery so near to the date of the race, spending weeks away from England when I should have been looking after the work at the factory. Not that we went into it in a light-hearted sort of way. Nobby Clarke, who came over with us for the first time this year to supervise the mechanics, did noble work in preparing the three cars, and all of us put in hours of work on minor adjustments, fuel testing and so on in the week before the race, apart from the normal routine practising.

For 1926 we had two strictly works cars, both standard short-chassis 3-litres, to be driven by Sammy Davis, Benjafield, Clement and George Duller, and a 9-foot chassis '100-m.p.h.' 3-litre—the catalogue term being a mere euphemism after Clarke had finished with it. This third entry came about as a result of 'Scrap' Thistlethwayte's dissatisfaction with his OE 30/98 Vauxhall, which he never seemed to be able to make go so fast as Clive Gallop's standard 3-litre. 'Scrap', a handsome, debonair playboy but no mean driver, wanted above all else to drive at Le Mans, but he knew he stood no chance with his 30/98, and Gallop (who had long since left us) invited him to share a Bentley's cockpit.

'All right—but only if it's a 9-foot chassis model,' 'Scrap' told him, and I agreed to our preparing the car 'Scrap' bought and running it from the pits as if it were one of the team on condition he could get a body on to this chassis that would meet the tough Le Mans regulations. Martin Walter of Folkestone eventually managed this after a good many difficulties, and a nice job they made of it.

We were a big party that year, arriving at the Hotel Moderne, where the mechanics always put up, and the Hotel de Paris, which was always our headquarters, by various forms of transport seven or eight days before the race. Clarke turned up at one in the morning, with Captain Head of *The Autocar*, who always helped with the timekeeping, Miller the electrician, and three tons of equipment in a 30-cwt. Ford truck which they had hired in Dieppe. The driver, it appeared, had entered into the competitive spirit rather too strongly, and full throttle for fifty miles played havoc with the heavy load, the nerves of his passengers and the water supply. In the pitch dark, miles from anywhere except a forbidding-looking château, the radiator boiled dry, and they had had to grapple with a massive and very fierce guard dog before they got any water. A second trip had been necessary when the French driver poured the water into a red-hot radiator, and by the time they arrived they were all in a demoralised state.

The French contingent was a strong one, with a pair of sleeve-valve 4-litre Peugeots, three works 3½-litre straight-eight Lorraines and a brace of 3-litre Aries, one of them in the hands of Chassagne, and all of them with experienced drivers like Brisson, Bloch and Mongin. This race, we realised, was going to be no walk-over for us; the opening laps demonstrated that, one of the big Peugeots coming round with a clear lead, which it held until the early hours of the morning when the broken road surface fractured its windscreen bracket. The driver then threw the entire windscreen into the pit, and, amid very Latin excitement a lap or two later, was disqualified. The other Peugeot went out with a flat battery soon after, and we managed to hold our position among the Lorraines without extending ourselves too much.

Duller was the first to go, after breaking the lap record while in the lead, burying himself in the sand at Arnage, digging himself out again, and finally retiring with valve trouble. Soon after dawn the short-chassis car came in with a broken rocker arm. That left us with Benjafield and Davis's car against the three Lorraines, and things became quite exciting during the morning when they managed to get past the third of the French cars while the second was in for a long call at the pits. It seemed obvious an hour or two before the end that we couldn't win, but with Sammy gallantly answering the 'All Out' sign, it seemed possible that we might manage second place.

There were just twenty minutes to go. Sammy had gone past the packed stands, with everyone shouting with excitement, only a few seconds behind the Lorraine, and was visibly gaining. And that was the last we saw of him.

My watch went ticking on, the hands moving past the ten minutes; the Lorraine went by, followed by one or two of the smaller cars; and Bertie Moir and I exchanged agonised glances. I know of no time in motor racing more awful than the moment when your car fails to appear, and it is hard to describe the agony of helplessness you go through while awaiting news. When the situation is as critical as it was in the last stage of that 24-hour race, it can take years off a pit manager's life.

At last, when the race was almost over, and Charles Faroux, the venerable chief of the Automobile Club de l'Ouest, was already making his way on to the track with the furled flag, the news filtered through. Sammy, it appeared, had followed orders and got past the Lorraine, but he had overtaken it very close to Mulsanne, had entered the corner much too fast, and had well and truly cast number 7 into the protective sand barrier. He was digging furiously, it was said, but when the flag fell there were still several hundredweights of sand round the Bentley's axle.

Poor Sammy! It can happen to the best of us, and he was so overcome with shame that I did my best to conceal my fury. After the previous year's failure, we had needed to win that Le Mans. That none of our cars completed the course was nothing less than a disaster, and I returned to London in an awful state of mixed self-recrimination, anger and depression. We simply couldn't afford to go on like this, wasting time and money and energy which could more profitably be employed in the production of cars to sell. . . . We would have to give up racing entirely; that was it, we would scrap the racing department and concentrate on making some money. Perhaps later?

At the next board meeting I announced this intention, to a new chairman and a new set of faces round the table.

CHAPTER ELEVEN

Woolf Barnato: Financier

I'VE said a certain amount about Woolf Barnato the sportsman, the international playboy, the racing driver, and this was the Babe I knew in the early days when he drove Bentleys at Brooklands and helped us a great deal in his record-breaking attempts. I knew at this time that there was another Barnato, the financier son of Barney, who had perpetuated the fortunes of his father and had even added to them through his numerous mysterious and intricately involved interests in the City; but I saw nothing of him before it began to occur to both of us simultaneously that this fabulous wealth and our poverty would require to be compensated in some degree if he was to continue to enjoy himself driving our cars. The moment when this was first discussed that evening in Grosvenor Square and we began to talk together about figures—other figures than revs per minute and miles per hour—this other Barnato emerged: Woolf Barnato, financier. It was a very interesting discovery.

Of course there were clues to the nature of this second Barnato: his single-minded determination, his unusual ability to concentrate, his moral toughness, and his extraordinary parsimony over little things, which made it impossible, for example, for him ever to offer anyone a cigarette. This apparent meanness, in contrast to his lavish hospitality, was a standing joke, and it was the ambition of many of us to get our fingers inside the gold cigarette-case which he always carried in a long, specially tailored pocket in all his suits. One of us—the indomitable Bertie Moir—did succeed and claimed to carry the scars from the flange of that gold case across his knuckles. Usually after the day's work the office staff would all gather at the Bristol opposite the new offices in Cork Street and have a few drinks before they went home. But the evenings when there was a round on the Company Chairman were very few.

Perhaps it's an oversimplification and also uncharitable to call this failing meanness. Barnato was very conscious of his wealth, and at a time when there was less social equality and less security, as well as a good deal more poverty than now, I think he was over-anxious not to appear patronising and to avoid giving the impression that he threw his money about. He never liked lending money, and anyone in debt to him was not allowed to forget the fact. Assets might be several million, his attitude seemed to suggest, but every pound note was sacred.

One of his business associates and friend, who is now a distinguished Air Marshal, was misguided enough to borrow a hundred pounds from him en route from America, funds having run short on the trip. On arriving back at Barnato's Grosvenor Square flat together, his friend, conscious of Barnato's anxiety, at once took out his cheque book. 'Do you mind awfully, Babe, I'm a bit low at the moment?' he said apologetically as he began to write at the desk. 'Can I give you some now and pay you back the rest later?'

Barnato's face was a study in disappointment and distress. 'Well, I don't know . . .' he began uncertainly, and glanced at the figure on the cheque he was being handed. It was £99 19s. 11d.

As a business man Barnato was uncommonly perceptive, quick on the uptake, quick to act and quite ruthless. In whatever he did, in work or play, what he wanted next to success was value for money. It was almost a mania with him, as it is with so many rich men. It has sometimes been said that he came into Bentley Motors only for the fun of the thing, because if he hadn't there would have been no more nice Bentleys for him to race, and that this was a shame when several of us, to whom the firm was everything, were dedicating our lives to it.

But like most things about Barnato, neither his motives nor the course of events were as simple as that. His sporting instincts were fundamental, and one of the things I discovered when I met Barnato the Financier was that he also allowed them to take a strong part in his business dealings. He knew that he was taking a gamble when he put money into the Company, but it was a calculated risk. There was a chance that he would lose on the deal, but there was also a chance that he might come out all square— or even make a lot of money.

In the event he didn't come out of it at all badly, in spite of the misgivings of his advisers. The gamble didn't come off and he received a lot of sympathy when he told people that he lost about

£90,000 in Bentley Motors. But against that he got an enormous amount of fun and pleasure from being able to race in the team, becoming as a result one of the most famous drivers of his day; and to be a successful driver meant a great deal to him. He gained the distinction of being associated with the *marque* Bentley in its years of greatest prestige; and he was not entirely above such nourishment to his vanity. He had the choice of any of our cars that took his fancy; and he always ran two 6½s, an open one for the country and for fun and a closed one for town and for splendour, and in 1930 requisitioned a brace of 8-litres (chassis price £1,850 each). Even at the lower rate of income tax that prevailed then, he was able to offset a large proportion of this direct loss in tax remission. 'I know nearly a hundred thousand went down the drain in Bentley Motors,' he told someone after it was all over, 'but on one diamond deal during that time I made a hundred and twenty thousand, so I can't grumble.' It wasn't everyone who saw it like that.

Our personal relations remained friendly throughout, thank goodness. Babe and I rarely discussed business, and I think this was partly because he looked on me as an engineer first, racing manager second, and business man third—a poor third. In any case he conducted his business largely through his ambassadors —his financial advisers. These gentlemen, who devoted themselves to preserving and expanding Barnato's fortune, heartily disapproved of their master's rash venture into the motor-car business, which they viewed with the gravest suspicion and of which they were totally ignorant.

Barnato's terms for participation were announced in May, 1926, and they included the devaluation of the existing £1 shares to a shilling, which meant a nasty knock for many of us. If we weren't quite beggars, however, there wasn't much choice but to accept if we were going to stay afloat; and of course the sudden relief from financial desperation after all those years was so wonderful that it took a bit of getting used to.

The broom was forcefully wielded. H.M. and Hillstead and a number of others decided that the new regime was unlikely to suit them, and resigned, and the sales department, beside being shifted to new headquarters, was entirely reconstituted. The showrooms' move to big new premises in Cork Street wasn't approved by everyone, even though we should now have space to show several cars at once. People were used to Bentley Motors being in Hanover Street. Cork Street, sometimes described as 'the street of the dead' by retailers, was not a good place for cars, and it was felt that it was bad policy to house all Barnato's cronies in the offices which they had appropriated for themselves on the floors above.

I was as discreet as I could be about all these changes and all the new faces in the old firm. It wasn't an easy position for me, liking and admiring Barnato as I did, regretting the departure of people I had worked with for so long and knowing at the same time that there was no alternative. Hillstead and H.M. both set up as agents themselves, H.M. taking over the lease on the old Hanover Street showrooms under the name of H. M. Bentley and Partners, the combination of name and locale drawing many of the old customers, and new ones who thought this was still the official Bentley headquarters.

At first my position as managing director was unaffected, but it wasn't long before one of Barnato's senior 'advisers' who had by then become a member of the board himself, invited the Marquis of Casa Maury, who had been a friend of Barnato's for some years, to join the Company and share the managing director's duties with me.

On the face of things, Maury's and my temperaments were likely to clash, causing friction if not fire. Although he was an astute business man, he gave the impression of being a social butterfly, a gay, light-hearted aristocrat with plenty of money of his own, a taste for the arts, a man who 'knew everyone'.

If this appointment was intended—and I am not for a moment imputing such a motive—as a move to bring about my resignation, then it failed, for I viewed Maury's playboy pranks and the fascination he held for women in the same light manner as he treated them himself. Apart from his business talents, Maury was no slouch, throwing himself into anything that came along—motor racing or engineering or the arts—with tremendous enthusiasm, and showing an unusual talent for anything he tackled. At Bentley Motors he added a further splash of splendour to our advertisements and catalogues, and his good sense of line in bodywork was shown in his own cars, all of which he designed himself. Maury and I had the same interest in motor racing and the same down-to-earth attitude towards it, and soon discovered that we had much in common. We survived happily as joint managing directors until all patience became exhausted, the bull was taken by the horns, and we were both removed from the chair. In our place, one of Barnato's advisers was appointed.

Bentley Motors at once ceased to be a tight, loyal, if occasionally bickering, family unit. 'Things'll never be the same again,' was the sort of comment one sometimes heard at the works now.

. . . . . .

The Company has experienced a very great demand for a chassis which will take the heavy and luxurious type of closed body and carry it in silence with a degree of flexibility on top gear, and will prove really fast when it is a question of maintaining a high average speed for long distances. After numerous experiments, a six-cylinder engine of 6,597 c.c. was ultimately decided upon as providing ample reserve of power and the requisite speed. In addition, those special features of the Company's four-cylinder engine which have proved so successful have been incorporated, and the result is a car which needs less attention and is cheaper to maintain than any other large high-powered car in the market today. Those many discriminating motorists who have been led to regard the Bentley as the leader in advanced points of design . . . will not be disappointed.'

That's how we introduced the 80-m.p.h. 6½-litre Bentley, the enlarged version of the experimental 4¼-litre car, in its first catalogue which we issued in 1925, a few weeks before its appearance at Olympia. We had sold quite a few—at the chassis price of £1,450—and had it well established on the market before Barnato's regime; but achieving this only by desperate measures, which included a trip by Bertie Moir and me all round the agents in a Weymann-bodied prototype, asking them to pay a deposit against future orders to be supplied at a special discount.

The response was typical of the support our agents always seemed to give us. The Bentley was a car that needed to be *sold* and not simply handed over in the showrooms after a few worn salesmanship clichés. The sort of people who bought a Bentley often demanded intimate knowledge of the mechanics of the car and several trial runs instead of the usual nip round the town, and this called for the qualities of an engineer as well as a salesman's enthusiasm. We were very fortunate in having many men like this among our agents, particularly in the north of England, whose love for the Bentley was as great as our own.

Yorkshire was always a good Bentley area, and there we were served by the Central Garage at Bradford, run by a canny man called Rose. His sales manager was 'Mac' McCalman, whom we first regarded as an awful pest because nothing seemed good enough for him. Time and again he would bring a car back to us with petty complaints, but I soon saw that there was sense in all his criticisms and that he knew what he was about. 'Mac', the finest car salesman in the country, has the dual attributes of absolute honesty and an unique ability to get on with people. Nobody could touch him at that time in his area of Yorkshire among the rich nobility, industrialists and millowners. They all trusted 'Mac' and would never dream of buying a car from anyone else. Later McCalman became sales manager for Lagondas, and to accompany him round the agents, as I did, with the 2½-litre post-war car was a complete education in the art of salesmanship.

At Blakes in Liverpool Bertie and I got the same warm reception and promise of co-operation as we had received everywhere else. And there I blotted my copybook by being very rude to an American, though I don't think he realised it at the time.

I am a great admirer of American cars now, but at that time they really were rather terrible, and when the President of the Studebaker Corporation, who had just arrived in a Cunarder, turned up for dinner with us all at the Adelphi, I should have warned myself to lie low if the conversation turned controversial on engineering matters. It did, and having been in the dining-room or the bar of that hotel since 1.45, I was tired and touchy.

'I've heard of your cars,' the American said, turning to me. 'Tell me, Mr. Bentley, in your firm, how does your engineer rate?' And then, giving me no time to reply, he told me that the engineer ought to rate exactly nowhere—he was of 'no account in the automobile organisation', just there to take orders from the sales guys. 'That's how we manage things, Mr. Bentley.'

I succeeded in getting some admiration into my voice when I told him, 'From the standard of your product, sir, I can well believe it.' And it went down very well.

Our sales guys had a few things to say from time to time, too, nearly always unexpected things, and very often illogical and contradictory things—although, to do them justice, they were only reflecting that strange and perverse thing, public taste.

'A nice low car, W.O., that's what we need; it's what every-one's asking for—something sleek and graceful.'

Ever accommodating, I would take out pencil and rough out something on the spot. 'Like this, with a really low roof line? About five feet?'

'That's it!' Their enthusiasm was always overwhelming, and I would allow it to run riot for a time while we discussed other details. And then I might put in casually: 'Of course this will mean 4-inch-deep seats and a ground clearance of $3\frac{1}{2}$ inches. All right?'

And then the trouble would start. No, the seats must be deep enough for a gouty dowager, and of course the overseas markets insisted on at least eight inches clearance for rutted tracks . . . and so on.

The $6\frac{1}{2}$-litre, which could easily be started in top gear (for those who hated changing), could cruise at 70 m.p.h. in top (for those who liked travelling fast), could accelerate from 0–50 in 12 sec. (for the sportier drivers), and could do all these things with an astonishing smoothness and silence with any sort of body-work up to an eight-seater landaulette, was intended to keep the salesmen quiet and to reach an altogether wider public than the 3 litre could ever hope to do.

But by no means did it satisfy all of even our strongest sup-porters. They would come into the showrooms and say, 'You know, there's nothing quite like a four-cylinder; now if only . . .' Foden, of the famous steam-wagons, was one, God bless him, for his devotion did us a power of good. He was pleased with his $6\frac{1}{2}$ all right. 'It's a very nice car, W.O., very nice . . .' and he hummed and hawed for a while. 'But you know,' he suddenly burst out, 'I do miss that bloody thump.'

It was a case of back to the drawing-board. A new four-cylinder they would have, and it would be a new one and a bigger one, for we had got everything we could hope to get out of the 3-litre. And so work was started, in the summer of 1926, on the $4\frac{1}{2}$, which in substance was the Bix Six less a pair of cylinders. And one of the first models was in the Le Mans team the next year.

Yes, of course we had given up racing; it was proving too ex-pensive, taking up too much of our time, and we weren't having any luck. We had finished with competition work entirely—but by November we were hard at work preparing the cars for the following June. It was inevitable with Barnato as Chairman, and

I had begun to realise the absolute necessity of wiping off those two humiliating defeats. You can't, having once won a race and then failed twice in succession, just lie low and hope that everyone will forget. They don't.

This time it wasn't simply a case of being a good thing to win. We just had to, and that was that. We built up a really disciplined organisation for 1927, rehearsing the drivers in their pit procedure, with the aid of a movie camera, until they could have done the job blindfolded. We arranged the oil filler so that by means of a quick-release cap and a hole cut into the bonnet, which now wouldn't have to be unstrapped and opened, and an overflow drained into a tray and operated by the clutch, we should save about 45 sec. per stop. Refuelling was simplified by the use of a giant funnel into which thirty gallons could be poured and allowed to drain in while other jobs were tackled. The ballast, which was always a headache (you can't imagine how difficult it is to secure inside a car the equivalent weight of three adults for twenty-four jolting hours), we placed as a massive, lead-filled steel bar between the dumb-irons, which incidentally gave us very useful additional structural strength and improved the handling characteristics after a refill when the tail became very heavy.

We made a lot of other modifications to the cars and improvements to our pit procedure. For instance we moved the signals away from the crowded confused area where everybody else's were, down the slight hill towards White House Corner so as to help the drivers to identify them, linking up by telephone, with a duplicate in reserve in case of a breakdown. In the pit we had a timekeeper for every car, each with a stacked reserve of watches, as we had discovered that we easily wore through the normal life-span of a stop-watch in the twenty-four hours. Weeks before the race, Clarke had his mechanics trained like a top-line circus troupe—petrol cans just so on the counter for the driver, everything to hand, everything arranged so that the car could be got away in the absolute minimum of time.

This roughly is how we arranged ourselves in the pit we occupied in 1927 and in succeeding years. Looking at them from the grandstand opposite, from left to right you would see first of all me in the corner, with a watch or two round my neck for checking the separating times (between our cars and any threatening opposition) or simply the lap times of any dangerous-looking car. Here, on my high stool, I could get instant news on all the lap times from the three timekeepers at their tables below me on my left, their stop-watches hooked on to little stands, and their charts, which they would progressively fill with careful pencilled figures as the race proceeded, in front of them.

To the right again you might see the pit manager[1] who acted as my number two and was directly responsible for instructing the drivers and passing information to them during pit stops, and supervised the mechanics. In any remaining unoccupied space would be Maury or perhaps one of the other directors who were interested enough to come over—but no other intruders. We had a very firm rule about that, which had at times to be applied with particular severity to the hordes of young women who followed the exploits of their favourite drivers around the circuits. What happened at the Hotel de Paris was one thing, during business hours another, highly decorative though they were.

At the right-hand end of the pit, like a market-stall keeper with his scurrying minions, would be Nobby Clarke and the mechanics, seven or eight of them, together with their fuel and oil, their stacked tyres and spares and tools of every description, in the years when it was allowed to supply them during the race. And here, too, you might catch a glimpse of one or two of the drivers off duty, lounging about smoking or refreshing themselves lightly at peaceful moments, dozing a while at night, and leaning over the pit counter anxiously in moments of crisis.

Let's complete this picture while we're about it. It's three in the morning, the first faint glow of dawn is showing over the pines towards the Hunaudieres Straight behind us. The grandstands opposite are less than half full and resemble the House of Commons at the climax of a nine-hour debate on sewage control. Every few minutes there is the faint sound of a rising exhaust note from White House Corner a mile down the track, followed by the sight of distant white beams from a car's headlights, searching out the gently rising road ahead.

Slowly, too slowly it seems at first, and then much more quickly, the exhaust roar and those twin tunnels of light increase in intensity, the car bursts in an explosion of sound into the pits-grandstand area, where the brilliant light of the arcs instantly kills the beams. Its passing is instantaneous and causes hardly a stir, its recession into the greyness suddenly undramatic.

1. In 1926 and 1927 he was Moir, 1928 Casa Maury, 1929 Clarke himself, and in 1930 Ivermee.

In our pit one of the timekeepers looks up from his chart. 'Number four coming up, sir,' he tells me, a routine reminder only, for we are being hard pressed and I have had my watch on him. Neither does Clarke along the pit need the information. Ten minutes ago the fuel churns were lined up in a precise row on the counter, the can of oil and overflow tray, the can of water ready alongside. He is there, leaning over alertly, ready to examine the car as well as he can from behind the barrier, for the track is forbidden territory to everyone except one driver at a time.

The sudden tension in the pits finds a response among the crowds. The word has gone round that an important pit stop is due; there is a stirring in the stands, and in the enclosure in front of them a few people who have been asleep on the ground make their way to the fence behind the safety pit.

This time the Bentley's roar drops an octave or two before it breaks into the glare of the arcs, rises momentarily once and then again as third and second are engaged, and the car comes slap alongside the counter. The pit looks like the railings of a crowded liner just before she goes down, with no one quite daring to jump overboard; and the only passenger who's going to take the plunge is the relief driver, standing beside Clarke, in overalls, gloves, crash-helmet and goggles, waiting without a word for the refuelling and servicing to be completed.

The driver is out the second the car stops; he's stiff and tired, but there is one more job before he can sink back on to the wicker chair inside with a glass of orange and a cigarette. The *plombeur* is there beside him with his wire and seals and pliers, moving quickly about his task, and the driver grabs the oil can, tips it up and leaves it to drain into the sump while he stuffs churn after churn of petrol into the funnel he has thrust into the rear tank. Clarke and his mechanics duck as first the empty oil can and then the churns in quick succession come flying past their heads.

Clarke can see that one of the rear tyres is badly worn and needs changing, and passes the word to Moir who shouts the instructions to the driver. The *plombeur* is still working on the last of the seals (no water is needed) when the driver loosens the hub cap with the copper-headed hammer, spins off the spare, slips the quick-lift jack under the rear axle and swaps the wheels around—not hurrying unduly, for we discovered long ago that precise movements are quicker in the long run. Last of all a quarter turn on the Bentley's sensitive shock-absorbers, a wipe over the lamp glasses and windscreen, and then he leaps up on to the counter as his relief jumps down on to the tarmac and slips into the cockpit. A touch on the starter and . . .

Two minutes forty-eight seconds. Not bad. The lead is down to three minutes, but the rival car will have to come in soon and with any luck its pause will be longer than ours.

．　　　　．　　　　．　　　　．　　　　．

I think quite enough has been written about the 1927 Le Mans and I'm going to say only a few words about it. In any case 1928 was a much closer and more interesting race, for the only serious opposition we had in 1927 was Chassagne's and Laly's 3-litre Aries. The crash at White House, when the new 4½-litre came through fast and hit a French Schneider, being followed into the ditch by both the 3-litre Bentleys and another French car, should have settled our chances in the race—just as today it would have killed all the drivers in their chassisless alloy or plastic shells.

In fact it was probably the luckiest thing that ever happened to us, not because the worst injuries were a few scratches, but because the story of the Benjafield-Davis car's survival, to limp home the winner 18½ hours later, made copy that was splashed across the pages of every newspaper on the Monday morning.

The last thing I want to do is to belittle Sammy's and Benjy's achievement, which was magnificent. When I first caught sight of Number 3 crawling into the pit after a long silent interval of uncertainty and appalling worry, her front wheel buckled, frame bent, and headlamp, wing and runningboard smashed, I was certain it was all over; and when I went down to White House nine hours later at dawn and saw the wreckage of the other four cars scattered along each side of the road, it seemed miraculous that our survivor was not only still running, but, after a long stop to tie things up with wire and string, was actually gaining on the leading Aries.

When the Aries came in and stayed for a long time due to starter trouble, we nearly caught up; but Chassagne had the car then, the gap widened, and we all began to lose heart.

It was around 1.30 on Sunday, with two and a half hours to go, when Clarke called to me just after the Aries had gone by, 'Did you hear that noise, W.O.?'

I nodded, guessing what his diagnosis would be. 'I think his cam-shaft drive's going. Better hang out the "Faster" sign'—an unkind suggestion in view of the state of the car.

A few laps later Benjy swept past the hunched figure of Laly peering into the open bonnet, and he was still there next time round.

Headlines, photographs, maps of the course, wildly inaccurate and journalistic reports—they were all there in every newspaper the next day: 'British Bentley Car Crawls out of Mass Wreckage to Win Great Race.' What better could we ask for? Le Mans was suddenly news as a result of that piece of misjudgement at White House; the Press recognised that, and it has remained front-page news ever since.

But it wasn't all on the credit side. If the $4\frac{1}{2}$ had run the full length of the race we should have discovered a slight frame weakness—the only way it could have been located—which, as you'll see, led to embarrassment and anxiety the next year, and might well have caused a far worse disaster than the one which had in effect concealed it.

The Autocar gave us all a huge dinner a few nights later in the private banqueting-room at the Savoy. After Bentley Cocktails, Tortue en Tasse au Sherry, Mignon d'Agneaus, Asperges de Paris and half a dozen other courses washed down with Clicquot 1919, Perrier Jouet 1917 and some exquisite Courvassier 1875, Sir Edward Iliffe rose as the Chairman.

'Gentlemen,' he began, 'I feel that there is somebody missing here this evening who ought to be present . . .' At that the curtains behind him were drawn apart and simultaneously there was an explosion and the air was rent by a familiar exhaust roar as Number 3 Bentley, still bearing the scars and mud of Le Mans, drove in to join us.

.   .   .   .   .

After many years of trying the Americans have at last won at Le Mans. It may come as a surprise to a lot of them that they very nearly did so some thirty years ago—in one of the most exciting of them all.

With the exception of Germany (Mercedes weren't going to be tempted into a works entry until two years later) all the major car-manufacturing countries were represented at Le Mans in

1928: Italy with an Itala (Alfa-Romeo waited until we retired from racing) in the hands of World Champion Robert Benoist and Christian Daubergne, France with Aries, and, what was most surprising, America with a Black Hawk Stutz and a trio of Chryslers, all in the hands of front-rank drivers. The Stutz was particularly formidable with its lower frame and superior cornering to the Bentley, and its 4.8-litre, eight-cylinder engine.

Lagonda were also there with 2-litre cars, and Alvis with their front-wheel-drive Smith-Clarke cars, more evidence that everyone was being forced to recognise that the news value of the race —all traceable back to the White House Corner mêlée— couldn't be ignored.

The 4½, a car which had very few teething troubles, was already well established by October[1] and had comfortably won its first race, the Grand Prix de Paris, two months before—though deprived of its prize money and even the cup because the organisers went bust. We entered a team of three of them, and the pairing of the drivers is worth recording because their performance—as well as their cars—very closely paralleled their temperaments.

Frank Clement and Benjy were our first string, Birkin and 'grand old man' Chassagne, then forty-seven, the second, and in the slowest of the cars were Barnato and Rubin; Birkin, Barnato and Rubin all in their first Le Mans. Barnato of course accepted his position without question; maybe he was Company Chairman and a very experienced driver at that, but he didn't know the Sarthe circuit or have any but second-hand knowledge of the subtleties of driving in a 24-hour race.

It was a beautifully sunny June day, and the start, with thirty-three overalled drivers pattering across the tarmac to thirty-three immaculately polished cars at the fall of the flag, was more impressive than ever. Away they went, Birkin thrusting a passage through the jostling field and coming round less than nine minutes later with his nose just ahead of Brisson in the Stutz. Brisson was a very good driver and the Stutz was obviously faster than I had thought it was going to be. The Chryslers were well up, too, and that didn't surprise me so much; I knew they were fast and reliable.

I let the team have their head as I knew the moral effect of these opening laps was important, particularly to the rather more

1. We tried to give ourselves nine clear months for preparation.

temperamental Continental drivers, with the result that first Brisson, then Tim, then Barnato, Clement and finally Tim again, all broke the lap record. Everyone was having enormous fun and the crowds were loving it.

Chiron in one of the Chryslers was first to go out, and then Tim, who was driving with terrific verve, failed to turn up. The news trickled through by the usual bush telegraph that he had had a puncture at Pontlieu, a minor blow but not a disaster, I thought, even though, to save weight, we weren't carrying jacks that year. The next thing we heard was that he had got going again after having to cut away the cords, and was proceeding—according to plan in this eventuality—on the tyre.

Unfortunately, and not at all according to plan, he accelerated into the seventies, instead of the 'reasonable speed' specified, drove at this pace all along the straight, and miraculously got as far as Arnage before the wheel buckled and sent him half into the ditch. Half an hour later Tim came running up the track, his spotless white overalls creased and covered in oil, and panting so hard that he could hardly cry out for a jack.

I didn't have to tell Chassagne what to do; the little grey-haired figure went trotting off, a jack under each arm, on the three-mile trek back to the car. This episode cost us three hours, and put that car right out of the running.

Our Lagonda friends took the next knock, Samuelson in their first car digging himself into the sand at Mulsanne and Baron d'Erlanger piling the second car into his rear. Half an hour later, with the car's headlamps and bonnet in an unnatural attitude and his own face cut about, he sailed past the pits and continued, with a wonderful expressionless nonchalance and regardless of frantic signals to come in, until the finish: a typical Baron performance.

It was also characteristic of the level-headed Benjy to come straight in when he felt roughness from his engine and a light spray of oil over his legs; there was no pressing-on-regardless about Benjy, and he knew that Frank Clement would be able to trace the trouble at once—which he did, to a broken oil pipe the repair to which put them way back in the field.

So at nightfall things were really critical, with the Stutz in the lead, the remaining Chryslers running sweetly, and everything in the Bentley camp depending on the stocky, relaxed figure of Babe, who had settled down to a steady and, as usual, deceptively slow pace behind the Stutz in the old crashed car from the '27 race. How I blessed his reliability and common sense that year, especially when Clement came in for the last time soon after midnight with a cracked frame!

Our hopes rose again when Barnato handed over to Rubin, after a magnificent stop, at the same time that the Stutz drivers swapped seats, and the Bentley came round on the tail of the American car on the following lap and with a hundred-yard lead on the next. What we didn't know was that the Stutz, with its 8-m.p.g. fuel consumption, had taken on forty-five gallons, and while the $4\frac{1}{2}$ was decidedly tail-heavy on corners with a full tank, the Stutz was positively unmanageable at above three-quarters speed.

What we did know then—which gave me a horrible sensation at the pit of my stomach—was that Clement's cracked frame had been caused by the steady once-per-lap strain it had suffered from a diagonal ridge across the road near White House, which had to be taken flat out for the long climb up to the grandstands. It had not been a freak fault but metal fatigue, and it could surely only be a matter of time before the same thing happened to Babe. I sat on my stool, clicked my watch at every passing of the Stutz —and crossed my fingers. There was nothing to do until daylight.

At dawn we were still running second, some way behind the Stutz again, and as soon as there was enough light I got out my binoculars and focussed them on the Bentley every time it went by. The half light was maddening, Babe was doing over a hundred past the pits, and I just couldn't tell for sure.

Up to that time we had never injured a driver (we never did) and it was a heavy responsibility to send Rubin off to chase the Black Hawk Stutz and hold off the Chryslers in a car I knew to be potentially dangerous, and yet it just wasn't sense to order caution at White House; better to retire now than do that. Rubin was ready to take the chance, and in fact drove away, clipped seconds off Brisson's lead and passed the American car while it was in for a refuel.

The last spell was sheer agony. The frame had outlasted the other car's by many hours, but it was bound to go sometime; the only uncertainty was when? Babe took over, and the Stutz pit, at last realising our danger, had hoisted the 'All out' sign to try to upset him. Might as well blow at a battleship! Babe, knowing that our only chance lay in Brisson overdoing things himself, and holding on a mile or two ahead, wasn't to be tempted. This was Babe at his finest—and he got his reward at 2.30 when the Stutz stripped a gear.

Four laps to go—only another 42 miles after more than 23 hours' racing. Surely we were home now. We watched the Bentley coming up from White House, and it appeared at first to be travelling slower than before; but then that rise was always deceptive.

Babe was doing barely seventy when he went by, and none of us needed the thumbs-down signal he gave us to confirm what we could all see. It was horribly apparent that the bonnet had slipped back and was now overlapping the dash. It could mean only one thing. The frame had gone, the radiator hose would have been detached, and the water must be pouring out.

How far and how fast could a $4\frac{1}{2}$ Bentley be expected to run in this hot weather without water? And how fast and reliable was a Black Hawk Stutz with a missing gear? There were no slide-rule answers; only prayer was left to us.

Somehow Babe nursed that sick, red-hot, suffering car round, and we heard its less certain roar coming up the rise again for the last time, and the flag came down on one of the closest-fought, most exciting—and for us most harrowing—Le Mans ever.

There is a wonderful photograph of Babe at the end, sitting on the back of the seat beside Rubin, bedecked in flowers and quaffing champagne, looking like a prep-school boy who's just scored the winning try. The transparent pleasure he got from moments like this was in perfect character, and in such extraordinary contrast to the keen business man playing the market.

Equally characteristic was Birkin's performance after the early catastrophe. We mustn't forget him. He and Chassagne worked their way slowly up through the field again, from nineteenth place to just behind the two steady Chryslers, and finally Tim, in a last dramatic gesture, went scorching round the last lap at the all-time record speed of nearly 80 m.p.h. *Finis coronat opus.*

CHAPTER TWELVE

Triumphs and Failures

NINETEEN-TWENTY-NINE; the Wall Street Crash, a dramatic drop in the stock market in England, growing unemployment, and the threat of a disastrous slump.

In any trade recession, nothing is more immediately affected than motor cars, and the most susceptible of all are luxury motor cars. Since 1927 things had not been going so badly with us. The works at Cricklewood and the service department at Kingsbury had both been expanded, and the fresh injection of capital had given us much of the new machinery and equipment we had badly needed. The obsolescent 3-litre had been withdrawn from production, the 94-m.p.h. 4½ taking its place for our sportier customers, who also had the choice of the faster short-chassis version of the 6½, with a different radiator, higher compression and twin carburettors—the Speed Six. For luxurious Continental touring or as a refined closed town carriage we provided the 6½ Big Six with a variety of coachwork at around the £2,000 to £2,500 mark; and finally we had the new 8-litre on the stocks.

How was this looming financial crisis going to affect us? Already by the autumn the trend was visible. In the first half of the year we had made our first-ever profit, thanks to the 6½, of £28,467, and on the strength of this we had erected a machine shop and new offices at Cricklewood. Now we could think seriously of re-forming Bentley Motors as a public company.

But by the end of the summer the sales decline was evident, and it was a decline that was well above the average for the season. For several years the volume of cheap, mass-produced cars had been growing, and there were fewer and fewer people prepared to pay the vastly higher prices for a hand-built vehicle. Now, with increasing competition, the catalogue prices of all these cars were being reduced as competition became keener. Obviously there were tough times ahead for us.

To cheer us up we had the best racing year ever. We just didn't seem able to put a foot wrong, and I don't think any British firm has ever had such a high proportion of successes in one year. We started off with Barnato and Benjy leading for the first nine hours of the Brooklands Double-Twelve, a sort of dress rehearsal for Le Mans run over two days in daylight because night driving had long ago been banned at that circuit. It was the Speed Six's first official outing, and nothing too worrying happened to it except that the dynamo drive sheared, and Benjy had to remove the component. He drove off again, after hurling it into the back of the car, but some time later we were told that we had broken the regulations and were disqualified. 'But I hope you'll carry on just the same, W.O.,' I was asked, 'just for the spectacle. The crowds are loving it and we've got to think about tomorrow's gate money.'

I'm afraid the answer was brief and rude. We never seemed to be able to make people understand that we didn't indulge in racing for 'the spectacle', or anything except what we could get out of it indirectly in the way of business; a scarcely sporting attitude, some may think, but to survive racing just had to be related to sales and nothing else.

Actually we didn't do so badly in the Double-Twelve, as Sir Ronald Gunter, a rich young man who was a sort of supernumerary Bentley Boy, and Sammy Davis in a 4½ kept the Bentley flag flying, were first on speed, and came home second after a terrific duel with an Alfa-Romeo, just .0003 behind on the handicap-marking formula.

Le Mans can only be described as a walk-over, with Bentleys 1—2—3—4, the Barnato-Birkin 6½ leading an impressive procession of the big green cars over the line at touring gait, although earlier we had had again to deal with a determined flock of American Chryslers and Stutzs. I had quite a time trying to hold the speed of the four cars down in the later stages that year, and at one point during the morning Jack Dunfee drew up to a crawl beside the pit and bawled out in exasperation, 'What do you want me to do—get out and push the bloody thing?'

Incidentally, this is a point worth bearing in mind when looking through—and perhaps drawing hasty conclusions from—statistical data on race results. It is too easy to assume that in every race every car has been fully extended. This applies to any race—quite apart from the weather and varying road conditions—and applies particularly to any study of the succeeding race speeds at Le Mans of cars that had refused battle when Bentleys were running there.

Nineteen-twenty-nine was Barnato's peak year, too. A week or so later he romped home first in the B.A.R.C. Six-Hour race at Brooklands in the same car. Clement and Jack Barclay won the Brooklands 500-Miles for us at over 107 m.p.h. with another team Bentley second, and in the Irish Grand Prix we took second to fifth places on handicap behind the supercharged Ivanovski Alfa-Romeo, though Kidston's was the fastest car there by 4 m.p.h.

So it went on, until the R.A.C. Ulster Tourist Trophy came round again in September, a race I regarded with caution because the handicap formula was all against our sort of cars. At dinner a few weeks before, Birkin had told me that, regardless of our plans, he was going to enter a 4½ Bentley, one of his first supercharged cars. 'You ought to come along as my mechanic,' joked Tim. 'Do you a world of good.'

To his astonishment I said, 'All right, I will.'

Bertie, on the other side of the table, seemed distressed at the idea. 'But you can't do that. It's much too dangerous. You can't go around sticking your neck out.'

We left it at that for the moment, Tim accepting the implied thrust at his driving with good humour. Bertie, however, knew that I hadn't put the thing out of my head, and came up with his trump card a few days later. 'Your life insurance,' he told me triumphantly. 'It doesn't cover you for racing—so that's that.'

But it wasn't. I had decided that, apart from the fun, it would be a good thing to discover just what the mechanics had to put up with and to show them that I was ready to stick my neck out too. I paid an additional premium for a covering clause, and set sail for Belfast with Tim and the others.

The T.T.s in those days, run over a thirteen-mile circuit just outside the city, were always pretty riotous affairs, with anything up to sixty cars and a quarter of a million excitable Irish spectators ranged along the banks and in the most hair-raising positions on the pavements in the villages. How more people weren't killed—until the 1936 disaster—I can't imagine, and why no driver or mechanic was ever killed at Ards, where everything from giant-blown Mercedes to Austin 7s beat their way around the narrow roads together for five hours, is a mystery.

Besides all that, in 1929 there were nasty little rainstorms which broke out on isolated sections, making the surface as treacherous as ice. Tyre adhesion, in fact, was a problematical thing and everyone was skating all over the place—all that is except Caracciola, who wielded the huge white Mercedes with incredible skill, and in spite of his formula handicap managed to beat the Austins and Campari's Alfa home.

So far as I was concerned the whole thing was terrifying to the last degree, with Tim at his most animated, scorching round the corners in great slides, flat out the whole time in an effort to hold the much bigger Mercedes. My morale was not raised by the sight of a $4\frac{1}{2}$ Bentley upside down at the top of Mill Hill, with a lot of people trying to push its two tons off Rubin and his mechanic, and then of Kidston's $6\frac{1}{2}$, which had already won Le Mans and the Six-Hour for us that year, settled astride a bank and a ditch.

Thank goodness that by then Tim had decided that Caracciola was beyond the reach of mere mortals, and had eased up a bit. I relaxed, and, considering refreshment was called for, reached down for the pile of oranges I had thrown into the cockpit at the last minute. The pace had been too hot for them, too; in fact I could hardly hold them—and somehow roast oranges didn't appeal.

About five hours later, filthy dirty, very wet and very hot, we drew in, consoled at least by a class win and second place in speed.

After all that fun and excitement, the return to London, to a worsening sales situation and a rapidly gathering crisis, was a sobering business. Barnato had gone to America, on business and in pursuit of a new wife, and it was obvious that his business advisers' attitude towards the firm was hardening and that their only ambition was to get their master out as soon as possible and at the minimum possible loss. I was in for a fight, and I knew my weapons were hopelessly inadequate.

When people ask me (and they are too tactful to do so often) why Bentleys went bust, I usually give three reasons: the slump, the 4-litre car, and the 'blower' $4\frac{1}{2}$s; in proportions of about 70, 20 and 10% respectively.

I'll have a few words to say about the unfortunate 4 litre later. The 'blower', or supercharged, $4\frac{1}{2}$ was the car in which I had done thirty laps of the Ards circuit with Tim. Tim, as you've seen, had a constant urge to do the dramatic thing, a characteristic which I suppose had originally brought him into racing. His gaily vivid, restless personality seemed to be always driving him on to something new and spectacular, and unfortunately our 4½-litre car was one of his targets.

To supercharge a Bentley engine was to pervert its design and corrupt its performance. Every engine we built was conceived with an eye first on reliability, then on smoothness and silence, and lastly on sheer power output. Of course we were after speed and acceleration, but not by any falsely induced means; and I always held that the supercharger applied to the Bentley engine was, by its nature, a false inducer. When we wanted higher performance we increased the engine size, from 3 to 4½ to 6½, and finally to 8 litres, with the intention of always retaining refinement and reliability.

I disliked the easy short cut provided by the supercharger which was against all my engineering principles. But unfortunately for the Company, Tim used his charm and persuasion to induce first Amherst Villiers to build a special blower for his 4½, next Barnato to give it his blessing, and finally the Hon. Dorothy Paget to put up the money for a works at Welwyn and to buy and modify the chassis.

These weren't the only people attracted to the idea by Tim's reputation and the current fashion for the supercharger. Bertie Moir joined him as racing manager, Clive Gallop as works manager, and quite a number of our regulars elected to drive them.

It was, I thought, the worst thing that could happen to us. They would still be Bentley cars, carrying with them the spurious glamour associated in the public's mind with the supercharger, and Tim would see to it that they were well publicised. They would also lack in their preparation all the experience we had built up in the racing department under Clarke over ten years. I feared the worst and looked forward to their first appearance with anxiety.

On June 29th Tim entered his for the Brooklands Six-Hour race; it soon retired. At Phoenix Park a fortnight later, the two 'blowers' stayed the course and came in 3rd and 8th, but not without their troubles. In the T.T., apart from Rubin and Birkin (and I mentioned a page or two back what happened to them) the third car retired with engine failure. Tim was also forced to retire in the 500-Mile race two months later, and in the J.C.C. Double-

Twelve the following May none of the 'blower' team lasted out the course.

This list can become tedious; what really counted was that the supercharged 4½ never won a race, suffered a never-ending series of mechanical failures, brought the *marque* Bentley disrepute—and, incidentally, cost Dorothy Paget a large sum before she decided to withdraw her support in October, 1930.

It is a sad story, with a sting in the tail. Because Tim managed to persuade Barnato to allow him to enter a team in the 1930 Le Mans (in which none survived) we were obliged, in order to meet the regulations, to construct no less than fifty of these machines for sale to the public.

.   .   .   .   .

I think it would be a good thing to add a touch of light to these dark pages by mentioning briefly what else happened to us in that last Le Mans of 1930—besides the performance of the 'blowers' —and then to say a word or two about the 8-litre.

The team that year was a good one, lacking only Jack Dunfee, who had done so well in 1929. I wanted Jack to drive with Sammy, but Sammy was so strongly insistent that he should take Jack's younger and much less experienced brother under his wing, that I had to give way in the end, and Jack instead drove with Bertie Moir's 'blowers'. Barnato, of course, came back from America for it, intent on doing the hat trick, and stimulated to a state of terrific determination by the presence there of Rudi Caracciola, surely next to Nuvolari the finest racing driver of the between-wars period, partnered by the veteran Christian Werner, in a works-prepared 7½-litre supercharged Mercedes-Benz.

I don't think Babe ever enjoyed himself as much as in that Le Mans when, after Tim had got past the Mercedes in the opening laps, then torn off his tyre tread and later blown up his car, the pursuit and harrying of Carach was left in his and Glen Kidston's hands. It was a battle royal, with the pair of them slowly wearing down the Mercedes by making it use its supercharger almost continuously instead of only in the emergencies for which it was intended. There was never more than a minute or two between the two cars, and the lead changed time and again through the night, until at twenty past three Babe began to draw slightly away. A lap later he was 90 sec. ahead, then 2 min.; progressively his lead increased until he was catching glimpses of Caracciola's tail light down the straight. At 4.20 a.m. the scream of the Mercedes' supercharger died away for the last time, and it came slowly into the pits with dimmed lights. It was all over.

I went round to the Mercedes pit at once to express my sympathy, noticing at the same time that there was water pouring from the car's blown gasket, and had a word with Caracciola. He was very disappointed, of course, but was his usual generous, friendly self. They had not expected to be so hard pressed as they had been, he told me. Their carefully worked-out race forecast, based on our last year's performance, had shown them with a full lap's lead at this stage of the race, confirmation that our policy of not extending our cars unnecessarily paid dividends.

'Never before had I seen such a smile on the face of the "Tiger",' Benjy wrote of me later in *The Bentleys at Le Mans*. But it was nothing to compare with the high-spirited grin of pure glee we all recognised through the oil grime on Babe's face when he came in for his next refill. I slowed his car, and the Clement-Watney $6\frac{1}{2}$, down by 10 m.p.h. after this as there was nothing left in the field to worry us, which again caused some wry cracks among the drivers.

Our retirement from racing after Le Mans was strongly criticised at the time, but I'm sure it was the right thing to do, just as it was wise of Jaguar to withdraw in 1956 at the peak of their success to concentrate their resources on production.

The 8-litre really did add some colour and splendour to the last months at Cricklewood. We decided to build this big car to compete with the Phantom II Continental Rolls-Royce, and to the dismay of our rival company, we priced it a shade above their car and gave it distinctly better performance and at least equal refinement.

Perhaps the car is best described in the words of others, in this case of the testing staff of *The Autocar*, on December 5th, 1930:

> It may seem slightly unusual to commence a description of a car's test by disagreeing quite thoroughly with a statement made by a representative of the manufacturer when introducing the model at one of the firm's functions, but so great appears to be the discrepancy between what one would naturally

expect and what is actually provided that a word or two of argument is essential.

At the time of the Olympia Show the 8-litre Bentley was introduced in such a way as to stress to the full the fact that it was designed to be that rather mysterious type of vehicle which is generally known as a town carriage; and undoubtedly a great many people who listened to that announcement went away under the impression that performance was the very last thing on which the car based its claim to consideration—so much so that certain people undoubtedly believed that the performance was sacrificed to obtain other possibilities.

Now, in the first place, although everybody knows what is meant by a town carriage, and, further, can realise the distinction between that and a sports car, it is not, in fact, easy to see where one type stops and the other begins. Quite apart from that, the one thing, the dominant note, of the new Bentley is its tremendous performance, and on that performance alone it stands right in the forefront as an equal, at least, of any other car in existence. One glance at the figures shows, as no sentences or phrasing can, that the big 8-litre is something out of the common run, even when allowances are made for the increase in engine capacity as compared with the 6½ litres of the earlier six-cylinder model.

Therefore, it is impossible to allow that the car can be described, or in any way regarded, as just a town carriage and nothing more; and to remain silent concerning, or in any way belittle, the performance factor is, from the sales point of view, to disregard the principal reason why this splendid car should succeed.

Had it been that the performance made the car difficult to handle on top gear at low speed, heavy to manœuvre in traffic or in a confined space, harsh or noisy, then the performance by itself might justly be regarded as simply that of a sports car, though few of these features are easily noticeable even in the modern sports car, unless it has been tuned for racing.

Quite on the contrary, this car can be driven really softly on its high top gear as slowly as a man walks, and can accelerate from that without snatch and without difficulty, and the whole time the engine, being well within its power, is silent and smooth; in fact, it is only really apparent that there is a big engine working under the bonnet at all, and that so high a top ratio is used, when the machine is accelerated from a crawl. For all practical purposes, therefore, the machine does its work on the one gear, in town or out of it, and it is with that one gear that it best suits the average driver.

The new gearbox is interesting, the longer movement of the lever from one slot to another being a little puzzling at first to anyone who is accustomed to the earlier models, a point emphasised because to start on second and then change at once to top is the obvious way of handling the machine. The gears are quieter than before, and will be quieter still when there has been opportunity to obtain more experience with this type of box.

The use of two broad shoes in each of the rear-wheel brake drums, instead of four relatively narrow shoes, has certainly improved the brake power, and certain alterations have made the vacuum servo motor seem more definite and more positive, so that to the driver it really appears as though he can feel the shoes touch the drums and thus command a more delicate control. But the great change in the machine, apart from its engine, is the way in which the car, travelling fast and with a saloon body, can be taken round curves and corners with its shock absorbers adjusted as for town work. It is true that when once one was accustomed to the earlier 6½-litre that model seemed as steady as could be wished—provided the shock absorbers were really tight—yet the new car is steady with easy riding springs and so puts the earlier model entirely in the shade, a thing due in great part to the big, stiff frame, though the fact that the springs are farther apart and the chassis lower may have a great deal to do with it as well; and this rigidity makes the big car almost as tractable as one of the smallest machines on the road, while it seems to have no side sway whatsoever on a fast corner.

It is possible, of course, to go right over the chassis, pointing out here and there where improvement is apparent, but when all is said, it is not a matter of detail improvement that makes the 8-litre Bentley what it is, for the thing that counts above everything else is the way in which the big machine does its work, and its great sense of latent power. Exactly this and nothing else is the real reason why so big a machine has a future.

Putting it another way, one can breakfast comfortably in London yet lunch at Catterick Bridge, and during the whole of a run of this type there was none of the intenseness that usually comes into fast driving; indeed, it was practically impossible to believe that the car was travelling at anything like the pace the speedometer showed, though subsequent tests showed that speedometer to be reasonably accurate. In spite of the average, not a single village or town was traversed at anything like the pace that is maintained by the driver of an ordinary car, and in most cases it seemed much more pleasant to go through at a genuine 11 to 15 m.p.h.

Apart from that, the best testimonial to the ease with which the car did its work lay in the fact that the occupants of the two front seats were conversing naturally during the whole of the run.

In France the Bentley has kept up a cruising speed of 70 m.p.h. without the engine seeming to do anything at all, and, if the long northern roads offer, can go right up to 100 m.p.h. on the flat with surprisingly little apparent effort.

PERFORMANCE—FIGURES

Acceleration	10–30 m.p.h. 4-2/5 secs.
Maximum speed	101.12 m.p.h.
Weight	48 cwt. 0 qr. 14 lb.

The standard 8-litre was a lovely car to drive. But my own was a rather special one, and it gave me what I think was my most memorable driving of all time. Mine was really a $6\frac{1}{2}$-litre chassis with the bigger engine, fitted with a very pleasant, if abominably square and ugly, Weymann fabric body.

What a blessing those Weymann bodies were! When metal coachbuilding resulted in a continuous and ever-varying chorus of rattles and squeaks and chirrups, and a weight that terribly handicapped performance, the fabric-and-wood Weymann body gave complete silence without any sort of resonance, and almost negligible weight. Their only disadvantage, in the eyes of chauffeurs and some proud owners, was that they could not be polished and never gave the same satisfactory shine as half a dozen good coats of paint on steel or aluminium.

My 8-litre had beautifully comfortable seats (and few people today seem to recognise how important this is) and it had a great feeling of spaciousness.

157

It was about as quiet as a car can be and could do 110 m.p.h. on the open road without apparent effort. I modified it to my own requirements in several little ways. For instance, I used a proprietary American windscreen wiper which operated on a horizontal rod, one blade catching the other and carrying it in a companionable sort of manner to the side of the screen when parked. The 8-litre also had the very first Bosch trafficators, which never failed or jammed at any speed. Steady retrogression seems to be the guiding principle of some people who have made trafficators since then.

Also, for a time, the 8-litre was steam-cooled. Both Rolls-Royce and ourselves, with our huge engines, were having boiling troubles in hot climates and over mountain passes. This was hardly surprising with radiator blocks in the stage of development which applied at that time. It simply wasn't possible to fit one large enough to deal with the immense amount of heat given out by an engine of 6 or 7 litres under very demanding conditions.

As an experiment, then, we fitted a tank to the bottom of the radiator, and the water from this was pumped into the cylinders, when it overflowed and returned to the tank. In this way the cylinder was always full to a certain level, and when it steamed the steam went to the bottom above the water level and rose up the radiator's honeycomb, where it condensed and came down again as water.

I drove the 8-litre all over Europe and at full bore up every pass I knew without any trouble and never lost a drop of water. The advantage of this steam-cooling was that it was lighter and the car ran at a uniform temperature almost from the start.

We did have a little difficulty in getting a positive pump to drive the water into the cylinder block and the engine was rather noisier because the valve clearances had to be increased. But I think we would have got these difficulties ironed out, and we were approaching the production stage, when a new and much thinner and more satisfactory radiator block came on the market and got us out of this little bit of trouble. I believe the Americans were doing similar work at this time, as they were having trouble with their big engines, too. They called this modification 'evaporative' cooling. Cement-mixers and other machines that have to remain stationary for long periods operate their cooling on the same principle today.

The performance of that old 8-litre was extraordinary, even by modern standards, and in some respects it combined the merits of the 8-litre and 6½-litre Bentleys. With its lighter 6½ gearbox, axle and frame, the acceleration was tremendous and the 8-litre engine made it only fractionally heavier. Just how spectacular the performance of that car was in 1930 can be judged by glancing at the road test of a standard 8-litre, included in the Appendices of this book. My own car was substantially lighter than this, of course, and the acceleration figures in particular much superior.

To digress a moment: we had a certain amount of trouble with the production 8-litre frame at first. The 6½ frame was not very rigid and was rather unsuitable for some of the heavy bodies that customers insisted upon, but the extra rigidity incorporated in the 8-litre frame produced complications which became evident when I began testing it. At that time there was almost no support between the dash and the dumbirons for cars with big heavy chassis. The result of this was that when the front axle vibrated up and down, the frame became excited in sympathy, and on the wrong frequency, with axle tramp resulting. I discovered this under hazardous circumstances. I was approaching a corner at just 80 m.p.h. when the tramp set in, and I got no results at all when I tried to steer round. I'm not sure to this day just how I got out of that one. This happened just before we were to deliver the first cars, so the long-term results of the episode looked as though they would be even more embarrassing. We were hard put to it to solve the problem entirely satisfactorily on the 8-litre, but we did so just in time by various modifications, including the mounting of rubber bushes to the bolts securing the body scuttle dash to the chassis dashboard. I tested the early cars individually myself before delivery at every possible speed and under every possible circumstance, to ensure this safety until I was satisfied that we had entirely cured this tramping nuisance.

.   .   .   .   .

The Olympia Show of 1930 was a sad affair for everyone, and for us it would have been worse if we hadn't had the huge and impressive-looking 8-litre on the stand. That we survived for another nine months is accounted for by the fact that we sold sixty-three of these expensive cars in the period before the liquidation. Kevill-Davies had meanwhile been brought back as sales manager, and had been spending weeks touring the country with a fleet of cars, staging special Bentley Weeks to back up the agents. We did everything possible to keep things going, but it was no good; the brakes were hard on and trade was grinding to a standstill.

I suppose what we should have done was to lay off most of the men (it would have been better for them in the long run anyway) and content ourselves with the erection of a few 8-litre chassis for the occasional overseas order. This is what the liquidator did eight months later, and by doing so succeeded in breaking even.

What we did instead was to design and market a new car, the 4-litre, of unhappy memory. 'We must have something to compete with the small Rolls,' was the Board's verdict. 'A car that will undersell it. It doesn't matter much about the performance, so we'll use the 8-litre chassis—we've got a lot of them hanging around the works. And we don't want any of W.O.'s expensive cylinder heads with four valves per cylinder. Push rods will do.'

I declined as politely as I could to have anything to do with the top half. 'I don't know anything about push rods, I'm afraid,' I said. 'I think you'd better get someone else to look after this cylinder head.'

The 4-litre was in effect a last desperate fling on which most of the firm's remaining resources were spent, but very few were sold because it wasn't a car that could be recognised as a Bentley at all. The Bentley clientele wouldn't have anything to do with push-rod engines, and its performance, particularly its acceleration in top gear, was appalling, the power-to-weight ratio being ridiculous by our standards. If only the huge, heavy 8-litre chassis hadn't been used we should at least have had a car with some pep in it. Instead it was a cumbersome makeshift, with an undoubted long-life expectation, but nothing else that anyone wanted.

·   ·   ·   ·   ·

The motor industry nearly always seems to be in a state of boom or depression, and, like a patient with a severe attack of 'flu who thinks he will never be well again, every slump seems like the last. The 1930–1 one was the worst of them all, and while it was on the trade felt that things would never be the same again. Bentley Motors, dependent on its goodwill and on the annual sale of a comparatively small number of luxury cars to the higher-income group, had of course been more strongly affected than any other firm. But we could have pulled through; there's no question of that, and the receiver was already proving it in the five months during which he looked after the firm.

Our continued existence depended on Barnato and his advisers; and, because Barnato and I never afterwards referred to the liquidation, I shall never know for sure just how strongly he was influenced by his financial advisers in his decision to let Bentley Motors go.

By the early summer the writing on the wall was as clear as a Guinness poster, and despair had set in in all departments. And then on 11th July a news item on the City page of *The Times* announced that the London Life Association had applied for the receiver, the sums of £40,000 and £25,000 being due under two mortgages. Captain Woolf Barnato, it stated, was unable to meet these debts. The last item could only be described as a figure of speech; besides, Captain Barnato was in America on an extended visit; he had been there for some time, engrossed in business and personal affairs. The troubles of Bentley Motors must have appeared distant and perhaps rather tedious, and it seems clear that he must have been strongly prejudiced by the reports from London which told him how his losses would be certain to increase unless he allowed the Company to go into liquidation. In America the slump was far more severe than it was in England, and I think the general sense of hopelessness in the business world there must also have had some bearing on his decision.

It was late in June, 1931, when I heard that Barnato wasn't prepared to put up any more money, and I realised what must inevitably follow. The position was reported to the debenture holders, who decided at once that they would have to appoint a receiver. His name was Patrick Frere, and I only wish he had been our managing director instead of Barnato's crony. He was easy to work with, got on well with everyone, and created an atmosphere of confidence that we had not known for months, by such acts as retaining the design staff in the hope that the tide would turn.

Frere even succeeded in keeping my spirits reasonably high. I had been horribly depressed at first, of course, but it was only a matter of weeks before I heard that a firm of good repute was interested in taking us over, and while things could obviously never be the same as they had been before, I already knew that I should be kept on as chief designer, with a seat on the board.

The firm was D. Napier and Son, Ltd., of Acton, a large and prosperous company which had made some of the finest cars in England up to 1925, but had now concentrated all their resources on aero engines. They were anxious to launch back into the motor trade, and by intending to do so with a luxury car of my design in the middle of such a serious slump, they showed a flattering confidence in our design department. By the end of July, when the negotiations with Napiers were officially announced, I was given leave by the liquidators to start work on this new car.

Their last car had been an overhead cam-shaft six-cylinder machine of excellent design, great weight and indifferent performance. The car we worked on during those months—the Napier-Bentley—had a single overhead camshaft six-cylinder engine, with four valves per cylinder, and had 'square' dimensions of 110 × 110 mm, giving a capacity of just over 6¼ litres. It was in some respects a scaled-down 8-litre, but the crankshaft was completely redesigned and made more robust; and it revved at a good deal higher speed than the older car. There was nothing very revolutionary about the chassis, which was both lighter and shorter than the earlier car's, and we used semi-elliptics all round for the suspension, although to achieve a lower floor level we dropped the frame after the front axle. This, with the shorter wheelbase and a general lightening all round, made it an altogether lighter car than the 8-litre.

Incidentally, Sewell told me only recently that he was a member of a team that almost got into production with another car which, on paper at least, would have been very interesting. This also had a single overhead camshaft, with inclined valves, and was a high-performance six-cylinder engine of 4 litres, 85 × 115 mm. Other features of this further aborted Napier were four valves per cylinder, two S.U. carburettors, a detachable head and a gross output of 120 b.h.p. which was to have propelled this 35-cwt. machine at an estimated 90 m.p.h. It was to have had a very rigid deep frame to combat the menace of flexibility that so many big cars suffered at that time, and very long semi-elliptic springs.

It certainly sounds a most interesting car. Apparently they worked on it for three years, and then Napiers were obliged to put it into cold storage owing to the sudden pressure of rearmament orders at the beginning of 1935.

I was feeling reasonably happy about our future plans—which also included a possible new aero engine—when the time came in November for the receiver to apply to the court for approval of the Napier contract. Terms had been agreed, everything seemed to be tied up, and this was to be nothing more than a formality. Frere had even treated the staff to a farewell dinner and theatre. Instead that day turned out to be the most disastrous in my life.

The court was in session, everything was running according to schedule, Napiers' representative had made known to the judge their price, when a figure rose and said, 'I am empowered by the British Central Equitable Trust to offer so much for the assets and goodwill of this Company'; a figure that was, by an extraordinary coincidence, a fraction more than that offered by Napiers.

There was a brief and horrible pause, and then Napiers' representative got up and asked for a brief adjournment to allow him time to consult his principals. This the judge granted, and shortly after the court heard Napiers' new and higher bid.

The other barrister was about to raise his price too when the judge informed the court that he was not an auctioneer and that there would be another adjournment until 4.30 in the afternoon when sealed final bids were to be handed in by the two opposing barristers.

I don't know by how much precisely Napier were out-bidded, but the margin was very small, a matter of a few hundred pounds. All I knew that evening was that the deal would not be going through after all.

The confirmation of this bitter news was in the papers the next morning.

'Bentley Motors—Purchase Surprise' ran the headlines. 'The expected absorption of Bentley Motors Ltd. by D. Napier and Son Ltd., the aero-engine makers, will not take place. An unexpected and last-minute bid yesterday afternoon secured the Bentley assets for a rival buyer, a syndicate known As the "British Central Equitable Trust". Nothing is known of the syndicate's intentions. Nor is any director of the Trust apparently identified with motor-manufacturing interests. It is therefore presumed that this financial corporation is acting on behalf of some firm as yet unknown.'

Days passed without news, during which I was in a state of acute anxiety. It was an odd and unpleasant sort of situation not to know who now controlled my future, and the firm which bore my name. I waited for an official word, but none came, and Napier could tell me nothing.

And then one evening my wife came back from a cocktail party at which she had overheard a man saying something which she understood to mean that his company had recently taken over the old Bentley firm. Later in the party she managed to find out the man's name from her hostess.

'It was Arthur Sidgreaves,' my wife told me. 'Who is he?'

'He's the managing director of Rolls-Royce,' I told her.

CHAPTER THIRTEEN

Lagondas

NAPIER couldn't have been nicer and did their best to cheer me up, confirming that of course I could still work for them, and that, in effect, I should only be transferring my offices from Cricklewood to Acton. When Rolls-Royce, however, decided they had other ideas about my future, Napier's goodwill towards me was put to practical test.

My service agreement with Bentley Motors, Rolls-Royce informed me, was still in force. I was not a free man to select my own future. I was, they made clear, part of the assets which they had purchased, together with all my office furniture, my medals and cups and trophies.

Napier replied, rallying nobly to my defence, by disputing this contention, and actually went so far as to take legal proceedings on my behalf. So there I was, back in court again, with the issue this time a strictly personal one. The judge ended the hearing with the announcement that, as it was presented, he could not give judgement in the case, and advised Napier to re-present it in different form.

By then Napier had already spent a lot of money on me, for the legal expenses alone had been considerable, and so, with the greatest reluctance, they told me they simply couldn't pursue things any further. I replied that I understood perfectly, and we parted on the best of terms.

I am deliberately hurrying through these winter months of 1931-2, sketching in the barest outline, and I think that's the best way. Even now I find it distasteful and depressing to think about them, though I try to do so as charitably as I can. I suppose the nadir was reached when I was instructed in a letter to sell my old 8-litre. I left it with Jack Barclay and walked home, without a car for the first time for goodness knows how many years, wondering if I should ever have another, and wondering, too, just how long I could expect the hundred pounds or so I had left to last.

A tiny ray of light was cast at this moment in time by Billy Rootes (later Lord Rootes). He had been an active and successful agent for Bentleys, and I knew him quite well; well enough, anyway, for him to be able to ask me, without so much as a blush, if I wouldn't mind doing him a favour. 'I'd be very grateful if you'd try this car for me,' he told me on the telephone one day. 'And I want your honest opinion on it.' The car in question was one his new Hillman Minxes, and for that particular weekend, and for almost every week-end for months afterwards, a Minx or one of their larger cars used to be made available for me. Not only was this exceedingly kind and thoughtful of Rootes, but I had the added pleasure of being able to tell him, quite honestly, that I thought the Minx was a very nice little car.

For several weeks I lived in a sort of vacuum of uncertainty and worry, avoiding meeting anyone I knew, and trying to keep fit by walking round and round Hyde Park. On top of everything else at that time, my marriage wasn't working out. I had re-married seven years before, but unfortunately we weren't temperamentally very well matched, and I'm afraid I may have been too dedicated to my motor cars. Anyway, we were divorced soon after Bentley Motors was sold up, when I married my present wife.

It seemed inconceivable that Rolls-Royce should want to employ me. What could they do with me? They had their own design staff, and it seemed to me that I would be as embarrassing as a prisoner of war after the armistice signing. I simply couldn't imagine what they might have in mind when I was asked to call at their London head office for an interview with Sir Henry Royce.

It might be called an exploratory interview, I suppose, and I have often wondered what was its purpose. The opening was not propitious.

'I believe you're a commercial man, Mr. Bentley?'

'Well, not really,' I said. 'Primarily, I suppose I'm more a technical specialist.'

'You're not an engineer, then, are you?' Royce asked in some surprise.

I didn't know quite how to answer this without appearing vain. And then I remembered from thirty years back. 'Yes, I suppose you could call me that. I think you were a boy in the G.N. running-sheds at Peterborough a bit before I was a premium apprentice at Doncaster.'

This was accepted with a nod, and I heard no more on the subject. Instead I was offered a job, on not ungenerous terms, a rather nebulous sort of job in their London showrooms as an understudy to Percy Northey who had, like nearly everyone at Rolls-Royce, been there since the company began. Northey, who had years ago brought a Rolls-Royce into second place in the first Tourist Trophy race, looked after the technical liaison with the works, and was due for retirement soon. I was to help him, to attend the morning sales conferences at ten o'clock when any technical points and criticisms were discussed, and ensure that the demonstration cars were in good order.

Whether or not I could have refused is a nice point, and one that didn't arise.

.   .   .   .   .

Rolls-Royce had acquired, apart from me and my name, the Cork Street showrooms, the works and offices at Cricklewood, the service station at Kingsbury, and a few 8-litre chassis. The showrooms and works were sold; the service station returned to Vanden Plas, from whom we had rented it; the sad survivors of an extinct motor car were shipped to Derby; I had been safely placed out of harm's way; and now—for not only had they paid a large sum for it but to let it die would reflect badly on them— they must justify their acquisition of the *marque*. In fact, the Bentley car must be reborn.

What sort of car was it to be? And was the person whose name it was to carry going to have any say in its design? The second question never arose, for I was not consulted in any way on either the 3½- or 4¼-litre Rolls-Bentley and only asked to comment on the design. The first remained problematical for a time.

When the clouds of the depression had been seen on the horizon from Derby, work had begun on a small 2¾-litre bread-and-butter economy car, a sort of scaled-down 20–25 h.p., and intended to be sold at a considerably lower price. It turned out eventually to be as complicated and refined a piece of machinery as its bigger brother, and as the only saving was in the weight of metal involved, the term 'economy' was a misnomer, and the prototype was put aside. Actually it was a very nice little car, carrying a rather dainty radiator on the same classic pattern as all R.-R radiators, with a good turn of speed, as I discovered when

I tested it at Brooklands.

Because Rolls-Royce could not think of anything else to do with me after they bought me up in 1931 (my person was, in effect, part of the deal) they put me on to this testing; and the car provided me with many months of pleasant motoring. It also gave me a few nasty moments, because I was supposed to do things with it that no private owner would contemplate attempting. I used to take this 3½ out from Derby and round a private circuit of my own. The main purpose of these runs was to test the brakes. It is necessary only to drive fast any quality car of the 1930s on the roads today to realise what tremendous advances have been made in brake development in the past quarter-century. Most modern drivers, with their disc-braked, 80-m.p.h. saloons, would be surprised by the brakes of a 1935 Rolls-Bentley by modern standards, although their servo system was about the best that could be had at the time, and it was efficient and light to operate. The one serious drawback was that it was prone to very sudden fade if the brakes were used continuously. With a top speed of around 90 m.p.h. the Rolls-Bentley was quite fast, too, and I learned on a recent trip up to Derby that I still hold the works record for the Red Gate–Derby run in a 3½-litre.

But it was a combination of axle tramp and brake fade that combined to finish my testing days once and for all. One day some time in 1936 I was putting the 3½ saloon through its paces, which meant treating the brakes unmercifully at corner after corner on my own special route to London. Unfortunately, someone had dropped a brick at the side of the road and on the apex of a rather nasty left-hand corner. I caught it with my nearside front wheel, and was at once subjected to the most appalling axle tramp. This meant I had no steering at all. So I tried to use the brakes, and found that I had none of these either, as they had faded quite away. With neither steering nor brakes, I calmly awaited my fate, curious to learn what I was going to hit. My victim was a Wolseley Hornet, approaching innocently and on the correct side of the road.

The little Wolseley was quite pulverised by the impact, which made an ear-splitting noise, hurled the owner harmlessly aside and threw me against the steering column. In a remarkably short space of time I was standing in the road beside the mass of rubble, finding my hand being shaken by the Wolseley owner, who was congratulating me on my merciful escape, and, instead of showing any hard feelings, helped me to replace a piece of the end of my nose that had been almost severed.

There was a police case after this episode, however, and for a time Rolls-Royce were anxious that there might be something more serious than the 'without due care and regard' summons that was eventually issued. I said, in perfect truth, that a tyre had burst, and was duly fined a modest £10. But I thought the magistrate gave me one or two curious glances during the proceedings, and on the way out of the court he took me aside and asked me in a confidential tone: 'Tell me, Mr. Bentley, what did really happen? I know you use that road for testing your cars.' I gave him an enigmatic smile and passed on.

The Wolseley owner, by the way, got a new car from Rolls-Royce; there was never any argument about that. And I never did such strenuous testing again; I found I had become rather thoughtful.

Second to the D.F.P.s and my own cars, I suppose I have done a greater mileage on the $3\frac{1}{2}$ Rolls-Bentleys than any other motor. It was, as I have said, very pleasurable motoring, too. Soon after the first $3\frac{1}{2}$s came on the market, I was asked to take one across the Channel and do what I could to break it. 'Go anywhere you like,' I was told, 'for as long as you like.' I left at once, taking my wife with me, and we had a very pleasant seven weeks in France, Italy, Switzerland and Germany, going up and down all the passes I could find, and doing long, fast runs between cities.

I found two main faults, which were later put right as a result of this tour. One concerned the radiator shutters. On one morning we did the Milan–Turin run of 120 miles at an average of just 78 m.p.h., and we could have done much better than this if I had not discovered that at sustained high speeds the shutters were forced shut by the wind pressure, and the water temperature consequently rose alarmingly, obliging me to slow up momentarily until the needle dropped sufficiently. The shutters were very effective on the passes, and I never had a moment's concern about boiling. Coming down, however, was different. I remember one evening descending the mountains to Cannes, using third and accelerating briskly between the hairpins, when the brakes faded until nothing was left.

I chanced upon my report on this trip the other day and as an example of what used to occupy me in those days (and also what

cars used to suffer in my hands!) I think it might be interesting
to reproduce it in full:

3000 miles in France, Switzerland and Italy on 2–B–4

Route		Miles
1st day	Dieppe, Senz, Dijon, Pontarlier	390
2nd	Lausanne, Martigny, Brig, Gletch	210
3rd	Grimsel Pass, Rurka Pass, Oberalp Pass, Schyn Pass, Julier Pass, Ofen Pass, S. Maria	205
4th	Stelvio Pass, Sondrio, Cadenabbia on Lake Como	160
5th	Como, Milan, Turin, Briancon, Galibier, Braincon	220
6th	Briancon, Cannes	265

Homeward Journey

1st day	Cannes, Saulier	420
2nd	Saulier, Dieppe	374

The following passes over 3000 feet were climbed:

	Feet
Stelvio	9050
Galibier	8400
Furka	8000
D'Isoard	7900
Oberalp	7620
Julier	7500
Grimsel	7130
Ofen	7100
Sestrieres	6660
Monte Genevre	6100
St. Pierre	3800
Schyn	3400
La Faye	3300

The car contained two people and 240 lb. of luggage.

The first day's run across France was done in torrential rain,
which practically never stopped. This severe test produced only
one very small leak at the corner of the windscreen, the sunshine
roof being perfectly watertight. Mud was, however, splashed over
the engine and the front side of the dashboard. The windscreen
wipers work rather slowly for this type of rain.

The car ran very well, but on cambered roads and on corners

one felt the overhang weight of the luggage, making it more of an effort to control the car. On bad pavé the car was very objectionable—the wings, lamps, etc., being very unsteady and the weakness of the frame in front causing the bonnet and body to rattle; this is the worst feature of the car in my opinion.

The second day was also very wet, and after a short time the windscreen-wiper cable broke, putting both the windscreen wipers out of action. The roads had many corners, and working the windscreen wiper by hand became very tiresome. This is a most annoying thing to happen on a tour and is a big job to put right, as the cables are buried in the body.

The third day brought out the best of the car, and the way it climbed the various passes was a revelation, and I have never been in a car which made these roads appear so ordinary.

The weather was not hot—60° to 65°; the water temperature never rose above 78°.

It was a very enjoyable day's run; the cornering, the gearbox, acceleration and handiness of the car enabled one to appreciate the scenery without the effort usually associated with driving over these twisting and hilly roads.

The fourth day included the Stelvio Pass, with its forty hairpin corners on the way up, and there was never any doubt of getting round with quite a lot to spare. The air temperature was 65° and the highest water temperature was 80°. The acceleration between the corners was excellent in spite of the weight carried.

The back number plate was knocked off on one of the corners and went over the side of the road. This was not the first time this plate had been hit. This standard position is really too low. The front wings also get hit if you are taking corners which require full lock.

Fifth day. This day's run included the two Autostradas from Como, Milan and Turin, and 120 miles were covered at an average of 75 m.p.h. The Galibier was also climbed at the end of the day in an effortless way which I have never experienced before. Once again the water temperature was under 80°.

When driving fast between Como and Turin the water temperature varied between 78° and 95°, owing to the wind pressure closing the shutters, while the oil pressure dropped 7 lb. below the usual average pressure owing to the oil getting very hot.

Sixth day. During the day's run, while trying to keep a set average speed which meant going down one of the smaller passes using third gear for acceleration, and braking rather hard before the corners after a very short time the brakes became very ineffective owing presumably to their getting very hot.

SUMMARY

Body details

1. Back number plate is too low.
2. Front wings have too little clearance when on full lock at outside edge.
3. Dust enters luggage compartment making the toolbox deep in dust. It also enters the fitted suitcases and makes one's clothes very dusty.
4. Window winder and door handles rattle owing to their getting very loose.
5. Wind roar round body is the most tiring feature of a long run and makes it almost impossible to talk without raising one's voice very considerably.

Chassis details

1. The weakness of the frame in front and the small and hard spring movement causes the car to be almost unbearable on bad pavé, and the wings, lamps, bonnet and body get rattled very badly, and is the most unpleasant feature of the car. It is also very bad when cornering on a road where there are bad potholes causing the front of the car to sidestep outwards.
2. Petrol consumption is very good—from 16 to 22 according to speed, etc. Oil consumption with these pistons (Aerolite) is very good, being over 2,000 miles to the gallon. Very little water was put in the radiator.
3. The brakes squeak very badly—standard linings.
4. The petrol pumps supply petrol satisfactorily at 9,000 feet and when temperature was 95° in the shade.
5. The car handles very much better when there is no weight in the luggage container.
6. P.100 headlamps do not make enough difference to glare when dimmed.
7. Esso or Azur petrol should be used. Some of the others are very bad and pink very badly, even when one-third retarded.

8. Although lamps were seldom used very little water had to be added to the accumulators.
9. No electrical troubles.

The $3\frac{1}{2}$ Rolls-Bentley was almost as fast as the $4\frac{1}{2}$-litre Bentley that we had first produced eight years earlier, and of course it was much lighter, and quieter with its six-cylinder engine. It also had the best gearbox—with synchromesh—that Rolls-Royce had ever produced. All that it seriously lacked was independent suspension at the front, and really fade-free brakes.

When I have mentioned this lack of independent front suspension, people have often retorted: 'If you were so keen on it why didn't you ever fit it into your own cars?' The answer was that at the time we designed the $6\frac{1}{2}$- and 8-litre, independent front suspension was too elaborate, too expensive and not sufficiently developed, just as an effective four-wheel braking system was not ready for the first 3-litre cars. We should certainly have got round to it in time, and of course we included it in the V12 Lagonda specification in 1937.

I had nothing, whatever, of course, to do with the designing of the $3\frac{1}{2}$-litre Rolls-Bentley, but it was quite an interesting experience for me to be an observer and a witness to the growing-pains and development of the car, particularly as I had suffered so many or the same headaches with our own machines. I was, however, 'kept in the picture', as the saying goes, and I remember the conference that took place and the memoranda that were circulated on the subject of the engine for the new car—the 'Bensport' as it was called in the works. For some months during 1932 experiments went on at Derby with Powerplus and Roots-type superchargers fitted on a small experimental engine and using aero-engine fuel.

This 25-h.p. engine, the J.1., with the induction on one side and exhaust on the other, had been designed to replace the 20/25-h.p. engine and provide the smaller Rolls-Royce with more power. This it did well enough, but at the expense of a noise level above R-R standards but well below contemporary sports-car standards. To use it in a new 'Bentley' seemed a sensible way of preventing it from going on the scrap-heap.

As may be imagined, these supercharger tests were rigorous in the extreme and the higher power output achieved was treated with the gravest reserve. Derby were determined that the new car should have a sporting flavour, in the tradition of its predecessor. But no risks were going to be taken; there must be no shadow of chance that the huge and unique fund of goodwill possessed by the company might be jeopardised by an unreliable car, even one appearing under another name.

If I had been consulted, I think I could have saved Derby the expense and time involved in testing the 'Bensport' with a supercharged engine. Quite apart from any difficulties regarding royalties that would be payable for the use of Powerplus or Rootes-type superchargers, the necessity for owners to have to use special high-octane fuel every time they filled up had to be considered.

Even in 1932, when it was at the height of its fashionableness, the supercharger still had a distinct flavour of the race-track about it and this Rolls-Royce was determined to avoid at all costs. Quite apart from all these disadvantages, Rolls-Royce cars and the supercharger were temperamentally alien to one another Very largely at Hives's persuasion, all ideas of using a supercharger, even a supercharger of their own manufacture, were finally dropped when gasket after gasket was blown during these trials, and the J.1 engine with atmospheric induction, which was all ready and awaiting a job, was used instead, with admirable results, in the chassis of the old experimental 18-h.p. Rolls-Royce.

Rationalisation was not a word often used in the motor business in those days, while today, of course, no one pretends to differentiate between a Rolls-Royce and a Bentley, although, as I believe the American advertisements put it, those who feel self-conscious about possessing a car with the square radiator can choose the alternative and save themselves a few dollars as well. But there was a certain sensitiveness at Derby about the use of standard Rolls components in a machine that did not bear the correct name, and I remember after a conference and test run at Brooklands with the first Bensport, now called the Bentley 3½-litre, 'The Silent Sports Car', that recommendations were made to design new types of milled nuts for the valve cover, new grips for brake and gear lever, a new petrol filler cap and floor mats with the letter 'B' engraved on them and numerous other minor modifications in order to distinguish the new car from its stablemates.

The 3½ Rolls-Bentley was an excellent car on the road, light and easy to handle, with surprisingly good performance allied to quietness. Later on it was spoilt, just as the 3-litre Bentley of a decade earlier had been spoilt, by customers who put on heavy, unsuitable bodywork, which inevitably, as before, led to complaints of lack of performance. So up went the capacity to $4\frac{1}{4}$ litres, and the same story began again.

The model was launched with the customary R-R. publicity—discreet, tasteful and most effective—in time for the 1933 Show, and at the Royal Hotel, Ascot, there assembled by invitation all the motoring correspondents worthy of the name for a luncheon and trial run. There were three cars for demonstration use, and on these Cox, the sales manager, Percy Northey and I were to take the gentlemen of the Press in turn round a triangular course. Naturally, the purpose was to impress, and it was thought advisable to post scouts around the circuit to ensure that the roads were clear.

It was a very good luncheon, and the three of us enjoyed our afternoon hugely. But the peak of the day for me came when I identified the proprietor of the hotel as the man who had once written a book called *An Innkeeper's Diary*. I had been amused to read in this that one of his guests at his previous hotel had been W. O. Bentley, 'a timid little man'. I invited him to come round with me in the front seat on the last lap of the day, when the brakes were feeling a little tired. By then my eye was well in and I felt I knew the road and the car thoroughly. I had him holding on like grim death before I skidded to a halt in front of his hotel again, and told him who I was.

.   .   .   .   .

After eighteen months or so with Rolls-Royce, and on the retirement of Percy Northey, I was appointed to a position that was little less indeterminate but which carried the title Technical Adviser to the Managing Director. I continued to look after the demonstration cars, both those attached to the London showrooms, which were, ironically, now situated below the offices in which the original Bentley 3-litre engine had been designed, as well as those belonging to the London agents.

This job was taken very seriously by the firm, and the cars were brought in turn by a chauffeur to my Addison Road house where I was now living, married to my present wife. There I tried them out, first sitting in all the seats in turn while I was driven round, usually taking over myself for a while and driving us both back to the office, where I would submit a report. The Continental Phantoms I would take down to Brooklands to see that their performance was up to scratch. It was also my business to test other cars, mostly high-performance cars which could be regarded as competitors to the Rolls-Bentley, and this I enjoyed immensely.

I was also expected to take both Rolls and Bentleys over to the Continent for long test runs, just as I had done in the old days with our own cars. The first of these was with one of the $3\frac{1}{2}$s, which I thrashed over the Italian and French passes and ran at high speed along the Routes Nationales for six weeks, the only sure way to discover hidden faults. Another time I took a Continental Phantom II Rolls-Royce on a similar trip and sent in a long report with a number of suggestions for improvements. For instance, on the Continental I got stuck on a corner 9,000 feet up on the Galibier Pass with the petrol boiling away merrily, and as a result the works moved the pipe lines clear of the engine and the pump to a cooler position along the chassis.

Not all these reports and suggestions were received kindly or acted upon. There was, as you can imagine, a certain suspicion of recommendations from an 'outside' engineer by the regular staff of the experimental department and the works, which was increased rather than reduced by being filtered through the managing director. As soon as I got wind of this attitude I made arrangements for direct liaison with Derby, and started making weekly visits to the works, getting to know the men there personally. To leave the dreariness of the London offices behind and head for Derby was like a tonic, and my days there were the happiest and most interesting of my time at Rolls-Royce. Not only did I succeed in damping down the quite understandable distrust they had for me at first, but I made many good friends, some of whom left to join me later and are still my friends today.

There was enormous talent at Derby, so much that it sometimes became congested, which led to frustration among some of the younger technical men. The standards of workmanship and attention to detail were extraordinarily high, and if (rather to my satisfaction) I occasionally found them making the same sort of mistakes that we had made at Bentley Motors, there was never the least suggestion of complacency.

I suppose I should have been grateful for a job that was well paid and which kept me in touch with all the good motor cars of the time, and I certainly couldn't complain of being overworked. But of course it was all rather tame and uninspiring after the exciting and adventurous days of Bentley Motors, and I could never quite throw off the feeling that I was nothing more than a hostage —a dangerous ex-enemy confined (with all reasonable comforts) to my Elba.

By 1934, Barnato, who had bought a substantial number of Rolls-Royce shares shortly before the liquidation, was on the new Bentley board. I saw him often; we were still good friends, if there was a trace of reserve in a relationship which was now on an entirely social level. Business was never discussed between us, and when we talked about the old days it was of our cars and our racing. It was never suggested, by Barnato or anyone else, at any time that I should become a director of Bentley Motors (1931) Ltd.

By an extraordinary piece of mismanagement we had never registered the name Bentley as a trade mark, a fact which the legal men at Rolls-Royce jumped on at once, and one of the first things I had been asked to do when I joined the company was to sign a document authorising them to apply for one in my name. In addition, and in consideration of my release from paying them a certain sum of money owing at the time of the take-over, I signed a contract which, in the event of my leaving them, debarred me from lending my name to the design of any car or aero engine for a period of ten years.

It was perfectly understood between us that as soon as my service contract expired I was free to leave the company. On my past record, this was indeed considered probable as soon as a likely job came along. I suppose, after all, that I could be considered a car designer rather than a car tester, and I was still only forty-seven.

Just the same, I was undecided whether I should leave the security of this huge company and cast myself into the mêlée again. Finally it was the persuasion of my wife and friends, who knew how frustrated I felt, that made me take the plunge. Though I've paid for it dearly, not for one moment since then have I regretted the decision.

. . . . . .

In June, 1935, an odd and totally unexpected thing happened. A 4½-litre Lagonda, driven by Hindmarsh and Fontes, won at Le Mans. It wasn't a very spectacular win and the speed was considerably below that of Barnato's Bentley for the first twelve hours in 1930, before he was slowed down. But it was a win and would mean a tremendous fillip for the firm which, like us, had recently gone into liquidation.

On the Friday before the race, I had had to be with Arthur Sidgreaves for most of the day. It was an occasion of some delicacy for me, for my contract had just expired and he obviously expected me to give my decision on the new five-year contract, on better terms than the first, which had already been drawn up. Over lunch we discussed this and that and I awaited the leading question.

Instead, he told me that Rolls-Royce were thinking of making a bid for Lagondas, a subject which was as delicate as my contract, for I had just heard from Dick Watney, who had recently left Rootes, that a friend of his was also about to buy the firm, and that he wanted me to look after the design side. I remained firmly noncommittal on the matter, contenting myself with asking Sidgreaves why on earth Rolls-Royce should think of doing such a thing.

Twenty-four hours later that 4½ Lagonda set off with fifty-seven other cars round the Sarthe circuit, and on the Sunday evening the unexpected news came through that it had won. Dick Watney heard from me first thing on Monday morning. 'Yes,' I told him, 'I'll come if the sale goes through.'

Thank goodness, Rolls-Royce were beaten to it this time by Watney's friend, Alan Good. Good was a Lincoln's Inn solicitor who had decided to break out of the legal rut into the uncertainties of sports-car manufacturing; and now I was back in it again—with him.

Lagonda is the name of a small town in America, the home town of a Wilbur Gunn, who emigrated to England sixty years ago and began building motor-launch, motor-cycle and three-wheeler engines, and then small utility cars. By 1935, when I went there as technical director, they had acquired through their 2-litre, 3- and finally 4½-litre cars a solid reputation for quite high-performance sporting machines. Somehow the company had staggered through the worst years of the depression, but had never really found its feet again, and when Alan Good took it over, the factory and offices at Staines were in a dreadful state. I was horrified when I went down to see them for the first time; it seemed impossible that a car that had won Le Mans had emerged from such a dilapidated wreckage, and I was thankful that responsibility neither for rebuilding and extending the works, nor the finances, were mine.

At the same time I was rather dismayed to find, contrary to what I had been told, that Dick Watney was to be the managing director instead of Alan Good. Watney, a likeable man, was not in my opinion a big-enough character to handle the responsibility, even with Good as Chairman over him. However, what mattered to me was that I was to be quite unfettered in the one field I knew something about, a change after the diversions and anxieties of Bentley Motors, the frustrations and politics of Rolls-Royce, and I felt quite light-headed with the sense of freedom.

At first, until the new buildings were completed, working conditions in the drawing-office verged on the ludicrous. It was an ancient tumbledown shed; the rain rattled on the corrugated iron, and spiders and water fell freely about us. I had known austere working conditions at Bentley Motors, but nothing quite like this.

As a first obvious step before we could get our own car on to the drawing-boards, we decided to re-vamp the 4½-litre model for which the works was already tooled up. It was a fundamentally sound if rather coarse basis on which to start, a six-cylinder, o.h.v. push-rod engine, sturdy, powerful, and with a quite outrageous crank-shaft roar. It seemed a long step—and a retrograde one—from the 8-litre and the dainty, involved and highly refined 3½-litre Rolls-Bentley. But we managed to get an agreeable high-performance car ready for the Show that autumn, with rubber-insulated engine mounting and suspension modifications providing greater smoothness and quietness, improvements to the combustion chambers giving about 140 b.h.p. at 4,000 r.p.m. (providing around 95 m.p.h. in top), and a host of other alterations such as the provision of synchromesh gears and a right-hand gear change. It was a good buy at around the four-figure mark, and later we put the engine into the V 12 chassis. In this form it remained in production until the war.

My period at Rolls-Royce had driven home once again to me the value of time for development: time, that luxury that only the most solidly founded firms can afford. The big Rolls-Royce Phantom III car, for example, was begun in May, 1932, with no

less than sixteen designers. Two years were spent on the completion of the main design, and the first experimental car was running
in June, 1934. But it was another sixteen months before the car
was even announced, and production didn't begin until May,
1936—four years in all. That was how Rolls-Royce achieved
standards of perfection against which other companies, without
their reserves of capital, couldn't compete.

We had produced the 3-litre Bentley in just twelve months. At
Lagondas we were given rather over eighteen months to have a
car ready for the Motor Show. 'When a renowned designer and
his assistants—in this case W. O. Bentley and his technical staff
—set themselves the task of evolving a car which shall rank in
the very forefront of machines,' wrote one of the motoring journals of the new V 12 Lagonda, 'it would only be a matter of surprise if that car failed to be outstanding.' To us it was a matter of
surprise that we got the car out at all. No reasonably conscientious
workman likes being rushed; and yet the yearly balance sheets
made the impatience of Alan Good and his backers—and also
the salesmen—inevitable. We did our best, and I think the V 12
Lagonda of 1937 could have been the best car for which I have
been responsible; but I would have given my right arm to have
had another two years to develop the car before it was placed on
the market.

The V 12 was a very short-stroke engine, with twelve cylinders
set in two rows in the form of a 'V'. The short stroke resulted, as
we had intended, in great smoothness and flexibility, and no car
that I have ever driven has given such an impression of quiet
effortlessness. The first road test spoke of the passengers dozing
in the back seat at 100 m.p.h.; this was quite practicable, too, for
the 4/5-seater body carried very comfortable seats. The performance at the top end was satisfactory and the top speed was well
over the 100 mark, but at the lower end there was plenty of scope
for improvement, and the 0–50 acceleration time was only just
under 10 sec. That, together with points of detail in the chassis
design and the steering, were things we would have put right if
the war had not intervened.

Soon after production began we put on a show at Brooklands
for publicity and general Lagonda prestige. Lord Howe and
Stan Ivermee took a V 12 and a 4½-litre down to the track to see
how far they could go in the hour. Both were completely standard
production models and both had our own saloon coachwork.

Brooklands, as anyone will tell you who drove there in 1938, was in a very bad state, and the V 12 damaged a tyre half-way through the run, and Lord Howe had to stop, jack up and put on the spare. In spite of this he managed 101½ miles in the sixty minutes, with a lap at over 108 m.p.h., while Ivermee did just under 96 miles in the same time.

This was good for business, but we had never thought of this big, refined sports carriage in terms of racing at all, and it therefore came as a nasty shock when Alan Good suddenly told me early in 1939 that he had decided we ought to run a team at Le Mans in June.

'But we're nothing like ready for that sort of thing,' I told him. 'If you really want to race the V 12 you must give us at least another eighteen months for preparation.'

Good was adamant. 'If it could be done with the old 4½ then there's no reason why we can't win with this. It's a much better car, and it's a much faster car.'

Of course he was right to want the prestige that a Le Mans win would bring the model, but to be left with less than six months to get the cars ready was patently absurd.

'All right,' I agreed after more argument. 'But let's be quite clear—and tell everyone else—that we're not out for a win this time. We're running for what we'll learn from the race.'

In fact we decided to run the cars at a set speed, regardless of what happened to the rest of the field, a mile an hour faster than the 1938 winner's, and see how things worked out. What really counted was what we found when we pulled the cars to pieces afterwards.

We nearly killed ourselves getting the cars ready in time. Stan Ivermee looked after the work, with Kemish, Sopp, Taylor, and one or two others, all from the old Bentley days. I suppose there was some sleep and food for them, but whenever I went down there they were always at it. The most fundamental modifications were the fitting of four carburettors and a much larger petrol tank, and the raising of the compression. But it was all the little bits and pieces (too technical to go into here) that took the time, as they always do in preparation work—so much time, in fact, that we could only try out one of the cars for an hour or so at Brooklands. The other had its first run down to Newhaven to catch the boat.

They looked very low and sleek, and formidable, too, we

thought, with their special two-seater bodywork. Arthur Dobson and Charlie Brackenbury were to handle one of them; the other, with his coat of arms emblazoned on the dark green cellulose, belonged to Lord Selsdon, and he and Lord Waleran ('The Peerless Peers') were to drive it under our control.

It was quite like the old days to be going in good company with a team to Le Mans again, and what made it even more pleasant was the welcome I received from everyone, from the customs officials at Dieppe to the scrutineers, and wonderful old Faroux himself, whom I had first met sixteen years earlier at the first Le Mans ever.

I got a shock when I saw the circuit for the first time again for nine years. From the speeds—the lap record had gone up to 96 m.p.h. against Tim's 89 m.p.h.—I should have guessed that there had been some radical changes to the corners and to the road. But I hadn't realised we were going to have this billiard-table surface, with every bend eased, the trees cleared to improve visibility, the road widened everywhere. This was more like track racing. The regulations showed that the whole conception of the race had altered. Now there were no hoods or screens, two-seaters were *de rigueur*, and it wasn't necessary to carry that great burden of ballast that had always been such a headache. Pit work was revolutionised by the use of gravity-fed petrol pumps and other aids, and mechanics were now allowed to work on the cars. You can see what this meant by comparing the time of 27 minutes that the winning Bentley in 1930 spent in the pits, when our pit work was really streamlined, and the 12 minutes the Selsdon-Waleran car was in the pits in 1939. The 15 minutes saved at 80-odd m.p.h. represented twenty miles in the race, or about 2½ laps.

After the 1—2—3—4 Bentley win in 1929, Charles Faroux had written, 'The moment has arrived when the French automobile industry must decide whether to reassert itself or allow the decline to continue.' Ten years later it had reasserted itself all right; there was no question of a few small blue cars tussling five hundred miles behind for the Index of Performance handicap prize. In 1939, besides Wimille's and Veyron's streamlined 3.3-litre supercharged Bugatti, there were big Talbots, Delages and a whole flock of very fast Delahayes, all in the hands of well-known drivers.

The Saturday was blazing hot, with the banners floating in the sun and, as always, what appeared to be half the population of France there, gaily dressed for their great annual fête. And they certainly got their money's worth. The start particularly was as wild as I have ever seen it, the Sommer-Bira saloon Alfa, Louis Gerard's Delage, Chinetti's Darracq and the big Bugatti all fighting it out just as if it was a half-hour sprint run.

With Stan Ivermee handling the pit with his usual efficiency and my wife looking after the only slightly less important domestic side, it was as pleasant a race as we could have hoped for, with the two green Lagondas running faultlessly and with only one unpremeditated call when Dobson's exhaust worked loose. They kept scrupulously to their stipulated 83 m.p.h., and slowly, as the French cars tore themselves to pieces, we found ourselves automatically working up through the field from tenth or twelfth place, until the following afternoon when, at four o'clock as the flag fell, there were only the Bugatti and Gerard's Delage (by then fit only for the wrecker) left ahead of us.

That was my last Le Mans, and I've never been back to the Sarthe circuit since. But it wasn't quite my last race. The Outer Circuit August Handicap was one of the few occasions when Ebblewhite, the famous handicapper, was thoroughly caught on the hop. He wildly underestimated the speed that the two Lagondas—the Le Mans cars without wings—could lap at, and Brackenbury and Selsdon were having to cut out at the fork so as not to embarrass him too much. Even so they were miles ahead of anything else, lapping under these conditions at 128 m.p.h.

A week or two later my wife and I were staying on holiday at the San Christophe Hotel near Miramar in the South of France. The sea was of the incredible shade of blue that only the Mediterranean can assume, the food and wine were beyond compare, that blessed sun blazed in a clear sky day after day—and the hellish doings of Adolf Hitler seemed a million miles away. But, dutifully and reluctantly, I drove the Lagonda up to the top of the hills behind Miramar one evening and switched on the radio. The six o'clock news came through, loud and clear and horribly depressing. Germany was poised to invade Poland; an ultimatum had been sent by Britain. Slowly we drove down the steep road back to our hotel.

The Riviera had already emptied and we were almost the only English people left in the town. By the time we had reached Dieppe, after being almost reduced to pushing the car for lack of petrol, the ominously threatening atmosphere had changed to one of wild disorder. Hundreds of cars were stranded all over the docks and the town, and I got a hollow laugh for pointing out that we had booked shipping space. In the end we sailed without the car like everyone else, and that drab port, Newhaven, looked drearier than ever as we steamed in for the last time on the packet boat.

.　　　.　　　.　　　.　　　.

At the end of 1936 my wife and I had moved from our London home in Addison Road to a house with a thatched roof and a beautiful garden in Colnbrook. From Millbrook House to Staines took only a quarter of an hour, and after eighteen months of driving from London to the Lagonda works I had had enough of it. The west London industrial fringe is not generally considered prepossessing, and it is true that there are some pretty terrible arears of scattered factories and bungalows spread out over a dead flat landscape. Colnbrook escaped all this, and, relieved of heavy traffic by the by-pass, has remained an unspoilt oasis in that steel-and-concrete desert. Millbrook was the happiest house I have lived in, and I think we should have stayed there longer if London Airport hadn't come and sat down outside our back door.

Any mild excitement in the Second World War seemed to happen at Millbrook rather than Lagondas. The factory was so craftily camouflaged that it never got a bomb splinter, even from the squadron that blasted Vickers at Brooklands which passed right overhead. But our house was neatly pin-pointed for enemy bomb sights by those famous barrage balloons Jessie I and Jessie II (Jessie I upped and away in a gale one night), and I sometimes suspected that these two plump girls, who were a part of the barrage for Hawker's factory, carried the painted message for Luftwaffe pilots that the factory where I worked turned out thousands of anti-aircraft rockets every day.

This was all highly important, if very tedious. But I was delighted to hear that our more distinguished products were taking part in the war, too. For the V 12 was to have a war career!

This came about because, shortly after Italy entered the war, Malta harbour was attacked by a squadron of unique and highly dangerous hydroplanes that can best be described as manned torpedoes. We received the first and highly secret information about them at Lagondas when we got an urgent appeal from the Admiralty at Bath saying that they were interested in the V 12 engine and could we come down at once for consultations.

Dick Watney arrived to find the Admiralty in a state of some excitement over a signal recently received from Malta describing this hydroplane attack. It seemed that they were very fast machines each manned by a volunteer who steered his craft with its 5 cwt. of explosive in the nose straight for the harbour shipping from its parent submarine. He was equipped with an ejector seat and a rubber dinghy and he had recourse to these when the hydroplane leapt over the harbour boom at some forty knots.

This feat was accomplished with the assistance of an ingenious arrangement by which the bevel-driven vertical shaft driving two contra-rotating propellers was swivelled out of the water, and back into it again when the obstacle had been passed. The engine, the naval signal related, was by Alfa Romeo, probably a 3-litre twin overhead camshaft one.

The Admiralty thought that the V 12, tuned to some 240 b.h.p. and with four carburettors as we had used at Le Mans, was the most suitable engine to power a similar craft to offset this Italian menace, particularly I imagine because of its low weight. Vospers were brought in for the hull, and we were told that the first machines would be expected within three months. This deadline was, in fact, met, although it meant a tremendous pressure of work at Staines and Southampton, and a very tight liaison between us.

Some time after the prototype was finished, the navy succeeded in capturing one of the Italian hydroplanes, which had run up on to the beach in Malta harbour and had failed to explode. The similarity with our own was astonishing, even down to small points of transmission detail, in spite of the fact that neither Vospers nor Lagondas had more than the most uncertain cabled details of the Italian machines.

Peter du Cane of Vospers did a number of highly dangerous trial runs in our boats, and I think they were finally developed as practical weapons of destruction; in fact experiments were also carried out with dropping them (manned by a dummy) from Sunderland flying boats at low level, although whether on impact the engine went through the hull I never discovered. I don't think they were ever used in combat, and I don't believe the Alfas did any more damage than the Lagondas.

The period 1939–45 was mostly drudgery, as I suppose it was for nearly everybody: a good deal of hard work, long hours and not much fun, though things were made gayer for us by the near-by 956 Balloon Squadron, whose officers often came in for dinner and parties at Christmas and for tennis parties in the summer. Millbrook was never empty or quiet, especially as we nearly always had a nomadic population of W.A.A.F. billettees, and my wife was perpetually busy with her W.V.S. work.

When at last I began to feel that my work at the factory and the night A.R.P. duties weren't really enough, I went to see my old C.O. of 4 Squadron from the R.N.A.S. days, who was now something important at the Admiralty, to ask if I could be of any use in the aero-engine line, but nothing came of that, and I went back to the aircraft parts, the bits and pieces for tanks and the even more unpleasant things like flame-throwers that we were turning out at Staines.

Towards the end of the war, with all the new machinery we had installed and the vast expansion in the size of the factory, it was quite clear that if we went back to cars we could do some quite big things. There seemed, in fact, nothing to prevent us from becoming a major producer in the motor-car market, and when it was obvious that the tide had turned, I began to think about our post-war car.

Alan Good wanted the V 12 back into production, and there was nothing I should have liked better. It would have been a very good car with all the development work we could have put into it. But, apart from the fact that all the jigs and dies had been scrapped, I wasn't at all sure that it was the car the post-war world was going to need. Obviously, I thought, there were not going to be so many people with money for a luxury machine as there had been, and the cost of motoring was going to be higher. Now that we had all the facilities for quantity production, it did seem unwise deliberately to take the risk with an expensive car, with its acute susceptibility to every trading recession. In this, I was entirely wrong!

In the end we decided on a medium-sized car aimed at the quality rather than the luxury market, a car designed for as high a performance as silence, comfort and a $2\frac{1}{2}$-litre engine would permit. The prototype was very like the current Lagonda, with a body we built ourselves, and performance was quite good, with a maximum around the 90-m.p.h. mark; and with independent suspension on all wheels, the handling was very pleasant. I didn't think we should have any trouble selling this at a competitive price, just above that of the Rover, thanks to the quotation we got from Briggs for making the bodies and frames. And 'The New 2½-litre Lagonda-Bentley' would be the first entirely new post-1939 designed car. So far so good. Now we had to announce and sell it.

The first advertisements duly appeared, and the first response was a prompt and very firm demand, backed by threat of legal action, from Rolls-Royce that we must withdraw my name at once from the car because it was an infringement of their trade mark. We had an immediate extraordinary board meeting at Lagondas, to which I brought my fourteen-year-old agreement. This was studied with care again, and then I said: 'Let me go up to see Hives and talk this over with him before we get mixed up with litigation. He's not an unreasonable man and I know him well.' Good and the others agreed, and I went off right away to see him at the Grosvenor where he was staying.

Lord Hives had now succeeded Sidgreaves as managing director, which made things easier. I think I've already made clear my admiration for Lord Hives, both as an engineer and as a man. If ever there was a testing time for our friendship, this was it.

In his suite I pulled out the contract and showed him the clause. 'There's nothing in here prohibiting me from using my name on a car,' I pointed out. 'It says that for ten years from 1932 I can't, except, and in smaller print, as the designer. And I've always presumed that after ten years it's permissible, otherwise there would be no point in having a time limit.'

'I agree with you,' said Hives after he had read through the document. 'That's how I would have read it too. I haven't seen this contract before.'

'Well, what about this case you threaten to bring, then?'

But, of course, as he pointed out, a trade mark was a trade mark, regardless of any private contract of this nature. At the same time he thought that it was hard on me and agreed to my suggestion that a new agreement should be drawn up prohibiting me, for a consideration, from lending my name to any motor car for life.

Hives, after agreeing to this in principle and stating the sum they were prepared to pay, said he would confirm it in writing. But unfortunately, although it was really a matter between Rolls-

Royce and me, Alan Good said he wouldn't have anything to do with it on these terms and announced his intention to go and see Hives and argue it out himself. I knew what the result of that would be. By strict legal definition I was entitled to nothing, and in any case Good's aggressive manner would be certain to get Hives' back up. Within a few weeks we were neck-deep in litigation.

Lagondas never had a leg to stand on, and when it was my turn to go into the box—dragged there very reluctantly I might add—I couldn't see how to present my evidence other than in favour of Rolls-Royce rather than Lagonda. The case cost Lagondas £10,000 and the use of my name on the car, and me the substantial sum of money agreed to by Hives, beside the agony of standing witness. There is no place I hate more than the inside of a British court when I am involved, and I have been in them much too often for my liking.

Catalogues were scrapped, advertisements altered, and now it was to be simply, 'The New 2½-Litre Lagonda—designed under the supervision of W. O. Bentley.' That was blow number one to the post-war car. The second was much more serious, the death-blow in fact so far as this company was concerned. We were then, in the mid-'forties, back to the old supply and manufacturing conditions that had prevailed when we had launched the original 3-litre. There was a shortage of everything—plant, raw materials and labour. But this time, under the Labour Government, everything was tightly controlled, and steel more severely than anything else. When we applied for some for the car we were horrified to receive an allocation for just a hundred bodies.

This is absurd, we said; we can't tool up for production on this basis and anyway what happens when we use that up? What sort of guarantee can you give us for the future? The Ministry of Supply refused us any guarantee, and Briggs, with too much other work to bother themselves with such uncertainties as this, declined to handle the bodies at all. So there we were, with a stack of orders to keep us busy for years, a beautifully equipped works, a new car—and nothing to build it with.

Some years before, the ownership of Lagondas had been taken over by a large finance house in the City who were not directly interested in the car business, although they were very satisfied to leave the firm in the hands of J. R. Greenwood (who had now succeeded Alan Good as Chairman after disagreements) and the rest of us at Staines so long as prospects were promising. Obviously they were not after this crippling blow.

There was nothing else for it, and with all regret, but very sensibly I think, Lagondas was put up for sale; and I was told to put the finishing touches to my own gravestone. I suppose there was no one better equipped than I to try to sell the design of the car for which I had been responsible, and I did the job with as much grace as I could, and with genuine enthusiasm.

I took the prototype down to Oxford and showed it to Sir Miles Thomas and Alex Issigonis after Lord Nuffield had expressed interest in it. But it wasn't really proletarian enough for them. My next call was at Jaguars at Coventry. They liked it too, but as it had a good deal in common with their own cars and would meet the same market, they didn't see how it could be fitted into their programme.

I think it must have been some time in the summer of 1947 when I met David Brown at London Airport and drove him in the prototype to the works. And this, of course, brings us to recent history. The deal went through, the David Brown organisation took over the half dozen prototypes and the engine design, which in ever increasingly developed form has since powered their D.B. Aston Martins; while our Lagonda chassis with the same unit was similarly developed and marketed, with increase bore and handsome Tickford coachwork, as the 3-litre.

That engine has had quite a long and successful life—some twenty-two years so far! And I see that the new V8 Aston Martin racing engine still leans heavily on it, especially in the design of the head.

.   .   .   .   .

In the post-war years, besides the 2½-litre Lagonda there were a number of other design exercises, which were interesting to work on, even if none of them came to anything. For instance, early in 1945, before the David Brown take-over, we set about two exercises for possible future planning. For the basic formula of the first of these we went back thirty years to another world war, and to the B.R. rotary aero engines, which were perhaps the most successful and certainly the most satisfying engines for which I was responsible.

I had been much impressed by the front-wheel drive Citroen design of 1934, and had driven one of these cars for many thousands of miles. The merits of driven front wheels in a small car are obvious, allowing a high safety factor combined with economy of space. I was convinced at that time that the future of the small car lay in the principle of the engine being over or adjacent to the driven wheels, and, with the immediate rejection as bad layout of the rear engine, we had to decide on the best transmission arrangement, bearing in mind the prerequisite that as much weight as possible must bear down on the front wheels for maximum adhesion and controlability.

There were two obvious lessons to be learnt: from the f.w.d. Alvis of the 'twenties, a remarkably advanced design by the distinguished Captain Smith-Clarke, and the Citroen itself. The Alvis suffered from the disadvantage of having the engine and gearbox too far back in the chassis, and the consequent weight distribution made them tricky cars and unpredictable to handle.

The Citroen, of course, had (and has to this day) the engine sensibly placed right over the front wheels, but this led to transmission complications with the gearbox out (very vulnerably) in front and driving back to the axle.

By combining aircraft-engine practice with the benefits of front-wheel drive I thought we might be able to learn some valuable lessons, and perhaps even get some way along the road towards the ideal small car. We therefore worked on a five-cylinder radial engine driving vertically down on to the front wheels. This was to be a very light unit with an aluminium head, air-cooled, with a cowled-in fan forcing the air on to the finned cylinders. The valves were to be inclined, operated by pushrods, and the cam gear followed Bentley Rotary engine practice, which itself was based on Clerget principles.

The combustion chambers were hemispherical, the pistons aluminium—in fact, the heaviest single component was the flywheel, which was necessarily quite substantial. Transmission was through an all-synchromesh gearbox. Originally I think the cylinder dimensions were to have been 63×72 mm, but we later enlarged these to $72 \times 69\frac{1}{2}$ mm; a slightly over-square engine with a capacity of some 1,360 c.c. and an R.A.C. rating at that time of 15 h.p.

We knew from the beginning that this would have been a very

refined engine, and with a high power output in relation to its size and especially its weight.

We also recognised that the balance problem would be quite tricky, and we therefore mounted it very flexibly, using a great deal of rubber. In practice the vibrations and the harmonic balance due to the very lightness of the engine were something of a headache. I have no doubt that we should have got round these drawbacks, given time, but we shelved this radial and continued the exercise on an entirely different level, intending to come back to it again if we did not succeed better with the new concept.

In retrospect I think this would have been a very good or a very bad car!

We worked next on an air-cooled flat-six. Although the layout was entirely different, of course, to the radial, the size and pattern were similar, and light weight was again to be achieved by using aluminium cylinders and pistons, and an aluminium head. The six cylinders were horizontally opposed, with the many advantages that this layout combined.

In addition, we arranged the transmission on the Citroen principle with the gearbox out in front driving back to the bevel-box. This allowed us to raise the centre line of the engine and obtain reasonable accessibility, which can sometimes be a difficulty with horizontally opposed engines, as those who have had a Jowett Javelin will know.

We thought at the time we were on to something original with the flat-six, but someone must have been working on the same lines, for very shortly after this a successful flat-six light-weight aero engine appeared in America.

The flat-six was to have had torsion-bar independent front suspension, but, like the Citroen, we thought a beam axle would be preferable at the rear, as without bevel-box drive shafts, etc., it would give us a lower unsprung weight. It would also be cheaper and lighter. In this case we could see no immediate benefit in having full independence.

Two considerations prompted us to put aside the flat-six, too, and concentrate wholly on the more orthodox $2\frac{1}{2}$-litre car. The first was our lack of facilities at Lagondas, which would have made the development both of this and the radial designs a long business, longer perhaps than the company could afford if we were not to miss the sudden tremendous demand for a small car that would be unleashed at the end of hostilities.

But I think we were also a little nervous about transmitting so much power through the front wheels, for the output of both engines was to have been quite high in relation to the intended weight of the car. Cord's experience with their front-driven machines influenced us, too. I had heard quite a number of disturbing stories about the handling of the Cord, and difficulties with the steering. Wheel-spin when accelerating hard with this car was also, I believe, something of a problem. Perhaps, we decided, this was a gamble we should not take after all.

But I don't think the few months we spent on these two designs were wasted as a great deal of interesting information came to light, and everyone concerned with them learnt many useful lessons.

After that, and after the Lagonda days were over, I was employed for a while in a consultative capacity over various projects, including the design of an air-cooled flat-four aluminium engine for an American. This was never intended for motor car use, but we tested it out for several months in a Morris Minor, with great success. Then there was a complete 3-litre car which I designed for Armstrong-Siddeley. This worked quite well, too, and they were very pleased with it, but decided in a moment of caution and economy that they ought to stay on the well-trod path. The Sapphire appeared instead. This Armstrong was really a 3-litre version of the $2\frac{1}{2}$-litre Lagonda, with a twin-camshaft 6-cylinder engine, and independent suspension all round, at the front by coils and by torsion bars at the rear. I was sorry to see it go.

. . . . .

More recently, I have 'gone into complete retirement', as they say! And never have I been more content with life. In 1959 we moved from our old and beautiful but very inconvenient cottage in Shamley Green into a new Colt bungalow we built in a part of the garden. I have regained a lot of my old interest in railways, and through the good offices of my friend Richard Hardy, now Divisional Manager of the Eastern Region, have even travelled again on the footplate several times—a bracing experience. Many other hobbies and interests give me satisfaction; and nothing gives me greater pleasure than the continued flourishing of the Bentley Drivers Club. The Bentley cult seems to be as strong today as it ever was, judging by the number you see on the road and the events that are run for them by the Bentley Drivers Club. This energetic body had begun operations some five years after the decease of the old Company under the initiative of G. K. Pelmore, Forrest Lycett, the Hon. G. W. Bennet and a dozen or more enthusiasts for the *marque*; and on 24th May, 1936, there was a get-together tea at the Old Bell Hotel in Hurley at which twenty-seven 3-, 4½-, 6- and 8-litre cars and about forty founder-members were present. Speed events at Brooklands, hill-climbs and trials followed, at which it was unthinkable to turn up in a car that was not in *concours d'elegance* condition; and teas, film-showings, cocktail parties and dinner-dances have added a pleasantly gay social touch to this unique and ever-growing body.

Today it is at its strongest, with Stanley Sedgwick as President, Colonel Darrel Berthon as Executive Vice-President, and Miss Barbara Gunstone as Secretary, and a host of voluntary supporters who have helped to make the club as influential as it is. There is a membership now of around 2,000 an impressive monthly magazine, and a calendar packed full enough to keep the strongest Bentley-phile contented. To me personally, the club has always been most generous, and it is a tremendous pleasure to receive greetings (and even presents) from members in America and South Africa, Australia, New Zealand and other parts of the Commonwealth.

Unfortunately my own position with the club was rather difficult at first when I was with Lagondas, but for the past twenty years or more I have kept in close touch, always attended the annual dinner and a number of the events, and have been honoured with the position of Patron. It is always a great satisfaction to see how beautifully the cars are kept and in what excellent hands they are spending their old age.

Cars have been my business for nearly fifty years now; they have filled most of my life, given me enormous pleasure and satisfaction—and worry and heartbreak. Four times—in 1914, 1931, 1939 and 1946—I have been pipped just when things looked promising; for the world of high-performance quality cars is an especially tough one, and I should think it is going to be even tougher in the future.

∙ ∙ ∙ ∙ ∙

Some years ago now, my wife and I gave a party in the old cottage where we lived in Shamley Green for the Bentley Drivers Club—the first of several we have since held. On the village green during the evening some seventy of the old cars assembled—3-litres, 4½s, 6½s and the odd 8-litre, none of them less than a quarter of a century old. As the English summer was up to its usual tricks and we couldn't use the garden as we had planned, our low-ceilinged rooms were packed to bursting, and the air was thick with smoke, with technical talk, racing talk and reminiscences. Dear old Bertie Moir—he was still alive then—handled the beer barrel with his usual aplomb, and there were many others there from the past, together with around 150 members of the Club whom I had never met before.

My wife and I had reconciled ourselves to some inevitable breakages, and a mess to clear up afterwards. But everyone was meticulously careful as well as good company, no one drank too much, and afterwards the rooms looked as if they had just been spring-cleaned—we couldn't even find a glass stain or a shred of cigarette ash on the floor.

As the last booming Bentley exhaust note faded away that night and one or two of us settled down to some late-hour talk about the old days, I felt that it had all been worth while.

Appendices

APPENDIX I

'The Bentley Boys': A Racing Record

These figures cover the period 1922–1931 and include only the follow-
ing races: Le Mans (marked by an asterisk), the Brooklands Six-Hour,
Double-Twelve and 500-Mile races, the Dublin Grand Prix, and the
Paris Grand Prix. Nor are the supercharged team's results included.

JACK BARCLAY ... ... Started in one race
1st once
WOOLF BARNATO ... ... Started in eight races
1st five times (three at Le Mans)
J. D. BENJAFIELD ... ... Started in eight races
1st once*
3rd once*
W. O. BENTLEY ... ... Started in one race
4th once
SIR H. R. S. BIRKIN, BT. ... Started in seven races
1st once*
3rd twice
4th once
JEAN CHASSAGNE ... ... Started in one race
4th once*
F. C. CLEMENT ... ... Started in fourteen races
1st four times (one at Le Mans)
2nd once*
3rd once
4th once*
H. W. COOK ... ... Started in two races
3rd once
S. C. H. DAVIS ... ... Started in five races
1st once*
2nd twice
J. F. DUFF ... ... Started in three races
1st once*
4th once*
GEORGE DULLER ... ... Started in three races
1st once

197

JACK DUNFEE	... ...	Started in three races 1st twice 2nd once*
CLIVE DUNFEE	... ...	Started in three races 2nd once
BARON D'ERLANGER	... ...	Started in two races 3rd once*
R. C. GALLOP	... ...	Started in one race
SIR RONALD GUNTER	...	Started in one race 2nd once
EARL HOWE	... ...	Started in one race
GLEN KIDSTON	... ...	Started in four races 1st once* 2nd twice
H. KENSINGTON MOIR	...	Started in one race
BERNARD RUBIN	... ...	Started in three races 1st once*
R. G. WATNEY	... ...	Started in one race 2nd once*

APPENDIX II

Production Figures of Bentley Cars

	Yearly total	Year	Total
3 Litre	145	1922	
	204	1923	
	403	1924	
	395	1925	
	295	1926	
	140	1927	
	45	1928	
	8	1929	
	4	after 1931	
			1,639
4 Litre	50	1931	
			50
4½ Litre	273	1928	
	260	1929	
	138	1930	
	56	1931	
	6	after 1931	
			733
6½ Litre	58	1926	
	127	1927	
	99	1928	
	129	1929	
	126	1930	
			539
8 Litre	100	1931	
			100

Grand total ... 3,061

Of the 3-litre cars 506 were 'Speed Models' and 15 '100-m.p.h.' models.

Of the 4½-litre cars 54 were supercharged.

Of the 6½-litre cars 171 were short-chassis 'Speed Sixes'.

APPENDIX III

The 6½-Litre Bentley

RACING RECORD IN MAJOR RACES

Le Mans Grand Prix d'Endurance ...   Entered twice, won twice.
Brooklands Double-Twelve ...   ...   Entered twice, won once,
                                     second once.
Brooklands 500-Miles   ...   ...   Entered twice, won once,
                                     second once.
Brooklands Six-Hours   ...   ...   Entered once, won once.
Irish Grand Prix   ...   .   Entered once, second once.
Tourist Trophy   ...   .   Entered once (crashed).

RACING RECORD OF LB 2332 ('OLD NUMBER 1')

1929	...	Le Mans	...	...	1st
		Six-Hours	...	...	1st
		Irish G.P.	...	...	2nd (1st in speed)
		Tourist Trophy	...	Crashed.
		500-Miles	...	...	2nd (1st in speed)
1930	...	Le Mans	...	...	1st
		500-Miles	...	...	1st

(This car, fitted with an 8-litre engine, was destroyed when it went over the banking at Brooklands in the 1932 500-Miles race.)

A report on the 6½-litre car compiled by the Bentley Drivers' Club, under the guidance of its President, Stanley Sedgwick. It was first published in *Motor Sport* in February, 1949, and is here reproduced in abridged form by courtesy of the Editor:

As early as 1925 it became apparent to the designer of the by then world-famous 3 litre, that an entirely different type of car was required, to meet the needs of a different class of motorist. Such a car should have the attributes of a high-speed touring chassis, should be capable of carrying the enclosed coachwork of the time, and should handle like a dignified town-carriage. The development of such a car was no mean task and W.O., ably assisted by his designing staff, set about designing a prototype based on their experience with the 3 litre. The six-cylinder evolved closely followed the well-tried layout of the 3 litre, but incorporated several new features.

The specification of the first production models was as follows:

Engine ... Six-cylinder, 100 mm. bore by 140 mm. stroke 6,597 c.c.
Four overhead valves per cyclinder.
Coupling-rod-driven overhead camshaft.
Compression ration 4·4 : 1.
Duralumin rockers, ball-end tappet screws.
Dual ignition by two magnetos.
Thermostatically controlled water circulation.
Celeron reduction gears, 30 by 60T.
Autovac fuel feed. Single Smith type 50 BVS/C carburettor.

Clutch ... Single-plate type, Halo-lined. Single-plate clutch-stop.

Gearbox ... B.S. type. Indirect ratios: 3rd, 1·278; 2nd, 1·823; 1st and reverse, 3·364.

Steering ... Worm and sector type.

Rear axle ... Spiral bevel gears, ratio 4·16 to 1.

General ... Wheelbase 11' and 12'. 33" by 6·75" tyres: 21" rims.
19 gallon petrol tank. 'Telegauge' petrol gauge.
Smith double-pole lighting and starting.
Road speed at 3,500 r.p.m.: 84 m.p.h.
Chassis price: £1,450.

The first models had a half-engine-speed dynamo, driven from the camshaft and located on the aluminium bulkhead as in the 3 litre, but the majority of these chassis were later modified to the engine-speed dynamo driven from the nose of the crankshaft, the radiator shell being altered to suit. Few, if any, of the original radiator shells are in existence today.

At this point it is convenient to deal with some aspects of the operation of that somewhat complicated, but nevertheless reliable type of camshaft drive, the coupling-rod crank-drive—frequently referred to incorrectly as the 'eccentric drive'.

Broadly the system consists of a helical gear-driven, three-throw crankshaft, having the crank throws at 120 degrees, to which are coupled three specially designed connecting-rods, which in turn are connected to a driven crankshaft of similar dimensions direct coupled to the overhead camshaft. The upper big-end bearings of these connecting-rods are fitted with an expansion-compensating device to counteract changes in crankpin centres due to temperature variations, and it is this device at the camshaft end of the coupling rods which appears so complicated to the uninitiated.

Another development introduced with the advent of the 6½ litre was the ball-ended tappet screw, designed to give 100% valve-tip contact with the tapper-adjuster screw, despite the use of overhead rockers, thus eliminating the centre-punch effect of the orthodox tappet-screw on the valve stem face, and, by so doing, reducing the need for tappet adjustment to very infrequent intervals.

Another refinement used for the first time as standard equipment was the crankshaft torsional damper of the conventional multi-disc type. Fitted to the front end of the crankshaft, this self-contained unit, when adjusted to slip at 60 to 80 foot-lbs., required attention only at infrequent intervals.

A thermostatically controlled circuit of unconventional design completed the layout of this very efficient power unit. It consisted of two distinct water circulation circuits regulated by a thermostatically controlled valve of ample proportions. In the 'cold engine' circuit the thermostat by-passed the radiator except for a small leakage to prevent freezing-up. With the engine hot, the valve in the open position allowed the coolant access to the radiator. The whole system of cylinder block circuits was concealed within the cylinder block and the front cylinder block jacket-plate.

The single Smith 5-jet Type 50 BVS/C carburettor supplied the mixture to a water-jacketed induction pipe of the 'Ram's Horn' balanced-flow type.

A starting device or strangler and a mixture control is incorporated in the design and consists of a cam-operated sleeve sliding over the well jet which, in the full-rich position, closes the air supply to the well jet, and in the full-weak position opens a series of holes in the base of the port block.

The steering-box, of the orthodox semi-reversible worm and segment type, was of entirely new design incorporating a meshing arrangement consisting of an eccentrically machined, slotted-valve bearing for the segment shaft. After removing the securing tab and slackening off the sleeve pinch-bolt, the rotation of this sleeve moved the segment into or out of mesh, according to the direction of rotation. End flat was adjusted by the methods common to all Bentley chassis, viz. the steel valve with inclined slots secured by two pinch-bolts at the base of the box casting.

As in the 3 litre, the brakes were fully mechanically operated, but the front brakes were 'push-rod' operated in order to utilise the considerable self-energisation developed by the torsional effect of the brakes on the front axle assembly. The method was a phase in the development of the 'reversed action' front brakes used so effectively at Le Mans.

The first 6½ chassis (WB 2551) took the road in March, 1926; in frontal appearance it differed slightly from later models by reason of the absence of the casing carrying the engine-speed dynamo driven from the crankshaft, as the dynamo was camshaft-driven at the rear end of the engine.

In September, 1928, there were rumours afoot that there was every possibility that a 'Speed Model' of this chassis was scheduled for development and very early production. Much development work was, in fact, proceeding behind the scenes and culminated in the production of an entirely new type of chassis to be known as the 'Speed Six'.

The first of these chassis to be laid down was No. WT 2265, and the principal alterations in design were as follows:

High-compression pistons, giving 5.3 : 1 compression ratio.

Twin S.U. carburettors. BM 7032 camshaft. 0.019 tappet clearance.

'C'-type gearbox with indirect ratios—3rd, 1.357 to 1; 2nd, 1.823 to 1; 1st and reverse 3.364 to 1.

3.84 to 1 rear axle ratio.

The radiator was redesigned—the sides were parallel whereas the standard 6½ radiator had a pronounced taper inwards at the bottom—and the winged B had a green label.

From a commercial standpoint the 'Speed Six' development had to include exploration of the probabilities and possibilities of this car superseding the now hard-pressed 4½ litre in the competition field. Intensive development work was carried out unobtrusively. Air-flow tests were made, the cylinder block was redesigned, port areas were altered, and brake endurance tests were carried out.

It is most interesting to read the report of Mr. Clarke on this chassis (LB 2332—see above) after winning the 1929 Le Mans:

(*a*) *During practice:* Slight steering instability reported and rectified by balancing the practice wheels and adjusting shock-dampers. Oil pressure—60 lbs.

(*b*) *During race:* Brake adjustment used up at the 20th hour.

(*c*) *After race* (Strip report).

Engine: Nothing to report. Exhaust valves and valve springs changed as a precautionary measure only.

Clutch: Nothing to report. Clutch-stop locating ears fractured.

Gearbox: Nothing to report. Mainshaft, first motion shaft and journal bearings changed as a precautionary measure.

Rear axle: Crown wheel and pinion—slight signs of pitting, otherwise O.K. Pinion thrust-race disintegrated. Otherwise O.K.

Brakes: Relined: two rear drums changed as a precautionary measure (local hot spot).

Frame: Small fracture through front engine-bearer engine-securing bolt hole. Signs of fracture where front wing stay palms connected to neutral section of frame channel due to 'fidgeting'.

Truly a remarkable strip report after a gruelling race of this calibre.

Altogether 544 6½-litre Bentleys were made, of which 171 were 'Speed Sixes' and of these, more than 70 are on the roads today in the hands of Bentley Drivers' Club members, including two of the team cars. GF 8507 (chassis No. HM 2868) is owned by J. D. Percy and is in its original form and beautifully kept. It was this car in which 'Babe' Barnato won Le Mans for the third time and, fittingly, it led his funeral cortège bearing floral tributes, driven by 'Babe's' chauffeur.

So concludes the story of truly one of the giants of the road, which never fails to impress wherever it appears. The majesty of the 'Speed Six' will continue for many years to dwarf motor cars of younger vintage.

APPENDIX IV

From The Autocar *January 24th 1920*

A TEST OF A 3-LITRE BENTLEY

A car which combines Docility in Traffic with Exceptional
Speed Potentiality on the Open Road

Although frowned upon by the authorities, limited by law and penalised
when discovered, speed is the greatest attribute of a car, and from the
car alone is it possible to realise to the full that peculiar feeling of
greatness, soaring almost to poetic heights, consequent on high-speed
travelling.

There are, however, certain private roads in our own country, and
nearly all the national highways of fair France, on which a racing
machine and an open throttle are not only allowed, but encouraged, to
the great joy and thankfulness of those drivers who know really where
the true pleasure of motoring exists.

Quite recently we were enabled to make a trial of the 3-litre Bentley,
a car designed to give a great speed, yet to remain tractable and docile
in the hands of an unskilled owner and to be suitable also for Britain
with British road conditions. The machine is one just completed, un-
tuned, unaltered and hand-built, with a rough, four-seated body carrying the mud of previous runs, lacking a hood, with a narrow windscreen—in fact, having bare accommodation for four people. Not very
handsome to look upon (test bodies seldom are), not altogether free
from straps and string, the car bore an air of something indefinable,
just a suggestion, perhaps, of what was to come, a knowledge, maybe,
of its own power; at all events, something which showed its breed
through the external work-a-day disguise.

Cars undoubtedly have a personality to the real enthusiast, to whom
they are not mere collections of steel and aluminium, but, animal-like,
show their spirit just so soon as the clutch bites home and feeling comes
to the driver through the narrow steel steering-wheel rim.

Our start was typical; the engine, responding at once to the electric
motor, emitted a steady roar from the exhaust; the crew, well wrapped
up, soon settled down to comfort in their seats, and, with one or two of
those little dabs at the throttle beloved by all Brooklands drivers, the
car moved off.

For the first part of the journey we travelled as steadily as could be wished over bad roads, betraying little of the engine's power, save when an occasional opportunity demanded rapid acceleration; the general behaviour of the chassis suggested an entire absence of effort combined with more than ordinary tractability, the power of either brake being something altogether extraordinary and impossible to believe, save from the evidence of actual experience.

THE ENGINE'S FULL SONG

All this was done with the air of a lithe, active and speedy animal straining a little on the leash. Presently a long stretch of familiar road, quite deserted, with a lining of trees, unrolled ahead. Each member of the crew, as if by instinct, settled farther down into the seat, drew in a deep breath, and inwardly said, 'Now!' Instantly the exhaust changed its note from a purr to a most menacing roar, the white ribbon of road streamed towards the car, while the backs of the seats pressed hard upon one's shoulder blades.

As the speed increased to over 70 m.p.h. the landscape leaped at us, wind shrieked past the screen, while the flanking trees and other objects seemed, not definitely and sharply contoured, but a blurred streak hurtling past as the roar of the exhaust rose to its full song. To such an accompaniment the pulse beats quicker, there comes an almost irresistible desire to burst into some wild war song, greater even than the immortal song of Roland—in defiance of the demons that howl invisible without. Every part of one's being urges greater speed in the fierce wild intoxication of a moment supreme above all others in the life sensations of man. A curve flashes past with just the suggestion of altered course, mayhap with a small shower of stones slung up from behind, but till the silver radiator rushed towards that dark unattainable line of the horizon, which seems so near yet never is attained.

BRAKES A PREDOMINANT FEATURE

Then the throttle comes back, abruptly the noise dies down, and the brakes take a hold upon the drums as all one's exaltation dies, leaving a curious sense of shame, as though for a moment one's soul had been exposed to the rude, not to say unsympathetic, gaze of other men.

But those fierce few minutes are worth much as a memory, even more than similar experience on the Big Benz or a low-flying aeroplane, for the Bentley is but a small machine by comparison.

The reader may say, 'This is all very well, but what of the car?'

Well, the best description of this car is one of its speed; for the rest, the brakes are the most predominant feature. Smoothly and without chatter, they draw the car up in an altogether incredibly short distance—so short, indeed, that one is still bracing for the smash when the car stops dead many yards from the obstacle.

RACER AND TOWN CARRIAGE COMBINED

There are, of course, numberless small things of note. The gears of the double oil-pump drive are noisy, somewhere in the engine something emits a peculiar penetrating grate every now and again, while much good oil is sprayed over the engine by the breather pipes. These are faults inseparable from the first chassis of a new design, are easily overcome and are no impediment to success.

The car holds the road all square, corners admirably and is well sprung. In England, as a short runs proved, the machine can travel without protest, chatter or difficulty on top gear at 10 m.p.h. or under, can pick up from that to high speed, or take a hill slowly and easily; in fact, the 3-litre Bentley—racer on occasion though it may be—is endowed with all the desired features for town carriage work of the most docile type.

For the man who wants a true sporting type of light-bodied car for use on a Continental tour—where speed limits are not meant to be observed, unless one is involved in an accident—the 3-litre Bentley is undoubtedly the car *par excellence*. Its comparatively small size renders it an extraordinarily easy car to handle, not only on the open road, but also in congested city streets.

APPENDIX V

From The Autocar, *December 5th, 1930*

8-LITRE BENTLEY SALOON

MOTORING IN ITS VERY HIGHEST FORM:
THE TREMENDOUS PERFORMANCE

It may seem slightly unusual to commence a description of a car's test by disagreeing quite thoroughly with a statement made by a representative of the manufacturer when introducing the model at one of the firm's functions, but so great appears to be the discrepancy between what one would naturally expect and what is actually provided that a word or two of argument is essential.

At the time of the Olympia Show the 8-litre Bentley was introduced in such a way as to stress to the full the fact that it was designed to be that rather mysterious type of vehicle which is generally known as a town carriage; and undoubtedly a great many people who listened to that announcement went away under the impression that performance was the very last thing on which the car based its claim to consideration —so much so that certain people undoubtedly believed that the performance was sacrificed to obtain other possibilities.

Now, in the first place, although everybody knows what is meant by a town carriage, and, further, can realise the distinction between that and a sports car, it is not, in fact, easy to see where one type stops and the other begins. Quite apart from that, the one thing, the dominant note, of the new Bentley is its tremendous performance, and on that performance alone it stands right in the forefront as an equal, at least, of any other car in existence. One glance at the figures shows, as no sentences or phrasing can, that the big 8-litre is something out of the common run, even when allowances are made for the increase in engine capacity as compared with the $6\frac{1}{2}$ litres of the earlier six-cylinder model.

Therefore, it is impossible to allow that the car can be described, or in any way regarded, as just a town carriage and nothing more; and to remain silent concerning, or in any way belittle, the performance factor is, from the sales point of view, to disregard the principal reason why this splendid car should succeed.

Had it been that the performance made the car difficult to handle on

208

top gear at low speed, heavy to manœuvre in traffic or in a confined space, harsh or noisy, then the performance by itself might justly be regarded as simply that of a sports car, though few of these features are easily noticeable even in the modern sports car, unless it has been tuned for racing.

Quite on the contrary, this car can be driven really softly on its high top gear as slowly as a man walks, and can accelerate from that without snatch and without difficulty, and the whole time the engine, being well within its power, is silent and smooth; in fact, it is only really apparent that there is a big engine working under the bonnet at all, and that so high a top ratio is used, when the machine is accelerated from a crawl. For all practical purposes, therefore, the machine does its work on the one gear, in town or out of it, and it is with that one gear that it best suits the average driver.

The new gearbox is interesting, the longer movement of the lever from one slot to another being a little puzzling at first to anyone who is accustomed to the earlier models, a point emphasised because to start on second and then change at once to top is the obvious way of handling the machine. The gears are quieter than before, and will be quieter still when there has been opportunity to obtain more experience with this type of box.

The use of two broad shoes in each of the rear-wheel brake drums, instead of four relatively narrow shoes, has certainly improved the brake power, and certain alterations have made the vacuum servo motor seem more definite and more positive, so that to the driver it really appears as though he can feel the shoes touch the drums and thus command a more delicate control. But the great change in the machine, apart from its engine, is the way in which the car, travelling fast and with a saloon body, can be taken round curves and corners with its shock absorbers adjusted as for town work. It is true that when once one was accustomed to the earlier 6½-litre that model seemed as steady as could be wished—provided the shock absorbers were really tight—yet the new car is steady with easy riding springs and so puts the earlier model entirely in the shade, a thing due in great part to the big, stiff frame, though the fact that the springs are farther apart and the chassis lower may have a great deal to do with it as well; and this rigidity makes the big car almost as tractable as one of the smallest machines on the road, while it seems to have no side sway whatsoever on a fast corner.

It is possible, of course, to go right over the chassis, pointing out here and there where improvement is apparent, but, when all is said, it is not a matter of detail improvement that makes the 8-litre Bentley what it is, for the thing that counts above everything else is the way in which the big machine does its work, and its great sense of latent power. Exactly this and nothing else is the real reason why so big a machine has a future.

Putting it another way, one can breakfast comfortably in London yet lunch at Catterick Bridge, and during the whole of a run of this type there was none of the intenseness that usually comes into fast driving; indeed, it was practically impossible to believe that the car was travelling at anything like the pace the speedometer showed, though subsequent tests showed that speedometer to be reasonably accurate. In spite of the average, not a single village or town was traversed at anything like the pace that is maintained by the driver of an ordinary car, and in most cases it seemed much more pleasant to go through at a genuine 11 to 15 m.p.h.

Apart from that, the best testimonial to the ease with which the car did its work lay in the fact that the occupants of the two front seats were conversing naturally during the whole of the run.

In France the Bentley has kept up a cruising speed of 70 m.p.h. without the engine seeming to do anything at all, and, if the long northern roads offer, can go right up to 100 m.p.h. on the flat with surprisingly little apparent effort.

PERFORMANCE FIGURES

Acceleration	10–30 m.p.h. 4-2/5 secs.
Maximum speed	101·12 m.p.h.
Weight	48 cwt, 0 qr. 14 lb.

APPENDIX VI

From The Autocar, *March 11th, 1938*

42-H.P. TWELVE-CYLINDER LAGONDA SALOON

When a renowned designer and his associates—in this instance W. O. Bentley and his technical staff—set themselves the task of evolving a car which shall rank in the very forefront of machines produced today, and have the backing of capital and modern works resources, it would only be a matter of surprise if that car failed to be outstanding. This is an impression of the atmosphere in which the twelve-cylinder Lagonda has been created.

Well over a year ago the car was first heard of publicly. The interval has been devoted to developing it from the early stages of an entirely new design to the point of production; and the waiting has been worth while to those who appreciate a fine car. It is a magnificent machine.

Opinion can be based upon the experiences of a particularly comprehensive test run, over several days, in which a wide variety of roads was covered, making up a total distance of more than 700 miles. Much can be conveyed by the bare comment that every one of those seven hundred miles was a delight. High opinion has been formed of the car as a whole, even from the standpoint that has to be taken, namely that it costs some £1500, and therefore should be superlative.

It is the short chassis version that has been tried, and this example represents the first of these cars with final-drive ratio now adopted, and other modifications incorporated, to undergo impartial test.

Somehow it seems almost an insult to so remarkable a car to take it feature by feature, and appraise each of them in the usual manner. It is as an entity that such a car stands or falls. Each major item of engine, chassis, and body must do its proper share in making up the car de luxe, and none be disproportionately prominent at the expense of others.

This desirable state of affairs has been achieved. The aim of those responsible was not to produce a car having sheer speed as its be all and end all, but one that should be naturally and easily capable of 100 m.p.h. at least, by reason of its engine design, and gearing, and provide really comfortable travel on the road.

Let these claims be examined in the light of unbiased experience.

As to performance, the Lagonda shows itself able to go up to well over the 100; its acceleration is tremendous. As to comfort, driver and passengers can sit in it all day and yet not wish for a change of position, and regular passengers comment that they cannot remember travelling in a car less affected by road surface or one in which even extremely fast cornering is as little apparent, so exceptionally does it remain level and steady, so slight is the evidence of mechanism working.

PASSENGER DOZING AT 100 M.P.H.

Vivid illustration comes from an actual instance during this test, when more than 60 m.p.h. had been averaged over a certain section of safe open road, devoid of hedges or obscured crossings, and the 100 reading had been shown, yet a back-seat passenger dozed meanwhile. There is no sense of strain upon the human factor, and it scarcely seems possible that the speed should be as high as is indicated.

Few roads in this country permit such motoring. Not always does one want it, of course; but as a result of there being so much in reserve, the Lagonda runs at speeds between 70 and 80 m.p.h. as good smaller cars do at 50 or 60. The most practical appeal of the car lies in the manner in which it wafts along at a small throttle opening and low revs, disdaining gradient, overtaking in a clean sweep with an extra touch of throttle, and ready to soar to the eighties and nineties wherever there is a chance and the driver wills. It is a wonderful motoring experience to see the speedometer needle at 90 up a long slope of the kind found on roads across Salisbury Plain and in parts of Dorset.

EASILY ACHIEVED HIGH PERFORMANCE

Performance is apt to be stressed. It is a great part of the car, but the merit of the sheer test figures, outstanding as these are as a set, is increased by the fact of their being obtained without apparently over-stressing the engine or making it noisy or rough.

On the other side of things, it is a docile, easily handled car, just as well able to fit in with the leisurely mood of driving. It can be moved off gently on second gear and top put in within a few yards, and it will creep about on top gear, accelerating smoothly from a crawl. When picking up from the lower speeds some slight pinking is evident; there is no hand ignition lever, the control being automatic in the two distributors.

In top gear the comfortable non-snatch minimum is 6–7 m.p.h., and the engine shows a fine capacity to pull against gradient at low speeds without a change down being necessary, though here may be mentioned a striking point peculiar to the new twelve-cylinder Lagonda among production engines of considerable size. It is capable of much higher crankshaft speeds than has been general practice with this size of engine. The red warning light on the rev. counter is set at 5500 r.p.m., and up to 5000 at any rate, is an everyday usable figure on the indirects if a driver should be so inclined. Thus the maxima on the gears are exceptionally high, and it can become a 'gearbox' car, greatly adding to the interest on occasion. Yet at the same time the engine has top-gear flexibility.

In considering the exceptional performance, it must be remembered that the V-type engine is of no more than 4½-litre capacity. The speedometer on this particular car displayed the unusual trait of becoming slower in its readings as the speed rose, being almost dead accurate at 10, 20 and 30, but 1 m.p.h. slow at 60 and 80, and showing the highest reading of only 98–99 when the car was timed at 103.45 m.p.h. This was at 5200 r.p.m. but, if conditions permit, the engine can go on increasing revs usefully, the power peak not having been reached. A lap at Brooklands track was covered at 97.95 m.p.h. Wind conditions were not helpful, though not adverse. Another interesting point is that in a quarter-mile, using the gears, a speed of 73 m.p.h. was attained.

For the gear change the best type of synchromesh is used on second, third and top, the lever being rigid and moving with a pleasing positiveness into each gear. The drop to first remains a plain double-declutching change, but is likely to be needed very seldom indeed, to judge by behaviour on steep and narrow hills of considerable gradient in the West Country, where there was all the power that could be wanted in second gear. Both second and third are so quiet running as to be unnoticed, and it is possible at some speeds for the driver to forget to change to third and find that it is already engaged.

The brakes, hydraulically operated through twin master cylinders, make the driving of this car a safe and confident procedure, and that is really all that need be said of them, though the exceptionally light operation must be mentioned. As might be expected, the steering is not low geared (3½ turns from lock to lock), and a most satisfactory balance has been achieved. It gives the essential accuracy of control up at the top speeds, with no trace of road-wheel movement, and is not heavy to turn when the car is nearly stationary. The clutch action, again, is particularly light, and the whole control and 'feel' of the car are completely different from what may have been associated with Lagondas of some years ago.

INDEPENDENT SPRINGING ADVANTAGES

Unquestionably, the independent front-wheel springing—in which a system of long torsion bars carried in the frame members is used—

gives not only the comfort of riding already emphasised, but also shock-free steering and an almost uncanny degree of road-holding. The driver comes up to a corner fast, turns the wheel, and the car goes round, with no after effects. There is no more than that in the process.

As to the driving position points, particularly at first a shallow wind-screen is noticed, but both wings are visible. The steering wheel is on the high side; the column is adjustable, and was not at its lowest setting. The handbrake lever is in an ideal position, lying horizontally to the right of the driving seat, and is of the fly-off type, proving dead-sure for holding the car on a hill. When the driver is wearing gloves, it is found to be a little too close to the seat cushion.

The placing of the central lever renders use of the near-side door awkward if the driving seat is adjusted well forward. For some reason, possibly the fact of the wings projecting beyond the point where the driver can actually see them, it proved a not altogether easy car to manœuvre at low speed in a tight space, though actually it is relatively compact.

There are some details applying to the car that has been tried which have since received attention for production. The main instrument lighting certainly needs improving; the dials are particularly clear by daylight, and the speedometer and rev counter needles of the 'dead-beat' type. Again, the foot-operated anti-dazzle switch could be more convenient. The head-lamp beam allows almost full speed at night, which says enough.

Exterior lines have been slightly changed in the latest cars, the striking fairing of the front wings becoming less accentuated. The front seat back-rests are adjustable for angle, which is a valuable point. There are two external mirrors which, adjusted to suit a given driving position, give a good view behind, except directly astern.

NEAT ENGINE

Considering what it comprises, the engine is neat. At least four sparking plugs look awkward to reach; the oil filler is well placed but the dipstick could be easier to withdraw. One of the S.U. carburettors has combined with it a thermostatically regulated auxiliary starting carburettor, no hand-mixture control being fitted; the engine fires at once, and pulls almost immediately from cold. Water temperature is observed to run low.

In a dummy spare wheel cover on the near side is the whole tool kit, as well as the operating mechanism for the hydraulic jacks. The luggage compartment in the tail is of good but not exceptional capacity. Duplicated petrol fillers are a practical point, and all fillers have quick-acting caps.

Appendices

PERFORMANCE FIGURES

0–30 m.p.h. through gears   4·0 sec.
0–50   „   „   „   9·7 „
0–60   „   „   „   12·9 „
0–70   „   „   „   17·9 „
Maximum on gears 1st   32 m.p.h.
   „   „   „   2nd   63 „
   „   „   „   3rd   86 „
   „   „   „   Top   103·45 m.p.h.
Weight, without passenger, 39 cwt. 2 qr. 14 lb.

APPENDIX VII

This account of our last race at Le Mans was written by the late Dr. J. D. Benjafield some fourteen years ago and remains the best that I know of our tussle with the Mercedes.

LE MANS 1930

Early in 1930 I received an invitation to drive for the supercharged team for the whole of the coming season, which I accepted without hesitation.

This is no place to describe the troubles and tribulations of those endeavouring to prepare a team of cars for a season's racing, with less than half the minimum of time normally necessary for such a project available. Anyway such was the position, and many were the nights that the 'Brains' of the side went short of sleep. In their optimism, three of the S/C 4½s were entered for Le Mans and, miracle of miracles, three cars left the Welwyn Works under their own steam, bound for Le Mans a week before the race. To say that they were ready for the race would be a gross exaggeration, and the amount of work done by the very able and interested mechanics during that last week was incredible. The drivers for the three cars were as follows: Car No. 1 Tim Birkin and Jean Chassagne; Car No. 2 Ramponi and Dr. J. D. Benjafield; and Car No. 3 George Eyston and Beris Harcourt Wood.

To add to our difficulties, we found that the fuel allowed by the regulations caused our engines to overheat, and in order to overcome this trouble it was decided on the Thursday afternoon (48 hours before the race) that all the supercharged team should run on pure benzol, which oddly enough was permissible, although a petrol-benzol mixture which would suit the engine was not allowed. Anyway, in order to get the best out of this fuel, it was necessary to raise the compression of the engines. To accomplish this, a plate had to be removed from beneath the cylinder block and it was only possible to complete this alteration on two of the cars in time for the race, and so only cars No. 1 and 2 came under the starter's orders. It was awfully bad luck for George and Beris, but there was nothing we could do about it and it was only through the courtesy and helpfulness of the Leon-Bollee works at Le Mans that cars Nos. 1 and 2 were ready in time. It was by no means the first occasion on which this firm had come to our rescue in a crisis of this

216

kind, and on behalf of the Bentley teams that have driven at Le Mans I would like to take this opportunity of thanking them.

By contrast, the official Bentley Motors Ltd. team of three 6½-litre was a haven of peace. The three cars were beautifully turned out, and split-pinned down to the last possible nut. They did indeed appear a worthy team of cars to uphold the good name of the country that had produced them. The drivers of the work's team were: Car No. 1 Captain Woolf Barnato (twice winner) and Lieut.-Commander Glen Kidston; Car No. 2 Frank Clement and Dick Watney; and Car No. 3 Sammy Davis and Clive Dunfee. By the way, the numbers used in describing the drivers of the two teams bear no relation to the numbers allotted to the cars in the race.

The works team and the supercharged team were quite separate, the pits of the former being managed by Mr. Clarke and those of the latter were in the able hands of Kensington Moir. And thus of the three Speed-Sixes and three S/C 4½-litres which had crossed the Channel a week earlier, five only were ready to face the starter at 4 p.m. on June 21st 1930. It was the first time we had failed to get all our cars on to the starting-line, though as a matter of fact the supercharged cars were hardly out of the experimental stage.

The mere fact that two of the supercharged cars were ready in time, in my opinion, reflected great credit on all those responsible for having accomplished so much in so little time, for it was not until the preceding autumn that a definite start had been made.

The entry for this year's race was a small one, totalling only nineteen cars, but what it lacked in quantity it certainly made up for in quality, as may be judged from the following list:

Car No.	Drivers
1. Supercharged Mercedes	Caracciola and Werner
2. 6½-litre Bentley	Clement and Watney
3. 6½-litre Bentley	Davis and Clive Dunfee
4. 6½-litre Bentley	Barnato and Kidston
5. Stutz	Phillipe and Bouriat
6. Stutz	Brisson and Rigal
7. 4½-litre Bentley s/c (non-starter)	Eyston and Harcourt-Wood
8. 4½-litre Bentley s/c	Ramponi and Benjafield
9. 4½-litre Bentley s/c	Birkin and Chassagne
10. Alfa-Romeo	Howe and Callingham
11. Talbot	Lewis and Eaton
12. Talbot	Hindmarsh and Rose-Richards
13. 2-litre B.N.C.	
14. Lea-Francis	Peacock and Newsome

15. Bugatti	Mesdames Mareuse and Siko
16. Tracta	Gregoire and Vallon
17. Tracta	Bourcier and Debeugny
18. M.G. Midget	Samuelson and Kindell
19. M.G. Midget	Murton and Neale

The withdrawal of No. 7 Eyston and Harcourt-Wood's S/C 4½-Bentley, left eighteen cars to face the starter on the Saturday afternoon at 4 o'clock. It promised to be one of the most exciting and toughly contested sports-car races ever held, for in spite of the invincible reputation Bentleys had gained in this particular race, the entry, small as it was, had a very definite international flavour. Germany, America, Italy, France and Great Britain were all represented, and any one of the first twelve might be in the lead after twenty-four hours' running, for the speed in the opening stages of the race was sure to be a hot one, resulting in a high casualty list especially heavy amongst the fastest cars. Who would be bold enough to rule out the possibility of the race being won by one of the new Talbots? The S/C Mercedes had a great reputation for speed and was being handled by very skilled and experienced drivers. As regards numbers, Bentleys had an enormous advantage and it was long odds in favour of at least one of the five finishing, with little or no trouble, which would mean a pretty high average speed. On the other hand, if the 'Merc' could stay the course, he was going to take a lot of catching.

At a luncheon given on the Wednesday before the race, at which the Mercedes personnel and the official Bentley Motors Ltd. team were guests, and into which by some mistake I managed to insinuate myself, there were enough lies told to sink a battleship. Each side outvied the other in the speeds they had clocked for the circuit, and the speed at which they got through any given bend, speeds which, as long as the laws of gravity obtained, must land one in the ditch. Perhaps this was the idea behind the slight exaggerations, but I prefer to think that it was more the effect of insidious, but none the less pleasant, alcoholism. That very beautiful and charming lady, the late Frau Caracciola, was with her husband and together with her long-haired dachshund, 'Fritz', entertained us most delightfully, so much so that there seemed to be some risk that this spirit of friendship might extend to the circuit and neutralise the spirit of competition. In fact, I pretended to deplore the whole thing and accused Sammy Davis and Dick Watney 'of fraternising' with the enemy. I have quite forgotten who was responsible for this luncheon party which was successful in bringing together the chief members of the two most important teams running, but it was an excellent idea, and one that might be repeated with advantage.

At long last the great day dawns; Saturday, June 21st, and it looks like being a scorcher; better that than wet, though a cloudless sky in the late afternoon makes the run down to Arnage pure hell, as it is here that the direction of the road is due west and the last two hours before sunset the light is very trying.

Shortly after three o'clock the cars are lined up in front of the pits in a staggered row, the engines are run for a few minutes to warm them up, switched off and the hard racing plugs are substituted for the softer road ones and once more the engine is started to make sure that all the new plugs are firing, and after two or three bursts up to two-five she is once more switched off and covered up with an old rug. With fifteen minutes to go, Babe Barnato (for the second year in succession) and Tim Birkin, last year's winners, with a couple of marshals in the back with a large yellow flag, set off round the circuit on 'The Lap of Honour', to declare it closed to the public and open for racing. And now with five minutes to go everyone except the opening drivers are herded off the road by the officials. Glen Kidston, Frank Clement and Sammy Davis are opening with the Sixes, whilst Tim Birkin and Ramponi are opening with the Hon. Dorothy Paget S/C $4\frac{1}{2}$-litres. Caracciola is starting with the Mercedes and as the largest car in the race has pride of place at the head of the line. At flag-fall he takes full advantage of this position and the long, low, white car streaks away with the supercharger screaming, closely followed by Kidston and Davis, and then a pack of cars which included Tim Birkin with No. 9 and Ramponi with No. 8. Only one car is left on the line, the six-cylinder B.N.C., which had been pushed into its place in feverish haste a few minutes before the start and which, now that the flag had dropped, refused to respond, and had to be pushed off the stage, in dire disgrace, while the Grand Prix d'Endurance is yet only five minutes old.

Owing to the narrow road to Pontlieu and the two bends on the Rue de Circuit, little passing can be done until they come to the Hunaudieres stretch, but once this broad straight stretch is reached No. 9 Bentley goes through the mob like a knife through cheese, so that by the time Mulsanne is reached, the Mercedes is still in the lead, but Glen and Tim are on his tail. Immediately after the bend Birkin forges ahead of Kidston, so that when they come into view of the expectant crowds in the grandstands the low-built, white Mercedes, with its supercharger whining shrilly, is well in the lead, Birkin and Kidston following in close formation, Davis somewhat detached but well within striking distance, ready and anxious to take up the running, should anything go wrong with the leaders. Further reserves are close at hand as both Clement and Ramponi are only a few lengths astern. It is indeed an unequal battle, at any rate as far as numbers are concerned, but whatever the Mercedes firm may have lacked in quantity, they made up for in quality, both as regards machine and drivers. To appreciate the finer points of the really first-class driver, is almost impossible as a mere spectator, however well placed, and in my opinion this can only be achieved by driving in the same race so that he may be kept under observation for a considerable distance. For instance, suppose one is lucky enough to have a seat in the grandstand, what does one see?—merely car after car roaring past on full throttle whether he be a 750-c.c. M.G. or a 6500-c.c. Speed-Six Bentley. Certainly one would have to be built of stone not to be thrilled by the sight of Tim Birkin sitting bolt upright in the S/C 4½ roaring by at 120 m.p.h. at what appears to be about six inches astern of the long low white Mercedes, the shrill whine of whose supercharger monopolises the sound waves. But as a mere spectator, one misses that superlative artistry possessed by few drivers, and by none in greater degree than Caracciola, that enables him to pass another car on a fast left-hand bend on a wet road with anti-camber. I actually saw him do this in the Tourist Trophy race, the year he won it, as he had passed me shortly before.

At any rate this race promises to provide ample entertainment for the mere spectator, for Ramponi's tail is just disappearing at the beginning of his second lap, when the two black Stutz driven by Philippe (de Rothschild) and Brisson, closely followed by Lord Howe's Alfa and the two Talbots, pass in his wake. Somewhat farther astern is a third group composed of a Bugatti with its feminine crew, a couple of M.G. Midgets and the little Tractas.

Whatever may happen in this Grand Prix d'Endurance de Vingt-Quatre Heures, one thing is certain, and that is that the Bentley-Mercedes duel alone should provide more than sufficient interest to amply repay spectators for coming. At long last could be settled the argument between the protagonists of each marque, as to which was the better and faster car.

Admittedly the numbers five to one seemed a bit unfair, and we had hoped that Mercedes would have sent a team of at least two or, better, three cars to represent them. The fact that they did not send more than one car suggests that one Mercedes would have sufficient speed in hand over any number of Bentleys, to make the result a certainty. Had the Bentleys of 1930 no more speed than that shown in previous years at Le Mans, Mercedes supposition would have been correct, but had they studied the figures of 1924, 1927, 1928 and 1929 with just a little imagination, they should have realised that W.O. does not stand still and that each year that the race was won by Bentley Motors Ltd., the average speed for the race showed a significant increase. That this supposition is correct I have not the slightest doubt, for nothing was farther from the Mercedes policy than to take a hiding from another nation's car, however great the odds might be. And it was a hiding that he got, fair and square; he was beaten by a better car and were the race run again as a match just between the two cars driven by Barnato and Caracciola, I have no doubt whatever which would prove the victor. It was no fluke, neither did the numbers provide anything more than a tactical advantage. Babe Barnato had sufficient speed to compel Caracciola to use his blower too much in order to keep up with him, and once this fact was established it was only a matter of time before the Merc 'blew up'.

Carracciola's second lap was completed at 86.48 m.p.h., and Tim Birkin who is now forging ahead of Kidston is chasing him, clocking just under 87 m.p.h. for his second lap and 88 m.p.h. for his third. On his fourth lap Birkin catches the Merc and passes him just before Mulsanne, putting his offside wheels well over the grass verge at a speed of little short of 130 m.p.h. to do so. Caracciola had the shock of his life, never dreaming that anything could overtake him. Unfortunately, Tim's car chose this most unsuitable moment to throw a tread from his offside rear tyre, but he has taken the lead and judging from the speed of his next lap, 6 minutes 48 seconds (89.69 m.p.h.), he intends to keep it. Only by keeping his supercharger in action the whole time can Caracciola keep up. On his sixth lap the fabric of Tim's offside rear tyre bursts, compelling him to reduce speed to 40 m.p.h. The time lost by completing the lap at this speed and changing the wheel at the pit drops Tim back to seventh place, behind all the other Bentleys and Brisson's Stutz.

At the end of the first hour Caracciola is in the lead having covered exactly 85 miles, Sammy Davis and Glen Kidston who are lying second and third are three minutes behind, Ramponi with one of the Dorothy Paget S/C 4½-litres is fourth, Clement fifth, Brisson sixth and Birkin seventh. The two new Talbots driven by Lewis and Eaton, Hindmarsh and Rose-Richards are running very regularly, quiet and fast, and now occupying the eighth and ninth places. Then come the small fry, all of whom are still running and all of whom, with one notable exception, are showing the greatest consideration for their big brothers, keeping well out of their way to facilitate their passing.

At two hours, the leaders are unchanged, but one very significant fact emerges—the gap between the Mercedes and the Davis and Kidston Bentleys has been reduced from three to two minutes, and this in spite of plenty of supercharger. This indeed augured well for the marque Bentley and never before had I seen a smile on the face of the 'Tiger' (W.O.) thus early in the race.

At 6.30 p.m., two and a half hours after the start, the regular fuel stops commence, the first of our lot to come in being Davis with No. 3 Bentley, who was lying second. He and Clive Dunfee do an excellent refill, the *plombeurs* affixing the official seals to fuel, oil and water-filler caps in 1 minute 40 seconds. It is only as Clive drives off with No. 3 that Sammy reports that five laps earlier his goggles of 'Splinterless glass' had been hit by a stone thrown up by another car, forcing particles into his left eye. In a flash he substitutes his spare goggles and carried on in spite of great pain without loss of time. Unfortunately all the good work done by Sammy served no good purpose, for this was the last we were to see of No. 3 Bentley. Running down the gradient towards the new Pontlieu curve, about two kilometres after leaving the pits, Clive Dunfee, having passed a Stutz, underestimates his speed, forgets the escape road and tries to take the bend: result—a sickening slither into the sandbank, where the car comes to rest, half-buried. Much frenzied digging by Clive, ably helped by the very disappointed Sammy, using the spare head-light glass merely served to expose a bent front anxle and two buckled wheels. For the team to lose its leading car in this manner is a bitter blow, but fortunately one that it can survive, thanks to the reserves being in close attendance.

The next car in is Ramponi with No. 8. He does the same work in longer time and hands the car over to Dr. Benjafield. And now an accident is avoided by the narrowest of margins, an accident that might have caused international complications. Just as No. 8 is gathering speed, Caracciola with the Merc. roars by at somewhere near the 120 m.p.h. mark. Ha, thinks Benjafield, now for a right royal dust-up; let's see if we cannot give the German something to stimulate him, and with this object in mind Benjafield jams the throttle even harder down. At last we're holding him and now, wonder of wonders, we are shortening the gap, and only when the gap between the two cars has shortened to a few yards does Benjafield realise the reason. Caracciola is slowing for the bend, the new bend which cuts out the run down to the village of Pontlieu. So many times has Benjafield driven on the old circuit that in the excitement of the chase he has forgotten the new bend, a kilometre or more short of the old hairpin, and thus he finds himself rushing downhill at an alarming rate, charging straight into the rear of the Mercedes. The road is far too narrow to attempt to pass, especially as the Mercedes is in the middle of the road, never dreaming that anyone would be mad enough to try and pass him in this position. By dint of standing on the brakes and engaging a lower gear at the earliest possible moment the Bentley was just got under control in time; in time to prevent its front springs boring a couple of nasty jagged holes in the petrol tank of the Merc. By the time the Bentley was got under control, there was hardly room for a cigarette paper between the two cars. It requires little imagination to realise what would have been said, and thought, had this accident not been avoided. Anyway that narrow escape plus the sight of No. 3 buried in the sandbank served to bring Benjafield to his senses, and behave with more decorum.

Different drivers, different temperaments, but on the whole, in a long race, a race of this kind, it is safer to go easy for a lap or two—play oneself in so to speak. Twenty-four hours is a long time and it is only on the rarest occasion that the few extra seconds lost by doing this would affect the result.

Glen Kidston with No. 4 is the next car in. In addition to the refuelling a wheel has to be changed so that the total stop takes 3 minutes 18 seconds. No sooner is Barnato away with No. 4 than Clement arrives with the other surviving Speed-Six. No. 2, and it remains for him to show us just how a refill should be done. Every movement is a purposeful one, so much so that he almost appears to be unhurried. His fingers are at the petrol filler cap as the *plombeur* cuts the seals—in goes the enormous funnel followed by the upturned petrol cans, which are no sooner emptied than they are replaced by full ones and as the cascade of empty petrol cans showering into the pit ceases, he is already tipping in the oil and as soon as oil appears at the overflow tap so is he pouring water into the radiator—this finished and a quick run round the car snapping the spring caps to and as the last seal is being fixed Clement leaps over the pit counters and Dick Watney is engaging first. Pretty to watch, all in 95 seconds—1 minute 35 seconds. It seems incredible, but so important is it to save every possible moment in the pit work when one takes into account the effort expended to save or gain every possible moment in the driving. Five seconds lost in pit work is just as long as five seconds lost in the driving. Clement is an old hand more experienced than any of us and it is once more an example of the difference between the good amateur and the first-class professional. Caracciola is the last to come in and, thanks to rather inferior pit work, the gap between No. 4, now driven by Babe Barnato, which is lying second since the demise of No. 3, is reduced markedly.

For the first time since the Bentleys appeared at Le Mans, they encounter serious tyre trouble. Year after year have they run for the whole 24 hours on one set of tyres, occasionally, perhaps, changing a wheel as a precautionary measure, but this year the supercharged cars, especially, are throwing treads all over the place. Norman Freeman ('Mr. Dunlop') is consulted, but fails to explain. The tyres used by the Mercedes, the Speed-Sixes, and the blown cars are the same, yet the two former are enjoying their usual immunity. No, there is nothing wrong with the tyres. The explanation must be sought elsewhere. Actually it was due to a combination of circumstances of which the more important were the heat (it was a very hot afternoon), the weight of the car (47 cwt.) and the rather high centre of gravity plus the high speed of the cars. Whatever the explanation there was no doubt about the fact, of which I had a sharp reminder, approaching Mulsanne on my fourth lap, for the tread of my offside hind wheel parted company with the canvas when the car was doing 120 m.p.h. It made a report like a gunshot, boring a large hole in the wing and shooting up in the air to some prodigous height so that it appeared to be about the size of a blackbird. For the moment I thought some other car had hit me, but as soon as I realised the truth reduced speed till the pits were reached and changed the wheel.

There is a considerable tension in the air—the Mercedes is still in the lead and is setting a cracking pace, but there are two Bentleys in close attendance, No. 4 having taken the place of Davis's car. The blown cars have lost time through the constantly recurring tyre trouble, but in spite of this at the end of the third hour Bentleys hold the second, third and fourth positions, two of the Stutz cars having insinuated themselves ahead of Birkin's car. These American cars have been putting up a most impressive performance. They are non-supercharged straight eights with a special head carrying two camshafts and having four inclined valves per cylinder. They are certainly not as fast as the Bentleys, but Brisson has shown what can be accomplished by steady driving in a race of this kind, for he has succeeded in bringing his car within two minutes of Clement's Bentley after three hours' running. However, all the good work done by Brisson is thrown away for Louis Rigal, who now takes charge of the car, runs off the road on his first circuit, ripping away the exhaust pipe, which has to be secured with wire. Again he gets going and, failing to learn his lesson, again he leaves the road doing still further damage to the underslung exhaust pipe. Result—driving fast past the Café de l'Hippodrome, flames shooting out from the shortened exhaust cause the car to catch fire and the fire gets well established before the driver becomes aware of the fact. However, as soon as he realises the position, he stands on the brakes, switches off the ignition, grabs the Pyrene and prepares to leap to the road whilst the car is still in motion. His foot, however, gets caught by the top of the door with the result that instead of jumping clear he trips and falls into the middle of the road. It seems impossible that Barnato roaring down the straight on full throttle can miss him, but swerving to one side he accomplishes a miracle and so a tragedy is averted. To add to the drama, the Stutz tank chooses this precise moment to explode, the flames and smoke rising to such a height that they can be seen at Le Mans, five miles away. And thus are the chances of this fine car thrown away.

Caracciola is the last to come in for refuelling—so far he has enjoyed a trouble-free run and has held the lead since the fall of the flag with the exception of Tim's short-lived lead. The pit work here is obviously ill-organised, and many valuable seconds are lost through insufficient rehearsal, seconds which have only been gained at the expense of the supercharger and can ill be spared.

It is at this stage of the race, with Birkin falling back through repeated tyre trouble, No. 3 having been collected by a sandbank, that Capt. Woolf Barnato decides to take up the running and go for the Merc. Anyway, this is the way that we drivers like to think it is, whereas in fact it is the 'Great Man', the *Chef d'Equipe*, or in plain English just W.O., who gives the instructions, playing his pieces like the Master playing chess. By dint of hard driving, shortly before 8.30 p.m., Babe has got on the Merc's tail, and precisely at 8.26 p.m. the Big Six, carrying the number 4, amid vociferous cheers from the British contingent, came roaring past the pits some 50 yards ahead of his German rival. On the next lap, however, by superb driving, Werner, who has taken over from Caracciola, is again in the lead with Barnato 100 yards astern.

This, however, does not disturb the Chief in the least, for it has only been achieved at a price, and a very high price too. We know from past experience that there is one certain way of blowing up a Merc engine and that is by too much use of the supercharger, and Babe is pushing him hard enough, so hard that to keep ahead it means blower most of the time. And now begins that historical Bentley-Mercedes duel, or better, that Barnato-Caracciola duel. A duel between two of the world's finest and fastest production sports-cars driven in each case by the most highly skilled and experienced men England and Germany could produce. Here was a test, a really fair test, under ideal conditions, the result of which would prove, once and for all, which was the better car. Furthermore, here was a test for all the world to see and read about in their papers the following day, a test that would be recorded in black and white in the daily press on the following day and better still in the motor journals in their weekly issues, where it would remain and be available for the enthusiast for all time. Thrilling thought, here was history in the making. So important is the result of this duel, affecting the prestige of the winning car for several years to come, that I propose to give you an extract from the chart kept by Bentley Motors Ltd. in so far as it related to the two cars concerned. I have to thank W.O. for giving me access to these figures (see over).

We drivers are getting rather tired of the wreck of No. 5 Stutz, the rear wheels of which are well out into the road, leaving only half the highway free, especially as it is still smouldering and this piece of the circuit is normally quite the fastest and where we big fellows count on being able to pass some of the smaller fry in complete comfort. At last, thank goodness, the officials are doing something about it—high time too, for in another twenty minutes it will be dark. They are connecting a tow-rope to the front of the car and trying to pull it off the road with a Bugatti. Just before dark the road is once more clear and we are very relieved.

Since there can be no doubt but that the Bentley No. 4-Mercedes

COMPARISON OF MERCEDES AND WINNING BENTLEY
LE MANS 1930

Lap	Time Mercedes hr. min. sec.	Bentley hr. min. sec.	Lead min. sec.	Leading car Mercedes	Remarks
1	07 23	07 42	0 19	Mercedes	Driver of No. 4 Bentley Com. Glen Kidston, R.N.
2	14 24	15 04	0 40	"	"
3	21 22	22 29	1 07	"	"
4	28 22	30 01	1 39	"	"
5	35 28	37 21	1 53	"	"
6	42 43	44 48	2 05	"	"
7	50 02	52 09	2 07	"	"
8	57 20	59 30	2 10	"	"
9	1 04 38	1 06 44	2 06	"	"
10	1 11 56	1 14 06	2 10	"	"
11	1 19 13	1 21 16	2 03	"	"
12	1 26 29	1 28 30	2 01	"	"
13	1 33 46	1 35 52	2 06	"	"
14	1 41 04	1 43 06	2 02	"	"
15	1 48 18	1 50 42	2 24	"	"
16	1 55 36	1 58 02	2 26	"	"
17	2 03 00	2 05 18	2 18	"	"
18	2 10 15	2 12 31	2 16	"	"
19	2 17 38	2 19 48	2 10	"	"
20	2 24 58	2 27 00	2 01	"	"
21	2 32 26	2 34 35	2 09	"	No. 4 into pit for fuel and tyre change.
22	2 39 52	2 45 26	4 34	"	Mercedes Pit for fuel.
23	2 50 52	2 52 41	1 49	"	Driver of No. 4 Bentley Capt. Woolf Barnato.
24	2 58 14	3 00 00	1 46	"	"
25	3 05 32	3 07 15	1 43	"	"
26	3 12 51	3 14 32	1 41	"	"

Lap	Time Mercedes hr. min. sec.	Time Bentley hr. min. sec.	Lead min. sec.	Leading car	Remarks
27	3 20 08	3 21 47	1 39	Mercedes	Driver of No. 4 Bentley Capt. Woolf Barnato.
28	3 27 30	3 28 56	1 26	"	"
29	3 34 45	3 36 09	1 24	"	"
30	3 42 10	3 43 22	1 12	"	"
31	3 49 32	3 50 41	1 09	"	"
32	3 57 03	3 57 51	0 48	"	"
33	4 04 34	4 05 05	0 31	"	"
34	4 11 54	4 12 11	0 17	"	"
35	4 19 15	4 19 23	0 08	Bentley No. 4	"
36	4 26 36	4 26 34	0 02	Mercedes	"
37	4 33 41	4 33 52	0 11	"	"
38	4 40 50	4 40 56	0 06	"	"
39	4 48 00	4 48 02	0 02	Bentley No. 4	"
40	4 55 17	4 55 10	0 07	Bentley No. 4	"
41	5 02 31	5 02 28	0 03	Mercedes	"
42	5 09 44	5 09 45	0 01	Mercedes	"
43	5 16 55	5 19 37	2 42	"	No. 4 pit for fuel.
44	5 24 22	5 27 00	2 38	"	Driver of No. 4 Bentley Com. Glen Kidston, R.N.
45	5 31 50	5 34 42	2 52	Bentley No. 4	"
46	5 46 14	5 42 12	4 02	"	Mercedes into pit for fuel.
47	5 53 23	5 49 42	3 41	"	"
48	6 00 34	5 57 14	3 20	"	"
49	6 07 43	6 04 51	2 52	"	"
50	6 14 50	6 12 23	2 29	Bentley No. 4	"
51	6 22 00	6 19 55	2 05	"	Mercedes into pit for fuel.
52	6 29 13	6 27 17	1 56	"	"
53	6 36 28	6 34 44	1 44	"	"
54	6 43 40	6 42 13	1 27	"	"

Lap	Time — Mercedes hr. min. sec.	Bentley hr. min. sec.	Lead min. sec.	Leading car	Remarks
55	6 50 53	6 49 37	1 16	Bentley No. 4	Driver of No. 4 Bentley Com. Glen Kidston, R.N.
56	6 58 03	6 57 06	0 57	„	„
57	7 05 09	7 04 37	0 32	„	„
58	7 12 10	7 12 06	0 04	„	„
59	7 19 13	7 19 29	0 16	Mercedes	„
60	7 26 24	7 26 55	0 31	„	„
61	7 33 40	7 34 18	0 38	„	„
62	7 41 05	7 41 39	0 34	„	Mercedes pit stop.
63	7 51 05	7 48 57	2 08	Bentley No. 4	„
64	7 59 11	7 56 22	2 49	„	Bentley in pit for refill.
65	8 06 27	8 07 04	0 37	Mercedes	Driver of No. 4 Bentley Capt. Woolf Barnato.
66	8 13 48	8 14 32	0 44	„	„
67	8 21 02	8 22 04	1 02	Bentley No. 4	„
68	8 31 46	8 29 25	2 21	„	Mercedes in pit for refill.
69	8 39 40	8 36 55	2 45	„	„
70	8 47 43	8 44 27	3 16	„	„
71	8 55 37	8 52 03	3 34	„	„
72	9 03 36	8 59 33	4 03	„	„
73	9 11 37	9 07 27	4 10	„	Bentley in pit for new tyre.
74	9 19 18	9 18 10	4 08	„	„
75	9 27 07	9 25 31	1 36	„	„
76	9 34 55	9 32 50	2 05	„	„
77	9 42 47	9 40 13	2 34	„	„
78	9 50 36	9 47 40	2 56	„	„
79	9 58 30	9 55 04	3 26	„	„
80	10 06 21	10 02 25	3 56	„	„
81	10 14 21	10 09 38	4 43	„	„
82	10 22 55	10 17 00	5 55	„	„

Mercedes retired—'Battery completely discharged'.

duel for the first half of the race was the incident of predominating interest, an analysis of the time-sheets should prove very helpful to those wishing to form an opinion as regards the relative merits of the two cars.

Let us consider first which car is the faster—regardless of wear, tear and damage to the engine. Caracciola's fastest laps were in the early stages of the race, his second lap being clocked at 7 minutes 1 second and his third in 6 minutes 58 seconds. For these two laps he had a clear course, having got away at the head of the mass, whilst Bentley No. 4 was being held in reserve at this stage of the race, and Glen Kidston, driving to orders, was content to be clocking round about 7 minutes 20 seconds. Tim Birkin, on the other hand, who admittedly was going flat out, and whose run was short but very sweet, put in one lap, his third, at the amazing figure of 6 minutes 48 seconds, giving an average of 89.69 miles per hour for the circuit. No other car clocked under 7 minutes, so that the Mercedes claim to be the fastest production touring car is true, with one exception.

Incidentally, all the sensational rubbish published in the press about elaborate team tactics adopted by the two Bentley groups to 'crack up' the Mercedes are entirely without any foundation in fact. Is it likely that any 'team tactics', however subtle and however brilliant, would direct one of its team to continue racing with a car weighing over 2¼ tons at speeds up to 130 m.p.h. on a bare canvas, having thrown the tread two or three miles before the place where the car could have been stopped? Nothing but the individual sheer dare-devilry of our beloved Tim would do this sort of thing. Madness, yes, but rather admirable madness. Tim's driving was brilliant, but very hard on the car—furthermore he never could resist the temptation to play to the gallery in the early stages of a race—if his car survived both these hazards in a long race, as they did, most ably and abetted by the more phlegmatic, but very little slower, Barnato in the 1929 race, he won. How often does one see the chances of a perfect car jeopardised in this way. It is doubtful whether Tim's effort was sufficiently sustained to really affect the Mercedes and this opinion is supported by Caracciola's subsequent regularity, his next fourteen laps after the disappearance of No. 9 showing no more than 5 seconds' variation, being between 7 minutes 15 seconds and 7 minutes 19 seconds. This is not the performance of a 'Pinked Rival'. To return to our time-sheet, it will be observed that Bentley No. 4 lying quietly in reserve during the Birkin-Caracciola duel and later whilst Sammy Davis is gently prodding the Merc in the rear, never being more than 2 minutes 26 seconds behind, and it is not until poor Clive Dunfee's mishap put an end to Bentley No. 3's chances that No. 4 is called up to the front line.

Glen Kidston has played his part admirably, handing over a motor car well placed and in perfect condition to his co-driver, after completing 22 laps. Thanks also to a better-organised pit-stop, by the time the Mercedes and No. 4 get going again 'Babe' is only 1 minute 49 seconds behind.

Having received orders to attack, Babe settles down to a spell of really brilliant driving, clocking the following times: 7.15, 7.19, 7.15, 7.17, 7.15, 7.9, 7.13, 7.13, 7.19, 7.10, 7.14, 7.6, 7.12, 7.11, and by this means having gradually worn away the Mercedes' lead, on the 36th lap we have the joy of seeing No. 4 2 seconds ahead. With the exception of the few minutes that the lead was held by Tim Birkin, before the bursting of his tyre, the Mercedes has led throughout, nearly 4½ hours since flag-fall. Babe is given an enormous reception as he passes the grandstand, for the chase has been a most exciting one for those fans who follow it with their stop-watches. That slow wearing away of the Merc's lead, the very inevitability, like water wearing away the rock, 3 seconds, 3 seconds, 2 seconds, 2, 13, 2, 12, 3, 21, 17, 14, 9, 6, 10, in fact nearer and always nearer until the dramatic moment of passing and triumphantly leading past the stands.

This was a piece of impertinence too great for the Mercedes to tolerate, and thus scattering all thoughts of discretion to the winds, greater demands than ever were made on the supercharger that by increasing his lap speed to 7 minutes 5 seconds. No. 1 came round first with 11 seconds to the good. The next lap was covered in 7.9 and 7.4, respectively thus reducing his lead to 6 seconds. This was followed by a 7.10 and a 7.6, leaving a mere couple of seconds between the two cars. To those of us with previous experience of the Mercedes, it was evident that this sort of thing could only end in one way, for by now the whine of his blower could be heard all round the course. And now the Bentley held the lead for two laps by only 7 and 3 seconds, before coming in for his refill.

By the time both cars had settled down after their refill, the drivers now being Glen Kidston and Werner, the Bentley led by 4 minutes 2 seconds. By means of a spell of brilliant driving, Werner suceeded in wiping out this deficit—considering that the major part of this spell was in the dark, since it did not commence till nearly ten o'clock, the figures are most impressive: 7.9, 7.11, 7.9, 7.7, 7.10, 7.13, 7.15, 7.12, 7.13, 7.10, 7.6, 7.1, 7.3, and at this point on the 59th lap he wrests the lead from Kidston and keeps it till a pit stop 4 laps later. This was probably the most brilliant sustained performance of the whole race, considering it was dark. What a pity the Mercedes pit-work was so poor, necessitating taking so much out of the car in order to make up for it. After the next stops for refill, it was evident that this last effort of No. 1 had been too much for him and that he had shot his bolt, for the Bentley increased a lead of 2.21 to 5.55 in 14 laps, doing the following times: 7.30, 7.35, 7.30, 7.34, 7.54, 7.21, 7.19, 7.23, 7.27, 7.24,

7.21, 7.13, 7.22, and here it was that the Mercedes faded out on lap 82, shortly before 2.30 a.m. on the Sunday morning. The official reason given for the Merc's failure was a short in the battery causing a sudden and complete discharge. We are inclined to take this with a grain of salt, having grave suspicions about a gasket!

However satisfactory the result of this duel is to Bentley Motors Ltd., there is no doubt but that the demise of No. 1 has largely taken the interest from the race. Further, Caracciola, Werner and their car have proved themselves most doughty and worthy opponents, possessed of true sportsmanship, ready to give and take knocks inseparable from this kind of competition.

The end of this struggle is the signal for going home, as with the exit of Mercedes it is obvious that Bentleys must win the race. So true is this in actual fact and so far ahead is the Barnato-Kidston Speed-Six that for the last 12 hours of the race it has to do nothing more than a moderately fast tour, to maintain itself in first place.

During the early hours of Sunday morning, the instructions given to Glen Kidston to keep No. 4 rolling round about the 7.45 figure per lap led to a rather amusing incident. Somewhere about midnight, Ramponi had become ill and was not well enough to drive No. 8 so that his partner Benjafield was compelled to take over. Having suffered from repeated tyre trouble during the Saturday afternoon and evening, together with some bother with plugs, Benjafield was four laps behind No. 4. However, since his instructions were to keep going at about 7.20, sooner or later he was bound to overtake and want to pass No. 4. It so happened that he got on to the tail of No. 4 just before Mulsanne and spent most of the succeeding lap in trying to pass it. This Benjafield succeeded in doing only after almost completing another lap by putting the offside two wheels of his car well over the grass verge at a speed in excess of 120 m.p.h. Not expecting to have to do this sort of thing with members of his own team, Benjafield is naturally annoyed and having regained the crown of the road turns round and shakes his fist at Kidston. This is more than Kidston can stand and as No. 8 is braking for Mulsanne, Glen runs up alongside and shouts, 'If you want to hot-stuff me, I can hot-stuff you,' and a bit of a barging match ensues for the corner, which is won by Benjafield, who, naturally incensed with the crass stupidity of it all, vents his wrath on the accelerator pedal, goes crashing through the woods running into the Arnage bends rather more quickly than advisable and thus having to brake correspondingly hard—result, up goes the umpteenth tread just after the pits, so that nearly a whole lap has to be covered at reduced speed plus the added ignominy of being repassed by Glen. Some hours later, after No. 8 has finally burst and Benjafield is in the Dorothy Paget *équipe's* pit, Glen Kidston comes down looking quite a bit sheepish and says, 'W.O. has sent me to you to apologise.' Benjafield thanks him and at the same time explains that there was no question of wishing to hot-stuff him or even, being nearly 40 miles astern, of catching him, but it was merely the result of two cars running to scheduled speeds, the speed of the leader being less than the following car. Anyway, explanation being completed, Kidston and Benjafield adjourned for a drink together.

Just before ten o'clock on Sunday morning, Tim comes into the pit with the engine of No. 9 making fearsome explosions. Trouble diagnosed as valves—car withdrawn. Benjafield is not so lucky—his engine blows up with a loud report near Hunaudieres—piston gone—just before 11 a.m. Just as he is about to set out on his long trek back to the pits, having parked the car on the grass verge, Louis Chiron appears from nowhere with a perfectly good Chrysler Coupé and drives him back. Thank you, Louis! And so with five hours still to go Bentleys are left with two cars in the race out of six entered—certainly these two are lying first and second and look like staying there, but it is woefully short of the standard set last year. However, on analysis it is not so bad, for the supercharged cars are really not out of the experimental stage and for two of them to last as long as they did is most encouraging. Whereas the official works entry, one car only is lost and that not through any mechanical failure.

And so it finished—Nos. 4 and 2, driven by Barnato and Kidston, Clement and Watney, respectively, toured home first and second, Bentley Motors Ltd. having won the race for four years in succession. It was also a colossal personal triumph for Captain Woolf Barnato, Managing Director of the firm, who by winning this race completed his hat-trick. By his performance during his duel with Caracciola he has proved himself one of the best drivers this country has produced.

Although the result of the race is a foregone conclusion many hours before the end, so enthralling is the sheer magnificence of the Bentley performance alone that the crowds return after an early lunch to cheer the victors in no uncertain manner. The cordial generosity of the French is most gratifying and it would have been difficult for them to have shown greater pleasure had they themselves been the winner.

Maybe I have conveyed the impression that this is a match between the two cars alone, if so please allow me to make a correction. Not only were several other cars running, but amongst them were the three other Bentleys whose fate has already been described. Of the rest the two Talbots driven by Lewis and Eaton, Hindmarsh and Rose-Richards, did remarkably well, being most impressive in the regularity of their running, finishing 3rd and 4th respectively, averaging 68 m.p.h. for the 24 hours.

Of the 18 cars that started, 9 finished, qualifying to take part in the race for the seventh Biennial Rudge-Whitworth Cup in the following year. The following is a detailed list:

THE EIGHTH GRAND PRIX D'ENDURANCE 1930 AT LE MANS

Car	Driver	Kilo-metres	Miles	Average m.p.h.
1. Bentley	Barnato and Kidston	2930	1821	75·87
2. Bentley	Clement and Watney	2832	1760	73·33
3. Talbot	Lewis and Eaton	2651	1647	68·63
4. Talbot	Hindmarsh and Rose-Richards	2625	1631	67·97
5. Alfa-Romeo	Howe and Callingham	2607	1620	67·50
6. Lea-Francis	Peacock and Newsome	2291	1424	59·33
7. Bugatti	Mmes Mareuse and Siko	2164	1345	56·04
8. Tracta	Gregoire and Vallon	2105	1311	54·62
9. Tracta	Bourcier and Debeugny	2013	1251	52·12

and the result of the

SIXTH BIENNIAL RUDGE-WHITWORTH CUP

		Figure of Merit
1. Bentley	Barnato and Kidston	1172
2. Bentley	Clement and Watney	1133
3. Tracta	Gregoire and Vallon	1054
4. Lea-Francis	Peacock and Newsome	1041
5. Tracta	Bourcier and Debeugny	1009

As we said good-bye the following morning to all our good friends we of the Hon. Dorothy Paget *équipe* basking in some of the glory reflected from the works team, and pretending to be all of the victorious team, little did any of us think that 1930 was the last time Bentley Motors Ltd. would compete at Le Mans. Of course we knew that the company had weathered several financial crises in the past, but never in our blackest moods had we ever considered the possibility of the complete eclipse of the company that had produced these wonderful cars, for the sake of a few thousand pounds. Surely such a car was a national asset, an asset sufficiently valuable to be subsidised by the state rather than that it should be permitted to be swamped by some financial jiggery-pokery.

From *The Bentleys at Le Mans* by J. D. Benjafield, 1948, and reproduced by permission.

Index

Index

Index

Index